Communities and Workforce Development

Communities and Workforce Development

Edwin Meléndez
Editor

2004

W.E. Upjohn Institute for Employment Research
Kalamazoo, Michigan

Library of Congress Cataloging-in-Publication Data

Communities and workforce development / Edwin Meléndez, editor
p. cm.
Includes bibliographical references and index.
ISBN 0-88099-316-2 (pbk. : alk. paper) — ISBN 0-88099-317-0
(hardcover : alk. paper)
1. Occupational training—United States. 2. Employees—Training of—United States.
3. Welfare recipients—Employment—United States. 4. Public welfare—Government
policy—United States. I. Meléndez, Edwin
HD5715.2.C613 2004
331.25'92'0973—dc22
2004025118

W.E. Upjohn Institute for Employment Research
300 S. Westnedge Avenue
Kalamazoo, Michigan 49007-4686

Cover design by Alcorn Publication Design.
Index prepared by Diane Worden.
Printed in the United States of America.
Printed on recycled paper.

To Bennett "Ben" Harrison (1942–1999).
Colleague, mentor, and friend.

Contents

Part 3: Recasting the Role of Community Colleges

Part 4: New Directions in Community Collaborations and Partnerships

Acknowledgments

The authors thank the many individuals who supported our projects and provided data, insightful comments, and suggestions. First, we would like to thank the many community organizations, community colleges, state agencies, and other workforce development organizations that opened their doors to us, provided valuable information on their programs, partnerships, and collaborations, and contributed so significantly to the various studies included in this volume. Literally hundreds of interviewees generously gave us their time and attention, facilitated our research, and made our time in the field truly edifying and enjoyable.

This volume was made possible thanks to the generous support of the Ford Foundation and all of our friends at the Foundation who have supported our work throughout the years. In particular, we would like to extend our greatest appreciation for their unwavering support to Melvin Oliver, Robert Curvin, Betsy Campbell, Cynthia Duncan, Frank DeGiovanni, Roland Anglin, John Colborn, and Miguel García.

We would like to express our gratitude to Gloria Salas and Alicia Fernández from the Office of Employment and Training Programs of the U.S. Department of Labor, who supervised the grant that supported the chapter on community colleges and welfare reform by Edwin Meléndez, Luis M. Falcón, Carlos Suárez-Boulangger, Lynn McCormick, and Alexandra de Montrichard. They encouraged us to undertake this research, were actively involved in the design of the project, and offered thoughtful guidance and feedback to our work throughout. Thanks are also due to the program directors and other staff who sponsored our site visits to the colleges—in particular, Elaine Baker, Community College of Denver; Linda Cole, Los Angeles Trade Technical College; Yvonne Hart, University of New Mexico at Valencia; and Mark Gunderson, Los Angeles City College. They were instrumental in the successful completion of this project by hosting our visits, revising the case studies draft, and offering many helpful comments.

Participants from the conference "Communities and Workforce Development," held in New York May 11, 2002, provided invaluable feedback and discussions on various papers included in the volume.

This conference was cosponsored by the Ford Foundation and New School University's Community Development Research Center. Other funders of our projects include the CBO Alliance, Policy Link, Common Ground, the Brookings Institution, and the Altman Foundation.

Various staff of the Community Development Research Center played a critical role in support of the research projects and papers included in the volume. Our most sincere gratitude goes to Nestor Rios, Dayna Antenucci, Belinda Loomis, and Melisa Oliveros for their hard work and dedication to this project. Special thanks to Brian Sahd, who joined the Center's staff for the supportive housing study, helped us with the research design, and conducted many of the interviews for the study. Similarly, we would like to acknowledge the invaluable contribution of Wendy Trull, research assistant, for the study on nonprofit organizations and private sector competition conducted by Milano Graduate School Professor M. Bryna Sanger and sponsored by the Brookings Institution.

We would like to acknowledge the publication of earlier versions of the chapter by M. Bryna Sanger, "Competing for Contracts: Nonprofit Survival in an Age of Privatization," by the Brookings Institution; the chapter by Lisa J. Servon, "Community Technology Centers: Training Disadvantaged Workers for Information Technology Jobs," by Blackwell; and the chapter by Lynn McCormick, "Innovators Under Duress: Community Colleges in New York's Workfare Setting," by the Community College Journal of Research and Practice. PolicyLink provided the funding for Michael A. Stoll's project and released the resulting working paper, which became the chapter "Workforce Development in the Information Technology Age."

Finally, we extend our special thanks to the W.E. Upjohn Institute staff, including Kevin Hollenbeck, Director of Publications and Senior Economist, and Benjamin Jones, the editor for the volume, for making this volume a reality.

1
Communities and Workforce Development in the Era of Devolution

Edwin Meléndez
New School University

Low-wage and low-skill jobs keep too many Americans poor and yield few opportunities for career advancement. The employment and training industry as a whole provides necessary support services, connections to employers, skills training, and other programs that facilitate job readiness, placements, and career advancement for disadvantaged workers and job seekers. However, we know relatively little about the institutions and programs that facilitate workers' transition to the workplace and advancement in careers. A growing body of evidence points to the recent emergence of new types of labor market intermediaries (LMIs) serving the disadvantaged. These are based on a broad range of institutions that differ markedly in scope and mission from the typical service provider of years past. In comparison with the typical employment program of a decade ago, the new breed of intermediary is more responsive to employers' demands, has a broader base of financial support, and interacts or partners more often with other organizations. A growing number of LMIs are focused on a specific industry or sector within an industry, and their services target fewer aspects of the employment service continuum.

The emergence of more dynamic LMIs is partly a response to the growing demand for workers, which was fueled by the economic expansion of the 1990s, but it has also been greatly shaped by at least two major policy shocks in the latter half of the decade: welfare reform and the revamping of federal employment training programs under the Workforce Investment Act (WIA) of 1998. The combined impact of these forces induced many organizations to become more active in workforce development, and many others transformed their operations and adapted to the new, more competitive and uncertain environment. The evidence discussed in detail in this volume suggests several important trends. For one, traditional service providers have had to adapt to a shift in focus from vocational training, often based on classroom pedagogy, to job readiness training that follows a "work first" philosophy. Other important developments include greater experimentation with program design, greater specialization among service providers, greater employer participation in workforce development programs, and greater collaboration among various institutions and service providers.

Equally important has been the transformation of traditional service providers such as community-based organizations and community colleges. Given the available evidence, it is difficult to generalize about the evolving role of community-based service providers, but undoubtedly community-based organizations (CBOs) were changed by federal system reform initiatives in various ways. While many CBOs were clearly adversely affected, others took advantage of the opportunities presented to implement successful strategies and adapt to new policy regimes. Community colleges became more active in workforce development programs. In many state and local jurisdictions, welfare reform created the conditions for greater participation by colleges in programs targeting the disadvantaged (Meléndez, Falcón, and Bivens 2003).

Community-based initiatives are playing an increasingly prominent role in the ongoing restructuring of the employment and training industry.[1] One of the most important developments resulting from a decade of intense experimentation has been that service providers have realized the benefits of collaboration with other organizations. Though some of these collaborations are really across institutional boundaries, such as those between CBOs and community colleges or employers, many have involved collaborations among service providers otherwise in more direct competition. The resulting division of labor has yielded a richer and more complex network of services, and many local employment systems have been strengthened as a result. But in other places, often where broad community-based initiatives were not implemented, the impact of federal reform has led to less inclusive and less efficient arrangements.

This chapter provides a broad look at the two major federal policy reform initiatives and how they have affected the employment services industry. In the final section, an overview of the chapters in the volume is presented.

POLICY SHOCKS AND DEVOLUTION

The enactment of the Personal Responsibility and Work Opportunity Reconciliation Act of 1996 (PRWORA) and the Workforce Investment Act of 1998 (WIA) has redefined the underlying philosophical foundations and program structure of the employment training system in the United States. PRWORA transformed public assistance into a work-based and transitory (or time-limited) assistance system. WIA consolidated the most important programs sponsored by the federal government and restructured the services offered at the ground level. Both acts transferred program authority to the states and allocated funding through block grants, redefining the role of local authorities and encouraging greater flexibility and autonomy. The enactment and implementation of these major policy initiatives coincide with one of the longest economic expansions and some of the lowest unemployment rates of recent decades. In conjunction, these forces transformed the policy context and the general operational environment for employment service providers.

From a public policy perspective, it is of foremost importance to understand both the influence of these changes on local employment and training systems and the strategies implemented by service providers to adapt and respond to the changes. One of the immediate effects of the joint occurrence of welfare reform and low unemployment was to encourage the participation of a wide spectrum of employers and service providers not previously engaged in serving welfare recipients. In the past few years, a significant number of employers began programs for the recruitment and training of entry-level workers.[2] Numerous organizations not previously involved in a training system targeting the most disadvantaged entry-level workers started collaborations to assist employers in launching such programs or initiated their own programs. Many of these organizations, such as temporary employment agencies, faith-based groups, some community colleges, and multiservice agencies, brought to the task relatively little experience in training the disadvantaged.

Increased competition among service providers, improvements in program design, and greater connections to the business community could very well be some of the most positive and long-lasting aspects of welfare reform. However, it is apparent from the studies included in this volume that these changes have also weakened some of the traditional employment and training service providers. From a public policy perspective, what really matters is whether the system improves services to targeted populations such as welfare recipients, disadvantaged adults and youth, dislocated workers, and others. Whether these services are provided by one type of intermediary or another should not be a significant policy concern in and of itself. However, in actuality it is very difficult to separate the question of who provides the services from the matter of whether services are provided to targeted disadvantaged populations. CBOs and other nonprofit organizations may have a more intrinsic or organic relationship to the communities where these populations reside and the organizations that provide related services, thus facilitating outreach and complementing services.[3] From a systemic perspective, the challenge is to improve the quality of services through better performance management of service providers while maintaining an equal or greater level of services for all targeted populations.

This section of the chapter examines in more detail the policy shock affecting the structuring of local employment services. The primary objective is to provide an overview of the policy context in which the industry has operated since the enactment of welfare reform, and of how these changes in policy have altered the operational premises of local employment services.

The Significance of Welfare Policy Reform for System Change

By the mid 1990s, policymakers were beginning to reach a consensus about the need to revamp the employment training system serving the disadvantaged. In the case of the Job Training Partnership Act (JTPA), most of the criticisms were directed, overtly or covertly, at service providers in general, and in particular at CBOs, as they represented the majority of service providers. The main criticism of JTPA-sponsored programs centered on the limited impact these programs had on participants' outcomes. For example, the well-known evaluation of JTPA by Abt Associates (Orr et al. 1996; Bloom et al. 1997; U.S. General Accounting Office 1996a) documents the small impact that these programs had in general. The explanations for modest and often disappointing results are well known by now. According to Grubb (1996), for example, some of the most important factors contributing to the limited effect of these programs were 1) the relative small scope of the intervention in terms of both skills enhancement and work experience provided to participants, 2) the inappropriate infrastructure of skills training providers and their inability to keep pace with new technologies and pedagogy, and 3) the separation that existed between classroom-based training and the occupational skills demanded by industry. Other weaknesses of the system include the fragmentation of funding streams, the intrusive role of politics in funding allocation, and an overly bureaucratic administrative structure.

Criticism of JTPA-funded training programs was mounting as the evidence from various demonstration and evaluation projects indicated that programs promoting work experience were more effective than conventional training programs providing education and classroom training when it came to transitioning welfare recipients to the labor force (Gueron 1986, 1990; Gueron, Pauly, and Lougy 1991). Programs in which welfare recipients volunteered to participate were more effective than mandatory programs, but all programs targeting welfare recipients were more effective when a variety of support mechanisms were available to program participants. Mandatory programs, before the enactment of PRWORA, were more effective when sanctions for nonparticipation were more strongly enforced. Although not all community-based training was ineffective and some studies provided evidence of modest impacts on various disadvantaged populations (U.S. Department of Labor 1995; Meléndez 1996), so-called work first programs targeting rapid attachment to the labor force and promoting work experience were less costly to implement and offered policymakers a clear alternative to the prevalent model of classroom training.

Aside from reforming the welfare system, enactment of PRWORA gave the first major shock to the employment training system. For the purpose of this discussion on the emerging role of community initiatives in an era of devolution, perhaps the most important development was the provision of Welfare-to-Work (WtW) grants totaling $3 billion, split between fiscal years 1998 and 1999. The policy regulations clearly articulated a work first approach to solving the employment problem of welfare recipients. Stricter work requirements and sanctions made it very difficult for service providers to exceed the allowable time for classroom training and other educational activities. Another consequence of the infusion of the WtW grants into local employment training systems was the need to attract many new service providers in a relatively short period. Consequently, local welfare offices implemented strategies to aggressively recruit and enhance the role of labor market intermediaries (Pavetti et al. 2000). Given the tight labor market and the magnitude of the federal infusion of resources, many nontraditional training service providers for the disadvantaged started new programs or expanded existing ones. These organizations include temporary employment agencies, faith-based and advocacy groups, multiservice organizations, community development corporations, and community colleges.[4] In short, one of the most interesting developments of welfare reform was to expand the organizational infrastructure for workforce development, which increased competition in the industry.

It is in the above context that we must understand the forces that are converging to promote system reform. To begin with, most research that assesses the factors contributing to successful employment programs points to the key role that a close connection to employers and industry plays in advancing program effectiveness (Harrison and Weiss 1998; Giloth 1998; Meléndez and Harrison 1997; Mueller and Schwartz 1998; Stokes 1996; USGAO 1996b). Effective programs are designed to reflect the rigor and routine of the workplace, establish clear workplace norms and expectations, and actively engage employers in curriculum design and instruction. The connection to employers is often structured as an internship where trainees gain work experience and employers get to know the prospective employees before hiring them. Collaborations with employers often extend beyond placement, focus on job retention, and are continued for a period of worker adjustment that may last from three to more than six months.

The infusion of new service providers and advocacy organizations, together with stricter regulations and a more active role for employers, brings yet another notable development: a renewed effort toward understanding organizational practices and an increased experimentation with new professional practices. For one thing, the emphasis on placements forced many organizations to focus on making connections with employers and having an up-front conversation about workplace expectations. Whether as a result of tight labor markets or because of new corporate leadership, employers' participation in WtW programs and collaboration with government agencies and training organizations has grown significantly in recent years.[5]

New programs serving welfare recipients have incorporated many of the features documented in the literature, such as effective job readiness, placement, and retention practices for disadvantaged populations. However, some experts contend that the design of new programs has been limited by the emphasis on job readiness and placement at the expense of basic and remedial education and skills training (Strawn 1998). In this view, a combination of skills-enhancing and work-experience activities is necessary for a more successful transition to work, particularly for those with low literacy levels and long-term detachment from the labor force. The release of various Welfare-to-Work program evaluations supports this contention. In a summary of the findings for random-assignment evaluations of 20 programs conducted by the Manpower Demonstration Research Corporation (MDRC), Gueron and Hamilton (2002) conclude that, although all strategies that were evaluated increased work for single parents and reduced welfare participation, the higher impact on five-year participants' earnings came from programs that used a mix of activities. The mix included both immediate job search and a combination of short-term, work-focused education or training and job search.

The impact of recent WtW evaluations on the workforce development field has been twofold. First, the evidence supports the validity of prior findings about work-focused employment programs. Second, the studies suggest the need for more evaluative research to focus on the relative effect of various program components. The findings from the 20 studies included in the National Evaluation of Welfare-to-Work Strategies are of particular interest (Michalopoulos, Schwartz, and Adams-Ciardullo 2000). In this evaluation, the results for the job-search first strategy were compared with those for the education-or-training first strategy at 11 different program sites. Though in general the job-search first programs had a bigger impact on five-year earnings than did those of the education-or-training first strategy, one of the sites (Portland) employing mixed initial activities outperformed all programs, and net annual gains in earnings exceeded $5,000.

Regardless of whether the long-term welfare policy shock to the employment training system is a positive or a negative one, in the short term it has induced experimentation, attracted new service providers to provide training for the disadvantaged, and promoted effective organizational and professional practices. However, while we must recognize these positive aspects of welfare reform in the short term, it is also necessary to discuss some of the dynamics that may have a negative effect in the near future. Obviously, one of the more challenging questions is how welfare participants who have received limited job-readiness training are going to fare when the unemployment rate is not as low as it was when most of these evaluations were conducted and employers are more demanding regarding minimum skills standards for employment. Or even in the context of favorable labor demand, what is going to be the impact of these programs on the so-called hard-to-serve welfare recipients, for whom more support services and long-term interventions are necessary to achieve positive outcomes than were for the majority of those in the first waves of WtW program participants?

The worst-case scenario might be one in which the next wave of welfare recipients reaches the time limits for benefits at a time when the unemployment rate is significantly higher than it was in the 1990s. There are enough indicators to suggest that the more recent welfare recipients entering into the employment and training system require support systems for a more varied and complex set of barriers to employment than did prior program participants. These types of hard-to-serve populations may require comprehensive support programs from CBOs that have been the most affected by the welfare policy shock. Whether the system as a whole has the capacity to help the hard-to-serve population remains an open question. Notwithstanding the uncertain legacy of welfare reform, its impact on the workforce development field provides a necessary context for understanding the enactment of the Workforce Investment Act.

WIA and the Restructuring of Employment Services

Congress finally enacted workforce development legislation in 1998 after several earlier attempts had failed to consolidate the major federal employment and training programs. Perhaps less ambitious than prior bills, WIA combined all major employment and training programs overseen by the Department of Labor but did not integrate programs overseen by the Department of Education (such as school-to-work and vocational education) that had been included in prior attempts (Meléndez 1997). However, WIA did mandate increased coordination of all programs at the local level and created Workforce Investment Boards (WIBs) at the state and local levels as the mechanisms for overseeing a more coherent integration of the system. In addition to employers and representatives from industry, the local boards incorporate a broad range of educational institutions and government agencies directly involved with workforce development programs and activities. One-Stop Career Centers (OSCCs) were given a more critical role in the system, as discussed in more detail below (Buck 2002; King 1999; Patel and Savner 2001; O'Shea and King 2001; U.S. General Accounting Office 2000).

The major goals of the new legislation are to increase flexibility at the local level and to provide clear guidelines for increased performance in the system. With the transfer of local program oversight to the states, the act requires that local jurisdictions evaluate system performance based on participant outcome measures such as placement and wages at placement, wage gains, and job retention. Full implementation of and compliance with WIA was mandated in 2000, but because of difficulties in data collection and the short time period with which to observe program completers' labor market trajectories, currently there are no available national data to evaluate the effectiveness of employment and training under WIA (U.S. General Accounting Office 2001, 2002, 2004).[6] In sum, WIA changed the landscape of employment and training programs for the disadvantaged in the United States by incorporating elements of competition and performance standards into policy design.

The critical question is how these changes in policy are affecting employment and training services to the disadvantaged, and more specifically, how these changes are affecting CBOs that have traditionally provided services to this population. In theory, one could conceive of a system targeting the most disadvantaged populations with minimal participation from the existing infrastructure of CBOs. In practice, it is difficult to separate the analysis of services to the disadvantaged and the training organizations since CBOs remain the primary service providers for the most disadvantaged program participants in the current system. WIA has the potential to adversely affect the current infrastructure of CBOs and, as a consequence, basic employment services to the most disadvantaged populations (Plastrik and Taylor 2001). There are three interrelated aspects of WIA that more directly affect services to disadvantaged adults. These consist of sequential eligibility for employment services, a performance-based certification system for service providers, and Individual Training Accounts (ITAs)—popularly known as vouchers—for adult training. Below, I will discuss each of these key policy and implementation issues and their potential impact on service providers' operations.

Sequential eligibility refers to the process through which participants in the publicly funded employment and training system have access to services under WIA. The act defines three types of services. Core services consist of outreach and intake, orientation and information on job openings, job search assistance and placement services, and follow-up services. Core services are universal, open to all job seekers regardless of employment status or income. In this way, WIA attempts to broaden the appeal to employers by providing employment services to all, not just to the more disadvantaged, thereby minimizing the stigma attached to state agency referrals to employers. Intensive services are offered to job seekers unable to find employment after receiving core services. These services are more specialized and include a more rigorous assessment of skills and barriers to employment, the preparation of an individualized employment plan and career planning, group counseling, and case management. Intensive services may also include other aspects of job readiness training such as communication and interviewing skills, and prevocational skills such as time management and introduction to computers. Eligibility for intensive services is restricted to unemployed workers with predefined barriers to employment, or to employed workers who may need intensive services to remain employed. Job seekers are eligible to receive training services only after the first two categories of services are exhausted.[7] The law also requires that job-training candidates must have the qualifications to be successful in order to receive ITAs and skills training.

Clearly, the concept of sequential eligibility of services under WIA reflects a work first philosophy. In this sense, WIA brought the employment training system into alignment with welfare reform. This is a continuation of a trend that actually started in 1992 with the amendments to JTPA that directed resources to the hardest to serve. Recent experiences with state implementation of WtW programs suggest great variability in local regulations and implementation of welfare reform. In many ways, the congressional intent to give more latitude and control to local authorities for the design of regional employment services can work to CBOs' advantage in their quest to redefine a role in the restructured employment and training system. Recent experience with programs targeting welfare recipients also suggests that CBOs possess the capability to develop effective organizational strategies, to redesign programs, and to adapt to a new policy environment.

Although it is generally a more punitive environment for CBOs under the new WIA regime for the reasons explained above, there are key local policy and implementation issues that may open the door to increased CBO participation. First, it is important to understand the coordinating role assigned to OSCCs. Under the new administrative structure set up by WIA, OSCCs have the responsibility for coordinating all services. How these services are distributed and structured is left to the discretion of state and local boards. The State Workforce Investment Board has the primary authority for establishing (after a public process of consultation) service eligibility guidelines and the standards for job placements and retention. These standards are subsequently used as benchmarks to certify service providers at the local level. WIA guidelines are flexible enough for each locality to structure OSCCs and training services to adapt to local conditions and encourage the participation of CBOs in the system. Research presented in this volume[8] indicates that CBOs' involvement and their role in the local system vary widely, depending on their prior involvement in the system and their ability to respond effectively to policy and regulatory changes at the state and local level.

CBOs have structured various types of arrangements with OSCCs and local WIBs. In a few instances, OSCCs are designed as community job centers, where CBOs serve both as managing partners and as service providers for core and intensive services. At the opposite extreme in terms of CBOs' participation are cities where CBOs act more as outside advocacy organizations focusing on the continuation of services to the disadvantaged but not directly providing those services—at least not primarily through contracts from the OSCCs. In between these two extreme examples of CBOs' role in the emerging system, there are many other cases of cities where CBOs have sustained and even enhanced their role in the local system. For instance, CBOs can obtain contracts to provide on-site core services to job seekers. In this "every-door-is-the-right-door" model, CBOs are contracted to provide intake for core services but often require authorization to provide additional services or are requested to refer clients to other service providers, depending on the type of services authorized by the OSCC. This relation is often structured as a contract for a minimum number of intakes, with provisions for adjustment. In this de facto fee-for-service arrangement, OSCCs' outreach is decentralized, more likely to have satellite services in low income communities, and more likely to reach hard-to-serve populations.

Another format followed by CBOs and OSCCs to structure a contractual relationship is that of having most of the intake, assessment and referral services centralized at the OSCC (typically in a central business district or downtown location), but of having what are now referred to as intensive services provided by CBOs dispersed throughout the city. This is a departure from past practice to the extent that job readiness training and other intensive services were part of a more comprehensive training package and contract. With the advent of WtW grants, job readiness training has been, in practice, separated from skills training. Indeed, job readiness has become the most prevalent service provided to job seekers, at the expense of skills training (Frank, Rahmanou, and Savner 2003). Under the new work first approach to employment services, it is becoming more common for CBOs to lose training contracts with community colleges and other service providers. CBOs may still be subcontracted to provide the bulk of support services and, on occasion, job readiness training as well.

It is apparent from the above discussion that there is a new division of functions emerging in the post-JTPA employment training system. CBOs are being pushed away from vocational training and asked to provide more case management and job readiness services. The use of ITAs for adult training is likely to reinforce this trend in the composition of services since many of the traditional educational institutions already operate under a tuition system more easily adaptable to payments with training vouchers than the cohort contracts used to structure CBO training services under JTPA. However, to the extent that job readiness services become a disproportionate share of services under WIA and are provided through contracts to CBOs, CBOs will continue to occupy a prominent role in the new system. There are many examples of community-based job readiness and placement programs that have grown dramatically with the advent of the work first approach. By focusing on job readiness and not on skills training, CBOs' employment programs have capitalized on a market trend, and many organizations have benefitted substantially from the new local policies.[9]

One of the most important offshoots induced by the WtW grants was to more actively engage community colleges in developing new job readiness and short-term vocational training programs for welfare recipients (Meléndez, Falcón, and Bivens 2003).[10] All indications are that community colleges are in an advantageous position to create vocational training programs as a bridge to their core educational—and tuition-based—programs. In fact, community colleges are better positioned to occupy a more prominent role for both youth and adult training under WIA than they were under JTPA. WIA also benefits community colleges by requiring that job seekers who apply for training services must have the qualifications to be successful. By stipulating that training program applicants be able to meet minimum criteria to enter the programs, this requirement benefits the best-educated job seekers and penalizes those job seekers who are not able to demonstrate a minimum level of literacy. "Creaming," as this practice is known in the industry, benefits trade schools and community colleges because admissions (and state subsidies and tuition reimbursements) are linked to students' ability to pass literacy and math tests. In other words, the community college system is already based on testing students' literacy level before they can enroll in college-level courses. Thus, community colleges can accommodate adult training programs under WIA with little or no adjustment to existing operations.

WIA provides two additional contractual mechanisms that CBOs can take advantage of. First, all youth services remain under a performance-based contract system. Youth services are excluded from ITA regulations affecting adult training, and CBOs providing youth services continue to do so without much change from the prior system. The second mechanism for CBOs to continue operating under contract allows them to enter into partnerships with employers to set up workplace-based programs where employers cover at least half of the training costs. The allocation of funding among different types of services and programs is left to the discretion of local authorities. It is reasonable to assume that collaborations with employers, particularly on those training programs that serve the needs of a broad group of employers in a regional labor market, are going to be favored by local authorities.

Thus, the evidence regarding whether CBOs have been successful in the transition to the new policy regime or whether they will become the predominant service providers for the disadvantaged workers' segment of the training market is inconclusive at this point. However, one inference from the above analysis can be made: Those CBOs that have established collaborative relations with OSCCs, community colleges, and other service organizations are in a better position to adapt their operations to the new policy regime than those that lack these connections and networking practices.

A second area of concern in how the implementation of WIA may affect participation of CBOs in the provision of services is the new certification system mandated by the act. Under the new law, the state WIB establishes performance standards and certifies service providers. Certifications are based on performance in labor market outcomes such as job placement, employment retention rates, and wages and benefits at placement. The data collected for certification purposes also serve to produce "consumer reports" on the performance of service providers participating in the system. The intention of the act is to provide data on service providers' performance that will help training candidates evaluate the quality of the programs and arrive at the best options available to them.[11] This market-oriented system is designed to encourage competition among service providers and to improve performance among alternative types of vocational and skill training vendors. The voucher system also is intended to diversify the training options opened to the disadvantaged. All service providers will have to undergo a periodic review and certification process to remain service providers.

Taken together, the tuition-like financing mechanism for adult training and the one-year grace period given to educational institutions are evidence that Congress wanted to favor community colleges for providing skills training services for disadvantaged adults, and to make it harder for CBOs to qualify and compete as training service providers. The legislative intent of favoring community colleges is consistent, as previously discussed, with the prevailing view embodied in policy and evaluation research that documents the limited impact CBO-based skills training programs have had on disadvantaged adults. But the advantage given to educational institutions is only relative, and has proven to be transitory. For one thing, it is not clear whether community colleges can adequately serve individuals with low literacy levels as measured by standardized tests. The evidence from the WtW grants suggests they can, provided that the financing and other supports are available to colleges. But whether colleges will be able to create and sustain the support services necessary for disadvantaged adults in the absence of specific contracts covering operating costs remains to be seen. Most state systems pay for students enrolled in for-credit courses and limit enrollment in remedial and noncredit courses. If the revenue stream generated by training vouchers is not sufficient to cover the increases in operational costs associated with serving special needs populations, there is simply no incentive mechanism for colleges to provide the support services necessary for disadvantaged adults to succeed in regular for-credit courses. By implication, there are no incentives for colleges to initiate non-college-credit vocational training programs.

Whether colleges find ways to create support mechanisms with the revenue streams generated by vouchers will largely determine whether they remain competitive in this segment of the training market. In the end, CBOs with the experience and complementary support programs may have the advantage in serving disadvantaged adults. Over time, effective community-based training providers are maintaining a niche in this market. In any case, given the structure of the act, there are currently few incentives for community colleges and other educational institutions that do serve disadvantaged adults to seek partnerships with experienced CBOs to develop joint programs.

Perhaps the greater challenge for local WIBs is to develop an information gathering and reporting system that is balanced and fair to all types of service providers. One of the critical problems that needs to be solved is how to report comparative data for different types of programs serving a diverse population. There is great variability among disadvantaged adults both in terms of the skills and experience they bring to the job market and in terms of the multiple barriers that may affect their successful placement and tenure in a job. It is conceivable that CBOs serving the most disadvantaged and community colleges serving those with higher literacy and education could be grouped together for comparing outcomes and for measuring program performance. Contrary to legislative intent, there may be a disincentive for some training programs to accept the hard-to-serve. As the above observations point out, CBOs may be placed at a competitive disadvantage to educational institutions in a comparison of program outcomes. WIA is extremely vague as to the method that will be followed to assess program effectiveness. But because the law mandates that consumer reports be issued regularly, states have begun to collect data to be able to develop the baseline information necessary to produce the reports.

In sum, by dividing services into three distinct categories and breaking the prior contractual connection between job-readiness services and vocational skills training programs, WIA changed the terrain. The above discussion suggests it is more likely in the future that different types of service providers will cater to certain types of populations. One pattern observed in many local areas was that WtW grants were given to large organizations that specialized in intake, assessment, and referrals, while the actual job-readiness training was subcontracted to smaller CBOs. Consequently, given that community colleges will continue to pursue the provision of vocational skills training, a new division of responsibility and specialization is emerging in the industry.

What, then, is the role that CBOs are assuming in the new WIA-structured employment training system? CBOs are beginning to define a niche as job-readiness and placement service providers for the most disadvantaged job seekers, whether through contracts directly from the OSCCs or through those from larger regional intermediaries. We observe a similar role when CBOs enter into partnerships with employers and community colleges, although such partnerships are relatively fewer for CBOs than the "intensive service" contracts. Ultimately, not all CBOs are positioned to respond to changing conditions in the employment and training industry. Whether CBOs will be able to succeed in this transition and reposition themselves in the emerging system remains an open question. What we do know is that preliminary evidence suggests that those CBOs that have responded to the challenges posed by federal policy devolution by specializing in job readiness and placement programs and entering into partnerships with OSCCs, with employers, and in some instances with community colleges, have been more successful than many in adapting their operations to the new policy regime.

NEW EVIDENCE ON CRITICAL RESEARCH QUESTIONS

This section summarizes the findings from the various studies presented in this volume. To facilitate discussion, chapters are divided into four subsections corresponding to the central themes of the book.

Emerging Labor Market Intermediaries

One of the long-lasting impacts of welfare reform has been to attract a host of nontraditional employment and service providers to the industry, increasing competition and engendering new practices for a more effective service delivery system. But even with these positive developments, many questions remain. Most of the new organizations implementing employment programs have emphasized job readiness and placements. The chapters in this section examine 1) whether these organizations provide services to hard-to-serve populations, 2) whether the new intermediaries are able to provide job skills training that facilitates career advancement in the new economy, and 3) how local political forces promote and finance effective employment systems.

State and local agencies, nonprofit organizations, and private firms are increasingly operating as employment service providers in local markets, sometimes together. The chapter by M. Bryna Sanger, "Competing for Contracts: Nonprofit Survival in an Age of Privatization," examines how new contracting arrangements introduced by welfare reform in various localities have forced nonprofits to compete with for-profits, and how these competitive demands are altering the way the nonprofit, often community-based organizations, do business. The nonprofit sector is facing increasing pressure to demonstrate its effectiveness. Many of the traditional employment service providers have adapted creatively to the new challenges, improving their performance, competing effectively on price, and developing innovative means to protect their missions. Many others, however, are struggling.

The author examines the experience of some of the strongest existing providers. Case studies include Opportunities Industrialization Center (OIC) and United Migrant Opportunity Services (UMOS) in Milwaukee and Federation Employment and Guidance Service (FEGS), Wildcat Service Corporation, and Goodwill Industries of Greater New York—big operators that have had a long history of public service provision. However, many CBOs and small and medium-sized providers have fewer resources with which to succeed in a more competitive, performance-based environment. Their new roles as subcontractors have been more limited and their success is still in question. Little technical assistance or management support has been available, except in cases such as Seedco's Nonprofit Assistance Corporation (N-PAC). Nonprofit innovations formed through collaborative and creative partnerships, private fundraising, and status changes (development of for-profit subsidiaries) represent healthy and promising adaptations. However, these are the exceptions. Most small nonprofits are struggling, and many may simply disappear from the industry.

In the following chapter, "CBOs and the One-Stop Career Center System," Ramón Borges-Méndez and Edwin Meléndez examine the positioning of CBOs in WIA-structured local systems. As stated in the Workforce Investment Act of 1998, the OSCCs are intended to become the universal point of entry for all federally funded employment programs. Job seekers use OSCCs to find jobs and information about occupational education programs, and to request and receive career development services. The evidence from the study indicates that the majority of clients are eligible only for a core set of job search services. Clients who are eligible for various social support services are often referred to other agencies. The implementation of WIA and welfare reforms modified CBOs' position as providers of core, support, and training services. This is the first study to examine the general positioning of CBOs as service providers after WIA was enacted. The authors identify how CBOs have been able to directly participate in and influence the development of OSCCs while maintaining their commitment to disadvantaged populations and communities.

Using a national, nonrandom scan of OSCC cases and structured interviews from 28 CBOs, Borges-Méndez and Meléndez assess the evolving relationship between OSCCs and CBOs in the provision of employment and training services. CBOs' positioning with the OSCC system, as Sanger argues in the previous chapter, has been uneven because of the sweeping changes brought by the law and by other local environmental and organizational factors such as federal devolution, and because of the mission, staffing, connectedness and financial resources of these organizations. The authors identify three types of CBO positioning, or contractual relationships, within OSCC systems:

1) CBOs as primary operators, 2) CBOs in peer-to-peer networks co-managing OSCCs with other stakeholders, and 3) CBOs as subordinate subcontractors. Overall, the authors conclude that primary operators and CBOs that participate in peer-to-peer networks have been equipped to assimilate the new mandates, such as work first and universal access, because of their authority in system governance, experience, and relational resources. Further, some of these CBOs are adding value to the system in areas like program integration. Smaller, less endowed CBOs have become subordinate contractors. Some even experience outright exclusion from the system.

The following two chapters focus on nontraditional service providers—unions and community development corporations (or CDCs) operating supportive housing. These service providers were attracted to the market in part by the new welfare policies and in part by their history in responding to the needs of a clearly established constituency. In the chapter titled "Union-Sponsored Workforce Development Initiatives," Beverly Takahashi and Edwin Meléndez compare union-led workforce development initiatives with community-based and other traditional employment programs. The chapter examines three union-sponsored initiatives within the framework of prevailing union and workforce development trends. New Unionism, which rejects "bread and butter" unionism's exclusionary policies, is the driving force behind union-sponsored workforce development initiatives. At the same time, factors such as industry, region, government policy, union leadership, and prior experience influence the structure of training initiatives.

The authors find that innovative, union-sponsored workforce development initiatives are capable of serving the training and employment needs of low-wage workers, unions, and industries. Unions can intervene at critical junctures of workforce development: they have special knowledge of workplace opportunities, they are connected to employers' recruiting networks, and they are able to provide ongoing training and mentoring in the workplace. In addition, innovative unions have the capacity to assist workers who face multiple barriers to employment by developing links to CBOs that serve the disadvantaged, or by structuring support systems similar to those established by CBOs.

Clearly, not all experiences of those entering the employment services industry were positive. The example presented by Alex Schwartz, Edwin Meléndez, and Sarah Gallagher in the chapter titled "Addressing the Employment Challenge for the Formerly Homeless: Supportive Housing in New York City" demonstrates that entry continues to be a challenge for organizations that have limited experience with employment services. CDCs in the field of supportive housing provide a cost-effective means of helping formerly homeless individuals stay off the streets and live healthier, more independent lives. However, because of welfare reform and increased pressure to move people off public assistance, supportive housing providers, like many other social service providers, have become more interested in increasing the employment opportunities available to their residents and program participants. This chapter examines the employment status of residents in supportive housing programs in New York City, the nature of their employment barriers, the benefits to them of employment, and the ways in which supportive housing organizations are attempting to meet residents' vocational needs. Despite increased program development and innovation, vocational programs run by supportive housing groups do not seem to reach a large segment of their target population. Because of the many obstacles they face, a relatively small number of residents in supportive housing are employed or participating in vocational programs. The study's recommendations for improving vocational support for residents of supportive housing are 1) to develop a better understanding of the market and set realistic outcome expectations to attract more supportive housing residents to the existing programs, and 2) to revamp operations to improve the effectiveness of programs in helping residents to succeed in a competitive labor market.

Overall, the employment services industry underwent a significant change in the composition of service providers as a result of federal reforms of welfare and workforce development policies. In response to these policy changes, and in an attempt to be responsive to the needs of disadvantaged populations, new players entered the industry and established providers adapted their operations. The new local policy regimes are established on the premise of increased market competition and performance compliance. The evidence presented by the different authors in this section indicates a tendency toward increased concentration in the industry with private vendors playing a more active role, particularly in large metropolitan areas where the most profitable opportunities exist. Far from conceding their position in the local system, many large nonprofit and CBO operators have taken advantage of the opportunity and solidified and expanded their position in the system. A new breed of nonprofits, which manages large contracts for local welfare agencies, and a new breed of CBO, which operates OSCCs, signal the appearance of mission-driven organizations that have successfully adapted their programs and operations, improved organizational performance, and implemented effective management systems to comply with the new regulatory environment.

Community-Based Workforce Development Initiatives for the Information Technology Sector

The second section of the volume focuses on one of the most important strategies currently being employed by a variety of labor market intermediaries. Different community-based organizations, unions, and other types of intermediaries are increasingly adopting sectoral strategies to target employment programs at specific industry subsectors. In essence, this strategy seeks to establish long-term relationships between the training and service providers and employers in a targeted industry. Some of the principles adopted by practitioners and organizations implementing the strategy include a dual-customer approach, training for the specific skills needed by industry, and job-retention support services. Rather than recruit and train workers for a wide range of industries and occupations, as is common practice in the industry, supporters of this approach select an industry cluster and focus their efforts on that sub-sector of employers in a given industry. This approach has several benefits, one of which is better outcomes for participants, but practitioners face tremendous challenges when implementing the strategy. These challenges start with financing the project, as conventional sources often find that the intervention is expensive and serves only a limited number of workers. Added to that, acceptance from industry has been slow.

This section takes a closer look at programs targeting subsectors of the IT industry as an example of sector oriented strategies. These programs are of great interest to the field since they shift training and job development toward a fast-growing sector of the economy. The authors examine whether training programs are effective in establishing links with industry and in providing career ladders for jobs that pay family-sustaining wages. The authors show that there are various community-based initiatives, often involving partnerships among several organizations, that have created successful sectoral strategies. The experiences of employees in these cases can, in turn, serve as models for other practitioners interested in implementing similar strategies.

The increased use of new information technologies in the economy presents new challenges and opportunities for workforce development organizations. In the first paper of the section, "Workforce Development in the Information Technology Age," Michael A. Stoll presents a broad overview of programs and effective practices targeting the information technology (IT) industries. Specifically, this chapter 1) examines the demand for workers and the rising skill requirements in IT jobs, 2) evaluates whether current workforce policy is positioned to meet the growing labor market needs in the IT sector, and 3) investigates how workforce development policy can help low-skill workers overcome barriers in the new economy labor market. A number of "best practices" are identified that are likely to link low-skill workers to IT jobs. These include employer links, relevant and timely skills training, a mixed approach to training, integrating community colleges, networking and collaboration among training providers, and post-employment assistance.

The purpose of the second chapter in this section is to discuss how the rise of the IT sector has opened a unique window of opportunity for community based organizations linking disadvantaged workers to the growing sectors of the economy. In her chapter titled "Community Technology Centers: Training Disadvantaged Workers for Information Technology Jobs," Lisa J. Servon examines whether community technology centers, a community-based type of skills training program, have responded successfully to the challenges of the IT sector. Though the Information Technology Association of America (ITAA) estimates the demand for entry level IT workers to be close to a million and these jobs tend to pay well, many of these positions are entry level and will go unfilled because they require specific skills which need to be upgraded continually.

According to Servon, the rapid change within the IT industry carries with it three primary implications for community-based skills training programs: First, workforce development programs must be responsive to industry needs and constantly update curricula to provide the skills demanded by employers. Second, the traditional concept of job ladders is called into question, since IT workers tend to move between jobs quickly, making traditional measures of job training less useful. Third, workers must become lifelong learners. Training must be seen less as a one-time effort than as a lifelong process because graduates of training programs will likely continue to need training after placement in order to keep their skills current. Although other institutions occupy important niches in the landscape of IT training, community-based training programs have placed the greatest emphasis on targeting, training, and placing disadvantaged workers in IT occupations. The chapter concludes by summarizing the lessons and best practices from the community technology centers' experience in the field.

In the last chapter of this section, Laura Wolf-Powers discusses general principles for policymakers and practitioners pursuing sector-specific career ladder strategies for low-income workers. In "Beyond the First Job: Career Ladder Initiatives in Information Technology Industries," Wolf-Powers presents the findings from case studies of employment access and career mobility in three community-based career ladder initiatives in the telecommunications and related information technology (or information infrastructure) industries.

The study finds that skills training in these sectors has been simplified by the existence of external certifications such as the Building Industry Consulting Service International installer certification and the Cisco Certified Network Associate certification. However, to develop interventions that help clients to progress along external career ladders, an organization must carefully identify articulation points between telecommunications and IT skill sets and investigate how access to the industry is structured in its particular labor market. Echoing the conclusions of other studies, the study finds that the participation of community-based social support and advocacy organizations in training consortia contributes to program success. The study also concludes that institutional and financial support from the public sector, especially at the local level among WIBs, could improve and expand career ladder initiatives for information infrastructure occupations.

The workforce development field has advanced tremendously over the past decade, in part spurred by policy reform, and in part because of advances in program development and learning from the field. Today we know much more about effective practices and how to implement programs that help disadvantaged workers with career advancement than we did a decade ago. The programs articulating effective skills development programs for the IT sector that are presented in the chapter are just examples of the advances that have been made in skills training in many industries. It is evident from the discussion that when gaining technical skills is important for the success of the programs, community colleges play a crucial role in structuring successful partnerships and effective programs. The changing role of community colleges and their positioning in a reconfigured industry are the central topics of the next section of the volume.

Recasting the Role of Community Colleges

Among the institutions that have taken the most advantage of policy reforms are community colleges. Many community colleges have created new programs to accommodate the growing demand for job readiness programs for welfare recipients. Often these programs are structured like career ladders, allowing former program participants to continue their training and education toward industry-sanctioned certificates and other credentials. Community colleges are well positioned to attract incumbent workers in need of the portable certifications of skill competencies necessary for career advancement. The chapters included in this section of the volume address the ability of community colleges to adapt to changing policy contexts and the role that colleges have played in restructuring the employment services delivery system. In many jurisdictions, their involvement has helped change the system into one that is more responsive to the needs of the most disadvantaged job seekers, more regional in scope, and more open to integrating other workforce development partners.

The first chapter in this section, "Community Colleges, Welfare Reform, and Workforce Development," by Edwin Meléndez, Luis M. Falcón, Carlos Suárez-Boulangger, Lynn McCormick, and Alexandra de Montrichard, examines how, and to what extent, community colleges have implemented WtW programs in response to welfare policy changes. The authors found that, in part, the community colleges' responses to welfare reform have been determined by the various regulations enacted by state legislatures, as well as by the implementation of those regulations and by funding allocations from local authorities. State regulations vary tremendously in terms of time limits and definitions of work-related activities. The degree of flexibility of state guidelines regarding the type of job training activities that contribute to program participants' job readiness is particularly important to community colleges' ability to design training programs. The study also finds that the extent to which community colleges have responded to the new policy initiatives has been determined primarily by internal factors such as the college leadership's commitment to a comprehensive mission for the college, the existence of programs and prior experiences serving the disadvantaged, faculty and staff attitudes toward non-degree programs, and ongoing relations and collaborations with local labor, businesses, industries, and social service agencies.

While most states enacted regulations to encourage community colleges and other adult educational institutions to enhance existing or create new programs targeting welfare recipients, some local authorities enacted policies that in fact made it very difficult for colleges to maintain programs serving welfare recipients. In "Innovators Under Duress: Community Colleges in New York's Workfare Setting," Lynn McCormick shows how New York City policies have influenced community college programs for welfare recipients. Under PRWORA, each state is granted flexibility in determining the mix of education, training, and workfare activities that it will allow. New York City's state and local policy environments focus on workfare rather than education. Through case study research of the city's community colleges, McCormick finds that, overall, the policy environment has had a chilling effect on new programming for welfare recipients. Nevertheless, some exemplary programs have emerged. The paper concludes that there are strong policy "entrepreneurs" outside of government whose responses influence government policies. The interplay between policy entrepreneurs and city and state officials makes the reinventing government movement a more complex and nonlinear process than scholars have indicated.

In the final chapter of the section, "Community Colleges as Workforce Intermediaries: Building Career Ladders for Low-Wage Workers," Joan Fitzgerald argues that community college vocational programs are uniquely poised to provide the training needed for low-wage workers to advance into better paying jobs. Most of the nation's community colleges have developed short-term training programs, some specifically for Temporary Assistance for Needy Families (TANF) clients. A few community colleges are attempting to build on these programs by offering courses and programs for students after initial placement to prepare them to advance on the job. Many community colleges also engage in economic development activities that provide technical assistance to businesses to help them become high performance work organizations. In both types of programs, however, community colleges act as labor market intermediaries that not only connect supply and demand but also attempt to influence demand. This chapter examines in more detail the extent to which community colleges can help to create better paying jobs as well as provide the training for people to fill them. The study presents three highly successful community college programs that focus on career ladders or wage progression. These programs have been successful in connecting poor people to jobs to which they otherwise would not have had access.

In summary, the community colleges' effective and creative response to the challenge posed by WtW policies has proven that they are capable of playing a major role in regional labor markets. In some regions of the country, community colleges have shown employers that their programs can become reliable partners in providing well-trained and reliable workers. To many state labor and social service agencies, community colleges have demonstrated that they have the capacity and experience to serve a large number of disadvantaged students by creating specialized support programs and by adapting their existing infrastructure to meet these students' needs. Moreover, to community-based and church-based organizations, and to business and industry groups, community colleges have demonstrated that they can engage in mutually beneficial collaborations. Community colleges above all can provide numerous educational programs for any partnership and can articulate short-term vocational training with long-term education.

An evident conclusion from the discussion presented in the chapters in this section is that, initially, community colleges responded to the WtW policy shock by strengthening and transforming existing programs. However, as colleges became more aggressive in recruiting welfare recipients, a critical mass of colleges created new, more advanced and farsighted programs that positioned the schools as comprehensive regional labor-market intermediaries. Given the colleges' experience with the WtW initiative and the prominent and favored role assigned by WIA to community colleges, it's no wonder that they, more than any other type of intermediary, are capitalizing on the restructuring of the federally funded employment system and becoming the primary providers of vocational training for adults and out-of-school youth.

Whether community colleges can continue to assume such a prominent role in the emerging workforce development system will be determined by their ability to transcend their focus on a traditional educational mission and expand it to be inclusive of, and integrated to, workforce development activities and programs. Indeed, the community colleges that have evolved into the most significant labor intermediaries in their regions see themselves as playing a more comprehensive role than that of traditional educators. Based on the findings from the studies presented in the volume, these community colleges have a clear mission to link education with industry and have engaged in strategies to forge alliances and collaborations with employers, government agencies, employer associations, and community groups. The next section of the volume examines community-based partnerships and collaborations in greater detail.

New Directions in Community Collaborations and Partnerships

Effective strategies to help the working poor advance have involved government, the private sector, educational institutions, labor unions, churches, CBOs, and social service providers. These institutions serve as labor market intermediaries that prepare and connect individuals to jobs and support them in their efforts to stay employed and advance professionally. However, given the diverse needs of the populations served and the wide range of employers targeted for entry level jobs, it is difficult for any one organization to provide a truly comprehensive array of support services to program participants or to engage in effective strategies to interest employers in their programs. Faced with this reality of increased demand for services at a time of more competition for financial resources to provide such services, organizations are exploring various ways of associating with one another to complement their program offerings. The authors in this section of the book address the lessons to be gleaned from effective partnerships and the factors that contribute to successful collaborations. They also examine the role that different institutions and actors have played in strengthening local and regional partnerships and collaborations.

The first chapter of the section is by Héctor R. Cordero-Guzmán. Titled "Interorganizational Networks among Community-Based Organizations," it examines two questions: 1) why do CBOs enter into networks with one another, and, 2) what are some of the main factors in successful interorganizational networks among CBOs engaged in workforce development and other community initiatives? The study's main finding is that although it takes a significant amount of effort to design, manage, and maintain interorganizational networks, the payoffs to networking can be substantial for CBOs in terms of additional services for community residents and more access to resources, information, and accrued knowledge. However, the author cautions that the complementarities between the organizations' competencies are critical. Lack of understanding of such complementarities, or a forced relationship for funding or programmatic reasons, will often lead to a failed partnership.

One of the most important challenges in the field is how to establish long-lasting relations between employers and training providers. What is the role for each of the partners? What are the benefits to employers of engaging in partnerships with CBOs? In the final chapter of the section and the book, "Corporate-Community Workforce Development Collaborations," Stacey A. Sutton examines employer perspectives and expectations with respect to building and sustaining collaborations with CBOs. She also looks at the usefulness of such collaborative relationships in creating opportunities for disadvantaged job seekers. The analysis is based on the examination of eight cases that are representative of a larger group of corporations actively engaged in starting and sustaining workforce development programs. Particular attention is given to the level of corporate involvement with CBOs—referred to as external or corporate connectedness—and the level of internal corporate support for and integration of workforce development practices, or their level of cohesiveness. In the end, according to the author, the best jobs are created in firms characterized by both strong external networks with community partners and strong internal support among management and coworkers. So it is not just networks that matter in creating good jobs; firms also have to be ready to embrace change.

The knowledge that exists in the workforce development field about partnerships and collaborations, their effectiveness, and the factors that motivate different actors to participate in these arrangements continues to be limited. However, the two chapters included in this section contribute much to our understanding of two types of community-based partnerships: those among various actors at the community level, and those between community actors and the corporate sector. The first is focused on a more coherent utilization of community resources, while the second is concerned with establishing bridges to mainstream employment opportunities for disadvantaged workers. Clearly, partnerships and collaborations have been instrumental in determining the workforce intermediaries that are more capable of taking advantage of the changes in policy that are redefining the employment services industry. They also have helped in facilitating the success of sectoral strategies, in structuring community college programs that serve welfare recipients, and in all aspects of the employment service delivery structure as examined by the various authors in this volume.

CONCLUSIONS

Workforce development is a relatively new intellectual and professional field. Although the "employment and training," "social services," "economic development," and corporate "human resources" fields preceded its development, it is only in recent years that these streams of intellectual and professional practice have converged to advance a new discipline. Workforce development as a field of study encompasses the traditional social and supportive services necessary for job seekers to succeed in the labor market, as well as employer services and employer-intermediary relationships that influence successful recruitment and incorporation of workers into the workplace, career advancement, and increased productivity.

In this volume we examine how programming by different institutions and innovative professional practices are converging to transform the employment services industry. It is widely acknowledged by practitioners and other professionals in the field that the employment services industry has undergone considerable evolution over the past decade. System reforms have been partly induced by the dynamics of a rapidly changing economic environment and by a succession of policy shocks during the 1990s. The long economic expansion of the 1990s created favorable labor market conditions for the low-skilled, entry-level segment of the market, a reversal of the previous decade's pattern in which the more educated workers benefited the most from economic growth. Consequently, during the past decade employers in many industries have been more willing to experiment with recruitment and training programs targeting the disadvantaged.

Throughout the volume, the authors present evidence documenting how various policy reforms at the national, state, and local levels have induced employment services providers to revamp their operations to improve placement, retention, and other outcomes for program participants. The most recent wave of system reforms began with the enactment and implementation of TANF and WIA. Taken as a whole, these reforms promoted the principles of universal access, integration of federal funding streams, devolution of policy to local authorities, and the philosophical primacy of work experience (work first) as a starting point for employment services. WIA focused on outcomes and performance-based management. As a result, many new programs were started by nontraditional institutions, many of the traditional programs underwent a rapid transformation of operations, and many others left the industry.

The studies presented in the volume constitute a first step towards a comprehensive assessment of the role that community organizations have played in the revamping of the employment services industry. One of the most significant developments in the employment services industry today is the evolution of traditional service providers into a new type of labor market intermediary that simultaneously focuses on both the needs of job seekers and those of employers. The new labor market intermediaries have achieved a fundamental transformation of their services, which were previously oriented towards the provision of employment services to job seekers at the expense of responding to the needs of employers.

One of the most meaningful conclusions that can be derived from the discussion presented by the studies included in this volume is that, while many institutions offer employment services, the participation of CBOs has been a defining element in the majority of successful initiatives. Community organizations are a critical component of an integrated approach to economic and social development. One of the most defining characteristics of the new type of labor market intermediary is its emphasis on partnerships, networking, and collaborations as a mechanism to leverage resources in a highly competitive environment.

Collectively, the authors of the studies present an extensive discussion and assessment of the role of partnerships in workforce development. The book includes several in-depth case studies of successful initiatives anchored by partnerships among employers, CBOs, educational institutions, and government organizations.

Finally, understanding the role of community-based initiatives and the diverse types of organizations and institutions that compose the employment services industry infrastructure is particularly important in the context of public policy reform. WIA is intended to promote competition among service providers and has made it more difficult for CBOs to participate in local systems as service providers. Yet, based on the evidence presented in the volume, CBOs continue to play a positive and synergetic role in the system. Collectively, the authors included in the volume advise policymakers to take into consideration the contributions from community initiatives when reauthorizing WIA and to strengthen the community-based training options available to TANF recipients. Both of these issues have been at the center of congressional debates as lawmakers proceed with the reauthorization of the two most important legislative initiatives in recent years.

Notes

1. In this context, we refer to community-based initiatives as those programs and collaborations that involve one or several community-based organizations, social agencies, or groups (e.g., religious) that have a primary focus on neighborhoods and disadvantaged populations. These initiatives often include partners from several institutions.
2. See Chapter 13 in this volume for examples of these programs.
3. For the discussion in this Chapter, CBOs are a subset of nonprofit organizations. CBOs will often have a community focus, and area residents primarily integrate their boards. CBOs also will often provide multiple services to residents. In contrast, nonprofit organizations are frequently affiliates of national membership organizations; they provide services to a broader area, and their programs tend to focus on employment.
4. See Chapter 2.
5. See Chapter 2.
6. The following discussion is based on an interpretation of the available literature on the topic, particularly of the studies presented by the various authors included in this volume. States are having difficulty collecting data under WIA in part

because of difficulties with information management. The costs, technical difficulties, and expertise requirements of implementing information management systems to collect performance data are limiting states' ability to meet WIA mandates. Thus, many states, at least until now, have been unable to report on all of these measures, especially those that require unemployment insurance (UI) records to measure earnings over the six-month post-program completion period.

7. In actuality, many local authorities have enacted regulations that allow for the provision of intensive services to qualifying participants after the initial assessment. In a few localities, training services are also made available to qualifying participants while they are still receiving intensive services. Since this has been one of the most confusing and contentious aspects of the law, it is likely that with the reauthorization of WIA the act will be clarified to allow for the immediate assignment of intensive or training services to qualifying applicants.
8. See Chapter 3.
9. See Chapter 3.
10. See Chapter 9.
11. To our knowledge, very few jurisdictions have actually implemented this aspect of the act.

References

Bloom, Howard S., Larry L. Orr, Stephen H. Bell, George Cave, Fred Doolittle, Winston Lin, and Johannes M. Bos. 1997. "The Benefits and Costs of JTPA Title II-A Programs: Key Findings from the National Job Training Partnership Act Study." *Journal of Human Resources* 32(3): 549–576.

Buck, Maria. 2002. *Charting New Territory: Early Implementation of the Workforce Investment Act.* New York: Public/Private Ventures.

Frank, Abbey, Hedieh Rahmanou, and Steve Savner. 2003. *The Workforce Investment Act: A First Look at Participation, Demographics, and Services.* Washington, DC: Center for Law and Social Policy.

Giloth, Robert P., ed. 1998. *Jobs and Economic Development: Strategies and Practice.* Thousand Oaks, CA: Sage Publications.

Grubb, W. Norton. 1996. *Learning to Work: The Case for Reintegrating Job Training and Education.* New York: Russell Sage Foundation.

Gueron, Judith M. 1986. *Work Initiatives for Welfare Recipients: Lessons from a Multi-State Experiment.* New York: Manpower Demonstration Research Corporation.

———. 1990. "Work and Welfare: Lessons on Employment Programs." *Journal of Economic Perspectives* 4(1): 79–98.

Gueron, Judith M., and Gayle Hamilton. 2002. *The Role of Education and Training in Welfare Reform.* Washington, DC: Brookings Institution.

Gueron, Judith M., Edward Pauly, and Cameran M. Lougy. 1991. *From Welfare-to-work*. New York: Russell Sage Foundation.

Harrison, Bennett, and Marcus Weiss. 1998. *Workforce Development Networks: Community-Based Organizations and Regional Alliances*. Thousand Oaks, CA: Sage Publications.

King, Christopher T. 1999. "Federalism and Workforce Policy Reform." *Publius: The Journal of Federalism* 29(2): 53–71.

Meléndez, Edwin. 1996. *Working on Jobs: The Center for Employment Training*. Boston: Mauricio Gastón Institute for Latino Community Development and Public Policy, University of Massachusetts Boston.

———. 1997. "The Potential Impact of Workforce Development Legislation on CBOs." *New England Journal of Public Policy* 13(1): 175–186.

Meléndez, Edwin, Luis Falcón, and Josh Bivens. 2003. "Community College Participation in Welfare Programs: Do State Policies Matter?" *Community College Journal of Research and Practice* 27(3): 203–223.

Meléndez, Edwin, and Bennett Harrison. 1997. "Matching the Disadvantaged to Job Opportunities: Structural Explanations for the Past Successes of the Center for Employment Training." *Economic Development Quarterly* 12(1): 3–11.

Michalopoulos, Charles, Christine Schwartz, and Diana Adams-Ciardullo. 2000. *What Works Best for Whom: Impacts of 20 Welfare-to-Work Programs by Subgroup*. U.S. Department of Health and Human Services series on National Evaluation of Welfare-to-Work Strategies (NEWWS). New York: Manpower Demonstration Research Corporation.

Mueller, Elizabeth J., and Alex Schwartz. 1998. "Why Local Economic Development and Employment Training Fail Low-Income Communities." *Jobs and Economic Development,* Robert P. Gilroth, ed. Thousand Oaks, CA: Sage Publications, pp. 42–63.

Orr, Larry L., Howard S. Bloom, Stephen H. Bell, Fred Doolittle, Winston Lin, and George Cave. 1996. *Does Training for the Disadvantaged Work? Evidence from the National JTPA Study*. Washington, DC: Urban Institute Press.

O'Shea, Daniel, and Christopher T. King. 2001. *The Workforce Investment Act of 1998: Restructuring Workforce Development Initiatives in States and Localities*. Report no. 12. Albany, NY: Nelson A. Rockefeller Institute of Government.

Patel, Nisha, and Steve Savner. 2001. *Implementation of Individual Training Account Policies Under the Workforce Investment Act: Early Information from Local Areas*. Washington, DC: Center for Law and Social Policy.

Pavetti, LaDonna, Michelle K. Derr, Jacquelyn Anderson, Carole Trippe, and Sidnee Paschal. 2000. "Changing the Culture of the Welfare Office: The

Role of Intermediaries in Linking TANF Recipients with Jobs." *Economic Policy Review* 7(2): 63–76.

Plastrik, Peter, and Judith Combes Taylor. 2001. *Responding to a Changing Labor Market: The Challenges for Community-Based Organizations.* Boston: Jobs for the Future.

Stokes, Robert. 1996. *Model Welfare-to-Work Initiatives in the U.S.: Effective Strategies for Moving TANF Recipients from Public Assistance to Self-Sufficiency.* Hartford, CT: Connecticut Business and Industry Association and RSS Associates.

Strawn, Julie. 1998. *Beyond Job Search or Basic Education: Rethinking the Role of Skills in Welfare Reform.* Washington, DC: Center for Law and Social Policy.

U.S. Department of Labor. 1995. *What's Working (and What's Not): A Summary of Research on the Economic Impacts of Employment and Training Programs.* Washington, DC: U.S. Department of Labor.

U.S. General Accounting Office (USGAO). 1996a. *Job Training Partnership Act: Long-Term Earnings and Employment Outcomes.* GAO/HEHS-96-40. Washington, DC: U.S. General Accounting Office.

———. 1996b. *Employment and Training: Successful Projects Share Common Strategy.* GAO/HEHS-96-108. Washington, DC: U.S. General Accounting Office.

———. 2000. *Workforce Investment Act.: Implementation Status and the Integration of TANF Services.* GAO/T-HEHS-00-145. Washington, DC: U.S. General Accounting Office.

———. 2001. WIA: *Better Guidance Needed to Address Concerns Over New Requirements.* Report to Congressional Requesters. GAO-02-72. Washington, DC: U.S. General Accounting Office.

———. 2002. *Workforce Investment Act: Improvements Needed in Performance Measures to Provide a More Accurate Picture of WIA's Effectiveness.* GAO-02-275. Washington, DC: U.S. General Accounting Office.

———. 2004. *Workforce Investment Act: States and Local Areas Have Developed Strategies to Assess Performance, but Labor Could Do More to Help.* GAO-04-657. Washington, DC: U.S. General Accounting Office.

Part 1

Emerging Labor Market Intermediaries

2
Competing for Contracts

Nonprofit Survival in an Age of Privatization

M. Bryna Sanger
New School University

Competition among private providers in the delivery of employment training services may not be new, but the entrance of a few national, for-profit corporations has recently begun to reshape the employment training industry following the lifting of restrictions provided for under Temporary Assistance for Needy Families (TANF). Corporate players are changing the rules of the game in areas with a long and stable history of public-nonprofit partnerships, and the competitive pressures that emanate from the "work first" imperatives are of particular concern—especially for community-based organizations. Thus, the question of whether privatization in a performance-based environment will result in better services or distort and ultimately drive out essential, mission-driven programs bears scrutiny.

New contracting requirements and competitive demands that force nonprofits to compete with for-profits can change their priorities, requiring them to choose between meeting the market test and maintaining commitments to their primary mission. After all, "work first" eschews, in large part, longer and more intensive education and training in favor of direct job placement and short-term job readiness skills. Federal mandates to the states for caseload engagement place significant pressure on states and localities to meet their placement targets. There is also a desire by local officials to reduce costs, improve performance, and circumvent the constraints on flexibility and innovation imposed by public employee unions. Several jurisdictions have chosen competitive, performance-based contract arrangements as a solution to these pressures, awarding million-dollar contracts to a few large, profit-driven corporations over community-based providers (Barnow and Trutko 2002).

This new service environment places enormous demands on all participants and will likely determine the success of many. High performing, mission-driven organizations must change to remain relevant. But regardless of their merits under a competitive, performance-based system, nonprofits and community-based providers have held a unique place in the civic infrastructure and historically have played a critical role in the job training and placement arena by providing specialized services for a diversity of needs in the community. CBOs losing out to for-profit providers may have profound effects on the quality and appropriateness of the services available—services that would change when product standardization is required to achieve economies. The speed and scale of change have allowed little systematic evaluation of CBOs' strategies and service records, and advocates of the poor, traditional providers, and public policy observers question the wisdom of rushing into public contracting with private firms. This chapter takes a look at nonprofits competing with for-profit providers in four jurisdictions. Our assessment of the likely effect of the changing environment pays particular attention to its impact on these indispensable social institutions.

The competitive contracting environment created by reengineered welfare reform delivery systems is a mixed blessing at best. Some of the market incentives have worked in the expected direction by improving organizational and service performance and increasing innovation and creative adaptations, as seen in a number of nonprofits. Likewise, as we shall see in upcoming chapters, many CBO-operated employment programs owe their success as well as their survival in this evolving industry to effective and creative interorganizational networking, which enables them to combine strengths and share administrative functions. Intermediaries play an important role in setting up these arrangements. Such examples do exist in the face of competition for TANF contract awards, including cases of for-profit–nonprofit allegiances. CBOs have historically capitalized on high quality placements and the professional training capacity that for-profit partnerships can provide. They now stand to benefit from their access to start-up capital and the technologically sophisticated systems needed to function under these new mandates. For-profits have in turn benefited from subcontracting arrangements with community-based providers, tapping into their local expertise while averting the political backlash that can arise from the commercialization of this sensitive service environment.

Our investigation has revealed, however, that mutually beneficial for-profit–nonprofit partnering, and even examples of successful nonprofit collaborations, tend to be more the exception than the rule under this system. As they compete for Welfare-to-Work contracts, nonprofits in our four sites are experiencing considerable stress in making the necessary shifts to become more businesslike in organizational design, management, staffing, and culture. The degree of difficulty experienced varies considerably among nonprofit and for-profit organizations of different size, experience, sophistication and philosophy. Nonprofits vary dramatically among themselves—as much or more than they do from their for-profit competitors. For this reason, the increasing seductiveness of large government contracts and a desire to make a difference in a reengineered human services industry must be tempered by a balanced assessment of mission and capacities. The pressure exerted by private-sector competitors in all our sites is considerable, and all CBOs understand the tall challenges they face.

THE RECONNAISSANCE MISSION

In the absence of any existing national survey data that examine the impact of these new competitive demands on nonprofit providers, we undertook a reconnaissance mission to seek out existing arrangements in jurisdictions that have introduced innovations in the provision of services. Four jurisdictions, San Diego, Milwaukee, New York, and Houston (see Table 2.1) were selected based on meeting our criteria: 1) introduction of competition among vendors from each of the sectors, and 2) a change in the number and character of contractors serving TANF clients. These case studies include big operators that have had a long history in the provision of public services, as well as medium-sized and smaller agencies that have limited access to the resources and capital necessary to compete in a performance-based environment.

We can discern three types of experiences. Many large, experienced and competent organizations are meeting the challenge and, in many cases, improving their organizational systems, staff, and programming.

Table 2.1 Overview of Contract Characteristics in Four Cities

	Houston	Milwaukee	New York	San Diego
TANF client placement	Clients assigned to 1 of 30 career centers by zip code.	Clients assigned to 1 of 6 geographic regions, each with a sole provider.	TANF contracts are referred by Human Resources Administration (HRA) first to a Skills Assessment and Job Placement Center (SAP) contractor. If still without employment, client will be referred by HRA to an Employment Services and Job Placement Center (ESP) contractor.	Clients are assigned to 1 of 6 geographic regions, each with a sole provider.
Providers and sites per provider	6 contractors, each with multiple career centers.	5 contractors, all serving a single region except 1 that has received 2 regions.	5 contractors with the SAP contracts, 12 contractors with the ESP contracts.	2 contractors run single regions, while both county officials and ACS State and Local Solutions run 2 regions.
Services provided to TANF clients	Centers are assigned TANF clients; receive case management services including assessment, employment planning, job readiness and job search; refer clients for intensive job and basic skills training and on-the-job training.	Contractors complete eligibility determination and provide complete services all the way through job training and placement.	SAP contractors receive TANF clients and provide skills assessments and services through preliminary job placement centers. ESP contractors are referred clients who are not placed by the SAP contractors; they offer more intensive employment services and job training and placement.	Centers are assigned clients; they handle all case-management duties including appraisal, assessment, and job search training; if clients do not succeed in finding employment, they are referred to a work placement network.

Bidding process	Request for proposal.	Request for proposal.	Negotiated acquisition process.	Request for proposal.
Contract structure and measurement parameters	Cost reimbursement: each contractor must achieve certain levels for eligible served, clients receiving continued service, clients entering employment, and clients employed above minimum wage.	Pay for performance: contractors must achieve and can receive bonuses for achieving an entered-employment placement rate, average wage rate, job retention rate, available health insurance benefits, full and proper engagement, and basic education/job skills activities. Two optional measurements (faith-based contracts and basic education/job skills attainment) may be substituted for the bonus portion of 2 of the above categories.	Pay for performance: SAP—payment is given for assessment, engagement in employment activities, job placement (higher rate for 30+ hours), with a bonus given for high wages and 90-day placement. ESP—a percentage of base rate or a flat fee is paid for placement and 90-day retention, while a higher flat fee is paid for high wages, left welfare, or placement for 180 days.	Pay for performance: certain amounts are paid for participant engagement, active caseload, 30-day employment, and 180-day employment.
Level of subcontracting	Relatively little.	Extensive.	Very little for SAP, extensive for ESP.	Very little.

SOURCE: Contract information provided by the following organizations: Houston Department of Human Services, Gulf Coast Workforce Board; Wisconsin Department of Workforce Development; Office of Contracts, New York City Comptrollers Office; County of San Diego, Contract Operations.

Even as they do so, however, the demands and philosophy of TANF impose programmatic emphases that compromise organizational values and challenge long-standing missions. Others, less fiscally sound, find it a struggle to develop the capacity to meet the financial and management demands of the contracts but have temporarily managed to stay afloat through a variety of innovative, short-term survival strategies. A third group is at more immediate risk, unable to make the sizable financial and organizational investments to compete, and unwilling to capitulate to the fundamental challenges to their missions that performance-based contracts entail.

In the sections that follow we discuss the current status of the nonprofit sector in the context of this changing environment. We next examine the differences in nonprofits' motivations for competing for contracts and the differential effects that their recent adjustments are having. We conclude by highlighting the potential dangers for nonprofits while citing a few promising examples of effective adaptations and solutions to the ongoing challenge of competition.

STAYING IN THE GAME

These have been turbulent times for nonprofits. The past two decades have witnessed phenomenal growth in the nonprofit sector, even as critics and expert observers have sounded the alarm. The future of the sector is under constant scrutiny, but observers' judgments about its condition depend upon whether they have an optimistic or a pessimistic outlook. Paul Light (1999) shows how today's policy environment has put pressure on nonprofits to change and has caused many organizations to feel the squeeze from several sides. Even so, he reminds us that the sector has grown in the dollars it receives from contributors and government, the size and professionalism of its workforce, and the degree to which it inspires career aspirations in a new generation who increasingly see the nonprofit sector as their destination (Light 1999). Nevertheless, the sector is being compelled to demonstrate its effectiveness. Increasingly compared with both the public and the private sector, nonprofits are being asked to justify their competence and relevance. Calls to demonstrate performance in program outcomes, good fiscal and organizational management, and efficiency have been mounting from a more sophisticated donor base, funding institutions, boards of directors, professionalized staff, and government. Reform movements are besetting the sector (Light 1997, 2000).

Government contracts and funding represent an ever-increasing portion of nonprofits' income. In 1982, 56 percent of all social services and 48 percent of all employment and training services financed by government were delivered by nonprofits (Salamon 1995, p. 88). Between 1992 and 1998, public support for employment and training nonprofits increased by 44 percent (Lampkin and Pollak 2002, Table 5.8). Today, the government-funded portion of social services' income remains high. Although recent data on sources of funding for nonprofit employment and training providers alone are hard to find, 1997 data on the portion of revenue that nonprofit social-service organizations received from government sources put the figure in excess of 52 percent (Lampkin and Pollak 2002, pp. 100–101). This figure probably underestimates the percentage among employment and training providers, where nonprofits still provide the bulk of services to state and local governments and for whom government funding historically made up the single largest source of funding.

While the increasing reliance of state and local governments on nonprofits to deliver social services has resulted in considerable growth, it has also made these organizations vulnerable to changes in government expenditures and policies. A study that analyzed the impact of federal welfare waivers on human services nonprofits in the 53 largest metropolitan areas from 1992 to 1996 found that 26 percent failed over the period (Twombly 2000b). Another study of 13,500 nonprofits most likely to be affected by welfare reform found that of the 83 percent that were providing core services (including employment-related services), revenue was growing, but for a majority of those, expenditures were growing faster. Only 41 percent of these nonprofits had positive net balances for the two years of the latter study, 1992 and 1994 (De Vita 1999, p. 221). These data highlight the considerable vulnerability that nonprofits have to policy and funding changes. Some are better capitalized and managed; others have more diverse funding streams allowing them greater resiliency and adaptability to changing policy demands and economic fluctuations.[1] And those nonprofits that fail are quickly replaced by new entrants—at a rate of three human service providers for each one that fails (Twombly 2000b). What seems clear amid the turnover is that greater competition, increasing dependence on government, and changing standards and expectations for nonprofit performance pose serious challenges for the future.

Fiscal, economic, and effectiveness crises represent ongoing challenges for nonprofit institutions, but Lester Salamon (1997) has identified a more fundamental crisis in the nonprofit sector as being one of legitimacy (Salamon 1997, p. 41). Salamon poses the problem as a fundamental moral and political challenge that questions the sector's continued *raison d'etre.* Wedded to a nineteenth century image of charity and altruism, public support for nonprofits in the wake of their commercialization, public partnerships, and professionalization appears to be on the decline, Salamon (1997) says:

> The nonprofit sector is thus being hoisted on its own mythology. Having failed to make clear to the American public what its role should be in a mature mixed economy, the sector has been thrown on the defensive by revelations that it is not operating the way its mythology would suggest. A massive gap has thus opened between the modern reality of a sector intimately involved with government and moving into commercialization in the wake of government cutbacks, and the popular image of a set of community based institutions mobilizing purely voluntary energies to assist those in need. (p. 42)

Nonprofits—both large institutions and smaller CBOs—engaged in Welfare-to-Work contracting are obliged to reexamine their missions, governance, and ways of operating, especially in a competitive performance-based service environment. Success requires that they compare themselves with private, for-profit firms and elevate market values in their decision-making about what challenges to pursue and how to pursue them. As nonprofits move through transition in this environment, they are more like the "shadow state," says Wolch (1990): ever in conflict about the autonomy they can maintain and the participatory or democratic objectives they can pursue. "As the sector struggles to maintain itself and develop, it faces a difficult dilemma: to rely increasingly on opportunities linked to state privatization initiatives (and, hence, subject itself to increasing state control), or to maintain independence of organizational purpose but face a continuing struggle for survival and resources. Either way, the sector's survival remains at risk" (Wolch 1990, p. 19).

BEING IN THE GAME BUT KEEPING YOUR SOUL

Nonprofits that succeeded in the bidding process in the four cities we visited were generally experienced service providers with a history of contracting to government and with missions focused on serving disadvantaged populations. Many, but not all, had provided case management, employability assessment, job placement, and training services under a variety of government funding streams and private philanthropic resources. Many also had some degree of skepticism about a future under a competitive contract process with for-profit organizations, but most were motivated to participate by a commitment to serve low-income populations, as was consistent with their missions.

Most of those we interviewed held the view that the world is changing. As Nancy Liu of the Chinese Community Center in Houston said, "If you are behind the wagon, then you are behind the wagon no matter what. It doesn't matter what kind of heart that you have. There is just no money for you to have a good heart and not see what the bottom line is."[2] Although the role of nonprofit providers in the design of new delivery systems and contracts varied and some long-term providers expressed dismay about the lack of consultation in the system redesign process, all felt that given their experience and mission they should have a role in a redesigned system. One nonprofit executive, Sister Ramonda Duvall, executive director of Catholic Charities in San Diego, described the motivation in these terms: "We bid because we didn't trust the city to deal fairly with the poor. We wanted to have a voice at the table. The for-profits have no mission or commitment toward the poor. We thought, 'Once they get a foothold, the nonprofits would be out of business.'"[3] In a presentation before a group of welfare administrators from around the country, Sister Duvall further described the motivation of Catholic Charities as emanating directly from its mission. The federal legislation compelled the organization, she said, to embrace "a unique opportunity to do it right" (Duvall 2000).

In Houston, the Community Services branch of the local AFL-CIO bid on a contract and won. Choosing to capitulate to the realities of prevailing policy rather than relinquish its role, Community Services competed in an arena that labor unions have historically opposed entering. Loath to undermine the role of public employee unions in providing public services, labor unions have consistently opposed the practice of contracting services out, and have opposed privatization in particular. However, the local AFL-CIO director, Richard Shaw, explained the situation in terms similar to those Sister Duvall used: that if allowing for-profits to compete was the direction the state was headed in, labor could not afford to sit out and lose its opportunity to be part of the competition.[4]

The nonprofit response to the changing environment is clearly a marriage of pragmatism and social mission. Among our interviewees, there was the recognition that this was the only game in town—a game where the players were eligible for far more resources than most had ever been awarded in a single contract before. (See Figure 2.1.) But this assessment was balanced by a view voiced by most of those we spoke to: that this was the business they were in, and they had a mission-driven belief that they could do it better. Amalia Betanzos, the President of Wildcat Service Corporation, which has a $54.7 million contract with the city of New York, was particularly enthusiastic about her organization's ability to thrive under a performance-based contract and eager to demonstrate Wildcat's superiority as a provider. "We have always exceeded our benchmarks so we are pleased with performance-based contracts," she said. "We want to get paid for our results and will do well under this system. If you are good, competition is useful—compared to for-profits, our motivations are different: This is our business—this is their opportunity."[5]

Many nonprofit heads even claimed they welcomed competition from the private sector because they found that the competitive pressures made them better, and that the financial structure of their operations and their long experience in the community dealing with employers and disadvantaged clients gave them a comparative advantage. Most of the nonprofits we spoke to—and the majority of nonprofit contractors who won bids in the latest round—were relatively well capitalized and had been in the business a long time. Compared to the new entrants into the system, Betanzos said, "we know exactly what we are."[6] Even so, asset levels, even for large nonprofits, are often rather low in comparison to the size of contracts they are taking. (See Figure 2.1 and Table 2.2.)

Goodwill Industries of New York, for example, is a large, well-established player nationally and in the New York provider community and has been in business for more than 80 years. It runs a thrift shop that recycles, repairs, and cleans used items like clothing and furniture to be

Figure 2.1 Nonprofit Income and Assets (2000) Compared with Contract Amount (2001)

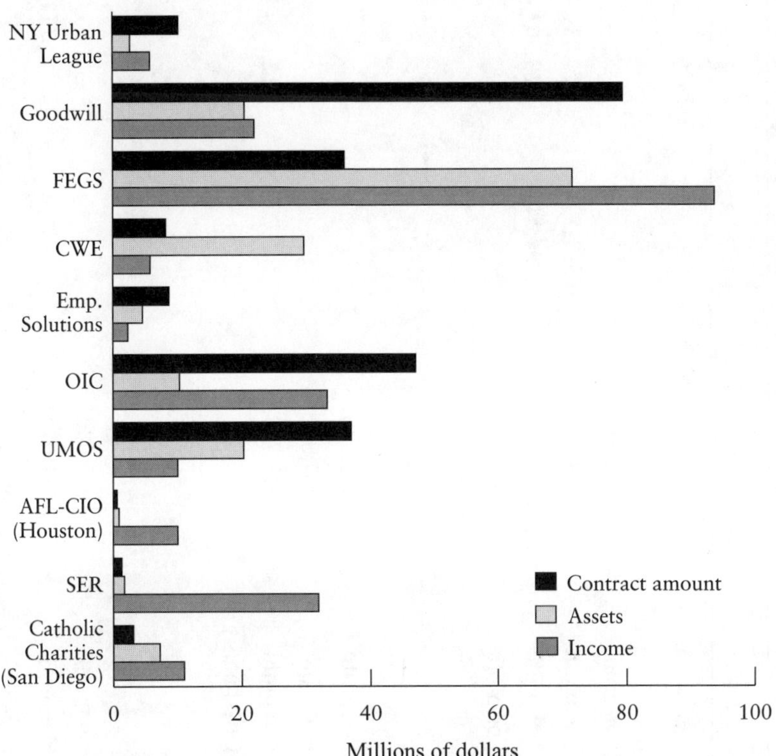

NOTE: Goodwill = Goodwill Industries (New York); FEGS = Federal Employment and Guidance Services (New York); CWE = Consortium for Worker Education (New York); Emp. Solutions = Employment Solutions (Milwaukee); OIC = Opportunities Industrialization Center of Greater Milwaukee; UMOS = United Migrant Opportunities Services (Milwaukee); SER = SER–Jobs for Progress (Houston).

SOURCE: Information from www.guidestar.org. Ten out of 13 contract providers for which data were available are included.

Table 2.2 County Contracts, Comparing Contract Size to Asset Level of Contractor

Contractor	Sector	Contract size ($)	Assets ($)	Income ($)
Milwaukee				
Contract period 2002–2003				
YW Works	For-profit	65,252,410		
UMOS	Nonprofit	66,517,591	20,391,592	10,031,453
OIC of Greater Milwaukee Inc.	Nonprofit	36,940,478	1,036,517	33,363,611
MAXIMUS	For-profit	36,940,478		
San Diego				
Contract period 1998–2002				
ACS[a]	For-profit	26,442,940		
MAXIMUS	For-profit	23,967,062		
Catholic Charities	Nonprofit	11,018,718	8,347,702	12,650,131
San Diego County Agencies	Gov't entity			
Houston				
Contract period 2000–2001				
Houston Works	Nonprofit	6,988,386		24,000,000
SER–Jobs for Progress	Nonprofit	1,311,072	1,176,734	3,144,020
Lockheed/ACS	For-profit	3,695,022		

Interfaith	Nonprofit	4,741,718		
Gulfcoast Careers of Harris County	Gov't entity	3,463,901		
Community Services Program of the AFL-CIO	Nonprofit	582,768	379,645	1,563,779
New York				
Contract period 1999–2002				
SAP Contractors				
Association for Research and Behavior	For-profit	17,797,500		
Curtis & Associates[b]	For-profit	26,932,500		
FEGS	Nonprofit	20,160,000	80,419,722	100,282,051
MAXIMUS	For-profit	3,000,000		
Goodwill Industries	Nonprofit	35,437,500	27,287,285	39,386,149
ESP Contractors				
America Works of New York	For-profit	30,630,000		
Career and Educational Consultants	For-profit	14,355,000		
Consortium for Worker Education	Nonprofit	8,250,000	33,836,345	7,531,841
New York Urban League	Nonprofit	10,197,000	4,780,896	8,182,268
Curtis & Associates	For-profit	35,805,000		

Table 2.2 (continued)

[a] IMS was sold recently by Lockheed Martin to Affiliated Computer Services (ACS), a technology firm based in Dallas. ACS is a Fortune 1000 company that operates 79 one-stops with 59 contracts in 36 locations around the country. Because most of the contract activity analyzed here came before the merger, reference will be to Lockheed Martin IMS throughout.

[b] Curtis & Associates was renamed Concera in 2002. In 1998, Benova Inc., headquartered in Portland, Oregon, was acquired by AFSA Data Corporation, itself a wholly owned affiliate of FleetBoston Financial Corporation. Benova acquired Curtis & Associates, headquartered in Kearney, Nebraska, in 2000. In 2002, Benova, Curtis & Associates, and the government contracting division of AFSA Data Corporation, headquarted in Long Beach, California, became the Concera Corporation. Concera specializes in contracting with federal, state, and local government agencies to provide a wide range of business process outsourcing solutions.

SOURCE: Information on assets and income from www.guidestar.org as of FY 2000. Blank = not applicable.

sold in its retail shops across the city. Goodwill uses these businesses to train the disabled, low-income populations, and youth for private sector employment. In an interview, CEO Rex Davidson identified the comparative advantages Goodwill has in philosophy and operations over its competitors (both for-profit and nonprofit) for Welfare-to-Work. Having its own business gives it independence in how it conducts on-the-job training. Goodwill's multiple funding sources—from its business activities and from philanthropy—reduce its dependence on government. "We have an efficient model to produce programs and service: we use for-profit management techniques and sophisticated systems of financial management which result in audits that always pass scrutiny," Davidson said. "We run businesses and embrace business-oriented management techniques. We are reliable, and our results are predictable. We have the lowest overhead in the country and can fund our operations up-front through high capitalization . . . We're here, and we'll be here when the money dries up." Furthermore, Goodwill supervisors can place clients in employment in their own industry. "We believe in the power of work," Davidson said. "If you don't work you can't learn to work . . . The dignity of employment—you can't replace that."[7]

Given its scale, reputation, experience, business-oriented values, and relationships with employers, Goodwill would appear to be an ideal contractor for the city. Indeed, it holds two of the largest contracts in New York City's reengineered welfare delivery system. However, challenges loom over the new mega-contracts. At a combined $84 million for the two contracts over three years,[8] the contract dollars represent three times Goodwill's asset base, an amount that makes the organization highly vulnerable to the city's funding and policy shifts. Although Davidson argued, "Competition is good. It makes us better, as long as it's not the be all and end all," Goodwill's performance at the time placed it below average among its competitors in the percentage of clients placed and in last place for retention—this despite its articulated commitment to follow up with clients on the job and its subcontracts with many CBOs that provide specialized services in the communities where they are located.[9] Whether Goodwill's performance problems stem from the scale of its operations, the performance of its subcontractors, or the city's generally acknowledged difficulties in referring an adequate number of assessed clients, it is clear that even highly capable and experienced providers are having difficulties in this environment.

The big dilemma for the large, stable nonprofits is whether they will compromise their mission of putting the client first and providing to each client what he or she needs. Performance-based contracts and current payment levels favor rapid placement of clients and few specialized services, which must be paid for out of the fixed maximum payments for which contractors are eligible. Many of the nonprofit leaders we spoke to bemoan the structure and incentives of the contracts themselves. The Women's Housing and Economic Development Corporation (WHEDCO), unable, on its own, to compete for a prime contract, became a partner with America Works and a subcontractor to Wildcat Service Corporation in the reengineered service delivery system in New York. WHEDCO's president, Nancy Biberman, describes the problem this way:

> The ESP [Employment Services and Job Placement] program and contracts were never intended to result in viable jobs for welfare recipients. The rapid reduction of the welfare caseload was the public policy mandate out of which the ESP program was created. The ESP contracts were children of shortsighted social policy and privatization ideology, which have proven both costly and inappropriate in the human services sector . . . The contracts were structured to provide financial incentives for 'rapid labor market attachment' (the expressly stated goal of HRA [Human Resources Administration] Commissioner Jason Turner). Consequently, at best they provided quick job placements and woefully unsatisfactory job retention outcomes. The policy has proven egregiously myopic. The current labor market contraction has left those with the poorest skills most vulnerable to layoffs. Had the ESP contracts been structured to enable participants to develop marketable skills before diving into low-wage dead-end jobs, perhaps long-term job retention could have been achieved. But the payment milestones in these 'performance-based' contracts, coupled with WEP [The Work Experience Program], forced even the most mission-driven providers into unconscionable work." (Biberman 2001, p. 4)

WHEDCO described itself as the poster child for employment and training providers because it embraces a holistic approach to meeting clients' needs. An association with America Works should therefore have boosted the visibility and legitimacy of America Works. In an arrangement brokered by the Local Initiatives Support Corporation (LISC), a community development intermediary, WHEDCO developed a for-profit subsidiary to partner with America Works on America Works' $30 million New York City contract. But the relationship quickly soured. As its partner, WHEDCO found America Works' service to clients inadequate and saw its profit-maximizing behavior as robbing clients of needed support services. Indeed, as a mission-driven nonprofit that served more than 50 percent of America Works' clients, WHEDCO had to cross-subsidize its payments per placement from America Works with other resources in order to provide the needed support services for its clients. "We barely broke even on the arrangement because we provided layer upon layer of solid supportive services," Biberman said. "But it was our investment that made America Works' performance so good."

WHEDCO terminated its relationship with America Works in the spring of 2001 because of serious differences in approach and philosophy. America Works objected to the time and cost WHEDCO incurred in providing additional social services, thereby hurting its bottom line. WHEDCO claimed that America Works' highly favorable performance outcomes reflected the significant investment WHEDCO had made in supplementing services, not the placements America Works made itself. Regardless, the strategy seemed to work for America Works, which currently outperforms all other New York City contractors on both placement and retention.

The dissolution of this relationship reflects a considerable disparity of values and approach that many feel characterizes profound cultural differences in the way non- and for-profit providers approach their work. WHEDCO was bound by its social service mission and unwilling to capitulate to a bottom line regardless of the economic rationale for doing so. The tension between contractual requirements and mission appears less troubling to private sector contractors. Indeed, when we queried Ed Gund, senior vice president and chief operating officer at IMS at the time, about the conflict between mission and contractual demands, he responded, "The quality and character of services are all contract driven. If you want a particular service, put it in the contract."[10] This was echoed by David Mastran, chief executive officer at MAXIMUS, a provider of program management, information technology, and consulting services to government agencies. "What gets measured and rewarded gets done," Mastran says.

Use of mechanisms like grant diversion and forming a temporary employment agency, which were central to America Works' strategy, appear less popular among other firms we have spoken to. With the exception of Seedco's limited liability corporation (LLC), few have used these mechanisms effectively and some, such as ARBOR, have rejected them outright, eschewing the documentation required and the loss in lifetime benefits that TANF clients experience when they use up precious months of their lifetime limit because of grant diversion.[11]

However, when for-profits collaborate with nonprofits, culture clash is a more common theme. For many for-profits, the use of nonprofits and smaller proprietary providers as subs and partners is a short-term necessity if they are to meet the service demands of their many new for-profit contracts. But in practice, private and nonprofit cultures seldom harmonize. The large for-profits dominating this field see their role differently from most nonprofits. David Heaney of MAXIMUS in San Diego stressed the importance of selecting subs with "services you need, political influence, a good fit philosophically and organizationally, and [a compatibility with your] culture."[12] In Milwaukee and San Diego the use of subcontractors was crucial for increasing both capacity and breadth of services. Local subcontractors—especially CBOs—were important for their political influence and their knowledge of the local culture and community resources. "We made some stupid decisions by not understanding the culture—though we should have understood it," said Jerry Stepaniak, a MAXIMUS executive. "We were under great scrutiny politically and the [state legislative] audits revealed some insensitivities on our part; MAXIMUS drops in a new place where politics and community relations can be a problem. There is a huge advantage to knowledge of the community and political culture. We've figured out how to tap that, either by collaborating with nonprofit subcontractors, or [by] becoming a major subcontractor for a nonprofit prime."[13]

Subcontractors, too, were held to performance standards. "There are explicit criteria that these subcontracts must reach through retention and number served," said George Leuterman, Stepaniak's predecessor as vice president for welfare reform. "We are a business. We have a contract. We hold your hands to the fire. If you do well, you get a good reputation."[14]

YW Works in Milwaukee also formed an LLC with private sector partners but severed its relationship after the first contract period for similar kinds of disagreements in style and values. Leuterman of MAXIMUS distinguishes between how for-profits and nonprofits view this work. "The county is our customer," he says. "There is a power inequality with the client, and we recognize it. But the client is not your customer. They are not paying you. We provide services for our client, which is the county . . . Our motto is, 'When you are doing something that is not in your contract, you are volunteering.' The nonprofits have more flexibility."[15]

Only in Houston, where contractors are paid on a cost basis for specified services up to a maximum, is there an incentive to vary the service package. Yet even in that city concerns have been raised about contractors choosing clients that are the easiest to serve to ensure higher success rates. The diversified funding streams that characterize many of the nonprofits, but none of the for-profits (like foundation and private fund-raising sources), can provide for cross-subsidy and cost-sharing among different programs, thus allowing them to pay for services clients may need but for which current contract amounts do not provide. Obviously the economic incentives built into these contracts offer much less latitude and pose a dilemma for mission driven nonprofits.

A recent development in Wisconsin following a state legislative audit in Milwaukee provides additional grounds for concern about the perverse effects—even for mission driven nonprofits—of the economic incentive central to the contract design (Johnson 2001). Milwaukee's contracts are comprehensive and include eligibility determination in addition to job readiness and placement services. The Milwaukee W-2 Advisory Panel recommended changes in the Milwaukee program in response to revelations by state audits that relatively few clients were advised by contracting agencies of the range of available services for which they were eligible. Further, the audits confirmed that few had been given adequate assessment of their needs, had been lifted out of poverty, or had been placed in more intensive education and training programs that might have led to self-supporting jobs. The implications of the audits were that contract agencies simply didn't offer services if clients didn't request them. The money saved by not offering them, presumably, represented cost savings to the contractors and contributed to their profits.

In response, under a newly funded arrangement, the state has allocated $5 million for a contract for county workers to assume the role at the "front door," undertaking client assessments and informing them of the services for which they are eligible, including job training and food stamps. Then they will be referred to the appropriate W-2 agencies. These changes are designed to insure that clients are made aware of their entitlements and the supportive services available. The need for changes like these, however, illustrates the potential conflicts between the cost saving (profit maximizing) incentives inherent in performance-based contracts and serving clients' interests. The legislative audit uncovered evidence of potentially serious consequences of the economic incentives inherent in the contract's design, absent systems to insure appropriate monitoring and accountability. These were dangers generally thought to exist only when for-profit firms provided the services: most observers viewed the values of nonprofits and their missions as insurance against contractual abuses. But both were found to have denied clients critical access to information about their eligibility for additional services and program resources. Whether or not these oversights were necessary to meet contract demands, we see that nonprofits may be forced to capitulate to market pressures, compromising their values to remain competitive with for-profits.

LIVING BY THEIR WITS

Large, stable nonprofits with large and diversified funding streams appear relatively secure. In may ways they resemble their for-profit competitors more than they do their leaner, less business-oriented counterparts among nonprofit providers.[16] But many nonprofits in the employment and training business that we spoke to are facing an insecure future in a changing environment. Some of the medium-sized and smaller organizations are regrouping, shifting their focus and looking for alternative sources of both government and private funding. These efforts to survive combine a search for new dollars, development of new areas of program growth, investments in improved management to achieve cost savings, and some efforts to embrace private market techniques. Some have developed for-profit subsidiaries to realize some of the benefits that accrue to the for-profit providers. Catholic Charities in San Diego was typical. That provider underwent a significant management reorganization, including the development of a more professionalized set of management and personnel systems, and introduction of a new generation of technology and information systems in order to be competitive and manage its recent contracts with the county. Similarly, Houston Works has modernized to such a degree that some contractors we interviewed described it as having become the leading edge in business technology—comparable to industry leaders like the for-profit Lockheed Martin IMS (now ACS State and Local Solutions—see Note 10).

A particularly innovative effort characterized one of the smaller nonprofits that won a $7.4 million contract in New York. Seedco, a highly respected medium-sized nonprofit with areas of investment that include community and economic development, workforce development, and housing, has built a collaborative with 15 CBOs. It provides them with technical assistance while helping them to provide employment training and job placement to TANF recipients under the New York City contract.[17] Organized as a subsidiary to the nonprofit Seedco, the Non-Profit Assistance Corporation (N-PAC) has structured a limited liability corporation named EarnFair to take advantage of a variety of private sector incentives such as the ability to use allowable tax credits as an eligible employer of welfare recipients. As an LLC, EarnFair can operate as a temporary employment agency and syndicate these tax credits, using the additional resources from their sale to subsidize increased and more intensive services to the clients it serves. Further, the N-PAC subsidiary runs the Welfare-to-Work program using the collaboration of CBOs and generates additional funding from a diverse set of resources including philanthropic and other public funds.

Seedco's president, Bill Grinker, an innovator in human services and a former HRA commissioner himself, described the vision this way: "We view ourselves as a management service entity. The key service provision is provided through CBOs. Our interest is in providing information systems, capacity, financial assistance, and technical, programmatic types of supports. While theoretically we are the prime contractor, we view the CBOs as partners rather than subs . . . Even so, these CBOs would most likely be closed out of these contracts had they not been able to come under the umbrella of a well managed, fiscally sound prime."[18] In actuality, N-PAC functions as a conduit for resources and information, "pooling together public and private grants and funds that it passes on to the subcontractor," said Tracie McMillan. "As a result, N-PAC has to rely on job placements for only 50 percent of its funding, freeing up considerable resources to invest in longer-term training" (McMillan 2001). Perhaps most important, Seedco manages the financial risk for the CBOs by basing their payments only partially on performance and the rest on a line item cost basis. The transparency with which each partner shares the performance data of its other partners creates pressure on each to be accountable.

The $7.4 million contract from the city represents only 20 percent of the resources N-PAC is allocating to this effort. The rest comes from the syndicated tax credits; other partners such as the United Way; the New York Community Trust; and LISC, a community development intermediary. These resources allow innovative programmatic designs that go well beyond what competitors could provide, specifically the for-profits. Indeed, the EarnFair model provides post-placement support services and case management for participants for two years. It operates as a temp agency but provides supervision of workers after placement with a private employer and provides additional supports on the job, including transitional services, fringe packages, counseling, and financing. Total wage packages are assembled that include the value of the Earned Income Tax Credit (EITC). "The EarnFair Model is a good example of Seedco's high standards for all our products," said Diane Baillargeon, Seedco's senior vice president. "The program design itself embodies some of the best thinking in the Welfare-to-Work field about effective interventions. We also have in place a plan for long-term financing. We're not looking for financing that consists of one big government contract, but for diverse revenue streams. Having seen nonprofits struggle when government contracts are cut, or living hand to mouth year after year, it's exciting to me to be working on economically sustainable financing for social purposes" (Seedco 1999).

A nonprofit in Milwaukee developed a simpler yet still innovative partnership to bid for a contract in that city. The YWCA partnered with CNR Health and the Kaiser Group to form a limited liability corporation to bid in one of Milwaukee's five contracting regions. In this arrangement, the YWCA became the managing partner of YW Works, controlling day-to-day operations, while Kaiser and CNR Health provided many of the management systems and technological supports (Yates 1997).[19] The Y had "a lot to bring to the table" since it had been involved since the 1920s in employment and training—especially nontraditional training for women, Rita Rinner, YW Works' chief operating officer, reported. When the first requests for proposals (RFPs) were released in Milwaukee for W-2, she said, "we wanted other expertise. We felt it was too risky to go it alone. CNR was a software developer, and we worried about the size of the budget and the risk of debt from a capitated payment if we failed. We needed technology, an MIS system, and help with reporting systems. Partners could help."[20]

These kinds of partnerships allow nonprofits to capture the benefits of private sector capital, efficiencies, and management expertise while operating in a manner consistent with their missions. Private sector partners helped to underwrite the risk, hire staff, and build needed infrastructure. In the second round of Milwaukee contracts, however, YW Works dissolved the relationship and bid alone. Whatever the initial advantages, cultural differences in style and values plagued the relationship. Once YW Works felt confident of its own managerial and technological capacity, it was less dependent on the partnership. Its private partners lost some interest as well. They found the environment and the bias against for-profits inhospitable. The political heat and the controversy that typically accompany the entrance of for-profit providers into a service area historically dominated by government and nonprofits made the arrangement uncomfortable. County providers around the state "have the view that private agencies can't be responsible with public funds," Rinner said.[21] But the arrangement served the short-term transitional needs of the Y and helped set it up for an independent operation with the capacity to go it alone.

Innovative partnerships served some nonprofits well. But other traditional employment and training providers were scrambling to stay in business. Many viewed the payment levels and schedules as unrealistically low under these contracts. A smaller contractor in New York who was unable to bid directly on any of the contracts became a subcontractor under two of the primes (one for-profit and one nonprofit). "Our reimbursement as a sub won't cover our costs," she said. "We'll have to fundraise to cover costs . . . But our key advantage is our diversified funding. We see government contracts as defraying costs, not covering them."[22] That observation rang true for Liu in Houston as well. "If you [as a local CBO] rely totally on government money," she said, "it is almost impossible for you to survive."[23] The contracts provide no incentive for long-term investment, and for the subs who must relinquish overhead to the prime, current payment schedules may pay only a fraction of the true costs of serving a disadvantaged client. But accepting these subcontracts allows for financial piggybacking and economies of scale in multiple program cost-sharing.

For small nonprofits, whose financial solvency depends upon their performance, reasonable numbers, high quality referrals, and timely payment for performance (which depends upon the administrative performance of both the county or city and the prime), the financial risks are clearly high. A generalized concern among the nonprofits we spoke to, all of whom are acting as subcontractors, had to do with referrals. They feared, first, that the city would not refer sufficient numbers of eligible clients in a timely fashion to the prime to support the heavy investment in program operations. And worse, they feared that the primes might 'cream' the most job-ready clients for themselves and refer out the most difficult and costly to place—those with multiple barriers to employment.

Diane Baillargeon was senior vice president of Seedco at the time I interviewed her and wrote this chapter; she now is president. Baillargeon is familiar with the plight of many CBOs. "There are already nonprofits—mostly small, relatively low capacity community-based organizations—[that] have gotten out of the business," she reported, "and I know personally of a number of organizations that simply have said, 'We can't compete in this business any longer,' and they have gotten out of it. Now, most of them are multiservice, social service, community-based community centers, and they are still operating their domestic violence program and their homeless shelter and all of that, but they are no longer in the workforce business. And I think that's a loss."[24]

In Houston, the system is designed to provide "customer choice."[25] No contract is signed with subcontractors and CBOs. Instead, training providers are chosen by the clients themselves after being counseled and given provider information by contractors at career centers. This system wreaks havoc on providers' planning processes, since they are unable to anticipate the demand for their services and the staffing those services might require. Furthermore, in order to attract and keep clients, they must provide considerable information and do aggressive marketing. These are investments that they have no assurance they will be able to recoup, and ones for which they typically haven't much expertise. Often CBOs invest considerable resources in initial recruiting and training before they refer clients to career centers to be certified, hoping they will return for more intensive services. These up-front investments are difficult for smaller nonprofits and CBOs to finance themselves. The process, known as reverse referrals, was seen as extremely costly for the nonprofits, but also necessary to ensure that at least some initial contacts would return to their organization. If they fail to find and attract a sufficient number of clients—who after all have a tremendous number of choices (over 6,000 qualified providers at last count)—thousands of traditional nonprofit providers may be forced to close their doors, seek new funding streams, or refocus their efforts on new service areas.

The current strategy of the municipalities we studied has been to find a few experienced contractors with good track records and sufficient technological and managerial expertise to provide the services and information necessary to ensure full participation and job placement of all eligible clients. Federal mandates and the terms of performance-based contracts require information systems to track and verify the progress of all clients in the system, and these demands often require sophisticated technology and management systems. Many of the for-profit providers have considerable advantages in providing these systems. Indeed, Seedco used the philanthropic resources it raised for its innovative effort to purchase MIS software from a subsidiary of MAXIMUS—allowing it the same kind of capacity for its LLC as the for-profit firms. But the development of these systems is expensive, even if they are bought "off the shelf," and few small organizations have the resources for those kinds of investments.

In New York and Milwaukee, nonprofit providers have had a long history and good performance record of providing employment and training services, yet many lack the necessary technological and managerial systems to manage performance-based contracts. Further, because the timing of payments depends on contractors' performance in Milwaukee, New York, and San Diego, and on systems to verify placements, considerable up-front capital is necessary to undertake these contracts. The for-profits have quite a few advantages over the nonprofits in assuming the risks. They have greater capacity to sustain operations in anticipation of future payment streams, since they have access to investment capital. Only a fraction of the nonprofits historically operating in the employment and training business have the ability to stay the course while they wait for payment. So serious was the threat to contractors in New York that the City was forced to provide some up-front working capital to float the start-up cost of their large TANF contracts.

Clearly the availability of working capital, an asset more likely to characterize the larger for-profit companies, is a key factor in how competitive nonprofit providers can be over time. As Richard Shaw of the Houston AFL-CIO put it, "First you have to have the money to spend the money, which is a real problem for small companies."[26] How well capitalized an organization needs to be to remain solvent in this environment depends in large part on the competence and efficiency of the public agency responsible for reviewing and authorizing payments. Timely and accurate payments and an adequate flow of client referrals to providers are an indication of the management systems and capability of public agencies, and their recent track record is not encouraging. Even large, well-managed nonprofits such as Goodwill and Wildcat worried about the city's capacity to insure that these functions ran smoothly.

New York's HRA has been notoriously poor at paying its vendors in a timely manner. So problematic has been this lack of capacity that the City has had to advance most of the contractors payments of up to three months to keep them afloat. The City has launched a new computerized system to receive vendor placements, make referrals, and speed up the process of calculating and verifying payments. Although the system promises to improve upon the City's speed of payments, as recently as 2002 vendors still complained about the backlog and the amounts they were owed. This falls particularly heavily on subcontractors whose payments flow from the City to the prime and then on to them. Biberman of WHEDCO, which subcontracts for two large primes, found her organization caught in the middle. "One of the most debilitating footnotes to this story involves untimely payments of the paltry funds available under these contracts," she said. "At any given time, our organization awaited at least $100,000 in receivables from prime contractors. We had no recourse to the City, although we tried. Indeed, when we learned that a prime contractor had already been paid by the City for the work we had done, the City officials told us that we should sue the prime for payment!" (Biberman 2001).

The concern over the ability of cities to refer clients resonates around the country. "It is the biggest issue we face," said Holli Payne of MAXIMUS. "It really is like pulling teeth trying to get these clients out of the system. The bureaucracy is horrible. For example, in Philadelphia there are 65,000 clients on welfare. MAXIMUS had a contract to serve 200, yet the City could not produce that many people for MAXIMUS to serve. They are inefficient and ineffective."[27]

ON THE BRINK

Smaller, community-based nonprofits, which historically have provided employment and training services to low-income populations, represent a large and diverse group nationwide. Before the Workforce Investment Act of 1998 (WIA), there were 163 federal programs that funded employment and training. Under these titles, tens of thousands of nonprofit and for-profit organizations have received contracts and grants. In New York City alone, more than 115 individual providers had one or more employment and training contracts under federal titles prior to the newly awarded TANF contracts and the commencement of the WIA programs.[28] Their capacity to compete in a more performance-based environment varies enormously, but most of the organizations we spoke to believed they would "get by" in the short run. Few small organizations had the ability to bid on the TANF contracts given the scale and organizational capacity requirements they entailed, and those that did often did so as a collaborative, such as in San Diego. There, a collaborative of nonprofits in the South Bay community bid to serve that community as the Metropolitan Area Advisory Committee. They did not, however, win the contract and are currently litigating the decision, questioning the fairness of the bidding process. In New York, where the bidding process was not the typical open competitive process but a negotiated acquisition, the city invited organizations to bid, and many historical small nonprofit contractors were closed out. A number of small, experienced providers lost their contracts with the city in what has been described as a shakeout.

Because of the scale of these efforts, however, most of the prime contractors in Milwaukee and New York by necessity have either solicited CBOs or responded to CBOs' requests to act as subcontractors or link with these organizations to provide training and support for clients with special training or social service needs. Under current bidding processes to select providers to serve TANF clients, many historical providers will continue to serve portions of the caseload, albeit to a limited extent. (There will be additional opportunities for many of them to compete for clients under the U.S. Department of Labor's (USDOL) WIA programs, but success under that system depends primarily on the selection of a provider not by jurisdiction but by customer.) Furthermore, many of the national for-profit providers (and large local nonprofits) like ACS State and Local Solutions and MAXIMUS have selected CBOs as subs, in part to mitigate the political backlash against them in the communities where they have won contracts. Subcontracts with CBOs have a number of valuable practical and political payoffs as for-profits enter new markets. In the short run they can learn from CBOs, which have a better understanding of particular client needs and a connection to the resources in the community that serve them. Beyond that, their association with well known and trusted community organizations provides some political cover, helping to co-opt and deflect criticism from groups that might otherwise be their opponents.

For the time being, then, many CBOs and smaller nonprofits may survive, even as they scramble to change their programmatic focus, seek other sources of public and private support, and serve the short-term needs of large contractors. Over the longer term, most observers we interviewed predicted that many of the weaker providers would scale back or close down. Since the industry varies enormously in quality and fiscal soundness, the consequences for many small providers may be dire. Their loss will have a mixed effect on the quality and range of available services.

Many small providers serve populations with special needs. Anita Moses, a small contractor who lost her contract when the city of New York reorganized its delivery system, said the old system had its merits. "Good CBOs in communities are linked to providers and understand the needs of their clients," she said. "You have them and you know them. Some CBOs are bad, some mediocre, but CBOs have unique advantages."[29] For example, The Chinatown Manpower Project in New York has historically served Chinese speaking clients, whose ability and willingness to benefit from training and employment services provided by a borough-wide contractor under the new service delivery arrangements are limited. Whether current contracting and referral arrangements can preserve the services that may be critical to special populations located in particular communities is questionable. Many fear that populations like ex-offenders, ethnic populations, and drug addicts may be poorly served. They also worry that welfare applicants from these groups, when they are diverted to job placement and employment training, may simply disappear, falling through the cracks of a system that has no capacity to meet their special language and cultural needs.

The career center contractor we spoke to in Houston, as well as interest groups there, fears the consequences of this shakeup. "In my opinion, when we lose the little guy [e.g., the small CBO], we lose the hard-to-serve clients, because that is who they trust and who they go to," said Lockheed Martin IMS head Carol Anderson. "They are not coming to my career center because I am there. They have to feel some reason to be comfortable and safe to come. When we lose the contract, we lose a lot."[30] But other observers saw the possible thinning of the provider ranks as being healthy, by reducing the number of weaker and less able providers and strengthening the field overall.

The smaller nonprofit contractors in Houston "do a lot more than what the performance standards measure," says Jesse Castanada, head of a CBO there, yet their dedication to their mission does not allow them to cut services even if current contract arrangements fail to reimburse them for their additional costs.[31] Mission drives the service policies of Castanada's organization, SER–Jobs for Progress of the Texas Gulf Coast, but two of the smallest CBOs with contracts have been placed on probation and threatened with contract revocation because of the difficulty they have had in getting their operations off the ground, and in part because of their unwillingness to capitulate on their service commitments in order to adhere to the economic realities of their contracts.

There is evidence that New York City's HRA is worried too. Current contract designs that provide incentives for immediate placement but allocate limited resources for longer-term support have not fared as well as expected. A recent summary on placement and retention rates of ESP contractors revealed average placement rates of 29 percent and retention rates of 9 percent at 90 days and of only 3 percent at six months. (Individual contractor performance varies greatly; retention rates at each milestone range from 2 to 28 percent and from 0 to 14 percent respectively.)[32] Many view the poor performance, especially in job retention, as being due to the lack of intensive services for clients with special needs. Historically, the providers most often serving these populations have been the CBOs.

So much controversy has attended the poor performance of and the weak support for CBOs in the contracting system that the city of New York recently awarded, through a negotiated acquisition process, 30 new contracts to serve special populations under WIA. The contracts were awarded exclusively to nonprofits, mostly CBOs. This represents a big victory for advocates who have questioned the viability of the current contracts to serve a caseload marked by daunting labor market barriers. It also reflects the city's increasing recognition that job retention among all contractors is very low. While only 21 contracts have so far been registered, these alone represent a large additional city investment in CBOs providing support services for the most difficult and vulnerable parts of the caseload, those clients with multiple barriers. The signed contracts already total more than $75 million. Although quite recent, they will provide sizable cash advances, more adequate funding, regularized reimbursements, and a recognition of the more intensive service needs that some clients have if they are to enter into and retain employment.

While risks abound for CBOs, the organizations themselves vary enormously in capacity, resourcefulness, and promise. Bill Grinker of Seedco's N-PAC described those nonprofits living on the brink as "a mixed bag in terms of capacity and ability to survive. Many will remain subs in the short run." The problem over the long run will be that, as the for-profits develop connections in the community, they will have less need for these CBOs and greater incentive to save the overhead devoted to managing them. Even for those CBOs that currently have contracts, there is the question of whether performance-based contracts will drive them out because of their lack of capital to sustain themselves while they wait for payment. Grinker also questioned whether the for-profits would continue to need the political protection they now enjoy through the connection they have with CBOs that serve as their subs. Moses, the long-term city employment contractor who lost her contract when the city administration reorganized service delivery in New York, viewed the selection process as entirely politically motivated, granting large contracts to mayoral favorites, politically connected for-profits, and large, established nonprofits. "What we will lose is the human element," she says. "Smaller providers are better than larger ones. Small nonprofits are driven by values and mission, and their staff is more concerned with people than numbers. All this gets lost in bigness—clients get lost."[33]

Richard Bonamarte, formerly the HRA executive deputy responsible for designing the original contracts, explained that the decision to select a few large contractors was based on a recognition that a major employment engine was needed to manage the large flow of clients, and that that would require providers whose scale of operations, systems capacity, and experience could handle a performance-based environment. Yet the design made an express attempt to protect the survival of the CBOs. "Many nonprofits, especially CBOs, have limited cash flows, low surpluses, and no professionalized financial systems and management capacities to deal with performance-based contracts," he said. "A major idea behind these contract designs was to allow smaller nonprofits to work as subcontractors under the primes and to reduce their exposure, to protect them and nurture them. They [the smaller nonprofits and CBOs] represent much of our infrastructure, and infrastructure takes so long to develop . . . You don't want to lose community-grounded organizations."[34]

Ironically, the CBOs see their exclusion as prime contractors in the selection process and their limited role as subcontractors as a repudiation of their contributions, and as the cause of their current problems. New York subcontractor Biberman described the situation facing nonprofit subcontractors as morally and financially untenable:

> The private and nonprofit contractors tend not to subcontract; the nonprofit contractors do more of it. In either case, prime contractor and subcontractor survival is predicated on doing as little work as possible. The city pays the primes only when they have certified that a recipient is in the labor force. *For the average community-based subcontractor, $1,700 is received at initial placement, $1,300 at 90-day job retention and $200 at 180-day retention!* Simple calculus coupled with the suspension of social mission drive[s] the implementation of these contracts in one direction: *placement only* . . . The subcontractors in these contracts are losing their shirts, both in financial terms and in the mutilation of their social missions, not to mention the morale of their staffs . . . Honorable community based subcontractors cannot[,] in conscience, work in this way; and so through philanthropic help and often at

> serious financial peril, they cobble together literacy assistance, social services, child care, etc. (Biberman 2001)

Thus, while small nonprofits have the motivation to stay alive and fulfill their mission, few have the resources and capacity to compete on their own, and many fear that, even as subcontractors, their future is in doubt. They complain of inadequate payment by the primes and of documentation and information processing demands that are as excessive and costly as when they reported directly to the city. In San Diego, contractors with case-management contracts refer clients to CBOs for particular services, but payments are capped, and performance-based contracts may impose severe constraints on small organizations that must wait for payment until a client has been employed and retained for up to six months. In Houston, where the contracts for case management at one-stop centers merge TANF clients with others served under USDOL titles, clients themselves select from the service providers that the city has qualified as eligible. Nonprofit and for-profit providers, therefore, compete for clients, and those with better connections and marketing expertise are likely to win out. Many CBOs have trouble competing in this environment.

CONCLUSION

Nonprofits are clearly sailing in uncharted waters. The new demands on nonprofits to compete in a reengineered welfare delivery system where market forces compete with traditional values has created real hazards. When missions collide with financial, managerial, and programmatic imperatives induced by new contractual arrangements, many nonprofits are forced to question their traditional roles as protectors of the poor and champions of progressive social values. Even so, many have adapted creatively to the new challenges, improving their performance, competing effectively on price, and developing innovative means to protect their missions. Many others, however, are struggling.

Much has been made of the inherent disadvantages that many nonprofits have in the new welfare service delivery markets, where they now compete with large, national for-profit firms (Ryan 1999; Frumkin and Andre-Clark 1999). They lack the management systems and the information technology needed to manage large and complex contracts. They have a comparative disadvantage in attracting government executives with welfare expertise, and they are constrained by their nonprofit status from raising capital in the financial markets. They lack both the capacity and the experience to handle the scale of operation that new contracts require. These are formidable handicaps.

But nonprofits in this industry have considerable strengths that national for-profit providers lack. As Baillargeon said, "They're really known entities in the community that they serve, they have a respected level of cultural competence, they offer other kinds of services, they already have preexisting connections to the target populations that we're talking about. I think, in fact, they will do very well."[35] Besides those attributes that Baillargeon ticked off, nonprofits have the ability to fundraise both from individuals and from major philanthropic organizations. These resources allow them to enrich their programs and provide additional services that contract dollars might not cover. In that respect they can often offer higher quality services than their for-profit competitors.

But we have seen that nonprofits providing welfare services vary as much from one another as they do from their private sector competitors. And many traditional providers have been closed out of the reengineered delivery systems we have studied. As a consequence, the adaptations nonprofits have made and their success in meeting the challenges show considerable variation. Some of the large, experienced nonprofits have a solid foothold in the markets we examined and appear to be holding their own. The speed with which all contractors have had to gear up, transform their systems, hire staff, and achieve placements has strained the resources of everyone we interviewed—profit and nonprofit alike. Early implementation has been rocky in many cases. While few data are available on the relative performance of individual contractors and subcontractors, the numbers we have uncovered in New York and San Diego suggest that no single factor can explain the wide variation in prime contractor performance in placements and retention. There is no obvious or consistent pattern by size of contract, size of organization, or sectoral status.[36] Since in theory referrals are randomly allocated by borough in New York, differences in client characteristics cannot explain the bulk of the disparities we observe. Start-up problems—many of which were the result of the city's performance—no doubt explain some of the variations. But nonprofits competing as primes appear, in general, to be no better or worse than their private sector competitors.

Competition first confronted these vendors when they had to respond to an RFP, and few made the initial cut. Existing providers, therefore, are likely to be those that were strongest. For example, Opportunities Industrialization Center (OIC) and United Migrant Opportunities Services (UMOS) in Milwaukee and Federal Employment and Guidance Services (FEGS), Wildcat, and Goodwill Industries in New York are big operators that have had a long history of public service provision. They were the most likely to succeed. Thus, the selection of a few experienced organizations, most of which were well-respected (and politically connected) providers in the community, left many CBOs and small and medium-sized providers out of the game. Few even had the ability to bid on these contracts, given the contracts' scale and organizational requirements. These CBOs' role as subcontractors has been more limited, and their success is still in question. Little technical assistance or management support has been available except in a few cases such as with Seedco's N-PAC, whose very design is structured to allow it to play the role of a management services entity.

Efforts like the one that created N-PAC are the sorts of highly focused initiatives that have the potential to sustain high quality operations that include smaller organizations in collaborative arrangements by which they can share resources and management systems. Networks of agencies can consolidate functions and share administrative tasks, and as a group they may be in a better position to attract funding, contracts, and capital financing. Some cost-sharing, particularly when it comes to expensive overhead, can help financially strapped smaller agencies be better able to compete for the available resources of intermediaries. It is also a promising strategy for strengthening the chances of experienced, mission-driven organizations threatened by new contracting arrangements.

These kinds of innovations—formed through collaborative and creative partnerships, assisted by private fundraising and changes in status (the development of a for-profit subsidiary)—represent healthy and promising adaptations. But, again, these are the exceptions. Most smaller nonprofits are having a hard time of it, and squeezing profit margins will retard creativity and productivity among even the most competent providers. Worse, such pressures will threaten the organizational mission and human service values that make nonprofit providers uniquely qualified to undertake some of the most difficult and important services now being outsourced. And those are the risks that attend the survivors. Others may simply disappear. As organizations learn to adapt to new funding, service, and management imperatives, so too must local governments adapt their program designs. Contracting is popular, but it is hard to do well, especially for providing human services. Public, nonprofit, and private providers have different comparative advantages. Evaluating the relative risks and rewards of various arrangements and choosing carefully requires experience and an interest in analyzing the impacts of alternative designs.

The dilemma involved in the design of New York City's performance-based contract is instructive since within it reside the incentive structures that affect the behavior of contractors. Paying too much for initial job placements and too little for job retention (in quality jobs with good pay and benefits) encourages contractors to provide little service or effort to find good jobs. But placing too much of the payment on the back end may impede cash flow and cripple contractors' ability to stay afloat. Thus, contract design needs to balance optimizing cash flow to contractors with setting milestones at the desired levels. It's a balancing act among three desires: to reduce program costs, to improve service quality, and to insure the fiscal stability of the contracting organizations. This is more art than science. But if employment training is to achieve its promise in a resource constrained environment, it will require more than the adaptation of nonprofit providers to demands for efficiency. Local government must do a better job of learning, through multiple iterations of contract design, to identify the right balance of incentives and supports. Only in this way can it preserve the viability of mission-driven and innovative nonprofits and allow them to compete without losing their souls.

Notes

This chapter was completed at the Brookings Institution and is derived from a larger project that was published as *The Welfare Marketplace: Privatization and Welfare Reform* (Washington, DC: Brookings Institution Press, 2003). It is reproduced in similar form here by permission.

1. Twombly's research points to the greater ability of larger, older nonprofits providing core welfare reform services to survive changes to the environment induced

by welfare reform. In part this reflects the longstanding relationships older nonprofits have with funders and other groups that may have buffered their operations. See also Twombly (2000a).

2. Nancy Liu (executive director, Chinese Community Center, Houston), interview by Philippe Rosse, August 3, 2000.
3. Sister Ramonda Duvall (executive director, Catholic Charities, San Diego), interview by the author, July 20, 2000.
4. Richard Shaw (chief executive officer, Community Services of the AFL-CIO, Houston), interview by Philippe Rosse, August 1, 2000.
5. Amalia V. Betanzos (president, Wildcat Inc., New York), interview by the author, May 16, 2000.
6. Ibid.
7. Rex Davidson (chief executive officer, Goodwill Industries of New York), interview by the author, June 7, 2000.
8. Goodwill won a $35.4 million Skills Assessment and Job Placement (SAP) contract for October 1, 1999–September 30, 2002, and a $49.4 million Employment Services and Job Placement (ESP) contract for December 1, 1999–November 30, 2002.
9. At the time of this writing, Goodwill had 12 subcontractors.
10. Ed Gund (chief operating officer and senior vice president, Lockheed Martin IMS), interview by the author and Paul Light, January 12, 2000. In 2001, the Lockheed Martin Corporation sold IMS to Affiliated Computer Services, which renamed it as its State and Local Solutions group. The IMS Corporation included Children and Family Services, Information Resources Management, Municipal Services, Transportation Systems and Services, and Welfare and Workforce Services.
11. The Personal Responsibility and Work Opportunity Reconciliation Act of 1996 (PRWORA) created a five year total lifetime cap on benefit receipt. Employed recipients whose jobs are partially financed through grant diversion run down the clock on this cap during their period of employment.
12. David Heaney (project director, San Diego, MAXIMUS), interview by the author, October 30, 2000.
13. Jerry Stepaniak (vice president, welfare reform division, and project director, Milwaukee, MAXIMUS), interview by the author, April 25, 2001.
14. George Leuterman (former vice president, welfare reform division, MAXIMUS), interview by the author, January 13, 2000.
15. Ibid.
16. In a paper titled "Nonprofit Organizations in an Era of Welfare Reform" that was presented at the 1997 meeting of the Association for Research on Nonprofit Organizations and Voluntary Action (ARNOVA), Carol J. DeVita and Eric Twombly used 1992 and 1994 IRS data to examine the number, types, and financial stability of human services organizations most likely to be affected by welfare reform. Of these, 83 percent offered core services. The study shows that these organizations faced financial uncertainty and increasingly stringent budgets. As a result only 41 percent reported positive net balance sheets for 1992 and 1994. De Vita (1999)

subsequently reported on these findings in her chapter of the Boris and Steuerle book.

17. Diane Baillargeon, senior vice president of Seedco and chief operating officer of the Non-Profit Assistance Corporation at the time, said as a Brookings Forum panelist in 2001 that Seedco had a waiting list of nonprofits that wanted to work under its umbrella, but the size of the contracts limited the number Seedco could work with, because it was at capacity. (Brookings Forum, "A View from the Frontlines: Innovations in Delivery of Welfare Services," Washington, DC, October 17, 2001.)
18. William Grinker (then-president of Seedco and its affiliate, N-PAC, of New York), interview by the author, May 18, 2000.
19. Rita Rinner (chief operating officer, YW Works), interview by the author, April 23, 2001.
20. Rinner, interview.
21. Ibid.
22. Rachel Miller (vice president for operations and fiscal affairs and director of workforce development, WHEDCO, New York), interview by the author, July 17, 2000.
23. Liu, interview.
24. Baillargeon, Brookings Forum.
25. This model is the prevailing one under the U.S. Department of Labor's Workforce Investment Act of 1998, which provides eligible clients with independent training accounts (ITAs) to use for training with qualified providers.
26. Shaw, interview.
27. Holly Payne (director of welfare services, MAXIMUS), interview by Paul Light, June 8, 2000.
28. Data provided by the New York City Comptroller's Office and the mayor's Office of Contracts.
29. Anita Moses (president, Education and Planning Institute, New York), interview by the author, June 27, 2000.
30. Carol Anderson (executive director, Lockheed Martin IMS, Houston), interview by Philippe Rosse, August 5, 2000.
31. Jesse Castanada (president, SER–Jobs For Progress of the Texas Gulf Coast), interview by Philippe Rosse, August 4, 2000.
32. Data provided by Swati Desai, executive deputy administrator for policy and program analysis, New York City Human Resources Administration.
33. Moses, interview.
34. Richard Bonamarte (former executive deputy administrator for contracts and procurement, New York City Human Resources Administration), interview by the author, January 25, 2002.
35. Baillargeon, Brookings Forum.
36. Public Assistance (PA) Summary Report, provided by Swati Desai, executive deputy administrator for policy and program analysis, New York City Human Resources Administration.

References

Barnow, Burt S., and John Trutko. 2002. "Analysis of Performance Based Contracting in Human Resource Administrative Programs in New York City." Draft paper prepared under contract to Human Resource Administration (HRA). New York: HRA.

Biberman, Nancy. 2001. *Recommendations for Structural and Policy Changes to Link Workforce Development and Economic Development: A Practitioner View from the South Bronx Field.* New York: Women's Housing and Economic Development Corporation.

De Vita, Carol J. 1999. "Nonprofits and Devolution: What Do We Know?" In *Nonprofits and Government: Collaboration and Conflict,* Elizabeth T. Boris and C. Eugene Steuerle, eds. Washington, DC: Urban Institute Press, pp. 213–233.

Duvall, Ramonda. 2000. Presentation at the American Public Human Services Association conference "Boosting Effectiveness in Urban Welfare Programs," Washington, DC, July 19.

Frumkin, Peter, and Alice Andre-Clark. 1999. "The Rise of the Corporate Social Worker." *Society* 36(6): 46–52.

Johnson, Mike. 2001. "County Workers Get Key W-2 Role: $5 Million Contract to Provide for Initial Assessments of Clients." *Milwaukee Journal Sentinel,* September 19, 3B.

Lampkin, Linda M., and Thomas H. Pollak. 2002. *The New Nonprofit Almanac and Desk Reference: The Essential Facts and Figures for Managers, Researchers, and Volunteers.* Washington, DC: Urban Institute Press.

Light, Paul C. 1997. *The Tides of Reform: Making Government Work,* 1945–1995. New Haven, CT: Yale University Press.

———. 1999. *The New Public Service.* Washington, DC: Brookings Institution Press.

———. 2000. *Making Nonprofits Work: A Report on the Tides of Nonprofit Management Reform.* Washington, DC: Brookings Institution Press.

McMillan, Tracie. 2001. "The Great Training Robbery." *City Limits* (May).

Ryan, William P. 1999. "The New Landscape for Nonprofits." *Harvard Business Review* 77(1): 127–36.

Salamon, Lester M. 1995. *Partners in Public Service: Government-Nonprofit Relations in the Modern Welfare State.* Baltimore: Johns Hopkins University Press.

———. 1997. *Holding the Center: America's Nonprofit Sector at a Crossroads.* New York: Nathan Cummings Foundation.

Seedco. 1999. "New Solutions for Changing Times." A report of Seedco and its affiliate, N-PAC. *Partnerships for Community Development* (July): 16.

Twombly, Eric C. 2000a. *Welfare Reform's Impact on the Failure Rate of Nonprofit Human Service Providers.* No. 9 in the series Charting Civil Society, from the Center on Nonprofits and Philanthropy. Washington, DC: Urban Institute Press.

———. 2000b. *Human Services Nonprofits in Metropolitan Areas during Devolution and Welfare Reform.* No. 10 in the series Charting Civil Society, from the Center on Nonprofits and Philanthropy. Washington, DC: Urban Institute Press.

Wolch, Jennifer R. 1990. *The Shadow State: Government and Voluntary Sector in Transition.* New York: Foundation Center Press.

Yates, Jessica. 1997. *Case Studies on Non-Profits' Involvement in Contracting for Welfare Services.* Washington, DC: Welfare Information Network. http://www.financeprojectinfo.org/WIN (accessed August 17, 2004).

3
CBOs and the One-Stop Career Center System

Ramón Borges-Méndez
University of Massachusetts Boston

Edwin Meléndez
New School University

Community-based organizations (CBOs) are long-standing and invaluable participants in employment and social services delivery systems. Among their strengths are their ability to represent communities that are often sidelined by other institutions and their capacity to deliver a broad range of social services to those communities as independent providers or as subcontractors of local and state governments. The one-stop career center (OSCC) system was started by the U.S. Department of Labor (USDOL) in 1994 and was formally established by the Workforce Investment Act (WIA) of 1998 as the institutional frontline outlet to deliver workforce development services to job seekers and employers.[1] The primary objective of this paper is to identify the factors that influence the positioning of CBOs in relation to local OSCC systems. The primary data for the study are provided by structured interviews with the heads and staff of 28 selected CBOs representing a cross section of organizations from around the nation. In some cases, we performed site visits and conducted multiple interviews.[2]

The implementation of WIA affected various aspects of CBOs' operations. CBOs faced funding problems in the transition from a contract to a performance-based system, as well as in fulfilling other reporting requirements demanded by the law (Plastrik and Taylor 2001). This difficult transition forced some CBOs out of the system; others chose to leave the WIA-funded system rather than change their programs or engage in the substantive costs associated with participating in the system. However, CBO engagement with the OSCC system has proven successful to the extent that CBOs have undertaken significant management and operational changes to accommodate the newer philosophical principles and operational guidelines established by WIA. Some of the most significant challenges involve service integration, staff development, and strategies for service coordination (Heldrich Center for Workforce Development 2002).[3] Many of the CBOs that adapted successfully to the WIA transition had previously implemented successful programs targeting welfare recipients. The Personal Responsibility and Work Opportunity Reconciliation Act (PRWORA) and the Temporary Assistance to Needy Families (TANF) induced greater devolution in programming and service delivery and increased the use of CBOs as subcontractors in a widely decentralized system of providers. CBOs were encouraged to participate in Welfare-to-Work programs because they are often cost-effective providers and can reach targeted populations (Nightingale 2001, 2002; Sanger 2000).

The contracting of Welfare-to-Work programs and the adaptation of CBOs to the new WIA regulations (in many areas implementing a strict work first approach) may have resulted in locking in CBOs to providing services for the very hard-to-serve or hard-to-engage populations that have been left behind by providers seeking more lucrative welfare markets (Sanger 2000; Withorn 2002). For small CBOs, achieving economies of scale and tracking outcomes in service provision are difficult tasks, which increasingly force them to become specialized service providers at the bottom of the subcontracting chain, serving few clients. This dynamic could be creating an entire class of subordinate subcontractors lacking influence in the overall structure of the local service delivery system. In the context of WIA, CBO specialization is most common in core and intensive services, less so in training services. Thus the potential for this kind of downward specialization is present. Notwithstanding previous case study research, which suggests that CBOs have had a difficult time adapting to new performance standards, more recent in-depth studies suggest that some large CBOs have been quite effective at creating management systems that satisfy performance-based contracting and at overcoming other WIA-induced compliance and performance issues. In terms of CBOs adding value to the OSCCs, the evidence from these case studies points to their significant contributions in such areas as program integration, outreach, network consolidation, and services to the hard-to-serve (Borges-Méndez and Meléndez 2002a,b; Meléndez, Kohler-Hausmann, and Borges-Méndez 2002; Meléndez, Donohue, and Borges-Méndez 2002).

In general, we found that the structural relationship between CBOs and OSCCs is more complex than simply one of inclusion or exclusion. The implementation of WIA has produced, as is suggested by the literature on the topic, a multifaceted landscape of CBO positioning. We found three discernible types of CBO relations to local OSCC systems: 1) CBOs as primary operators of OSCCs, 2) CBOs in a peer-to-peer network comanaging OSCCs, and 3) CBOs as subordinate participants in OSCCs. These three types of CBO positioning in the OSCC system are explained in more detail in the next section of the paper. The two sections after that discuss the regulatory, environmental, and organizational factors that influence CBO positioning. Evidently, CBO positioning is influenced by the legal framework of WIA and the greater autonomy in implementation it gives to local authorities and stakeholders. The main finding in this regard is that the WIA regulatory regime has not produced a uniform set of conditions for CBO inclusion. Positioning, to a large extent, is historically and contextually bounded. In addition to examining the regulatory regime, we identify and discuss important environmental factors such as the characteristics of job seekers, communities, and local labor markets, variety and density of intermediaries, and the politics of devolution at the local and state levels which interact with the regulatory regime. Equally important for CBOs' positioning are their history and background, their commitment to certain sets of values and mission, and other organizational characteristics such as size, staffing, leadership, and the networking capacity or connectedness of these organizations to other stakeholders. Overall, our findings suggest that a combination of regulatory pressures and environmental factors are inducing forms of CBO specialization in the provision of workforce development services. Further, CBO specialization and adaptation bear significant costs to CBOs in terms of the resources and professional expertise needed to successfully meet regulatory demands and in terms of their historical commitment to serving disadvantaged populations. CBOs regularly find themselves managing the dilemma of commitment versus compliance. The last section of the paper draws the policy implications of the research.

CBO-OSCC TYPES

The first step in the analysis is to define the relationship between CBOs and OSCCs and then categorize CBOs based on the proposed typology of CBO engagement with the OSCC system. The relationship between CBOs and OSCCs is defined strictly based on their contractual responsibility to local authorities in relation to the operations of the OSCCs. To support our definitions and typology we carried out an extensive bibliographic review of the first four years of the implementation of WIA, which included academic material, program evaluations, government documents and reports, and websites on workforce development. In this research, we also identified programs and cases in various parts of the country that could provide insight into the dynamics of CBO positioning, and we looked at whether previous systematic research on the positioning of intermediaries in emerging workforce development systems suggested identifiable types of positioning, especially for CBOs. The bibliographic research was accompanied by interviews of a broad group of practitioners in workforce development, academics, government administrators, and representatives of foundations, think tanks, and professional associations. Using this information, we selected 28 organizations from around the nation for our inquiry. We then conducted in-depth interviews with the organizations' directors and staff, and on several occasions we went on site visits.

Upon reviewing our cases we have identified three broad types of contractual relationships:

1) CBOs as primary operator and manager of one or many OSCCs. In these cases, local authorities have delegated most or all OSCC operational authority to CBOs. CBOs are responsible for engaging other partners in providing services, deciding on the allocation of core, intensive, and often, training services; and collecting and evaluating performance data for subcontractors. This relationship is illustrated in Figure 3.1. Though we found three variations of CBOs as primary operators, in each case the CBO acts as the primary decision maker in regard to the allocation of services. It can provide these services directly or subcontract them to other CBOs and service providers. In some circumstances, these CBOs operate multiple OSCCs in the city or region.

2) CBOs in a peer-to-peer network with other CBOs (and other stakeholders) sharing operations and management of one or many OSCCs. This relationship is illustrated in Figure 3.2. In this type, one of the CBOs operates as managing partner but a local authority is often in charge of approving service provision and the monitoring and collection of performance data. Partners in the network often share in the delivery of services, and components of system management are shared among various operators.

3) CBOs as subordinate participants offering specialized services at OSCCs held and managed by other organizations. Figure 3.3 illustrates this relationship. In these cases, CBOs are subcontractors of core, intensive, or training services and do not share any responsibilities for system management with other service providers.

Based on the criteria explained above for the CBO and OSCC typology of contractual relationships, we classified the selected cases into groups corresponding to the three types of management and service delivery roles reported by the CBOs. Table 3.1 summarizes the distribution of cases by type of CBO operator. A little more than half of the cases (16) selected for the study fall into the category of CBOs as primary operators of OSCCs. Of the remaining cases, five were classified as peer-to-peer and seven as subordinate OSCC operators. The distribution is not intended to show the numeric predominance of one type over others but rather to flesh out the ideal types we have outlined and investigated. Also, some CBOs can be classified both as primary operators and as peer-to-peer because of the broad scope and extension of their programmatic activity. The selection, though strategic, does seem to indicate that the inclusion/exclusion dichotomy is a rather narrow way of discussing and representing CBO positioning, and that some CBOs have managed their successful transition into the new regime while absorbing the local environmental pressures. This is not to say that CBOs on the opposite side of the equation have been experiencing subordination and further exclusion. The rest of this section of the study presents a detailed discussion of the characteristics of CBOs based on the typology of cases identified above.

Figure 3.1 Types of CBO Positioning

Three Variations of CBO as Primary Operator

1.

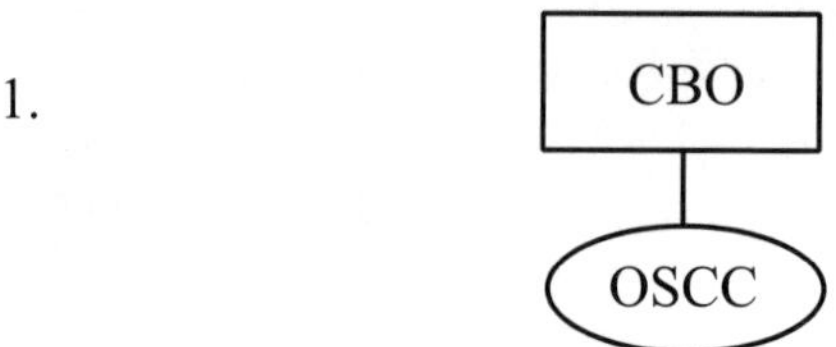

The CBO manages a single OSCC, or the CBO is an OSCC.

2.

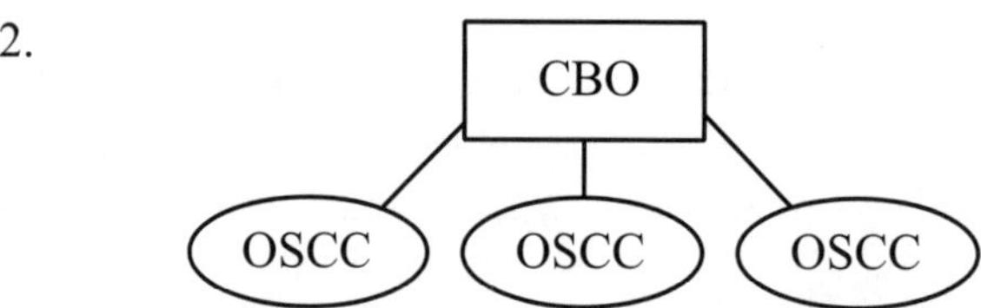

The CBO manages multiple OSCCs.

3.

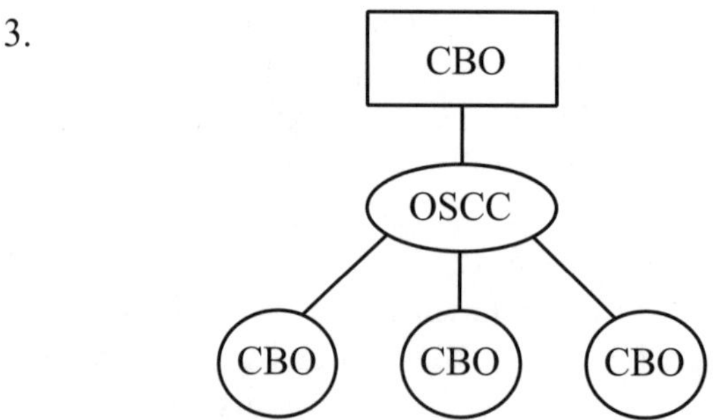

A large CBO manages an OSCC and hosts other CBOs as partners that provide specialized services.

Figure 3.2 Types of CBO Positioning

CBO as Peer-to-Peer Operator

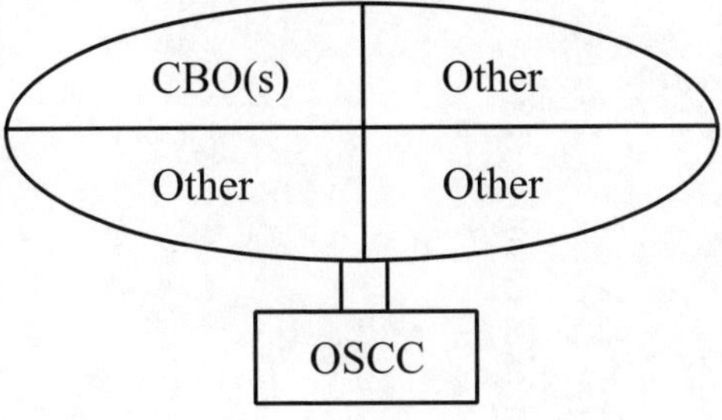

CBO(s) in horizontal/networked relation with other stakeholders.

Figure 3.3 Types of CBO Positioning

CBO as Peripheral Operator/Participant

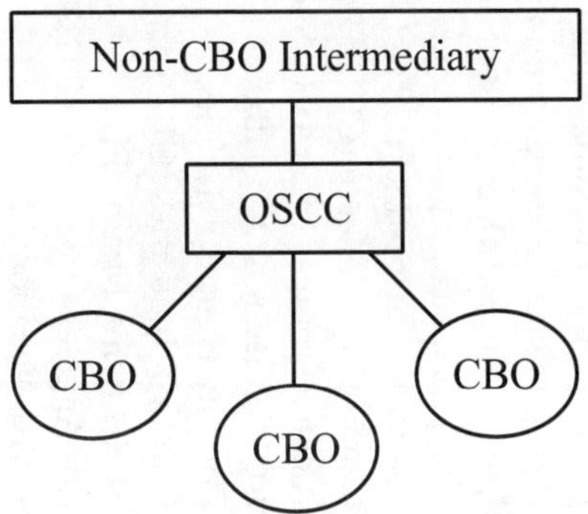

CBO as small, peripheral subcontractor or OSCC satellite.

Table 3.1 Cases by Type of OSCC-CBO Positioning

Type of operator	Name of organization
Primary	Unity Council (UC), Oakland, CA
	El Proyecto del Barrio, Los Angeles, CA
	New Community Corporation (NCC), Newark , NJ
	Opportunities Industrialization Center West (OICW), Menlo Park, CA
	United Migrant Opportunity Services (UMOS), Milwaukee, WI
	North Texas Human Resource Group (NTHRG), north-central Texas counties, TX
	Career Resources Inc. (CRI), Louisville, KY
	Central City Concern (CCC), Portland, OR
	Asian Resources Inc. (ARI), Sacramento, CA
	Job Connection (JC), Atlantic City/Cape May, NJ
	Friendly House (FH), Phoenix, AZ
	Goodwill Industries (GI), North Charleston, SC
	SER-Miami, Miami, FL
	Los Angeles Urban League (LAUL), Los Angeles, CA
	Jewish Vocational Services (JVS), Boston, MA
	SER Metro-Detroit, Detroit, MI
Peer-to-peer	Denver Employment Alliance (DEA), Denver, CO
	Chicago Jobs Council (CJC), Chicago, IL
	San Diego Career Opportunities Partners (SDCOP), San Diego, CA
	Boston Career Link CBO Partnership, Boston, MA
	Detroit's Workplace of Jewish Vocational Services (DWP), Detroit, MI

Subordinate	HART, Hartford, CT
	Hartford Construction Jobs Initiative/Jobs Funnel, Hartford, CT
	Southeast Works (SEW), Portland, OR
	Acercamiento Hispano/Hispanic Outreach (AH/HO), Columbia, SC
	Opportunities Industrialization Center (OIC) Phoenix, AZ
	Arizona Call-a-Teen (ACAT), Phoenix, AZ
	American Youth Works (AYW), Austin, TX

CBOs as Primary Operators

CBOs that are primary OSCC operators do collaborate with a broad range of mandated partners, exert leadership and stewardship, and attract and sponsor other actors who may want to be part of the OSCC. However, in such a scenario, one CBO tends to front or "underwrite" the costs associated with providing services, complying with local regulations, and maintaining the institutional and physical infrastructure of the OSCCs (and satellite centers). That is, one CBO is the anchor and manager of the OSCC. In more general terms, CBOs have become the backbone of some local and regional social and employment service delivery systems, often participating actively in the governance of these systems. The interdependence between CBOs and the delivery infrastructure can be attributed to diverse factors ranging from the historical expertise of organizations to the local implementation of outsourcing services. It is worth noting that local and state administrators and elected officials often see CBOs (and other intermediaries in service delivery) as a flexible management option, particularly in comparison to state bureaucracies. They often use subcontracting to CBOs as a way to bypass or sidestep frontline implementation problems related either to program interfacing or to human resource management in the public sector.

The evidence gathered regarding the general characteristics of CBOs that function as primary OSCC operators is summarized in Table 3.2. The data suggest that most of these CBOs are well positioned to assume a leadership role in the OSCC service delivery system. They are often large, multiservice organizations operating facilities in various localities within the city or metropolitan area. They have assumed a leadership role in the community, and their board members are often well connected to local government. Given their management experience and size of operation, these CBOs have adapted their operations not only to comply with the numerous and cumbersome regulations induced by WIA but also to add to the system through the enhanced coordination with other organizations, the integration of services from various funding sources, and the legitimacy to orchestrate system operations.

When CBOs assume direct responsibility and authority for managing OSCCs, it is often the case that local Workforce Investment Boards

Table 3.2 Description of CBO as Primary OSCC Operator

- Mostly old (20 years +), large CBOs with multimillion dollar budgets ($8+ million) and various sites in a geographic area.
- Often affiliate of national umbrella organization. Can be stand-alone CBO.
- Some available resources for adaptation and experimentation.
- Clear mission statement, often grounded in group identity and geography.
- Operates in large metropolitan and diversified labor market.
- Internal multidivisional specialization with professional staff, often with special division to manage workforce development services and various OSCCs (or one very large OSCC).
- Has incorporated some performance-management practices into service delivery.
- Commonly provides core, intensive, and training services in an integrated fashion, or at least core and intensive without subcontracting.
- Strong function as a political steward in local affairs (as well as an important service provider).
- Government may charter operation/management of the entire public WD and OSCC system to CBO. CBO can be the backbone of WD system.
- Also performs public accountability and advocacy roles.
- Board members tend to have political visibility.
- Networking is important yet not the gravity point of its activity in the WD system. Can behave as an independent player. Can keep competition at bay through political mechanisms.
- Relation with employers can be strong and collaborative.

(WIBs) authorize a list of providers heavily composed of CBOs. Service providers can become WIB-certified through a well structured and competitive process, or through a more flexible and negotiated approach that includes other social, political, and economic considerations, such as the need to meet service gaps in particular distressed geographic areas or neighborhoods. As a primary OSCC operator, a CBO may guide the development of OSCCs along various lines of specialization, depending, for instance, on the mission and practical and philosophical stance of the organization in regard to economic development. For example, a CBO may guide an OSCC to strongly combine support service provision with core and intensive services. Others may assemble services to strongly emphasize career-ladder development in targeted industrial sectors and in close contact with employers.

CBOs in a Peer-to-Peer Network

CBOs can also join forces to manage OSCCs as members of a peer network. Local authorities may choose to delegate the management and operation of the local OSCC system to a structured collection of CBOs. These collaborations or partnerships are likely to be multilevel, with some partners having greater responsibility for providing programmatic expertise, infrastructure, financial, or political resources. There can also be a division of labor with regard to the various services and contributions that individual CBOs bring to the network. In general, the philosophical thrust of the network is a commitment to system-wide collaboration and horizontal connectedness among stakeholders of various kinds. The management of the system is widely perceived as a joint effort between CBOs, and between CBOs and other stakeholders. The peer-to-peer network can be a sub-network of service providers nested or interconnected to a more encompassing network of public, private, and nonprofit organizations. This CBO network can also serve as a voice of collective action to achieve various objectives, such as the modification of allocating formulae, performance targets, and inter-jurisdictional coordination. At a more substantive level, network relationships do intend to meet WIA-driven mandates, but they also combine a great deal of activity aimed at promoting and evolving so-called high-road strategies, which often look beyond work first approaches. Relations with employers can be strong and collaborative yet place a strong emphasis on the creation of good jobs and corporate citizenship.

As summarized in Table 3.3, CBOs in peer-to-peer networks and collaborations tend to be midsize or large organizations, often managing various sites, and largely commanding budgets of over $8 million. They are willing to experiment with new ideas on networking, such as horizontal interorganizational relations with multiple stakeholders. CBOs operating in these networks perceive system management as a joint task of many partners. In addition, they are strongly interested in connecting workforce development to multiple policy areas to deal with regional economic restructuring, urban sprawl, and the declining quality of jobs. For them, workforce development requires strong leadership to advance stakeholder participation in the system and to elaborate strategies that complement standard work first practices under WIA,

Table 3.3 Description of CBO Peer-to-Peer OSCC Operator

- Can be either old, large CBO with multi-million dollar budget ($8+ million) and various sites; or midsize CBO with less than $10 million budget, founded more recently and located on one site.
- Can be a local/regional organization, or an affiliate of a national one.
- Willing to experiment with new ideas, especially on networking. Has leveraged funding from foundations and other agents for this kind of activity. Interested in innovations in WD beyond the mandates of the law.
- Mission statement grounded in group or functional identity, but with commitment to system democratization, equity, and horizontal interorganizational relations.
- Perceives system management as the joint task of many partners pulling their strengths together. Engages in peer-to-peer networking and shares in a division of labor on the management, design, and provision of WD activity and products.
- Internal multidivisional specialization with professional staff, often with dept. to manage WD services and various OSCCs. Strategic interest in integrating WD to other policy areas to deal with regional problems and economic restructuring (sprawl, new economy, quality of jobs). WD treated not as a traditional human/social service, but as a matter of long-term human/social development. Complementary WD activity to challenge simple work first approach.
- CBO can be very involved in WD politics and other political issues. Strong voice for stakeholders' participation.
- CBO leadership participates in broader coalition or organization that has system-wide governance aspirations or functions (association of providers and CBOs; WD councils/coalitions).
- Networking advocates high-road strategies of WD. Strategies pursue long-term goals and attempt to mitigate the negative effects of economic restructuring.

such as career-ladder development—the so-called high-road strategies of workforce development.

CBOs as Subordinate Participants in OSCCs

In recent years, the restructuring of social service delivery systems has diversified the avenues of inclusion, allowing many different kinds of intermediaries to participate in social support functions. But, the restructuring has created mixed opportunities, including outright exclusion for some CBOs. In the process of implementing WIA at the local level, a significant number of CBOs are connecting to OSCCs as subordinate participants. This pattern of subordinate engagement is not necessarily a negative situation, yet it shows that in some employment support systems, CBOs may lack the operational scale and political clout to preside over the operation of an OSCC. In this context, the CBO may not relate directly to the WIB or any other public agency, but it can act as a subcontractor to a larger contractor upstream in the service supply chain, which connects the OSCC to the rest of the governance and employment support system. As such, the CBO offers a very specialized or narrow service, acting as a gateway to a special population. As depicted in Table 3.4, the CBOs engaged in this fashion include small, faith-based organizations as well as organizations that serve specific populations such as immigrants and refugees, youth, and persons with disabilities.[4] For the most part, they were founded recently, although some may have a longer history, dating to the 1960s. Their funding base tends to depend on one major source, with complementary funding coming from the local or national philanthropic sector. CBOs as subordinate participants have little flexibility to experiment with service delivery, and they tend not to hold systematic relations with employers. These CBOs show interest in networking and collaborating in system-building but lack the resources to do so because such activities require and consume staff. Their strategic outlook on connecting workforce development to other policy areas is also rather narrow, unlike CBOs in peer-to-peer networks.

CONTEXTUAL AND ORGANIZATIONAL FACTORS INFLUENCING CBO POSITIONING

CBOs' history, mission, and leadership are associated with representing and advocating for disadvantaged populations and with providing a broad range of social and human services to them. Much of their history and mission are also linked to a specific geography such as a neighborhood or barrio, or a section or district of a city, where they stay in close contact with their constituents. CBOs also show ample philosophical diversity and uphold values of equality, diversity, and multi-

Table 3.4 Description of CBO as Subordinate OSCC Operator

- Predominantly small CBOs; less than $2 million budget; recently founded, although some have a longer history dating to 1960s. One location. Some midsize CBOs as well have left WD activity.
- Local/neighborhood organizations. May have affiliation to national organization, but that is not the rule. Some CBOs have been created by local government.
- Dependent on government funding received directly or through some intermediary. May have small contact with local and national philanthropy.
- Strong group identity and commitment to special populations.
- Little flexibility to experiment. Financial hardship is felt rapidly.
- May manage OSCC. Little capacity for performance management.
- Little internal functional specialization. Maybe 1–2 people devoted to WD.
- Connects to WD system as a provider of very specialized service, or as a gateway to special population. Participates as partner through time-sharing or part-time staffing in OSCCs managed by other agents.
- Board concentrates on internal management issues and maintaining basic contact with outside world.
- Would like to network and collaborate in WD system, but it is costly and time consuming given the CBO's small resource base.
- Marginal contact with employers.
- Little or no say in local political affairs.
- Little strategic capability to connect WD to broader policy issues (except through coalition-building).

culturalism. Sometimes CBOs have different approaches and capacities for community development depending upon their experience and time of foundation. For example, Unity Council, El Proyecto del Barrio, Opportunities Industrialization Center West (OICW), New Community Corporation, and United Migrant Opportunity Services (UMOS) were founded in the 1960s as a response to the disenfranchisement of mostly minority populations and disadvantaged workers. Although they have undergone organizational changes since, they have remained committed to serving those targeted populations. Further, they have expanded their services to reach other populations, such as more recent immigrants and refugees, and people with disabilities. More recently founded organizations align themselves with some of the same philosophical principles, yet focus their identity on a specific social or human service. Central

City Concern (1979) in Portland, Oregon, emerged to provide solutions to homelessness; Career Resources (1996) in Louisville, Kentucky, evolved out of specific efforts to provide employment services; Asian Resources (1980) in Sacramento, California, arose as a social service provider for immigrants and refugees; and Job Connection (1990) in Atlantic City, New Jersey, separated from the county to become an organization focused on employment issues.[5]

CBOs' diversity, history, and mission influence their involvement in programmatic areas, which can take various forms. Long-term history and commitment to targeted issues and populations may be a source of legitimacy and political clout, a competitive advantage for participating in local workforce development systems. CBOs report that previous experience managing programs under JTPA or for welfare recipients helped them to be chosen to participate in WIA-funded programs. Programmatic commitment can make a CBO a better synergy-building organization in a peer-to-peer system because it is considered a trusted partner. Multiple commitments in a programmatic agenda, however, can also work in the opposite direction, pushing an organization into isolation and contributing to its marginalization from the system. Hartford Areas Rally Together (HART) in Hartford, Connecticut, for example, has wanted since the early implementation of WIA to operate an OSCC satellite near the Puerto Rican/Latino neighborhood. Because of its commitment to a broader urban economic revitalization strategy that included workforce development, the organization aggressively tried to link its workforce development program activities to urban revitalization. After some public protests of the city's workforce development policies, which included a traffic blockade in front of the State House, and numerous meetings with government officials, HART decided to develop its own job center. The organization's strong position on this, however, slowly changed as it realized how difficult it was to provide workforce development services disconnected from the OSCC system. Eventually, the HART job center opened an OSCC satellite operation in its facilities to enhance services to the community.

Another important consideration influencing a CBO's positioning is the web of interorganizational relationships CBOs establish with their surrounding environment in order to meet their mission and service commitments. Such relationships tend to change through time and are historically bounded. In the implementation of WIA, great emphasis has been placed on the newly acquired autonomy and flexibility of local actors in deciding program features and workforce development policy. CBOs that are OSCC operators must contend with mandated partnership requirements. In such a context, CBOs' connectedness to other community organizations and government agencies is an important factor in facilitating the formation of partnerships and collaborations to serve the needs of both job seekers and employers. Historically, CBOs, for different reasons, have not been well connected to some of the types of organizations that may be crucial to developing effective workforce development systems, such as business associations, employers, and professional organizations. For CBOs, establishing, nurturing, or redefining these relations consumes valuable resources and often requires the use of additional professional expertise not readily available in the organization.

In the cases we looked at, CBOs' connectedness took on various expressions regarding their positioning in the OSCC system, especially for those that we catalogued as peer-to-peer operators. In Detroit, Jewish Vocational Services connects to another strong primary provider like SER Metro-Detroit to manage the city's OSCC system.[6] For the Denver Employment Alliance, connectedness has served to minimize bureaucratic entanglements, make referrals seamless, and improve geographic and cultural access to services by promoting centers at more friendly locations than in downtown government buildings. For the Chicago Jobs Council, a membership organization comprising more than 100 CBOs and advocacy organizations, connectedness is related not so much to direct service delivery but to accountability, governance, and advocacy for disadvantaged workers. The organization seeks mainly to improve inclusiveness for CBOs at various levels of policy implementation, but especially at the OSCC level.

Primary operators also seek to use their connectedness to manage OSCCs, often as effectively as peer-to-peer operators. In the greater Detroit metro area, SER has sought connectedness to preserve a regular interaction with employers, since one of its workforce development strategies has been to keep a high profile as a large volume provider of services under WIA. Primary operators, however, tend to be more dominant and self-reliant agents in the context of the systems they work in. This is a pattern, for example, that we observed in strongly contested and very complex local systems such as in Los Angeles. The

Los Angeles City OSCC system, which partially overlaps with the Los Angeles County system, relies on 11 CBOs to manage its 15 OSCCs. CBOs, for the most part, tend to operate with relative autonomy in relation to one another and to keep direct relations with the local WIB and with the Community Development Department that shares authority in managing the public system. In contrast, subordinate operators usually lack strong connectedness to other local organizations. As mainly small organizations, they have high transaction costs, must deal with staffing shortages, and face overwhelming service demands from the neighborhood. Networking, partnerships, and collaborations become an intermittent activity that is pursued very narrowly depending on the specific issue under consideration.

The types described above are not solely the result of implementation of the law. But WIA, with other welfare reforms, established new rules which set in motion diverse patterns of positioning among CBOs. As CBOs sought adaptation, following the law came to involve much more than just implementing technical mandates. Significant organizational and political challenges were part of assuming the challenge of using the newly gained flexibility that came with WIA. For some CBOs, the shift has been enabling, but for others it has not. What are the more specific characteristics of the new regime and their effect on CBO positioning?

POLICY CHANGE AND CBOs' POSITIONING

CBOs were operating in an increasingly competitive environment even prior to the implementation of the Personal Responsibility and Work Opportunity Reconciliation Act (PRWORA) of 1996 and the Workforce Investment Act (WIA) of 1998. Federal reforms in welfare and employment services simply reinforced an existing trend of excluding CBOs from participating in local employment services. While the exclusion of CBOs from the delivery of employment services has probably increased overall, numerous CBOs have been combining their historical comparative advantages with newer practices to adapt to the revamped policy regimes (Cordero-Guzmán 2002; Folkman and Rai 1999; USDOL 2001; Borges-Méndez and Meléndez 2002a,b; Meléndez, Kohler-Hausmann, and Borges-Méndez 2002; Meléndez, Donohue, and Borges-Méndez 2002; Nightingale 2001, 2002; Plastrik and Taylor 2001). For instance, relatively large CBOs with a long history as service providers were more capable of negotiating their way into the new local regimes and defending their position as system stakeholders. In these systems, CBOs seemed to become primary and peer-to-peer operators. The politics of implementation also created conditions in some regions in which WIBs and local authorities had to rely on CBOs to become strong partners, often as OSCC operators, simply because local government agencies did not have the outreach or operational capacity to deliver services. At times, local and state agencies have delegated the management of the local public system, beyond the management of OSCCs, to CBOs (Chicago Jobs Council 1998; Kogan, Wolff, and Russell 1995; Mariani 1997; McIntire and Robins 1999; National One-Stop Team 1996; USDOL 1998; Salzman et al. 1999).[7] Examples of an increased role for CBOs in the operation of local systems include organizations such as New Community Corporation (Newark, New Jersey), Central City Concern (Portland, Oregon), OICW (Menlo Park, California), and SER Metro-Detroit, as well as conglomerates of CBOs in the cities of Boston, Milwaukee, and Los Angeles.

The implications of the transition to WIA for CBOs as service providers are still unfolding. In reality, WIA has been under implementation for only about five years as of this publication date. Most jurisdictions are just now moving out of the initial stages, having undertaken to lay out WIBs and OSCCs, recruit core partners, establish performance standards, and formulate strategic development plans. Although no large-scale survey study of CBO adaptation to shifts in policy exists, various comparative case studies of CBOs' (and of other service providers') compliance with WIA regulations identify some short-term responses and patterns of adaptation to shifts in the local regulatory structures (O'Shea 2000; Watrus, Torkelson, and Flynn 1996; Trutko and Barnow 1999; D'Amico et al. 1999; Kogan et al. 1997).[8] These changes are the first set of factors to influence the likelihood of CBOs becoming OSCC operators. Below we document the changes, relying on seven analytical categories often used in the literature for the analysis of WIA.

Philosophy

There are two salient philosophical shifts in WIA of particular relevance to CBOs. First, WIA grants greater control and flexibility to local authorities in the overall management of public employment services. At the same time, WIA also raises the stakes, in terms of systemic accountability and compliance with performance standards, and requires local authorities to implement performance management. WIA encourages the use of market-driven mechanisms to satisfy employment and training needs and demands by creating Individual Training Accounts (ITA). Through these tuition-like vouchers it encourages trade schools, private vendors, and community colleges to participate in the system as training providers. However, under WIA, short-term, work first approaches to employment became significantly more important than training (Frank, Rahmanou, and Savner 2003). Second, WIA also demands that local workforce development systems be driven by customer satisfaction—that of both employers and job seekers. In theory, levels of satisfaction among job seekers and employers have to be periodically surveyed as part of performance reports. But, at the same time that the law encouraged greater accountability and introduced more stringent performance management mechanisms, there was a reduction in the training dollars available, and therefore fewer incentives for CBOs to participate in the system.

CBOs reported difficulties with the philosophical shift in welfare and workforce development policy. Not all CBOs have been acquiescent in making this shift, yet the changes ultimately seem to be percolating into the mission statements of CBOs. The philosophical blending of prior programmatic commitments with new service demands does not mean they have abandoned their historical commitment to represent (mainly underprivileged) communities or to serve particular populations (Withorn 2002). However, there is a noticeable change to a new discourse that puts some distance between itself and the more militant, populist discourse from the War on Poverty era. It is also noticeable that mission statements now incorporate newer principles such as organizational efficiency, outcome measures, funding diversification, accountability, entrepreneurialism, re-engineering and strategic planning, and reducing welfare dependency. For CBOs to assimilate some of these newer principles—many taken from the private sector—oftentimes entailed changes in staffing, new approaches to client outreach and case management, casting a public image, and revamping operations. This philosophical shift, it is worth noting, is infused by an overall reformist movement that has captivated a significant part of the entire nonprofit sector and some levels of government (Kettl 2000).

Second, the most striking philosophical change for CBOs has been in accommodating work first approaches to employment. Many CBOs have stated that these approaches must be connected to, or evolve into, more complex interventions if they are to improve the employment outcomes and advancement opportunities of disadvantaged workers over the long haul. CBOs are quite aware of this dilemma, yet they are financially strapped by the overall bias of the act and the mandated funding streams that primarily support work first programmatic and placement activities. Finally, the philosophical shift has implied rethinking tactical approaches to organizational and economic survival. In the new policy regime, performance-based agreements, vendor competition, and customer choice are forcing CBOs to explore new programs, collaborations, and network affiliations to remain competitive (Borges-Méndez and Meléndez 2002a,b; Meléndez, Kohler-Hausmann, and Borges-Méndez 2002; Meléndez, Donohue, and Borges-Méndez 2002; Plastrik and Taylor 2001).

Governance and Oversight

WIA created Workforce Investment Boards (WIBs) to replace Private Industry Councils (PICs). A state-level WIB (appointed by the governor) is responsible for overseeing local WIBs. The local WIB has jurisdiction over a specific area. WIBs, in contrast to PICs, are not allowed to be direct service providers. They are primarily a policy body with oversight authority for WIA funding, though other funding streams may be delegated to the WIBs for operational integration at the local level. WIBs are also in charge of setting certification policies and procedures for local service providers. The composition of local WIBs is set up to have representatives of the private business sector, government, labor, education, and other local stakeholders. WIBs are financially accountable to city or county government, or a combination of them.[9] By the sunset of JTPA, PICs appeared to have evolved into passive bureaucratic-administrative agents; it is assumed that the WIBs will replace them with entrepreneurialism and synergistic engagements with multiple sectors (public, private, and nonprofit).[10] In some locales, WIBs remained practically identical in composition to PICs.

The shift from PICs to WIBs created numerous challenges to local areas, such as defining an optimum board size, given the unmanageable number of mandated partners, and recruiting local industry leadership. In some locales, CBOs are represented at the board and participate in decision-making. In particular, some large CBOs or coalitions of CBOs have had significant input in the governance affairs of local systems. This is especially true in cities and locales where CBOs are active players with political clout and have a track record in workforce program administration from the previous JTPA regime. In these locales, some large CBOs have been hands-on managers of the transition, deeply engaged with some of the WIBs' decisions on levels of funding for OSCCs, certification policies for service providers, and strategic orientations to grow the local employment system (Fitzgerald and Sutton 2000; Borges-Méndez and Meléndez 2002a,b; Meléndez, Kohler-Hausmann, and Borges-Méndez 2002; Meléndez, Donohue, and Borges-Méndez 2002). However, in most areas, CBOs reported feeling alienated from the decision-making process and lacked adequate representation on local WIBs.

CBO participation on local WIBs is to a large extent a function of the CBO's own board's political activism and engagement with the local employment system. In our interviews, CBO managers insisted on the critical role of CBO board leadership in formulating and implementing a pragmatic plan or vision to guide CBO positioning within the system. Politically, board leadership can provide an important source of political stewardship, especially if board members are involved and participate in broader political affairs. The strength of the CBO board leadership, however, may be related to how many of its members come from the private sector. Most CBOs interviewed consider strong private sector membership to be a critical aspect of developing successful workforce development programs and of establishing effective working relations with employers and local WIBs. Gender, racial, ethnic and multicultural diversity in board membership are also critical to the CBO's capacity for building networks and associations with a broad range of stakeholders. In addition, board leadership can act as a buffer between the CBO and government in regard to performance-compliance issues. Finally, CBO board leadership can act as a critical linkage between the CBO and its ability to connect workforce development to other policy arenas and issues such as economic development, housing, and health—policy areas that may improve the quality of jobs. In summary, board political clout, managerial expertise, and diversity are all critical factors in the ability of CBOs to adapt to changing policy regimes. Most CBOs attribute participation in the local WIB's governance and a good part of their success in becoming OSCC operators to strong board leadership.

Service Delivery Structure

WIA seeks to increase flexibility and local autonomy in service delivery while also increasing service, promoting universal access, and integrating programs. Because of these objectives, WIA increases service delivery demands upon local systems. One-stop career centers are institutionalized as the frontline, integrated service delivery mechanism. Under WIA, 17 categories of programs, funded through four separate federal agencies, are required to provide services through the OSCC system; the four federal agencies are the departments of Labor, Education, Health and Human Services, and Housing and Urban Development (U.S. General Accounting Office 2000b). All of these programs are not required to be available on-site at OSCCs, although there are some mandated partners that must have a presence at OSCCs and share a portion of operational costs. OSCC operators are selected and certified by local WIBs, and OSCCs can be operated by different types of agents: CBOs, unions, for-profit companies, city and county governments, and universities and community colleges. They often oversee three types of services: core, intensive, and training. The mix of such services is determined by WIA regulations and by local factors.

The new service delivery requirements challenged CBOs to modify their delivery capacity. The shift to universal access, although very much compatible with the historical commitment of CBOs to promote and preserve equity in service provision, implied devoting significant resources for outreach among new constituencies and providing services to them. The new clients sometimes are located beyond the immediate geographic boundaries of CBO activity. In the context of complying with WIA, the implementation of universal access and the work first mandate implied expanding the client base and doing more intense follow-up activity. In recent years, CBOs have been pushed to do more with less while working with populations that have multiple barriers to employment. The relative concentration of some types of workers or populations within the client base of communities makes this task much more difficult and significantly affects the positioning of CBOs. In addition, the relatively larger size of welfare caseloads at the county (or city) level during the early implementation of WIA offered many CBOs opportunities to participate in workforce development through work first programs. As case loads declined and Welfare-to-Work funding dried up, however, these entry opportunities diminished. Among those CBOs that developed work first programs, many report that they have not been able to upscale their services beyond work first into retention or training services and are beginning to experience exclusion from core operations of the systems, or have become marginal (niche) subcontractors.

Planning, Program Development, and Staff

JTPA stipulated two-year cycles for programming. WIA, by contrast, demands that WIBs develop five-year strategic plans for their workforce development areas. These plans are annually revised and subjected to public scrutiny. Strategic plans have to be approved by the state WIB, which then submits a unified strategy to the federal Department of Labor. Providers receiving more than a certain level of funding from local WIBs are also required to submit strategic plans, especially providers in charge of managing OSCCs.[11] The demands of a plan with a five-year strategic horizon implied ridding the CBO organizational culture of "back-of-the-envelope" planning or of rigid request-for-proposal (RFP) driven program development. The new planning outlook would have to combine long-term strategies of sustainability with performance evaluation considerations, giving particular attention to retention, customer satisfaction, and program integration. The implications for program development that derive from a more competitive environment are apparent. In the new regime, funding allocation and re-approval as vendors would be connected not to pre-negotiated contractual levels but to actual performance in a range of core, intensive, and training services.

Responses to the new planning and program development demands varied among CBOs. Some large CBOs, already having experienced the political and economic challenges of a prior era, actively engaged in adaptive practices, especially in diversifying funding portfolios (including government contracts) and, to the extent possible, reduced dependency on government funding. The shift from contract-based to performance-based, at the most immediate level, implied fronting significant funds in developing and complying with the new policy mandates without assurances of recovering expenditures and investments in the new WIA-induced infrastructures. In contrast, smaller CBOs experienced a difficult time in adapting to the new planning demands. Changes in the planning horizon and in the orientation of programs—for instance, into more work first approaches and customer choice—required leadership and boards of directors in CBOs to become more proactive in terms of engaging the private sector and newer partners.[12]

CBO size and specialization were important determinants of how CBOs responded to the demands imposed by planning new programs and adapting resources and capacity to the local performance regimes. In this context, CBOs' deployment of human resources and staff became a major force in determining CBOs' positioning within the OSCC systems. Large CBOs had more flexibility in restructuring the organization. For instance, the professional development of CBO staff facilitates compliance with the stronger, performance-driven approach brought by WIA. CBOs also developed new marketing strategies, which they deployed at various levels and through multiple media. CBOs intending to become visible and effective at recruitment hired marketing specialists and technology managers. Practically all primary operators have developed a new battery of instruments to meet the outreach requirements of programs targeting welfare recipients and the WIA mandate for universal access. Similarly, reaching out to employers has also entailed revamping the skills of job developers and traditional case managers or social workers. In part, CBOs met these challenges by promoting cross-training, teamwork, and learning from experience within the organization. Finally, CBO positioning in the OSCC system has been influenced by the resources devoted to strengthen management systems in areas such as case management, participant tracking, performance reporting, fundraising, and accounting.

Market Competition

WIA opens the local systems to increased competition among service providers through the use of Individual Training Accounts (ITAs), a tuition-like, portable training voucher. The reasoning behind ITAs is to encourage trade schools and community colleges to develop more programs targeting disadvantaged populations, while providing more training options for workers. However, to most CBOs, the idea of market competition through training vouchers was an entirely new concept. In our interviews, most CBOs—large or small—reported that they were not prepared to enter into such competition for various reasons. First, competition increased turf battles for funding, clients, and service delivery markets. This dispersed the political influence of CBOs and thus their ability to engage in meaningful decision-making in the restructured local employment services system. Second, trade schools and community colleges coming into the ITA market were likely to be better equipped than CBOs to compete for tuition-like funds and clients. In fact, WIA was structured to give an initial advantage to community colleges by providing a one-year grace period for initial certification. Many CBOs perceived that the field was not level even before competition was unleashed. Third, increased competitive pressures came simultaneously with demands for greater accountability and performance, which for many CBOs represented a management challenge given the inordinate volume of data collection and reporting required for participating in the program. Finally, the implementation of ITAs introduced a great deal of uncertainty for CBOs: Would ITAs contribute to draining resources from nonprofits into the private sector? Would ITAs be captured by the new providers and leave CBOs simply to specialize in core and intensive services? Would ITAs be available, or would they become too difficult for the CBOs' constituencies to get access to (Trutko and Barnow 1999)?

Despite these barriers, some CBOs that are large primary operators and some CBOs that are in peer-to-peer networks redesigned their programs and management system to participate in the ITA program. Redesigning programs to benefit from ITAs, however, depended on having a strong history of providing employment services and training facilities in-house, like OICW in Menlo Park. Some primary operators have created sister or affiliate branches that provide the training service sought by ITA clients, like SER Metro-Detroit. In this regard, the CBOs that could integrate ITA into a pre-existing training infrastructure or experience have benefited. In addition, strong connections to the private sector and good relations with city and county government greatly influenced the successful use of ITAs by CBOs. Getting to be a training provider certified by the local WIB and setting ITA expenditure levels are critical to the feasibility of using the ITA program. Both are negotiated processes that involve local authorities, WIBs, and providers, especially since ITA expenditure levels are not preset by federal authorities.

Local competitive conditions and relations among providers also influenced CBO positioning within the OSCC. Not all cities, counties, or regions show the same mix and density of labor market intermediaries or have the same history regarding collaboration and networking among stakeholders. Large and densely populated markets are often contested by large and experienced intermediaries. The Los Angeles metro area is a case in point. In its markets, smaller CBOs face higher entry barriers and operational costs. In such cases, large CBOs may be able to make their way into the system through their political capabilities or by demonstrating their comparative advantage in the provision of services. The Los Angeles Urban League's (LAUL) political clout facilitates its positioning as primary operator in a heavily contested market for workforce development services. Smaller CBOs may simply stay away from WIA funding or become subcontractors providing very specific services. Alternatively, in a few locales CBOs decided to work together and form collaborations. The success of this strategy depends upon the history of networking and operational collaboration in the area. The greater Boston area contains examples of these kinds of collaborative relations. In Boston, Jewish Vocational Services (JVS) in collaboration with the Economic Development and Industrial Corporation's Office of Jobs and Community Services (EDIC/JCS) and the Higher Education Center, manage one of the city's three OSCCs. In locales with smaller and less competitive labor markets and relatively weak government agencies, some CBOs have become central operators in the system, often in charge of managing the entire OSCC system. In Menlo Park and Detroit, OICW and SER, respectively, anchor the local systems. In Detroit, SER and two other organizations, JVS and Ross, administer the local OSCC system under a charter from the WIB. In all of these circumstances, WIBs are responsible for shaping the structure of local or regional employment services markets through the chartering of OSCCs and certification policies. Local discretion by WIBs and flexibility in policy implementation, however, can push the process in one of two directions, either facilitating or hindering CBOs' access to the market.

Program and Funding Streams

Under JTPA, low income was a criteria for program eligibility for adults, youth, and displaced workers. WIA preserves those three main target groups but shifts to universal access regardless of income. In addition, with the new emphasis on universal access WIA imposed requirements on the 17 programs spread across four departments. Title I of WIA absorbs most of the JTPA programs. Other changes fall under other title sections of the act. Title II replaced the Adult Education Act with the Adult Education and Family Act. Title III amended the Wagner-Peyser Act, which established the Employment Service. The Title III section transformed that service into the foundation of the OSCC system by requiring that its information and labor exchange activity be provided as part of the OSCC system. Title IV amended the Rehabilitation Act of 1973, which set requirements for vocational rehabilitation (U.S. General Accounting Office 2001a,b).[13] A number of those programs, like Welfare-to-Work and the Migrant and Seasonal Farm Worker Employment and Training Program, are currently being phased out and new ones are being created for faith-based organizations.[14] At the level of OSCCs, services stemming from these diverse streams and programs, then, are required to be funneled into a three-tier (sequential) system of core, intensive, and training services (U.S. General Accounting Office 2000a,b).

Historically, CBOs have been quite capable at integrating services that have multiple funding streams (Nightingale 2001). WIA, however, posed a newer challenge, in two ways. First, the consolidation of program and funding streams came with more stringent demands of performance accountability (especially on job retention) and customer satisfaction among job seekers and employers. Thus, significant resources were necessary to harmonize case data and accounting management systems to meet and report on the new standards. These resources for adaptation were, for the most part, nonexistent, except where some of the funding for the early implementation of the act may have been politically negotiated to address the specific needs of CBOs, which were operating as subcontractors (U.S. General Accounting Office 2002; Borges-Méndez and Meléndez 2002a,b; Meléndez, Kohler-Hausmann, and Borges-Méndez 2002; Meléndez, Donohue, and Borges-Méndez 2002). Mainly, it has been the large primary operators, such as OICW in Menlo Park, the Los Angeles Urban League, and SER Metro-Detroit, that have been able to carry forward with program integration, although not without problems. The technology, staff, and continuous client satisfaction surveys for multiple programs and multilingual populations that receive services across various sites are extremely difficult to maintain. Various administrators commented that their organizations seem to be "working to maintain the system" instead of working to improve the quality of services. Second, internal program and service integration within any particular provider would require partial harmonization with other kinds of partners in various settings. The need for harmonization would clearly emerge in the processes of implementing OSCCs, of creating chains of service provision, of meeting the partnership requirements of the law, or of implementing networks of providers in order to organize and process referrals. Given that many providers do not necessarily provide all three kinds of core, service, and training services in one location, these networks help organize the various types of services among providers. In terms of external harmonization, greater local autonomy and flexibility in service integration are likely to create both negative and positive networking externalities for CBOs and other agents (Cordero-Guzmán 2002; Harrison and Weiss 1998).[15] Increased interaction in the form of networks, partnerships, and collaborative programming and service delivery could become not only laboratories of innovation, but nodules of friction and conflict.

Performance Standards

JTPA was a contract-based system in which funds were allocated to providers according to pre-negotiated and preset levels of service provision. WIA is a performance-based system in which providers are partly reimbursed for achieving performance targets. JTPA placed little emphasis on retention and follow-up of clients, whereas WIA establishes strong provisions of systemic accountability that require data to be gathered on services provided, placements, and retention (up to a year after placement). The Department of Labor requires data from OSCCs on 17 performance indicators and periodic customer satisfaction surveys of job seekers and employers. WIA also ties cost reimbursement to meeting performance targets.

The issues of performance and accountability are shaped by the power dynamics of intergovernmental relations and the devolution of the federal system.[16] During the implementation of WIA, for CBOs to meet new standards in retention, follow-up, and customer satisfaction entailed filling out more paperwork and taking on greater bureaucratic loads. Many CBOs reported that enhancing services and gaining inclusion implied implementing changes in staffing, managerial philosophies, coalition-building, and partnership development. In some regards, by doing so CBOs are opening themselves to greater public and political scrutiny. In antagonistic political environments, such openness may not be in CBOs' best interests, as it can be used not to effect constructive policy change but to narrow the range of inclusion of CBOs in public policy making. The prospect of having to disclose performance under unfriendly or punitive political conditions has certainly affected the political calculus and thus the choices of CBOs. In many local contexts, the technical difficulties of raising performance levels and achieving those higher levels in service delivery are inevitably transformed into political justifications to further shed CBOs from service delivery systems (Borges-Méndez and Meléndez 2002a,b; Meléndez, Kohler-Hausmann, and Borges-Méndez 2002; Meléndez, Donohue, and Borges-Méndez 2002).[17] OICW in Menlo Park, for instance, reported that there was a continual battle for placement and retention numbers, referring to the difficulties in claiming a successful placement after program participants have undergone various sequential programs. Also, OICW indicated that the prospects of forming partnerships between CBOs and community colleges have been discouraged by the performance reporting requirements of WIA. Some community colleges see reporting requirements as intrusive and excessive.

THE GENERAL INFLUENCE OF THE LAW ON THE TYPES OF CBO-OSCC POSITIONING

From the discussion of the multiple dimensions of the law, various observations are pertinent. First, CBOs that are primary and peer-to-peer operators of OSCCs have been able to accommodate some of WIA's philosophical principles, like the work first mandate, within the broader scope of their historical mission. Such has been the case with large multidivisional, multiservice CBOs like LAUL, OICW, UMOS, SER Metro-Detroit, and New Community Corporation, which have a long-standing and well established history of program and political management. This gives them the flexibility to modify program structure without changing their mission. Although they are in disagreement with work first approaches to workforce development, these organizations adapted to the change and combined it within other initiatives, like career ladders and skills training, that complemented the short-term outlook of the work first approach. Also, at times, they negotiated program modifications to work first, such as changing OSCC funding allocation formulae, using their leverage as recognized service providers and political stewards within their jurisdictions. Admittedly, these are large organizations with above average annual budgets and more than 20 years of existence, among other attributes. However, midsize CBOs, with solidly established track records in specific functional areas such as health, education, or human services have also become successful OSCC primary operators or are partnering in established OSCCs. This may be attributable to their specialized expertise and performance as service providers rather than as all encompassing CBOs. Small CBOs, mainly recently founded ones, seem to be more likely to become subordinate subcontractors to the extent that they have less resources and organizational capital to invest in program restructuring without significant shifts in their overall mission objectives.

Second, CBOs that have become primary and peer-to-peer operators directly participate in the governance of the public employment and OSCC systems. That is, CBOs are service providers but they are often also members of their local WIBs and active participants in the decision making process along with local administrators. In addition, this participation in governance of the system serves as a connection to other collaborations that are formed by such interaction, like industry-focused workforce development initiatives or partnerships with professional associations. CBOs acting in more subordinate roles participate more indirectly or sporadically in the governance of these systems, although on occasion large CBOs become the conduit for smaller CBOs to participate in the governance of the local system.

Third, the introduction of ITAs has produced a mixed effect upon CBO positioning. ITAs are difficult to access and monitor. Even some of the large CBOs that have become primary operators have not been able to use them. Only CBOs that have close-knit and multilevel workforce development programs with employers seem to be capable of using and promoting ITAs among their clients. The integrated programs include training, curriculum development, and joint fundraising, among other features. SER Metro-Detroit and OICW fit this description. ITAs, for the most part, are too difficult to handle by CBOs in subordinate roles.

Fourth, WIA, and welfare reform in general, demands program and funding stream consolidation, and thus much program coordination and harmonization on the part of service providers. CBOs that are primary and peer-to-peer operators have been able to manage this challenge through various kinds of efficiency-enhancing activities or through networking with other organizations. For instance, CBOs have implemented service quality-control practices, have created technological management units and service matrices, have cross-trained staff to facilitate multi-program interventions, and have diversified collaborations. CBOs in subordinate positions cannot accommodate or manage these dynamics for various reasons, including organizational size, lack of partners, inhospitable political conditions, or lack of human resources. But among larger CBOs, the North Texas Human Resource Group has been actively engaged in training OSCC frontline staff. OICW has strongly pursued technological modernization to improve case management across programs. Boston Career Link, an OSCC, has sought harmonization through intensive networking and collaborative integration between CBOs with distinct competitive advantages in fields ranging from health and human services to accounting and management.

Fifth, the mandate and challenge of universal access has placed CBOs in a double bind—both philosophically and in terms of service delivery. Historically, CBOs have served as advocates and service providers for a broad range of populations and constituencies. However, this commitment can hit resource limits when various other factors are considered for service delivery, such as the capacity to handle an increased volume of clients, shifting neighborhood demographics that demand newer cultural competencies, or a rapidly deteriorating job base in the region. CBOs that were able to become primary operators and peer-to-peer operators had the capacity to underwrite and execute the scaling up of operations. They may have upgraded through any of several avenues, such as creating newer entities to improve financial sustainability, absorbing smaller CBOs with relevant attributes and competencies, entering into partnerships with other organizations, and changing or adding geographic locations. For instance, SER Metro-Detroit has created, or spun off from itself, various organizations to optimize relations with employers in order to advance a high-volume placement strategy. The San Diego Career Opportunities Partners organization has tackled the dilemma through a more horizontal organizational structure that promotes partnerships outside of contractual Memorandums of Understanding (MOUs). El Proyecto del Barrio in Los Angeles has simply decided to aggressively diversify operations into workforce development from a strong service platform and expertise in health and human services.

Finally, under WIA, complying with the newly created performance standards seems tremendously relevant to CBO positioning. Some CBOs said that the decision to establish an OSCC, a satellite center, or not to participate in the system rested upon the prospects of complying with the new standards.[18] Among the factors given by CBOs that weighed on their decision whether to participate in the OSCC system were 1) cost of human resources and technology, 2) additional (and apparently irrelevant) paperwork, 3) inter-jurisdictional conflicts, 4) added general uncertainty in program planning, and 5) simple objection to incomprehensible indicators that had no practical application. Notwithstanding, primary operators have taken up the challenge of adapting to the new performance regime. LAUL has incorporated into the management of its three OSCCs a complex system of quality control that links programmatic and organizational performance at various levels, including staff performance, program outcomes, and staff training needs determined by client feedback. And OICW in Menlo Park has decisively taken over the shaping of the client tracking and performance system in light of San Mateo County's inability to get an electronic data base and card system up and running.

CONCLUSIONS

The impact of the implementation of WIA on CBO positioning has been uneven. Changes brought upon CBOs by WIA are not the sole influence on their positioning. Other environmental and organizational factors are at play, such as policy devolution, the history and mission of CBOs, and the quality of connectedness to other actors in local workforce development systems. These factors have triggered differentiated responses on the part of CBOs and multiple paths of adaptation.

Some large, old, and well-established CBOs have been able to adapt to the changes and to incorporate some of the fundamental mandates of the new law, such as the universal access and work first approaches. In the process, however, they have also used the operational flexibility granted by the law to local agents to challenge, and on occasion to modify, some aspects of the implementation of the law at the local level, such as OSCC funding allocation formulae, responsibilities in system-wide management, multi-jurisdictional data management standards, and partnership requirements. As primary operators of OSCCs, some CBOs have gone a step further, combining and interconnecting work first approaches with other long-term outlooks to workforce development. These may include career-ladder development, complex and multilevel collaborations with employers, industrial cluster development strategies, and strong social service support to assure retention and long-term individual and family stability. Conversely, other, smaller CBOs with far less resources experienced a more difficult transition, having either to exit the system or become subordinate subcontractors. Both responses, however, pose a dilemma for all CBOs, one that has to do with the search for pragmatic approaches to combining commitment and performance—two goals that can be at odds with each other in the context of CBOs having to serve, represent, and advocate for disadvantaged workers that are increasingly disenfranchised by welfare reforms.

This complex interaction between CBOs' overall commitment to serving disadvantaged populations and their necessity to provide services under the pressures of more stringent performance standards creates several organizational dilemmas. At the programmatic level, CBOs have become the main integrators of various funding streams from WIA and other sources from the areas of education, disability,

Medicaid, Housing and Urban Development, social policy, and transportation. WIA contemplated this kind of interface to produce integrated workforce development systems yet made few proposals and offered few resources for CBOs to do so. By remaining in clear compliance with the law and going beyond the mandate, CBOs have added value to the system in this role.

CBOs have also shown operational flexibility in terms of covering new geographic areas and neighborhoods, attending to new populations, implementing technological improvements, promoting the cross-training of staff, and articulating increased coordination with new agencies. CBOs who became OSCC operators have often implemented internal capacity-building strategies. Some organizations are already following all-encompassing improvement strategies built on models and principles of "total quality management," "learning communities," "non-profit sustainability," "leadership and multicultural development," and "customer satisfaction," as well as using more traditional tools drawn from the world of organizational management and community development (community organizing, empowerment, and activism). These ideas are being extended to shape OSCCs' operations. It is worth noting that several stakeholders sponsoring these strategies for capacity building, such as the National Association of Workforce Boards or the National Governors Association, also play a critical role in lobbying for their constituents at policy making levels of government. CBO activity in this regard appears more scattered and disconnected. In some cases, CBOs may be affiliated with national umbrella organizations or may be chapter affiliates of a larger matrix organization; such affiliations offer some opportunity to become more actively involved in policy setting activities. CBOs at the local level, especially those working within peer-to-peer arrangements and broader community development programs, have come together on a more organized and permanent basis, forming service provider coalitions and influencing a workforce development policy agenda.

Notes

1. According to the U.S. General Accounting Office (2001a, p. 6, n. 10), "Labor introduced the one-stop concept in 1994, when it began awarding implementation grants to help states bring Labor-funded employment and training programs into a single infrastructure." Also, before WIA, some states had reformed their employment and training programs and had created OSCCs, along with other reforms in social welfare policy.
2. We carried out these site visits as an indirect result of other research projects on related issue involving the following organizations: Los Angeles Urban League, OICW, UMOS, SER Metro-Detroit, CETA, Asian Resources, Boston Career Link, and JVS-Boston.
3. Numerous cases of partnerships and promising practices are in Clymer, Roberts, and Strawn (2001) and in AFL-CIO Working For America Institute (2001). The specific profiles of the cases and organizations are available at http://www.workingforamerica.org/documents/HighRoadReport/highroadreport.htm.
4. For a list of faith-based organizations in workforce development see Bender (2003).
5. In our list of cases we have organizations that might qualify as faith-based organizations, as they were founded by religious or ecumenical coalitions or movements. Through the years, however, they have become more secular in their service provision activity. This is the case with OICW, Goodwill Industries, and the Jewish Vocational Service (JVS) in Boston and Detroit.
6. SER is an acronym for Service, Employment, and Redevelopment–Jobs for Progress. SER Metro-Detroit is a multiservice, community-based corporation established in 1971. For more information, see its Web site, http://www.sermetro.org.
7. Most of these reports, as well as a whole host of implementation manuals and guidebooks on WIA institutional infrastructure, can be found at the Web site of the Employment and Training Administration, http://www.doleta.gov (accessed Spring 2003).
8. Recently a large-scale survey of faith-based organizations was made available. See Bender (2003).
9. According to the U.S. General Accounting Office (2001a, pp. 11–12), "There are 54 state workforce investment boards and approximately 600 local boards (including District of Columbia, U.S. Virgin Islands, Puerto Rico and Guam). WIA listed what types of members should participate on the workforce investment boards, but did not prescribe a minimum number of members. Also, it allowed governors to select representatives from various segments of the workforce investment community, including business, education, labor, and other organizations with experience in the delivery of workforce investment activities to be represented on the state boards. The specifics of the local board membership were similar to those for the state." Also, according to a recent study by the Charitable Choice Center and the University Center for Academic and

Workforce Development at the University at Albany, State University of New York (SUNY), "On April 17, 2002, USDOL issued a Training and Employment Guidance Letter (No.17-01) requesting: 'that states take actions to broaden the number of grassroots community-based organizations, including faith-based organizations, which partner with Local Workforce Investment Boards (WIBs) and the One-Stop Career Centers.' " The report adds, "On July 1, 2002, USDOL became the first federal agency to award grants targeted specifically at states and intermediary organizations. As a result, $17.5 million was awarded to 12 states and 29 organizations in an effort to link faith-based and grassroots community organizations to the One-Stop Career Center system" (Bender 2003).

10. On PICs becoming passive bureaucratic entities, see Lafer (2002). On trying to make WIBs more active agents, see The Workforce Board Development Series, published by the National Association of Workforce Boards. The series includes titles such as *Workforce Board Leadership: Advice from Experienced CEOs* (2001), and *Putting Your WIB on the Political Map: Tips on Marketing, Communications and Public Relations* (2000). The NAWB is a member of the Business Coalition for Workforce Development, a group of 35 national business organizations "helping employers set up effective training and employment systems under the federal Workforce Investment Act" (National Association of Workforce Boards 2000, p. 3).
11. The required level varies, being determined and negotiated locally.
12. On the overall adaptation of CBOs to performance-based contracting see Sanger (2000). Other important works on the adaptation of nonprofits (CBOs among them) to structural changes in subcontracting, devolution, and privatization are Boris and Steurle (1999) and Smith and Lipsky (1993).
13. See the text of the full act at http://www.doleta.gov/reports/docs/legislation (accessed July 2, 2004).
14. A summary of the cutbacks can be found in the U.S. Department of Labor's *Summary of ETA Fiscal Year 2003 Request*, at http://www.doleta.gov/budget/03reqsum.pdf (accessed July 2, 2004).
15. One of the objectives of the Annie E. Casey Foundation's Jobs Initiative has been to support and document patterns of collaboration and networking in various cities. See Fleisher (2001) and Annie E. Casey Foundation (2001). The Annie E. Casey Foundation publications can be downloaded from http://www.aecf.org.
16. The essays in Sawicky (1999) provide an overview of the governmental changes that have taken place in various policy areas as a result of devolution. For more comprehensive and in-depth accounts of federal devolution and of the last major welfare reform, see Conlan (1998) and Weaver (2000). For some of the implications of the New Federalism and devolution on social policy research methodologies, see Bell (1999) and King (1999).
17. These observations unfold from the authors' research on four cases of the value-added contribution of CBOs to the OSCC system.
18. A "satellite" is a reduced-functions OSCC that can depend on a formal OSCC and does not have all of the partnership and service requirements of a full-blown

center. A satellite can be used to offer services in far away locations or places (neighborhoods, workplaces) that may not need all of the services demanded by the law. Satellites can be used and created for other strategic or outreach purposes as well, such as to increase the participation of organizations that cannot afford to run OSCCs or that cannot meet some of the certification requirements established by WIBs.

References

AFL-CIO Working For America Institute. 2001. *High Road Partnerships Report: Innovations in Building Good Jobs and Strong Communities.* Washington, DC: Working For America Institute. http://www.workingforamerica.org/documents/HighRoadReport/highroadreport.htm (accessed July 2004).

Annie E. Casey Foundation. 2001. *Products from the Annie E. Casey Foundation's Jobs Initiative: A Catalogue of Innovations in Workforce Reform.* Baltimore: Annie. E Casey Foundation.

Bell, Stephen H. 1999. *New Federalism and Research: Rearranging Old Methods to Study New Social Policies in the States.* A discussion paper in the Assessing the New Federalism project. Washington, DC: Urban Institute.

Bender, April M. 2003. "The Relationship between the Workforce Investment Act and the Charitable Choice Initiative." Charitable Choice Center Document 315.265.409, University Center for Academic and Workforce Development, State University of New York. Paper presented at the 2003 Biennial National Research Conference held in Washington, DC, June 4–5.

Borges-Méndez, Ramón, and Edwin Meléndez. 2002a. *OIC-West Value-Added Contribution to OSCC System Performance.* Washington, DC: U.S. Department of Labor, Employment and Training Administration.

———. 2002b. *Los Angeles Urban League Value-Added Contribution to OSCC System Performance.* Washington, DC: U.S. Department of Labor, Employment and Training Administration.

Boris, Elizabeth, and C. Eugene Steurle, eds. 1999. *Nonprofits and Government Collaboration and Conflict.* Washington, DC: Urban Institute.

Chicago Jobs Council. 1998. *Five Stops on the Road to Improving Chicago's One-Stops: Strategies from the Midwest to Make Chicago's Workforce System Work for Everyone.* Chicago, IL: Chicago Jobs Council.

Clymer, Carol, Brandon Roberts, and Julie Strawn. 2001. *States of Change: Policies and Programs to Promote Low-Wage Workers' Steady Employment and Advancement.* Philadelphia: Public/Private Ventures.

Conlan, Timothy. 1998. *From New Federalism to Devolution: Twenty-Five Years of Intergovernmental Reform.* Washington, DC: Brookings Institution.

Cordero-Guzmán, Héctor R. 2002. "Interorganizational Networks Among Community-Based Organizations." Paper presented at the conference "Communities and Workforce Development," sponsored by the Ford Foundation and the Community Development Research Center, Milano Graduate School of Management and Urban Policy, New School University, held in New York, May 11.

D'Amico, Ronald, Ruth Fedran, Mary Kimball, Michael Midling, and Sengsouvahn Soukamneuth. 1999. *An Evaluation of the Self-Service Approach in One-Stop Career Centers.* Final report. Menlo Park, CA: Social Policy Research Associates.

Fitzgerald, Joan, and Stacey A. Sutton. 2000. *One-Stops: Something for Everyone?* Report prepared for the U.S. Department of Labor. Washington, DC: U.S. Department of Labor.

Fleischer, Wendy. 2001. *Extending Ladders: Findings from the Annie E. Casey Foundation's Jobs Initiative.* Baltimore, MD: Annie E. Casey Foundation.

Folkman, Daniel V., and Kalyani Rai. 1999. "The New Role of Community-Based Agencies." In *The Welfare-to-Work Challenge for Adult Literacy Educators: New Directions for Adult and Continuing Education.* Larry Martin and James Fisher, eds. San Francisco: Jossey-Bass, pp. 69–82.

Frank, Abbey, Hedieh Rahmanou, and Steve Savner. 2003. "The Workforce Investment Act: A First Look at Participation, Demographics and Services." Center for Law and Social Policy (CLASP) Program Update (March): 1–19.

Harrison, Bennett, and Marcus Weiss. 1998. *Workforce Development Networks: Community-Based Organizations and Regional Alliances.* Thousand Oaks: CA: Sage Publications.

Heldrich Center for Workforce Development. 2002. *One-Stop Innovations: Leading Changes Under the WIA One-Stop System.* An ETA occasional paper. Washington, DC: U.S. Department of Labor, Employment and Training Administration. http://www.heldrich.rutgers.edu/Resources/Publication/85/PromisingPracticesFullReport.pdf (accessed July 8, 2004).

Kettl, Donald F. 2000. *The Global Public Management Revolution: A Report on the Transformation of Governance.* Washington, DC: Brookings Institution.

King, Christopher T. 1999. "Federalism and Workforce Policy Reform." *Publius: The Journal of Federalism* 29(2): 53–72.

Kogan, Deborah, Katherine P. Dickinson, Ruth Fedran, Michael Midling, and Kristin E. Wolff. 1997. *Creating Workforce Development Systems that Work: An Evaluation of the Initial One-Stop Implementation Experience.* Final report. Menlo Park, CA: Social Policy Research Associates.

Kogan, Deborah, Kristin Wolff, and Martha Russell. 1995. *Changes in the Hir-*

ing Process: New Actors, New Practices, and New Challenges. Final report. Vol. 1: Findings and Implications. Menlo Park, CA: Social Policy Research Associates.

Lafer, Gordon. 2002. *The Job Training Charade.* Ithaca, NY: Cornell University Press.

Light, Paul C. 2000. *The Tides of Reform: Making Government Work, 1945–1995.* New Haven, CT: Yale University Press.

Mariani, Matthew. 1997. "One-Stop Career Centers: All in One Place and Everyplace." *Occupational Outlook Quarterly.* 41(3): 2–15.

McIntire, James L., and Amy F. Robins. 1999. *Fixing to Change: A Best Practices Assessment of One-Stop Job Centers Working with Welfare Recipients.* Seattle: Fiscal Policy Center, Institute for Public Policy and Management, University of Washington.

Meléndez, Edwin, Katherine Donohue, and Ramón Borges-Méndez. 2002. *SER Metro-Detroit Value-Added Contribution to the One-Stop System Performance.* Washington, DC: U.S. Department of Labor, Employment and Training Administration.

Meléndez, Edwin, Issa Kohler-Hausmann, and Ramón Borges-Méndez. 2002. "UMOS Value-Added Contribution to One-Stop System Performance in Milwaukee." Paper presented at the conference, "Communities and Workforce Development," sponsored by the Ford Foundation and the Community Development Research Center, Milano Graduate School of Management and Urban Policy, New School University, held in New York, May 11.

National Association of Workforce Development Boards. 2000. *Putting Your WIB on the Political Map: Tips on Marketing, Communications and Public Relations.* NAWB's Workforce Board Development Series. Washington, DC: National Association of Workforce Boards.

———. 2001. *Workforce Board Leadership: Advice from Experienced CEOs.* Washington, DC: National Association of Workforce Boards.

National One-Stop Team. 1996. *National Learning Laboratories: "One-Stop" Career Centers: Making a Difference in Local Communities.* Washington, DC: U.S. Department of Labor, Employment and Training Administration.

Nightingale, Demetra Smith. 2001. *Program Structure and Service Delivery in Eleven Welfare-to-Work Grant Programs.* Report submitted to Department of Health and Human Services. Princeton, NJ: Mathematica Policy Research.

———. 2002. "Work Opportunities for People Leaving Welfare." In *Welfare Reform: The Next Act,* Alan Weil and Kenneth Finegold, eds. Washington, DC: The Urban Institute, pp. 103–120.

O'Shea, Dan. 2000. "Looking Beyond the WIA: Migrating from 'Programmatic' to 'Systemic': Workforce Development in States and Localities."

Comments delivered at the Association of Public Policy and Management's 22nd annual research conference. http://www.utexas.edu/research/cshr (accessed Spring 2003).

Plastrik, Peter, and Judith Taylor. 2001. *Responding to a Changing Labor Market: The Challenges for Community-Based Organizations.* Boston: Jobs for the Future.

Salzman, Jeffrey, Katherine P. Dickinson, Ruth Fedrau, and Melissa Lazarin. 1999. *Unemployment Insurance in the One-Stop System.* Final report. Washington, DC: U.S. Department of Labor, Employment and Training Administration.

Sanger, M. Bryna. 2000. "When the Private Sector Competes: Lessons from Welfare Reform." Paper presented at the annual Research conference of the Association for Public Policy Analysis and Management, held in Seattle: November 2–4.

Sawicky, Max B., ed. 1999. *The End of Welfare? Consequences of Federal Devolution for the Nation.* Armonk, NY: M.E. Sharpe.

Smith, Steven Rathgeb, and Michael Lipsky. 1993. *Nonprofits for Hire: The Welfare State in the Age of Contracting.* Cambridge, MA: Harvard University Press.

Trutko, John, and Burt S. Barnow. 1999. *Vouchers Under JTPA: Lessons for Implementation of the Workforce Investment Act.* Research report. Arlington, VA: James Bell Associates.

U.S. Department of Labor (USDOL). 1998. *Ensuring High Quality Career Centers Through Chartering: USDOL One-Stop Career Centers System Building Capacity Grant.* Final report on grant activities. Washington, DC: U.S. Department of Labor, Employment and Training Administration.

———. 2001. Five-Year Research Plan for the U.S. Department of Labor, Employment and Training Administration (USDOL/ETA). Prepared by the John J. Heldrich Center for Workforce Development at Rutgers University. Washington, DC: U.S. Department of Labor, Employment and Training Administration.

U.S. General Accounting Office. 2000a. *Workforce Investment Act: Implementation Status and the Integration of TANF Services.* House subcommittee testimony of Cynthia M. Fagnoni, director, Education, Workforce and Income Security Issues; Health, Education, and Human Services Division. GAO/T-HEHS-00-145. Washington, DC: U.S. General Accounting Office.

———. 2000b. *Multiple Employment and Training Programs: Overlapping Programs Indicate Need for Closer Examination of Structure.* Report to the Chairman, Committee on the Budget, House of Representatives. GAO-01-71. Washington, DC: U.S. General Accounting Office.

———. 2001a. *Workforce Investment Act: Better Guidance Needed to Address*

Concerns Over New Requirements. Report to Congressional requesters. GAO-02-72. Washington, DC: U.S. General Accounting Office.

———. 2001b. *Workforce Investment Act: New Requirements Create Need for More Guidance.* Statement of Sigurd R. Nilsen, director, Education, Workforce, and Income Security Issues, before the Committee on Health, Education, Labor, and Pensions, U.S. Senate. GAO-02-94T. Washington, DC: U.S. General Accounting Office.

———. 2002. *Workforce Investment Act: Improvements Needed in Performance Measures to Provide a More Accurate Picture of WIA's Effectiveness.* Report to Congressional requesters. GAO-02-275. Washington, DC: U.S. General Accounting Office.

Watrus, Robert, Emily Torkelson, and Elizabeth Flynn. 1996. *One Stop Career Center Systems: Lessons from the Field.* Seattle: Northwest Policy Center, Graduate School of Public Affairs, University of Washington.

Weaver, R. Kent. 2000. *Ending Welfare as We Know It.* Washington, DC: Brookings Institution.

Withorn, Ann. 2002. "Friends or Foes? Nonprofits and the Puzzle of Welfare Reform." In *Lost Ground: Welfare Reform, Poverty, and Beyond,* Randy Albelda and Ann Withorn, eds. Cambridge, MA: South End Press, pp. 145–162.

4
Union-Sponsored Workforce Development Initiatives

Beverly Takahashi
DePauw University

Edwin Meléndez
New School University

In recent years, unions have sponsored an increasing number of workforce development initiatives that target the disadvantaged. Thus far, however, union initiatives have received less attention in the literature than initiatives sponsored by government, industry, community-based organizations, or community colleges. Therefore, while knowledge of workforce development strategies for the disadvantaged has increased, the lack of scrutiny of union initiatives leaves important questions regarding these initiatives unanswered. In particular, we are interested in ascertaining what unions do in workforce development and what is different about union-led initiatives as compared to community-based or other more traditional workforce development programs. To answer these questions about union participation in workforce development initiatives, we examined three union-sponsored initiatives within the framework of what is known about workforce development projects that target the disadvantaged and what is known about unions. The initiatives are the San Francisco Hotels Partnership Project, the Philadelphia Hospital and Health Care District (HHCD) 1199C Training and Upgrading Fund, and the Wisconsin Regional Training Partnership based in Milwaukee.

In comparison to community-based training programs, union-led initiatives have the distinct advantage of benefiting from formal and informal ties to employers and to their recruitment networks. Unions' ties to employers facilitate access to better employment opportunities than those usually open to disadvantaged populations through neighborhood-based social networks, and they typically provide more advancement opportunities as well. Employment programs are often financed through collective bargaining agreements and involve a close collaboration with employers. Since employer demand for skills is the entry point for design and development, union-led training programs are best described as "demand pull" models. In these models, training is often part of a more comprehensive package of services offered to employers. In contrast, the vast majority of training programs are designed with a focus on helping job seekers. Employers' demand for specific skills and their concerns about worker productivity play a lesser role in design.

New unionism, which rejects traditional unionism's exclusionary policies and limited training programs, is the driving force behind union-sponsored workforce development. At the same time, factors such as industry, region, government policy, union leadership, and prior experience influence the structure of these training initiatives. The results of this study reveal that each initiative follows a distinct pattern that can be characterized by its dominant focus. In San Francisco, the focus is on the workplace; in Philadelphia, education and vocational skills training drive the initiative; and in Wisconsin, industrial modernization and employer services form the engine that propels the initiative. In any case, the success of the initiatives studied suggests that it would be beneficial to ensure that these and other successful initiatives attain broad recognition among unions. Business, government, community colleges, and community-based organizations should become familiar with demand pull workforce development models to promote multi-institutional partnerships and to ensure that their lessons and successes can be duplicated whenever and wherever feasible.

In the following sections of the paper, we provide a more detailed discussion of the problem and a framework to assess the elements that contribute to the success of union-led workforce development initiatives. The next sections present a general overview of the cases studied and the criteria for their selection. The final sections offer a comparative analysis of the cases and expand on the findings and conclusions of the study.

WHAT DO UNIONS DO IN WORKFORCE DEVELOPMENT?

Workforce development for the disadvantaged is more than simply job training. It consists of a constellation of activities, starting with orientation to the work world, recruiting, placement, and mentoring, and continuing through follow-up counseling and crisis intervention (Harrison and Weiss 1998, p. 5; Giloth 2000). Workforce development strategies must resolve issues regarding the acquisition of skills and the provision of supports for participants who often must overcome barriers like the need for child care and transportation, unfamiliarity with English, limited work experience, and a lack of credentials. Most crucially, successful workforce development strategies must provide the skills demanded by industry and the links to the recruiting networks of employers.[1] However, if the disadvantaged are placed in low-paying marginal positions, it increases the odds that either they will be looking for another job in the near future or they will lose motivation and drop out of the labor market. In short, successful workforce development strategies targeting the disadvantaged must develop a dual focus on both the population served and local industry.[2]

Even if good jobs are available, disadvantaged workers are not always aware of opportunities for training and placement. Also, because of prior negative experiences, they may even mistrust the training provider or lack the belief that training leads to jobs. To overcome these obstacles, the participation of community-based organizations (CBOs) is often necessary. Because of their deep roots in the community, the trust they have established, their prior training experience and an understanding of the needs of the disadvantaged, CBOs are most suited to the task (Meléndez 1996). However, community-based organizations often require additional resources. According to Harrison and Weiss (1998), community-based programs that establish long-term relations with employers, government agencies, support services, and community colleges seem to be the most effective ones. Therefore, CBOs may form linkages with school-to-work and one-stop centers, foster closer relationships between training programs and industry, and strive for greater integration of community programs within the existing web of community colleges and postsecondary institutions serving the disadvantaged.

Regardless of what type of labor market intermediary sponsors training initiatives for the disadvantaged (given the complexity of issues involved in workforce development and the high costs involved in implementing programs), initiatives are most successful when they are collaborative efforts that draw on the resources of several institutions. And as is the case in any successful collaboration, they require strong leadership, clear guidelines, a coherent strategy, institutional capacity, sufficient funding, and joint vision (Cordero-Guzmán 2002).

Unions have been involved in training for a long time. Unions do not have a reputation as institutions that provide training for the disadvantaged. This is due to labor's history of practicing exclusionary policies in the craft and building trades, where unions fiercely controlled the entry of new members and, in the process, excluded minorities and women from some of the best paying jobs. Nevertheless, several progressive unions have been involved in training initiatives for many years.[3]

The labor movement has begun to commit to training the disadvantaged. Both union membership and union leadership include growing numbers of minorities and women, many of whom have jobs in or represent the unionized low-paying service sector which provides a lot of the low-skilled, entry-level positions available to the disadvantaged. Labor is making efforts not only to increase union membership through organizing but to imbue the movement with a new fervor.[4] As part of instilling this new fervor, labor seeks to redefine itself as a "social movement" with deep roots in communities, and especially in communities of immigrants and minorities.[5] The labor movement is seeking to go beyond what has been known as "bread and butter" unionism by addressing issues that concern not only its own membership but regional economies and society as a whole.[6]

The AFL-CIO has responded to these deep-seated challenges in the labor market and in the economy by organizing "high-road" partnerships. The AFL-CIO Working for America Institute (2001) defines these as partnerships that "actively engage business with unions in the process of trying to increase skill demands and improve the quality of today's and tomorrow's jobs."[7] Union-sponsored training programs for the disadvantaged—some of whom are union members in need of career ladders or a job change because of physical disability or layoff—have become an integral part of a strategy to revitalize the labor movement and to reposition it in the New Economy. This can entail promoting the revitalization of industries with a strong union presence through modernization or industrial reorganization, unionizing new sectors of the economy, or building partnerships to promote stable regional economies.[8] New unionism is committed to actively shaping a future built on good jobs through the strong support of communities.[9] According to the AFL-CIO, "Just as regions serve as the building blocks to the economic borders of the new economy, communities are the structural centerpieces to the new labor movement."[10]

Unions know a lot about the workplace and can assist management in creating training curricula that impart core skills; unions can also provide follow-up supervision and mentoring for new trainees.[11] Since unions share a common interest with management in making companies viable and competitive, not only can they assist in modernizing efforts, but they can also ally with management and communities to create public policy that is favorable to industries in need of modernization.[12] This can be done at the same time unions are serving the needs of incumbent and disadvantaged workers participating in training programs. When modernization or industrial reorganization occurs harmoniously, both employers and unions can benefit (Korshak 2000, p. 15).

It is apparent from the above discussion that unions have a relative advantage over more traditional, community-based labor market intermediaries in that they already have strong links to employers and industry. These links help them to target occupational training that is in demand by employers and facilitate the placement of trainees. They also enjoy the potential benefits of collective bargaining for the financing of programs and for the establishment of support systems in the workplace. However, given their relative inexperience in recruiting and training populations with multiple barriers to employment, unions face a number of challenges in establishing employment and training programs or, more generally, workforce development initiatives. Our examination of the selected cases presents a more detailed picture of the interplay of these different forces shaping the participation of unions in community-oriented workforce development initiatives.

CASE STUDIES

This study provides an analysis of innovative, union-sponsored workforce development initiatives that provide training to the disadvantaged, and it delineates factors that circumscribe the development of effective initiatives. We also provide a preliminary framework in order to assess how these initiatives perform as labor market intermediaries. The principal data for this paper were obtained by conducting a study of three union-sponsored workforce development initiatives. Because of the necessity of observing initiatives in as broad a context as possible so that the interactions of all relevant groups of stakeholders are accounted for, we adopted a comparative case studies method.

Of the many partnerships in existence throughout the nation, we chose the San Francisco Hotels Partnership Project, the Wisconsin Regional Training Partnership, and the Philadelphia Training and Upgrading Fund.[13] After conducting a review of the literature on workforce development and holding discussions with a number of selected labor officials, we devised a set of research questions. These questions, included as Appendix 4A, provided the basis for a structured interview protocol that served both as a necessary benchmark for ensuring an in-depth analysis and as a framework for comparative inquiry. Afterwards, we visited each site and interviewed program directors, program staff, and representatives of collaborating agencies. We also interviewed representatives of community colleges, government agencies, community-based organizations, and employer associations that were able to provide additional information regarding the initiatives' performance and effectiveness. In some cases, supplementary interviews were conducted by telephone following the on-site visits.

The case studies reveal that the manner in which unions perform as labor market intermediaries varies greatly. In one case, they perform a role more usually associated with that of a community college by formulating and conducting training courses for both management and employees. In another case, unions perform the role of community-based organizations by establishing the high levels of trust necessary to recruit the disadvantaged and provide them with appropriate supports. Finally, unions, aided by a strong partnership with industry, functioned as an intermediary by orchestrating and coordinating the efforts of government, community colleges, and community-based organizations. In the following sections we summarize the defining elements of each case.

The San Francisco Hotels Partnership Project

The hospitality industry is one of the fastest growing economic sectors in the San Francisco Bay Area. However, it is also an industry that is changing rapidly from factors like increased customer demand for new services, technological advances, and the changing nature of the workforce. Because the hotel business is highly competitive, hotels must be able to provide increasingly high levels of guest service. This, in turn, increases the need for more highly trained, flexible managers and workers who can communicate with guests and perform numerous duties in a friendly manner.

Entry-level positions in unionized hotels in San Francisco provide some of the best jobs for low-skilled workers—the wages are high, and 95 percent of workers have medical insurance. Before the 1994 contract agreement that established the San Francisco Hotels Partnership Project, labor relations between the hotels and unions were, to put it mildly, strained. The friction depleted union resources and made it difficult to conduct organizing drives. Unionized hotels, for their part, were unable to make the changes that were necessary if they were to remain competitive with nonunion hotels.[14]

Labor and management conducted a joint study to analyze the problems facing the hotels in the San Francisco market. The study concluded that many things needed to be fixed, including training, communication, the grievance mechanism, the sick-leave system, and the way the hotels' kitchens and restaurants operated. As a result of these efforts, The San Francisco Hotels Partnership Project emerged in 1994 as part of a collective bargaining agreement among a multi-employer group of 12 first-class hotels. This group represented many national hotel operators, including Hilton, Hyatt, Westin, Sheraton, Fairmont, and Holiday Inn, as well as two of the hotel industry's major unions: the Hotel and Restaurant Employees Union (HERE) Local 2 and Service Employees International Union (SEIU) Local 14 (now merged with HERE Local 2). Because the needs of the hotels varied greatly, the bargaining agreement called for a "living contract," which allowed the parties to meet during the contract's five-year term to address unforeseen problems and forge a true working partnership between labor and management.

The partnership recognized that the workforce was multilingual and extremely diverse and that management often was unfamiliar with the special needs of their employees or the difficulties they encountered in performing their jobs. To ensure the participation of this multilingual, diverse workforce, meetings and classroom training sessions are simultaneously interpreted in Spanish and Chinese. Written project and training materials are also available in English, Spanish, and Chinese, and in some cases classes are taught in Spanish or Chinese.[15] Not only were there communication barriers to deal with, it was necessary to change attitudes, increase trust, and improve workers' language skills, as well as help workers cope with the difficulties that low-wage, largely female workers face. Problem-solving teams have emerged as the project's basic tool. To increase the level of trust, neutral third-party facilitators lead teams, and representation on project teams is staffed at a ratio of two-thirds workers, one-third managers (matching the actual composition of the hotels). The goal is to develop innovative, hotel-specific solutions to issues such as training, job design, workload, job security, hotel operations, and grievance resolution.

In 1998 the project, jointly funded by a state of California Employment Training Panel (ETP) grant and the local hotel and restaurant labor-management education fund, conducted a massive training program of more than 1,600 union and managerial employees. The goals were to improve job retention, make transfers easier, provide career ladders, and delineate baseline skills. The initial program provided the project with a baseline for all future job retention, transfer, and promotional training programs. It provided the average employee with more than 100 hours of classroom and on-the-job training.[16] The Project has also conducted a successful pilot to train room cleaners, bussers, and other hotel employees to become hiring hall banquet servers during the busy holiday season. More than 200 entry-level workers learned new job skills in a higher job classification, laying the basis for follow-up career ladders and training programs. [17]

The San Francisco Hotels Partnership Project has helped to develop newly unionized hotel restaurants, revamped the hiring hall to improve the quality of the hotels' banquet service, and instituted a massive joint training program that improved communication, teamwork, and performance. English as a Second Language (ESL), high-school equivalency test preparation, and remedial math courses are among several training programs offered to union members and funded through employer contributions and grants. SAT test preparation courses are offered to union members and their children. In addition, an affiliation with the City College of San Francisco serves to facilitate the expansion of educational opportunities for hotel employees. The college offers a one-year certificate program in hospitality services as well as avenues to pursue associate and bachelor degrees. The project has also implemented a novel sick-leave program and provided career ladders and job security for employees while enabling unionized establishments to remain competitive with nonunion hotels. Union jobs in the hotel industry remain the best entry-level positions available to low-skilled workers in San Francisco. As of mid-2004, the starting salary for room cleaners is $15.36, while that of dishwashers is $15.61. As nearly 80 percent of positions fall into the low-skilled category, unionized hotels, through their wage effects on nonunion hotels and in a tight labor market, have increased the incomes and improved the working conditions of low-skilled workers.

The San Francisco Hotels Partnership Project's primary focus is the workplace. The trust exhibited between labor and management, the effort to build a worker's community by breaking down barriers posed by ethnic and linguistic differences, and the commitment to provide low-skilled, predominantly minority workers with career ladders is a notable departure from the activities associated with traditional unionism. The partnership, a response to the needs of industry, low-skilled workers, and unions, seeks to alter the culture of the workplace by changing the attitudes of all stakeholders in the project. The initiative is largely self-contained, dependent for its survival on its capacity to improve workers' productivity and the competitiveness of unionized hotels, provide employer services that support the expansion of the market share of unionized hotels, and increase the density of union membership while serving the career needs of union members. The partnership has received recognition in the hospitality industry nationally and serves as the model for other HERE locals seeking to replicate its success.[18]

The Philadelphia Hospital and Health Care District 1199C Training and Upgrading Fund

The Training and Upgrading Fund was established in 1974 as part of the first collective bargaining agreement signed by the Hospital and Health Care Workers Union 1199C, an affiliate of the American Federation of State, County and Municipal Employees (AFSCME), and by major hospitals and health care employers in the Philadelphia region. Union membership was largely composed of African Americans employed as service workers—the non-professional, non-technical hospital staff that worked as nurse aides, housekeepers, and laundry workers. The union, rooted in the civil rights movement of the 1960s, had a strong commitment to equal opportunity.[19] However, service personnel were poorly paid and for the most part were stuck in entry-level jobs that offered little chance of advancement. Yet hospitals had, as a result of technological innovations in the medical industry, an increased need for staff with specialized training and professional degrees. Since most nursing and technical programs were full-time programs and few programs existed that offered remedial education to those in need of it, the educational opportunities available to service workers were scarce.

The union, intent on establishing the training fund as part of the first bargaining agreement, was able to convince management that by contributing 1 percent (today that figure is 1.5 percent) of the amount paid out in gross salaries, their need for a more highly trained workforce would be at least partially met. The Philadelphia Hospital and Health Care District 1199C's Training and Upgrading Fund moved from site to site until 1990, when the training program established the Breslin Learning Center on South Broad Street to keep up with technological change in the health care industry and to provide workers with career upgrades and advanced education. Three educational benefits were provided for union members: 1) a full-time scholarship for members seeking advanced degrees in health care, 2) tuition reimbursement for members seeking certification, and 3) continuing education courses. Although the training fund could only be used for educating union members, the need for adult public education (especially in disadvantaged communities) was great. Almost immediately, additional monies were made available by government agencies to provide educational programs to the public. In fact, the training center was designated a Local Education Agency, which allowed it to offer high school equivalency training and testing. The union also received funding through a Comprehensive Employment and Training Act (CETA) grant in 1977 to assist unemployed workers in obtaining health care positions through the use of the union hiring hall. The grant contained a provision that allowed the fund to design upgrading ladders for union members in entry-level positions. These workers trained for positions as registered nurses, practical nurses, respiratory technicians, medical record keepers, or skilled craftspersons while the center simultaneously trained welfare recipients to qualify them for the positions vacated by upgraded union members.

In 1991, when mergers, industrial reengineering, and hospital restructuring led to massive layoffs of hospital workers, the center trained these displaced workers. A grant from the U.S. Department of Labor (USDOL) allowed hospital workers to select one of the following full-time, 16-week training programs offered by the learning center: nurse aide, home health aide, mental health/mental retardation technician, or claims processor. By the time welfare reform legislation was passed in 1996, the center was training a second or even a third generation of union members, their families, and their friends, and had provided years of service to the community and the health care industry. Welfare reform posed both a threat and a challenge. Hospital workers, who had already witnessed massive layoffs because of industry consolidation, were fearful that welfare reform would take people off the welfare roles only to push them into hospital jobs on a lower wage scale, displacing incumbents. However, since hospitals were redeploying their workforce and were not in a position to hire, the jobs that were available were largely those of nursing home aides, an occupation with high turnover.[20]

Training welfare recipients who face multiple barriers for positions in nursing homes is arduous for all concerned. Few programs have been able to achieve the success of the Learning Center's Project CARRE (Creating Access, Readiness and Retention for Employment).[21] The program is open to Temporary Assistance to Needy Families (TANF) recipients and non-custodial parents who reside in the region, but recruitment is performed by the center itself, since few participants are referred to the program by welfare agencies. Because of the center's deep roots in the community and the trust it has established, most applicants hear of the program through word of mouth and many are friends or relatives of union members. The success of the program can be attributed to several factors. Applicants are carefully assessed, pre-screened for drug use, and informed about the nature of the job and the work requirements. In addition, the program tries to replicate during the training period as much of the real work experience as possible. Once in the program, participants are provided with a case manager who assists with transportation and child care needs and any other obstacle that might arise. Upon completion, the participant is provided with job counseling and job placement services. Once a position has been secured, a retention case manager continues to assist with support services, and a one-year tracking system is put in place. If the graduate is placed in a union nursing home, a workplace coordinator keeps alert to any attendance problems so that early intervention can prevent firing. Trainees are also encouraged to begin thinking about attaining LPN certification.

The Training and Upgrading Fund's focus is on providing education for both union and non-union participants. The fund offers more than 40 courses, and provides credentialing to participants in a number of fields, as well as opportunities to obtain academic degrees.[22] At the same time, the Philadelphia Training and Upgrading Fund, over its 20-year history, has acquired many of the characteristics of a community-based organization. Its community roots allow the fund to recruit by word of mouth and by networking informally with other community-based organizations. The fund also provides case management assistance to every client and helps clients with child care and transportation needs.

The fund began as a response to a need in the health care industry for technically trained and credentialed employees and is financed in part through the contractual commitment of employer members. At the same time, the fund has only limited involvement in restructuring the workplace because the forces shaping the industry are most often beyond the initiative's control. In order for the fund to meet its commitment to the 30 percent of union members whose training is not provided for by collective bargaining agreements and to nonunion workers in need of educational assistance, it depends on funding from the government and from foundations involved in training workers who face multiple barriers to employment.

The Wisconsin Regional Training Partnership

The Wisconsin Regional Training Partnership (WRTP) is a multi-employer, multi-union undertaking whose goal is to promote industrial revitalization through workplace education, modernization, and workforce development. To accomplish this goal, the partnership utilizes the efforts of employers, workers, unions, community-based organizations, government agencies, and the Milwaukee Area Technical College. Several factors contributed to the development of the partnership. Like many other major manufacturing cities during the 1980s, Milwaukee lost a sizable portion of its industrial base to the surrounding suburbs, right-to-work states, and overseas companies. With plant closings, the number of dislocated workers swelled. Aided by federal legislation, the Wisconsin State AFL-CIO received the sole source contract to handle dislocated worker projects throughout the state. In 1986, the state AFL-CIO formed Help in Reemployment (HIRE) with the Private Industry Council of Milwaukee, the Milwaukee Area Technical College, and other partners. The HIRE center was opened to bring the services available to dislocated workers together under one roof. It provided the initial experience for the union's involvement in skills training programs.[23]

Then, in 1991, the Governor's Commission on Workforce Quality warned of an impending shortfall of skilled workers. To reverse this trend and to prevent further erosion of union membership, the Wisconsin State AFL-CIO enlisted the assistance of the University of Wisconsin's Center on Wisconsin Strategy (COWS) to develop a broad-based strategy. The strategy advocated by COWS recognized that by cooperating with employers to modernize and increase industrial capacity in unionized shops, unions could increase their membership without having to resort to costly organizing campaigns. Then, unions aided by a strong partnership with industry could serve as intermediaries in coordinating the efforts of government, community colleges, and community-based organizations while actively seeking to shape public policy.

In 1992, the Wisconsin State AFL-CIO formed the WRTP with its industrial union affiliates and their employers to support the development of high performance workplaces and family-supporting jobs. As the economy began to improve and unemployment rates dipped, the tight labor market only exacerbated the need for skilled workers. The rate of worker turnover rose, and employers were forced to turn to temporary agencies to fill openings. One out of three manufacturers said they lost business because they could not find enough qualified workers. However, while employers were scrambling to find workers, the unemployment rate in Milwaukee's central city neighborhoods was over 20 percent. The high level of unemployment was attributed to residents not having job skills and living far from most jobs, poor network-driven job access systems, and inefficient training programs. At the same time, Wisconsin's welfare reform program, Wisconsin Works, further depressed wages by requiring that all former recipients of Aid to

Families with Dependent Children (AFDC) work full time even though some jobs paid sub-minimum wages. As welfare rolls cleared, more money became available for training programs that served the needs of the most difficult-to-place welfare recipients—those facing multiple barriers to employment.

Milwaukee's problems attracted a generous grant from the Annie E. Casey Foundation as well. After obtaining the required matching funds, the Milwaukee Jobs Initiative (MJI) established an employment and training program in several industries that linked inner city residents to industrial jobs. Participants in the program are primarily unemployed and low-income residents of central city neighborhoods. Nine out of ten are people of color, half receive TANF, Medicaid, or food stamps. Half also lack high school diplomas. Many have criminal records or lack work experience or are mothers of young children. The Milwaukee Jobs Initiative enlisted the WRTP to develop workforce development programs in the manufacturing sector.[24] The WRTP leadership sought to change the traditional approach followed by employment services providers, which the leadership referred to as a "push" model, or more precisely, as a supply-push model.[25]

The WRTP focuses on providing employer services while program participants work, more like a broker of employment training than a traditional services provider. Employer services include a variety of services intended to modernize operations and make employers more competitive in the marketplace. The ultimate goal of these services is to create a working collaboration with employers in the creation and stability of good jobs. These services may include consultancies for technology improvements, cooperation on common industry problems with the recruitment and training of workers, and training for front line supervisors in a variety of topics for team building and improved productivity. In a "demand-pull" model, although training becomes part of a more comprehensive package of employer services, the question of designing training and responding to employers' demand for skilled workers is crucial.

In the early years, the WRTP's program was small. It was held in check in part by the requirement that trainees go through a customized curriculum developed in partnership with the Milwaukee Area Technical College, which was designed to meet the needs of a particular manufacturer and could last up to 16 weeks. Once the curriculum was established, recruitment assistance was sought from community-based organizations. Next the participants were assessed and training funding for each applicant was sought from the appropriate government agency. Upon completion of the program, trainees were placed in the jobs specifically designed for them. While this process gave the WRTP the opportunity to gain experience in supplying the supports workers needed during training and once they were placed, the program was so customized that the scale the WRTP was seeking could not be attained. Perhaps as important, employers were oftentimes discouraged by the lengthy process.

To expedite the process, the WRTP designed a standardized curriculum that helped reduce the lead time for training courses. In this "on-time" training model, a core set of skills that could be useful across the industry was identified and a four-week training program was instituted. Upon completion, trainees were placed in positions that had not been customized for them. While this called for increased training and mentoring in the workplace, the WRTP could train a far larger number of applicants. With the expansion of the program, the WRTP was able to carry out a series of agreements with a network of community-based recruitment agencies in the central city. However, because trainees are placed, for the most part, in surrounding suburbs in companies with around the clock shifts, it became necessary for the WRTP to enlist the cooperation of local government to provide around the clock child care and transportation. In some instances the WRTP was actually able to get the city to change bus routes.

The WRTP is, without doubt, one of the most successful union-sponsored workforce development programs. Perhaps the crucial factor in the program's success is its focus on sustainable partnerships with employers for supporting high performance workplaces.[26] Clearly, such partnerships have thrived partly because of a tight labor market during the late 1990s. But the WRTP offers a cost-effective alternative to the use of temporary agencies, with clear long term benefits such as a better-prepared workforce and lower turnover. Unions are able to structure mentoring programs to make sure that new workers have a smooth transition to the job, learn specific skills while on the job, and seek advancement opportunities over time. In addition to offering the core elements of a successful partnership and profiting from the benefits of a sustained economic expansion, the WRTP fits in with the overall strategy of state government to expand technical education and increase the number of skilled workers. The University of Wisconsin and COWS provided assessment of technical needs and strategic planning in the early days and continue to be an excellent resource. Disadvantaged job seekers benefited from complementary support services provided by community-based organizations through state-financed programs.

The partnership is assisting or incubating new initiatives in the construction, data networking, health care, hospitality, and transportation sectors. In 2000, it established its first new partnership, the Milwaukee Hospitality Employment Partnership, in which four major hotels joined with HERE Local 122 to institute a joint labor-management training initiative whose goals include improving customer service, training the current workforce for higher-level jobs, and finding qualified workers for entry-level jobs. The WRTP is also working closely with community groups, immigrant rights groups, and neighborhood associations.[27]

In sum, the Wisconsin Regional Training Partnership began as an effort to assist in the modernization of small- and medium-sized manufacturing firms in Wisconsin's metalworking industry by facilitating industrial retooling and providing a sufficiently skilled workforce. Since most of the firms involved were relatively small and lacked the resources necessary to modernize and upgrade their workforce, they needed assistance to obtain loans and help in developing appropriate industrial and workforce development strategies. The Wisconsin Regional Training Partnership has operated as a labor market intermediary, coordinating the efforts of several key players. The partnership, with the cooperation of the Milwaukee Area Technical College, demarcated core skills with the least common denominator and the greatest transferability. This shortened the training time needed and ensured that the project could achieve the scale necessary for its success. Collaborations with community-based organizations were essential so that the initiative could have a steady supply of new recruits who received the support services necessary to maintain them in the program. Mentors and peer advisors provided support for new employees while both unions and employers attempted to improve the culture of the workplace. The partnership's ability to attract funding has also been crucial to its success.

COMPARATIVE ANALYSIS

The cases studied indicate that, although they have common ground in serving union members in the workplace, union-led workforce development initiatives offer a variety of formats and experiences. The San Francisco Hotels Partnership Project's primary focus is on altering the culture of the workplace by changing the attitudes of all stakeholders in the project. Although the initiative is associated with City College, a credential- and degree-granting institution, the partnership performs the role of educator itself and is not dependent on the services of the college to conduct training courses. The Philadelphia Training and Upgrading Fund's major focus is on providing education for both union and non-union participants. With contributions from employers for the union members, the fund offers more than 40 courses and provides credentialing in a number of fields, as well as opportunities to obtain academic degrees. At the same time, the Training and Upgrading Fund, over its 20-year history, has acquired many of the characteristics of a community-based organization. It received funding for training from traditional federal government–sponsored programs such as CETA, the Job Training Partnership Act (JTPA), TANF, and the Workforce Investment Act (WIA). In its effort to help retool small- and medium-sized manufacturing firms, the Wisconsin Regional Training Partnership has brought together fundamentally interdependent players. The partnership has been sustained by the common need for expertise in retooling and the multiple provisions necessary to transform the workplace and expand the size and skills of the workforce.

Despite obvious differences in the mechanisms and strategies these unions employed to achieve their objectives, we were able to discern common lessons from the case studies. As regards the research questions posed at the outset, a comparative analysis of the case studies resulted in the following findings.

Successful union-led initiatives responded to specific industry needs. Each initiative responded to and was structured by industrial requisites. However, in each case, the effectiveness of the initiative was enhanced when union leadership, government policy, and the regional environment were supportive of and worked in tandem with industrial needs.

In San Francisco, the initiative was informed by the participating hotels' need to upgrade service and improve efficiency in order to offset the vulnerability of unionized hotels to competition posed by nonunionized hotels. A booming regional economy and a tight labor market provided further incentive for management to participate in the initiative to ensure worker retention and a workforce with appropriate skills and commitment. HERE Local 2 and SEIU Local 14 were induced to join with management in a commitment to transform the workplace because of two major factors. The first was the loss of union density in the hotel industry. The second was the desire of union officials to obtain permission to organize through the streamlined process known as "card check" in the large number of hotels then under construction. This process involves the employer's agreement to recognize the union if a majority of workers sign an authorization card (which is far easier than holding elections). The initiative was also structured by an industry-wide need for additional workers during peak times of the year. This allowed for an enlarged role for the hiring hall, which in turn provided career ladders to incumbent workers and job outreach to the community.

In Wisconsin, many small- and medium-sized manufacturing firms required modernization and reorganization in order to expand and, in some cases, to survive. Wisconsin, historically, has been a state with a strong commitment to the manufacturing sector, making it more likely that the governor and key officials would support the modernization effort. On the labor side, union leadership had endured innumerable plant closings and years of declining membership and was anxious to arrest the downward slide. Another contributing factor was the state's welfare reform policies, which had resulted in reduced caseloads and the availability of funds that could be used to assist with the more difficult cases that remained.

In Philadelphia, changing industrial technology had increased the need for credentialing, technical training, and academic degrees, while hospital reengineering and downsizing had increased the need for career ladders for the lowest-income workers. Union leadership had a more than 20-year commitment to serving the educational needs of those least able to find opportunities. A number of factors created an incentive for government and foundations to provide the Breslin Center with sufficient resources to meet its commitment to the community. The decline in manufacturing in the region and the loss of well-paying jobs for low-skilled workers, the ghettoization of minority workers in the inner city who found themselves far removed from employment possibilities, and the demands of welfare reform on the system to provide jobs for recipients facing multiple barriers, all contributed to increased support.

Skills training in union-led programs targeted occupations in high demand by local employers and provided opportunities for career advancement for low-wage workers. Union training of low-wage workers goes beyond training for job skills. It includes training necessary to transform the workplace, making establishments more competitive and more gratifying and rewarding for workers. In Wisconsin, a core curriculum was devised in conjunction with the Milwaukee Area Technical College. In San Francisco, joint labor-management committees formulated the curriculum. In Philadelphia, the Breslin Center, guided by state credentialing and licensing requirements, determined the curriculum.

In all cases, the initiatives were connected to credential-granting institutions. In San Francisco that connection came later, whereas in Philadelphia and Wisconsin it existed from the project's inception. In both Philadelphia and San Francisco, developing career ladders was an essential component of program design. In Wisconsin, although manufacturing jobs were relatively well paying, career development assistance was provided by all companies, each of which had, at a minimum, tuition assistance programs. Most also offered on-site courses, learning labs, and apprenticeships.

In all the cases studied, continuous and extensive relations with employers and industry provided numerous benefits to disadvantaged workers. In Wisconsin and San Francisco, labor and management relationships resulted in a joint partnership. Employers' participation in curriculum design ensured that course content was aligned with industrial standards and focused on the competencies most in demand by the local job market. In Philadelphia, although unions served as the first source of employment, labor-management relations were more circumscribed and less formalized.

Employers' participation in the program also facilitated the retention of incumbent workers and new hires. All the initiatives attempted to change the culture of the workplace and the attitudes of incumbent workers to new trainees. Wisconsin did much in this regard, adding both mentoring and peer advisors to the workplace. San Francisco worked hard to build trust between labor and management and a sense of community among employees. Philadelphia, although it made an attempt to improve the reception of new employees by incumbent workers, had less capacity to control the climate of the workplace because of the greater number of worksites and more limited employer involvement.

Union-sponsored training programs were able to incorporate effective practices and partnerships for supporting the participation of disadvantaged populations in their programs. The recruiting practices of the initiatives were divergent. In San Francisco incumbent workers were recruited; in Philadelphia recruitment occurred by word of mouth (the Training and Upgrading Fund received as many as 200 calls a week) and informal contacts with community-based organizations; and in Wisconsin recruitment was performed by community-based organizations formally affiliated with the project. Because employees in both the health care industry and the hotel industry deal with the public, participants were screened for past criminal behavior. All the initiatives accepted individuals in need of remedial education and all provided some degree of follow-up supervision.

Unions often have firsthand experience in dealing with the problems of workers who face multiple barriers to employment. In both Philadelphia and Wisconsin, each program participant was assigned a case manager who assisted trainees in obtaining child care and transportation, as well as providing job preparedness, job placement, and job retention services. All initiatives provided education to improve cognitive skills and English language skills and helped participants prepare for high school equivalency exams, in addition to providing training in core industrial skills. In Philadelphia, educational opportunities were the most extensive.

In San Francisco, employer contributions and grants provided funding. In Wisconsin, funding was received from Welfare-to-Work monies, foundations, and government and employer contributions. In Philadelphia, funding was received from Welfare-to-Work monies, foundations, and government grants, whereas employer contributions were used to support training for union members.

Finally, the programs selected for review maintained working arrangements and connections with community-based organizations. In Wisconsin, several community-based organizations formally participate in the initiative. In fact, in some instances, they are housed in the same building complex. The connections to CBOs facilitated recruitment and outreach, the provision of support services, and integration to the workplace. In San Francisco and Philadelphia, the relationship is less formalized. However, as the case of the Philadelphia Training and Upgrading Fund demonstrates, innovative unions have not only proven their commitment to communities, they often act in a manner that resembles a community-based organization.

In these cases, successful union-led workforce development initiatives structured win-win arrangements that benefited employers, union members, and the community. Innovative unions are motivated by the need to increase union density, provide career ladders to union members, ensure the viability of firms, prevent wage shocks, and honor their commitment to those workers who, without the benefits of collective action, would be deprived of a living wage. As part of the effort to prevent further erosion in union membership and to preserve and expand industries that provide good jobs, unions have increased their participation in training programs for the disadvantaged. Training the disadvantaged also allows unions to take advantage of funding that is available from government and foundations while at the same time solidifying relationships with union members, community-based organizations, and employers. This in turn increases labor's political clout, or its ability to influence public policy.

In Wisconsin, innovative unions realized that expanding employment in existing union companies was a less expensive path towards increased union density than organizing non-union companies. In San Francisco, faced with industrial gridlock and the possible closure of several hotel restaurants, labor and management cooperated to improve union density, job security, and career ladders for incumbent workers. In Philadelphia, training initiatives satisfied a long-standing union commitment to social and economic justice and provided career ladders and training to union and non-union members alike.

Employers profited from improved labor relations, increased efficiency and productivity, and from having a workforce with industry-related skills. Employers also benefited from the training initiatives being linked to a rigorous assessment of the industrial and employment needs of the particular industry involved. Training increased trust between management and workers, lessening the number of grievances filed and strengthening teamwork and flexibility.

CONCLUSION

Although the number of union-sponsored initiatives has increased in recent years, our case study research indicates that unions have been involved in training for a long time. Because of labor's history of practicing exclusionary policies in the craft and building trades, unions have not been viewed as institutions that provide training for the disadvantaged. However, in recent years the New Economy, new demographics, and a new social commitment on the part of unions have fashioned a "new unionism." New unionism is involved in building career ladders for union members and training the disadvantaged, and these goals are intricately linked to ensuring the survival and expansion of not just unions but unionized firms. It reaches out to women and minorities—including many that work in the low-wage service industry. By organizing in low-wage communities and setting employment standards in industries that employ low-skill workers, unions protect themselves and build alliances with communities.

Union-sponsored training programs for the disadvantaged—some of whom are union members in need of career ladders or a job change because of physical disability or layoff—have become an integral part of a strategy to revitalize the labor movement and to reposition it in the New Economy. This can entail promoting the revitalization of industries with a strong union presence through modernization and industrial reorganization, unionizing new sectors of the economy, and building stable regional economies that can expand opportunity and provide for a broadly shared, equitable distribution of wealth. To accomplish this end, labor is committed to actively shaping a future built on good jobs through the strong support of communities.

Union-sponsored initiatives have borne a resemblance to more traditional labor market intermediaries. Our research indicates that effective initiatives share many similar characteristics with effective labor market intermediaries, including a knowledge of industrial needs, the ability to make job projections, an awareness of the needs of disadvantaged employees, the capacity to provide support services, strong ties to communities, adequate resources, and effective administration.

The cases also suggest that innovative unions recognize that in order to insure a firm's viability it may be necessary to participate in modernization and reorganization efforts that increase efficiency and productivity. In industries experiencing high turnover rates and labor shortages, where employers often utilize the services of temporary agencies, innovative unions intent on increasing density and preventing wage deterioration realize that training disadvantaged workers is a cost effective alternative. Increasing workers' productivity as a result of skills training leads to savings on billing rates, finder's fees and other costs associated with high turnover staffing arrangements—savings that often offset the cost of implementing the program.

Although the three union-sponsored workforce development initiatives presented in this study diverged in key aspects, together they imply that such initiatives can provide good jobs for low-income workers, training to those who face multiple obstacles, and career ladders to both incumbent workers and new hires. The data from the case studies indicate that unions can intervene at critical junctures in workforce development. Unions have special knowledge of the workplace and of job opportunities, they are connected to the recruiting networks of employers, and they are able to provide training and mentoring in the workplace after employment has been achieved.

Union initiatives have some advantages in structuring training programs for the disadvantaged as compared to community-based programs, or even as compared to training programs sponsored by community colleges and other educational institutions. We have mentioned the unique position of unions as regards their connections to employers and that these connections offer an advantage when structuring industry-wide initiatives following a sectoral approach.[28] Unions are well positioned to focus on workplace issues that are of critical concern to both employers and incumbent workers. In some instances, as in the case of the HHCD 1199C in Philadelphia and of the Hotels Partnership Project in San Francisco, unions benefit from collective agreements for financing of training for incumbent workers. These programs use their financial support to structure career ladders and opportunities within the same company and industry. In addition, unions have demonstrated that they occupy a unique position in structuring partnerships that involve a wide cast of stakeholders, including community organizations, educational institutions, and government and local foundations.

The effectiveness of the initiatives conclusively demonstrates that unions are capable of playing a major role in training programs that target the disadvantaged and that their participation in such programs should be encouraged. They have been able to show employers that they are reliable partners in devising core curricula and providing workers with appropriate skills. The projects we have looked at demonstrate to the workforce development industry that unions have the capacity and experience to serve significant numbers of the workers facing multiple barriers to employment.

Notes

1. A shortcoming of employment training programs is that many offer little or no training at all. In addition, classroom training is often disconnected from the needs of employers in a particular industry and has no significant impact on either basic or vocational skills of program participants. For the role of connecting the disadvantaged to employer networks see Meléndez and Harrison (1998, p. 3).
2. According to a report by the General Accounting Office (USGAO 1996), effective second-chance training programs require four key features:
   1) Ensuring that clients are committed to training and getting jobs
   2) Removing barriers, such as lack of child care and transportation, that might limit the clients' ability to finish training and get and keep a job
   3) Improving clients' employability skills, such as getting to a job regularly and on time, working well with others while there, and dressing and behaving appropriately
   4) Linking occupational skills training with the local labor market
3. An example of a progressive union with a strong history of training the disadvantaged is the National Health and Human Service Employees International Union, whose SEIU Local 1199 runs the Employment, Training and Job Security Program in New York. For an example of a successful manufacturing collaboration in Chicago, see Swinney (2001).
4. At the beginning of John Sweeney's tenure as president of the AFL-CIO, he promised to adopt more militant tactics, pledged to spend millions of dollars on bringing new members into the fold, and launched "Union Summer," a program meant to recall the civil rights movement's "Freedom Summer" of 1964. For more information regarding labor's renewed commitment to its core values see the AFL-CIO Web site, http://www.aflcio.org.
5. For a historical account on unions' stance on immigration and how the AFL-CIO has evolved to support a more pro immigration policy, see Briggs (2001).

6. Resolutions made regarding the American economy at the AFL-CIO's twenty-third biennial convention include attaining full employment, a federal fiscal policy that invests in America, equitable tax principles, a national manufacturing jobs policy, a service sector where jobs must be "good jobs," an industrial policy that confronts economic change and fosters economic development and technological innovation, helping cities help themselves, building a transportation infrastructure, and rethinking deregulation. See http://www.aflcio.org/convention99/res15.htm.
7. On this topic, see also Herman (2001).
8. The use of workforce development initiatives and the formation of high-road partnerships to unionize new sectors of the economy, build strong regional partnerships, and shape public policy have been endorsed in several of the reports published by Working Partnerships USA under the joint leadership of the South Bay AFL-CIO Labor Council in San Jose, California, and the Economic Policy Institute in Washington, DC. These publications include "Walking the Lifelong Tightrope: Negotiating Work in the New Economy" and "Growing Together or Drifting Apart? Working Families and Business in the New Economy."
9. Dan Swinney, director of the Midwest Center for Labor Research, states that labor and communities "must take responsibility for the creation of jobs, welcoming the responsibility for good management, productivity, and efficiency as well as justice."
10. Taken from the AFL-CIO's Web page, "The Road to Union City: What is a Union City?" (accessed January 2004).
11. Taken from David Eberhardt and Phil Neuenfeldt, "Letter from WRTP Co-Chairs," included in the Wisconsin Regional Training Program's *Mentor Training Guide.*
12. For a discussion of research that indicates that new work systems and labor-management cooperation efforts are most enduring and effective when implemented in unionized settings, see Mishel and Voos (1992) and Appelbaum and Batt (1994).
13. The AFL-CIO High Road Partnerships Report (2001) listed 14 partnerships, though there are many more in existence. These cases were selected because they met the following four criteria: 1) each had sufficient longevity and was of sufficient scale for the initiative to have reached full stride so that judgment could be rendered regarding the program's success, 2) each initiative had at some point received Welfare-to-Work funds and had experience in dealing with disadvantaged workers who face multiple obstacles to employment and career development, 3) each was a union-sponsored initiative in an industry that employs large numbers of low-skilled employees with short-term training needs, and 4) each has served as a prototype for subsequent initiatives in the industry. Initiatives were also selected to offer geographic diversity.
14. Nonunion hotels were able to institute innovations, such as placing coffee pots and fax machines in guest rooms. By contrast, the unionized hotels would have to negotiate such changes, because virtually every employee function is regu-

lated by narrow job classification, seniority lines, and sometimes archaic work rules.

15. One facilitator described the impact of interpretation: "Over and over again, people would come up to me and thank me from the bottom of their hearts. Native English speakers would say, 'I can't believe how much I have missed by not being able to communicate with a person in their native language. I never had an opportunity to find out what (the person) thought. This really has enriched me.' Non-native English speakers would say (through the interpreter), 'I never expected to have translators.... Thank you for giving me a voice.'" This quote appeared in the information flyer provided by the San Francisco Hotels Partnership Project.
16. In addition, since the union and the multi-employer group recognized that some workers viewed training as a disguised way to get rid of old employees by holding them to increasingly high standards, the core skills taught were those identified by the employees themselves. They were skills that are easily transferable, including communication, critical thinking, problem solving, and teamwork (Moy 1998).
17. Although the partnership created a number of job opportunities for Welfare-to-Work recipients in a pilot project funded by the San Francisco Department of Human Services, the lion's share of training is offered to incumbent workers. Thus, the project begins where many training initiatives end—in the workplace after a job has been secured. This indicates that even after employment is achieved, there remains a continuing need for training.
18. HERE Local 11 in Los Angeles has affiliated with community colleges in the city and has begun to institute similar training activities.
19. The Pharmacists Union, the precursor of 1199C, conducted a strike in 1936 to allow Blacks to work in Harlem pharmacies.
20. Among a number of reasons for the high turnover were the following: 1) the population of nursing homes had become older and sicker than in years past and 80 percent of care was administered by nursing aides, most of whom were women, 2) the job is strenuous and back injuries are common, 3) homes must be staffed around the clock and new employees get the least desirable shifts, 4) most nursing homes are in the suburbs while many of the trainees live in the inner city, transportation is a major concern and the linkage between the inner city and suburbs during peak times is poor—during off hours it is sometimes nonexistent, and 5) the need for child care at unconventional hours presents yet another difficulty for women employees.
21. Project CARRE is a work first program that offers 20 hours per week of paid work experience and requires participants to undergo clinical experience in a nursing home for an additional 20 hours. It is a full time, 40 hour per week, 16 week program. Requirements are a sixth grade reading and math level, no felony conviction, testing drug free and free of communicable diseases, the ability to lift 50 pounds, the willingness to travel one hour to work, and the ability to work all shifts, including evenings, weekends, and holidays. Those who do not meet educational requirements are placed in remedial classes and then retested.

22. Education and training programs include offerings in computer skills, pre-nursing courses, GED test preparation, medical claims processing training, child care worker training, a practical nursing program, Spanish for health care workers, and training for therapeutic support aides in addition to remedial education in math and English. In 1997 the Adult Education Labor Consortium was formed for the purpose of offering basic refresher courses, GED reviews, and ESL classes to union members and community residents.
23. These services included helping dislocated workers cope with financial and emotional stress, career counseling, re-training services, and job placement. However, technological change and industrial reorganization left many laid-off workers unprepared for new industrial job responsibilities such as working in teams and using statistics in quality control. At the same time, local unions were discovering that many of their remaining members had similar shortcomings and were inadequately prepared to operate new computer-controlled machinery and equipment.
24. Currently much of the WRTP's $1.5 million budget comes from the Milwaukee Jobs Initiative, funded by the Annie E. Casey Foundation and other sources, and a from a USDOL demonstration grant.
25. In a July 2000 interview, Eric Parker, executive director, Wisconsin Regional Training Program, asserts: "The traditional service delivery model [push system] begins with the in-take of individuals, assessment, counseling, maybe training, and a (typically disappointing) job search. The participants are being pushed back out into the low-wage labor market. By contrast, our model [pull system] begins with the market demand. We identify family-supporting jobs, then we identify viable candidates (through our network of community partners), then we get them eligible for funding purposes, and then we subcontract the just-in-time delivery of training. The employer commits to employing the participants on the front end so long as they successfully complete the necessary training."
26. Parker, the WRTP's executive director, summarizes the organization's partnership formula in the following statement: "The partnership helps employers find qualified workers, unions increase their members, and communities access better jobs; and the partnership develops leadership in the business community and labor movement to advocate changes in public policy."
27. These include the YMCA, UMOS, HIRE Center, Milwaukee Community Service Corps, Northeast Development Corporation, Harambee Ombudsman Project, Community Justice Center, and Rapha Ministry Center, among others.
28. Sectoral initiatives have gained acceptance in the workforce development field as effective strategies providing career paths for disadvantaged populations. See for example Seigel and Kwass (1995).

Appendix 4A

Interview Protocol

Motivation and context. What motivates labor unions to engage in training programs that target the disadvantaged? How do factors such as industry, region, government policy, union leadership, and prior experience influence the structure of these training initiatives?

Links to employers. What is the role of employers in determining the content of skills training? What are the connections of training programs to employers and industry? What formal and informal mechanisms exist to establish and maintain these connections?

Program Design

- **Recruitment and case management.** How are workers recruited to participate in the programs? What are the criteria for selection? How is participant progress monitored? How effective are these programs in targeting the disadvantaged? Are they examples of innovative outreach practices?

- **Support services.** What kind of support services are provided or facilitated to overcome barriers to employability? How are these services integrated to programs, and how are they financed?

- **Links to CBOs.** What are the connections between training programs and community-based organizations? What formal and informal mechanisms exist to establish and maintain these connections?

- **Training.** What combination of job readiness, basic skills, and soft skills is offered to participants? How are the types of skills and the curriculum determined?

- **Certifications and career ladders.** Are training programs connected to credential-granting institutions and do they offer transferable skill competencies, certification, or more advanced degrees? Is the potential for career ladders an explicit consideration of program design and development?

Retention and other employer services. What kind of post-program participation follow-up is provided? To what extent do programs deal with supervisor attitudes and expectations in the workplace? To what extent do programs deal with the attitudes of incumbent workers? Is changing the culture of the workplace a priority, and if so how is this accomplished?

Impact on unions. Have unions benefited from participation in these initiatives? Have the initiatives increased union density? Have they increased political clout, or the ability to influence public policy?

References

AFL-CIO Working for America Institute. 2001. *High Road Partnership Report: Innovations in Building Good Jobs and Strong Communities.* Washington, DC: Working for America Institute. http://www.workingforamerica.org/documents/HighRoadReport/alook.htm (accessed May 21, 2004).

Appelbaum, Eileen, and Rosemary Batt. 1994. *The New American Workplace: Transforming Work Systems in the United States.* Ithaca, NY: ILR Press.

Briggs, Vernon M. Jr. 2001. *Immigration and American Unionism*, 2d ed. Ithaca, NY: Cornell University Press.

Cordero-Guzmán, Héctor R. 2002. "Interorganizational Networks Among Community-Based Organizations." Paper presented at the conference "Communities and Workforce Development," sponsored by the Ford Foundation and the Community Development Research Center, Robert J. Milano Graduate School of Management and Urban Policy, New School University, held in New York, May 11.

Giloth, Robert P. 2000. "Learning From the Field: Economic Growth and Workforce Development in the 1990s." *Economic Development Quarterly* 14(4): 340–357.

Harrison, Bennett, and Marcus Weiss. 1998. *Workforce Development Networks: Community-Based Organizations and Regional Alliances.* Thousand Oaks, CA: Sage Publications.

Herman, Bruce. 2001. "How High-Road Partnerships Work." *Social Policy* 31(3): 11–19.

Korshak, Stuart R. 2000. "A Labor-Management Partnership: San Francisco's Hotels and the Employees' Union Try a New Approach." *Cornell Hotel and Restaurant Administration Quarterly* 41(2): 14–29.

Meléndez, Edwin. 1996. *Working on Jobs: The Center for Employment Training.* Boston: Mauricio Gaston Institute for Latino Community Development and Public Policy, University of Massachusetts Boston.

Meléndez, Edwin, and Bennett Harrison. 1998. "Matching the Disadvantaged to Job Opportunities: Structural Explanations for the Past Successes of the Center for Employment Training." *Economic Development Quarterly* 12(1): 3–11.

Mishel, Lawrence, and Paula B. Voos, eds. 1992. *Unions and Economic Competitiveness.* Armonk, NY: M.E. Sharpe.

Moy, Debbie. 1998. "Labor and Management Build Skills in the Hospitality Industry." *Workforce Investment Quarterly* 5(1): 27–34.

Seigel, Beth, and Peter Kwass. 1995. *Jobs and the Urban Poor: Publicly Initiated Sectoral Strategies.* Somerville, MA: Mt. Auburn Associates.

Swinney, Dan. 2001. "A Labor-Led Workforce Training and Education System: Practical Opportunities and Strategic Challenges." *Social Policy* 31(3): 23–32.

U.S. General Accounting Office. 1996. *Employment and Training: Successful Projects Share Common Strategy.* House subcommittee report of Carlotta C. Joyner, director, Education and Employment Issues. GAO/HEHS-96-108. Washington, DC: U.S. General Accounting Office.

5

Addressing the Employment Challenge for the Formerly Homeless

Supportive Housing in New York City

Alex Schwartz
Edwin Meléndez
Sarah Gallagher
New School University

Supportive housing provides a cost-effective means of helping formerly homeless individuals stay off the streets and live healthier, more independent lives (Culhane, Metraux, and Hadley 2002). Motivated in part by the increased pressure brought by welfare reform to move people off public assistance, but also by the desire to help the formerly homeless lead more rewarding lives, supportive housing providers have become more interested in increasing the employment opportunities available to their residents. This chapter examines the employment status of residents in supportive housing programs, the nature of their employment barriers, the benefits of employment, and the ways by which supportive housing organizations are attempting to meet residents' vocational needs.

Understanding the employment challenges posed by the formerly homeless is particularly important in the context of serving so called hard to serve populations, those that encounter multiple barriers to employment. In many ways the conceptual problem presented by the development of services for the homeless[1] is similar to that of providing services for long-term welfare recipients who, in addition to lack of employment experience and other barriers directly related to their job skills and readiness, often also face mental health, substance abuse, and many other barriers that seriously impede their employability. For these types of disadvantaged populations, conventional employment goals are often not attainable, at least not without significant investments in support services. Even then, when specialized programs are in place, many of these program participants cannot be expected to sustain full-time employment, whether for reasons of physical or mental disabilities or because of various other conditions that impede their workforce participation.

For this study, we formulated three core analytical areas of inquiry. First, we developed a set of questions to ascertain what the barriers to employment are for the homeless. We wanted to know to what extent the formerly homeless population diverges from typical participants in an employment services program. Second, given these multiple barriers to employment, we wanted to investigate what were the employment goals and benefits for the homeless. This question is important because it determines the types of programs that are offered to the homeless.

Finally, we examined the services necessary to serve the homeless population and looked at model programs that offer comprehensive and effective services. Evidently, programs serving the homeless must provide an array of support services that go beyond the conventional package offered by other employment programs. Our task was to determine the most important services, the proportion of support services provided, and by whom: the supportive housing organization itself or in partnership with other employment services providers.

We selected the supportive housing organizations and facilities for this study from a database of supportive housing providers and residences provided by the Supportive Housing Network of New York (SHNNY), a coalition of 160 nonprofit supportive housing agencies in New York State. The research was based largely on interviews with staff at the participating organizations, including executive directors, vocational staff, residence managers, and case managers. In addition to conducting staff interviews at 20 of the agencies, we held focus groups for residents at four supportive housing facilities.

Approximately one quarter of the residents in the supportive housing facilities covered by the study were employed either full or part time. Employment was considerably lower among residents living with a mental illness or HIV/AIDS, while residents with a history of substance use tended to have higher rates of employment. Many of the barriers identified pertain to residents' soft skills (such as dealing with authority, anger management, lack of motivation, high absenteeism, tardiness, and difficulties adjusting to workplace routines and expectations) or their hard skills (such as weak basic skills, literacy levels, and specific job skills). As is common in programs serving disadvantaged low-income populations, one-quarter to half of all the residents lack a high school diploma or General Equivalency Degree (GED). Another barrier is a lack of incentive, which is often associated with the low wages that residents are likely to earn if they do work. However, many of the impediments for employment went beyond purely labor market related factors. For instance, mental illness presents a barrier because of social and behavioral issues such as paucity of speech and lack of affect (emotional expressionlessness).

Loss of disability benefits proved to be a major concern for the formerly homeless. Due to a real or perceived threat to Medicaid and other benefits, residents receiving Supplemental Security Income (SSI) and Social Security Disability Insurance (SSDI) seem to have the least incentive to find employment. Another important barrier involves the limited ability of case management staff at supportive housing facilities and day treatment programs to actively and consistently encourage residents to seek employment. This inability may stem from several factors, including the frequent turnover of case management staff, inadequate training, lack of information, lack of time, and the need to respond to frequent crises and other emergencies. Last, the expiration of time-limited welfare benefits did not seem to compel recipients to seek employment.

Regarding the second analytical area of inquiry, our findings suggest that employment is perceived in the supportive housing community more as part of a therapeutic path towards recovery from health and social problems than as a route to financial independence. The most commonly perceived benefits of resident employment were the building of self-esteem, integration into mainstream society, the improvement of mental health and a sense of well being, and the added structure and purpose in residents' lives. Economic self-sufficiency was a goal for only a select few of the more highly functioning residents.

The study's final area of inquiry focused on the delivery of employment services for the formerly homeless. Effective programs targeting the hard to serve must not only address a broad range of labor market related barriers, such as the lack of soft or hard skills, but also the added burden of chronic health problems. Many participants in employment programs for the homeless have health problems that make sustaining a regular work schedule very difficult. Program managers must find employers and occupations that offer sufficient flexibility to accommodate medical appointments and absences due to illness.

To determine best practices in the field, we examined the variety of approaches that supportive housing providers utilized to enhance residents' employment opportunities. Of the 20 facilities studied, 14 offered some form of vocational program. Most of these vocational programs were small and relatively new, with annual budgets seldom exceeding $500,000 and often amounting to much less. Programs rarely have more than two to three dozen participants at a time and often offer vocational programs for a larger target population than supportive housing residents, who in many cases constitute only a small portion of all the vocational clients. Most of these programs offer a wide range of job readiness services, case management, and retention services. Two-thirds of the organizations provide vocational training for specific occupations, though several organizations interviewed felt it was more effective to refer residents to vocational programs at other organizations than to institute their own vocational programs. In general, vocational programs tend to place residents in full-time jobs, even though supportive housing staff tended to think that part-time work was the most that residents could handle.

We conclude that despite increased program development and innovation, vocational programs operated by supportive housing groups have not yet reached a large segment of their target population. A relatively small number of residents in supportive housing are employed or participating in vocational programs. Two sets of issues emerge from this study. One is the struggle vocational programs face in attracting supportive housing residents; the other concerns the effectiveness of programs in helping residents to succeed in a competitive labor market. Although economic independence is probably not a realistic goal for most residents of supportive housing, many, including those with mental illness, could still benefit from competitive employment given the opportunity and necessary support. Supportive housing groups and other service providers need to examine the efficiency of supported employment and long-term pre-vocational training as a pathway to competitive employment.

The chapter is organized according to the three analytical areas presented above. The first part examines the employment status of the residents at the 20 supportive housing facilities and the nature of their employment barriers. The second part takes a brief look at the perceived benefits of employment for residents of supportive housing. The third part examines the ways by which the supportive housing organizations are attempting to meet the residents' vocational needs. The final part offers conclusions and recommendations.

EMPLOYMENT STATUS OF RESIDENTS

The supportive housing organizations and facilities were selected not so much as a random sample but to reflect the field's diversity along several dimensions. As presented in Table 5.1, 20 organizations ultimately participated in the study, 14 of which provided vocational services. For each organization, one facility was selected to study in depth. The supportive housing residences selected for the study range in size from 14 units to 652. Seven facilities focus exclusively on people living with mental illness, three on people living with HIV/AIDS, and four target formerly homeless people who do not have diagnoses of mental illness or HIV/AIDS, although some of them have histories of substance abuse. The remaining six residences serve a mixed population, including people living with HIV/AIDS or mental illness, other formerly homeless individuals, and, in some cases, "community residents" (low- and moderate-income individuals who may not be disabled or formerly homeless).

Few residents of the supportive housing facilities included in the study worked. On average, about one-quarter of the residents in the 20 facilities covered in this study were employed either full or part time. However, there was wide variation in the proportion of working residents. At the high end, at least 50 percent of residents were employed full or part time at three residences. At the other extreme, less than 15 percent were employed at six facilities—nearly one-third of the entire sample (see Table 5.2). The incidence of employment varies among different population groups residing within supportive housing. It appears

Table 5.1 Overview of Selected Supportive Housing Organizations and Facilities

Organization	Facility	Year facility founded	Number of supportive housing facilities	Total supportive housing units	Number of units in facility	Offer vocational services	Population served
Bowery Residents' Committee	Los Vecinos	1995	12	648	35	Yes	Mixed
Brooklyn Community Housing and Services	Oak Hall	1990	3	136	74	Yes	Mixed
The Bridge	Park West House II	1996	12	326	14	Yes	Mental health
Catholic Charities, Brooklyn and Queens	Monica House	1992	6	402	78	No	Mental health
Clinton Housing and Development Corp.	300 W. 46th Street	1996	4	215	70	No	Mixed
Common Ground Community	The Times Square	1994	3	1,068	652	Yes	Mixed
Community Access	Gouverneur Court	1993	4	285	136	Yes	Mental health
Federation Employment and Guidance Service (FEGS)	White Plains Road	1996	3	150	52	Yes	Mental health
Friends Home Group	Friends House in Rose Hill	1996	1	50	50	No	HIV/AIDS

Housing Works	East 9th Street Residence	1997	2	68	36	Yes	HIV/AIDS
Institute for Community Living	Warren Street	1995	9	429	14	Yes	Mental health
The Jericho Project	Jericho House	1991	4	168	48	Yes	Homeless
Jewish Board of Family and Children's Services	Abraham Residence III	1997	1	68	68	No	Mental health
The Miracle Makers	Miracle Makers Adult Housing	1991	1	175	175	No	Homeless
Neighborhood Coalition for Shelter	NCS Residence	1984	3	800	66	Yes	Mixed
Project Greenhope Services for Women	Greenhope Houses	1990	2	55	36	Yes	Homeless
Project Return Foundation	Jerome Court	2000	5	200	40	Yes	HIV/AIDS
Services for the Underserved	The Majestic	1996	22	600	55	Yes	Mental health
VIP Community Services	Abraham Apartments	1999	5	261	27	Yes	Homeless
West Side Federation for Senior and Supportive Housing	Westbourne	1997	12	1,275	128	No	Homeless

SOURCE: Authors' calculations, based on interviews with the supportive housing providers.

Table 5.2 Employment Status of Supportive Housing Residents at Selected Facilities

Supportive housing provider	% working FT or PT	Total working	Facility population type
Institute for Community Living	91	11	Mental illness
West Side Federation for Senior and Supportive Housing	54	69	Homeless (public assistance)
The Jericho Project	52	29	Homeless (substance abuse)
VIP Community Services	41	11	Homeless (substance abuse)
Common Ground Community	41	257	Mixed
Clinton Housing and Development Corp.	28	19	Mixed
The Miracle Makers	27	47	Mixed
Brooklyn Community Housing and Services	26	19	Mixed
The Bridge	21	3	Mental illness
Services for the Underserved	21	11	Mental illness
Neighborhood Coalition for Shelter	20	11	Mixed
Project Greenhope Services for Women	16	24	Homeless (substance abuse/mental illness)
Housing Works	14	5	HIV/AIDS
Bowery Residents' Committee	12	4	HIV/AIDS
Catholic Charities, Brooklyn and Queens	12	9	Mental illness
Federation Employment and Guidance Service (FEGS)	11	6	Mental illness

Friends Home Group	8	4	HIV/AIDS
Jewish Board of Family and Children's Services	4	3	Mental illness
Project Return Foundation	0	0	HIV/AIDS
Mean	26	29	
Median	21	11	

SOURCE: Authors' calculations, based on interviews with the supportive housing providers.

to be considerably lower among residents living with a mental illness and HIV/AIDS than among other groups. It is noteworthy that facilities catering to people with histories of substance abuse tend to have considerably higher rates of employment than facilities geared to people with mental illness or HIV/AIDS. When facilities house mixed populations, people living with HIV/AIDS or mental illness (sometimes both) tend to have lower rates of employment than their neighbors.

Of the three residences with employment rates of at least 50 percent, only one—the Institute for Community Living, on Warren Street—focused on people with mental illness. This supportive housing provider actively integrates employment into its overall treatment program. The other two facilities serve a more general homeless population, including a large percentage of individuals with histories of substance abuse but not with severe mental illness or with HIV/AIDS. Most of the residences with intermediate levels of employment (i.e., between 15 and 41 percent) served a more heterogeneous population, housing people with different backgrounds and disabilities. However, within these facilities, residents living with HIV/AIDS or mental illness were much less likely to be employed than their neighbors.

For example, in the Times Square, the largest supportive housing residence in the sample, 40 percent of the facility's 632 residents were employed in 2001 (see Table 5.3). However, over 80 percent of these were either "community" residents—low- and moderate-income individuals, few of whom had histories of homelessness—or original tenants, who moved in before Common Ground acquired the facility in 1990. Excluding residents 60 years and over, some 87 percent of the "community" residents were employed either full or part time, including 37 percent of the original tenants. Of the formerly homeless residents under 60 years of age at the Times Square, the subgroup with the highest employment rate—47 percent—is subsidized by the city's Department of Homeless Services. These residents generally are not diagnosed with HIV/AIDS or mental illness. In contrast, of the 47 residents under 60 supported by the HIV/AIDS Services Administration (HASA), only one was employed, and of the 135 residents with mental illness under 60 years of age supported by the city and state's NY/NY program, just 13 percent were.

The high incidence of unemployment among residents with mental illness is consistent with national trends. Only about 15 percent of

Table 5.3 Employment Status of Times Square Residents by Population Group, 2001

	All residents			Residents under 60		
	Total	Number employed	% employed	Total	Number employed	% employed
AIDS	50	1	2	47	1	2
Mental illness	151	21	14	134	17	13
Homeless	80	27	34	57	27	47
Original	85	13	15	27	10	37
Community	266	203	76	227	198	87
Total	632	265	42	492	253	51

NOTE: Residents with AIDS are funded by New York City's HIV/AIDS Services Administration (formerly Division of AIDS Services); residents with mental illness are funded by the city/state program New York/New York; formerly homeless residents are funded through the city's Department of Homeless Services. "Community" residents come from New York's general population and generally are not disabled and do not have histories of homelessness.

SOURCE: Authors' calculations, based on interviews with the supportive housing providers.

people of working age with severe mental illness are employed in the United States, although surveys of the mentally disabled population consistently show that about 75 percent want to work (McReynolds, Garske, and Turpin 2002). The U.S. Department of Labor's (USDOL) Job Training for the Homeless Demonstration Program found that participants with mental illness had significantly lower job placement rates than other homeless populations. Whereas more than half of unmarried males and the chemically dependent found employment, the same was true for just 33 percent of the program's participants with mental illness (USDOL 1998). Similarly, when persons with severe psychiatric disability seek vocational services, their success rate is only about half of the rate for those with physical disabilities (McReynolds, Garske, and Turpin 2002). Persons with mental illness also tend to be underrepresented in vocational service programs. National reviews of vocational rehabilitation have found that only 2 to 4 percent of people who receive mental health services receive vocational rehabilitation at any given time (Bond et al. 2001).

BARRIERS TO EMPLOYMENT

The very issues that lead people into supportive housing also pose formidable barriers to employment. Previous studies, including the evaluation of the Corporation for Supportive Housing's *Next Step: Jobs Initiative* (Corporation for Supportive Housing 1997; Fleischer and Sherwood 2000; Proscio 1998) stress several common characteristics of the supportive housing population that can impede prospects for employment. Besides low levels of educational attainment and minimal work experience, these may include mental illness, HIV/AIDS, and substance abuse. Interviews with providers of supportive housing and vocational services brought out a large number of employment barriers, not all of which relate directly to the resident's disabilities, education, or employment history.

All of the supportive housing providers discussed the limitations posed by residents' disabilities and backgrounds. These limitations were most acute for residents with mental illness and for those living with HIV/AIDS. Staff and residents cited more than 50 barriers (see Table 5.4). These may be sorted into several broad categories, including 1) social, behavioral, or medical impediments, 2) inadequate skills or work history, 3) inadequate incentives and encouragement, and 4) employer resistance.

By far the most frequently cited barrier to employment involved difficulties adapting to the routines and expectations of the workplace. Many of these problems fall under the rubric of inadequate soft skills, such as difficulties dealing with authority, weak anger management skills, social skills, or problem-solving skills, lack of motivation, absenteeism, and tardiness.[2] In some cases, supportive housing staff members felt that the residents' mental illness made them too unsuitable for regular employment, either because their behavior and manner would not be acceptable or because they would not be able to tolerate the stress. Several respondents voiced concerns that too much stress or anxiety on the job could cause residents to relapse into substance abuse or experience a worsening of their mental illness (i.e., decompensate). At a resident focus group, two participants said they would not take any job without first consulting their psychiatrists to see if they could "handle it." Both expressed concern about having too much stress. These concerns about mental illness extend beyond residents with diagnoses of schizophrenia and other psychiatric disorders. Vocational and supportive housing staff often commented on the presence of residents with undiagnosed mental illness.

Another set of barriers clustered around the residents' skills, education, and work experience. Most residents lack the basic skills necessary for many types of employment and have little, if any, paid job experience. Few residents in the supportive housing facilities studied had more than a high school education, and many had less. Individuals without a high school diploma or a GED make up one-quarter to one-half of residents at most sites. While a number of residents have completed at least some college, including a very few with advanced degrees, they represent a small fraction of the supportive housing population. These low levels of educational attainment were noted by staff, who frequently remarked that many residents had very weak reading, computational, and other basic skills. In some cases, the residents' lack of skills reflects not just their limited educational attainment but various developmental disabilities as well.

Most residents have an intermittent or erratic work history, little of it in the formal economy. In the case of those with mental illness, it was

Table 5.4 Number of Organizations that Identify Barriers to Employment

Barrier	Mental health community (6)	HIV/AIDS community (3)	Homeless/ community residents (4)	Mixed (MH, HIV, homeless) community (7)	Total (20)
Social, behavioral, and medical barriers					
Loss of benefits	4	2	3	6	15
Mental health issues	4	1	2	5	12
Fear (of failure, of losing housing, of taking on too much, or of success)	3	1	2	3	9
Lack of motivation to find and retain employment	3	1	2	2	8
History of substance use	1	0	2	4	7
Personality issues/interpersonal skills (poor attitude, inability to deal with authority)	0	1	2	4	7
Lifestyle—i.e., prostitution, chaotic drug use/relapse	3	1	1	2	7
Behavioral issues	1	1	1	1	4
Low self esteem	1	1	0	2	4
Can't handle responsibility of a job—getting up on time	1	1	1	1	4
Physical health issues	2	2	0	0	4
Stress of training or working	0	1	1	1	3
Comfortable/stable at supportive housing program	1	1	0	1	3

Self-sabotaging behavior	1	0	0	1	2
Need flexible schedule for medical and SSA appointments	0	1	0	1	2
Learning or developmental disabilities	0	0	2	0	2
No stable support network	1	0	0	1	2
Disruptive family or family background	0	0	1	1	2
Residents wanting too much too soon	1	0	1	0	2
Involved in other activities (such as day treatment)	1	0	0	0	1
Lack of practical resources (i.e., clothing, services)	1	0	0	0	1
Hard for residents to trust	1	0	0	0	1
Age of resident	0	0	1	0	1
Inadequate skills and work history					
Lack of education	3	1	4	3	11
Lack of skills (hard and soft)	2	1	1	4	8
Lack of or poor employment history	1	0	3	3	7
Low literacy level	1	1	2	2	6
Lack of prevocational skills	1	0	0	0	1
Budgeting problems	1	0	0	0	1
Language barrier	1	0	0	0	1

Table 5.4 (continued)

Barrier	Mental health community (6)	HIV/AIDS community (3)	Homeless/ community residents (4)	Mixed (MH, HIV, homeless) community (7)	Total (20)
Inadequate incentives and encouragement					
Programs underestimate resident's potential—don't expect people with mental illness to work, don't understand role or push employment	2	0	0	2	4
Lack of staff to focus on vocational services	2	0	0	1	3
System barriers—too many appointments or steps required by VESID, SSI, etc.	2	1	0	0	3
The state of treatment for the mentally ill (such as clubhouses)	2	0	0	1	3
Job developers place people in undesirable, low paying, demeaning work	2	1	0	0	3
Practitioners unable to evaluate clients' skills and vocational needs	1	0	0	0	1
Lack of preparation by referral agency	0	0	0	1	1
Employer reluctance to hire residents of supportive housing					
Discrimination by employer and public perception of mentally ill and methadone patients	4	0	1	2	7

Criminal record	0	0	2	0	2
Stigma of being HIV-positive or mentally ill in the workplace	0	1	0	0	1
Employers have had bad experiences in the past	0	0	1	0	1
Fluctuations in the labor market	0	0	0	1	1
Other barriers					
Child care needs	0	0	0	1	1
Need to support children who live elsewhere	0	0	1	0	1
Housing issues (such as looking for housing)	0	0	0	1	1

SOURCE: Authors' calculations, based on interviews with the supportive housing providers.

pointed out that many residents became ill in their early 20s, precisely at the time when their peers were starting their careers. As a result, many residents of supportive housing not only lack the basic literacy, computational, and cognitive skills necessary for most jobs, but are also without the understanding of workplace norms that comes with job experience. Many residents are in their late 30s or older and have not held a regular job in years, if ever. Those with the least work experience, particularly if they are in their thirties or older, are the least attractive candidates to employers.

A third barrier to employment revolves around the incentive to work. Many residents of supportive housing see little to gain by working and in some cases much to lose. Residents receiving Supplemental Security Income (SSI) and Social Security Disability Insurance (SSDI) seem to have the least incentive to join the workforce, especially if they believe doing so requires them to relinquish their Medicaid benefits. Staff and residents alike voiced concerns about the loss of government entitlements that might ensue if residents became employed. Few residents and only some staff were aware of recent measures passed to increase work incentives for recipients of SSI and SSDI, but even the most thoroughly informed staff members said that loss of benefits remained a daunting barrier to employment.[3] Indeed, one agency employs a full-time benefits specialist on its vocational staff to keep residents informed of changing eligibility requirements and to help them navigate the system. The issue of benefits came up repeatedly at all four resident focus groups. Participants were wary of having their benefits cut off once they became employed. They were especially worried about whether they could regain their benefits should they become unemployed again.[4]

A related barrier to employment is the low wages that most residents are likely to earn if they were to work. Most participants at all four focus groups agreed that they could not support themselves at less than about $15 per hour, a wage few thought they could command. Most felt it was not worth it to work for less, especially if the job did not provide health insurance. Only a few participants said they were willing to accept a lower wage as a way to gain a foothold in the workplace. Most thought of employment as a way of moving out of supportive housing and into a home of their own; however, they didn't feel they could ever earn enough to do so.

The expiration of welfare benefits did not appear to be a significant incentive for employment among residents of supportive housing. This may reflect the fact that many residents are disabled and receive SSDI or SSI, which are not subject to time limits. It may also reflect the fact that New York State guarantees a reduced level of public assistance (Safety Net Assistance—noncash) for all individuals and families that have exhausted their time-limited welfare benefits. Only a few staff reported having public assistance recipients ask them for help in finding employment. Similarly, employment did not emerge as a particularly urgent priority at one focus group of mostly public assistance recipients, and the impending expiration of benefits did not seem a major source of concern. Although most of the participants at a second focus group of public assistance recipients did want to work, none felt compelled to do so by time limits.

The stability that formerly homeless residents have attained with supportive housing and a modest amount of public assistance may be another disincentive to employment. It was remarked that many residents are used to their current routines and are not motivated to change them, even though they receive limited income from public assistance or disability benefits. Having had chaotic lives, they seek stability. Since they live in subsidized, permanent housing and receive food stamps, they do not see a pressing need to increase their incomes through employment. In the case of supportive housing residents living with HIV/AIDS, residents and staff felt they had especially little incentive to work. Not only are people living with HIV/AIDS particularly dependent on Medicaid and other government benefits, it is difficult for them to balance employment with their need for medical services; specifically, it is hard to schedule health-related appointments while working. Moreover, it is also hard to find jobs flexible enough to accommodate absences due to illness.

Further dissipating the incentive to work are case managers and other social service staff who, several vocational providers said, do not actively encourage residents to seek employment and strive for economic independence. Vocational staff felt that case managers seldom encouraged residents to seek employment for three reasons: lack of time and resources, lack of training, and lack of financial incentive for them to go beyond their basic job description. Case managers, staff members sometimes said, are often so busy responding to various emergencies that they can rarely take the time to encourage more highly functioning residents to look for employment opportunities. Also, if residents express a desire for an expensive item such as a computer, or a wish to take up a new occupation, it was felt that case managers were likely to ignore these comments rather than explain the necessary steps it would take to achieve this goal and provide encouragement to do so. One facility director said that case managers tend to have little experience in or knowledge of vocational rehabilitation and are not adequately informed of the resources available to help residents obtain employment. Case management positions, she explained, are typically entry level and are most often filled by people straight out of college. They are still learning the ropes and are not educated about the resources that exist in vocational training and rehabilitation. Most of their time is spent on "troubleshooting, responding to crises." They have little time to refer residents to vocational services or otherwise encourage them to seek employment. Compounding the problem, turnover is usually quite high among case managers, in part because of low salaries, making it difficult to sustain a vocational culture within supportive housing organizations.

Some respondents also felt that staff members at the day treatment programs in which some supportive housing residents participate do little to encourage them to seek employment. Indeed, some interviewees stated that day treatment programs preferred to have supportive housing residents remain in their current programs than to have them create vacancies by moving into a vocational program or a job.

Other employment barriers included reluctance of employers to hire persons with mental illness, HIV/AIDS, a history of substance abuse, a criminal record, and other characteristics of the supportive housing population. Some respondents believed that residents were afraid of feeling stigmatized by their coworkers. Others said that the poor health of some formerly homeless residents also constituted a serious barrier. In addition to living with a mental illness and HIV/AIDS, residents often suffer from diabetes, hypertension, heart disease, asthma and other chronic conditions. A few respondents mentioned weak or nonexistent social support networks to help residents deal with the stresses of employment. Finally, some felt that vocational support and welfare systems were not sufficiently responsive to the needs of supportive housing residents. In particular, they felt that agencies such as the New York

State Department of Education's Office of Vocational and Educational Services for Individuals with Disabilities (VESID) imposed too many hurdles in the form of multiple interviews and delays for residents, causing them to become discouraged and lose interest in employment.

Benefits of Employment

The supportive housing groups, including those that do not provide vocational services, were nearly unanimous with regard to their views on the benefits of employment. Executive directors and case managers alike emphasized the importance of employment in building the self-esteem and confidence of residents and integrating them into mainstream society. Few if any expressed much hope that employment would pave a path of economic self-sufficiency for more than a handful of residents. Instead they stressed the benefits of employment for the resident's mental health and overall sense of well being. They said that employment, even a few hours a week, gives people a sense of purpose, a feeling that they are engaged in something positive. Employment also provides some structure and purpose in the residents' lives. As an unemployed participant in a resident focus group put it, employment "would give me a reason to get up in the morning, something to look forward to." Some felt that employment helps people develop stronger social skills and indeed helps them develop some of the skills desired for living in supportive housing.

Several respondents did discuss the financial benefits of employment, but few thought that it was reasonable to expect residents to become financially independent. Several also cautioned that the nature of some residents' mental illness made it unlikely that they would be able to work continuously into the future; some suffer periodic breakdowns that make them unable to work for periods of time.

Approaches to Employment

The study included organizations that do and organizations that do not provide vocational services for their residents. As was said earlier, of the 20 supportive housing providers studied, 14 offer some form of vocational services. Most of the vocational programs are small and relatively new. They typically involve a continuum of services, from initial assessment to post-placement support, almost always with a heavy dosage of case management. Several of the organizations with vocational services do not focus exclusively on residents of supportive housing; in some programs supportive housing residents constitute a small proportion of all vocational clients.

A few of the six organizations that do not provide vocational services would like to do more to help their residents secure a place in the labor force. Some of them have experimented with vocational support in the past, and others are planning to hire vocational staff in the future. Most said they did not have the financial resources to institute vocational programming. Instead, they rely on case managers to refer residents to vocational programs offered by other organizations. Some also hire residents for part-time jobs at their facilities.

Program Overview

The supportive housing organizations' vocational programs are quite small. Most employ five or fewer full-time staff and seldom have budgets in excess of $500,000—and sometimes much less. They rarely have more than two or three dozen participants at any one time. While some vocational programs focus almost exclusively on supportive housing residents, others serve a broader population. For example at Community Access's supported employment program, about 30 percent of the 198 participants live in supportive housing. However, only one or two of these participants reside at supportive housing operated by the parent organization; the rest come from facilities run by several different organizations.

The supportive housing providers with vocational programs differ more in the number of services provided than in their basic approach. Most of the organizations offer vocational services as a separate, standalone program, often based at a central location (often a supportive housing residence). One or two groups provide vocational service programs at multiple supportive housing facilities. In a few instances, vocational services are integrated within other programs. For example, Project Return's vocational services are part of a larger drug rehabilitation program. Similarly, supportive housing providers sometimes fold vocational services into day treatment programs and psycho-social clubs.

Work Readiness Training

Common to all 14 organizations offering vocational services is a concern with work readiness. All provide counseling and case management services to help residents adapt to the routines and expectations of the workplace. All provide some form of vocational assessment, in part to determine the most appropriate programs and referral.

Virtually all the groups provide some form of job readiness training. This can vary from long-term day-treatment or intensive psychiatric rehabilitation programs to two-week classes on a range of soft skills. The longer-term programs typically focus on persons with mental illness and do not necessarily aim exclusively at preparing clients for employment. For example, the largest vocational program run by Services for the Underserved (another supportive housing provider specializing in the mentally ill) is its Brooklyn Clubhouse, a psychosocial clubhouse. A structured therapeutic setting for persons with mental illness, the clubhouse program includes supported employment—mostly internships—for clients.[5] More broadly, it prepares people for employment by providing a task-oriented day. The agency views the clubhouse's overall programming as providing pre-vocational support. By requiring clients to sign up for specific activities and tasks, the clubhouse provides a structured day, which can help them adapt to the structure and routines of the workplace.

Most of the programs promote work readiness on a shorter-term basis. They usually involve individual or group meetings with vocational counselors and case managers as well as classroom instruction on a wide range of soft skills, including such topics as resume preparation, interviewing skills, job search skills, and anger management.

Several of the supportive housing groups offer supported employment, usually within their organizations, but sometimes with other organizations as well. Most of the programs involve part-time work and are limited to a few months. The goal is to provide work experience in a nonthreatening environment as a stepping stone to competitive employment. Most often, supported employment involves front desk, food service, building maintenance and other low-skill jobs at the parent organization. A few organizations also offer "assisted competitive employment" for supportive housing programs. These programs provide job coaches and other supports to help individuals (usually with mental illness) cope with regular employment. For example, The Bridge's Assisted Competitive Employment program employs two staff to work as job developers and job coaches for about 30 clients. Post-placement support includes individual and group counseling, regular phone contact with clients, and occasional visits to the job site. Staff members also speak to employers when requested to by the client.

Several programs integrate work-readiness or soft skills with their hard-skill vocational training. The Institute for Independent Living, for example, runs a three-week pre-employment course as a prerequisite for its vocational training courses. The work readiness training instructs people on how to complete employment applications, prepare resumes, identify realistic career goals, and develop strategies for job retention. The course also includes mock job interviews and provides assistance in medication and money management.

Some of the smaller vocational programs offered by supportive housing providers focus exclusively on work-readiness and refer clients to other programs for training in specific vocations. The Jericho Project, a supportive housing organization serving homeless individuals with histories of substance abuse, employs three vocational counselors and one job developer. The vocational counselors are based at specific supportive housing residences and help residents develop short- and long-term career goals and identify necessary steps to reach these goals. They also provide post-placement assistance to help residents retain their jobs. While some residents are placed in jobs directly, others are first referred to vocational training programs to develop more advanced skills. The agency's job developer assists residents with their job search, helping them sharpen their interviewing skills and improve their resumes.

A small number of organizations provide instruction in reading, writing, and other basic skills as well as English as a Second Language. Most of the groups refer residents to community colleges and other institutions for this kind of support. The Center for Urban Community Services (CUCS), for example, contracts with a community college to provide basic skills training at its supportive housing facilities.

Hard-Skills Training

Two-thirds of the organizations that offer vocational services provide some form of vocational training (i.e., hard skills training) for specific occupations or industries. Most often these programs are very small and focus on food services, building maintenance, case management, and other jobs routinely carried out by the parent organization. In some cases, training is intertwined with the organizations' supported employment programs; in others, it is provided in a classroom setting. For example, the Institute for Community Living operates four-week training programs in janitorial services, food services, and computer applications as part of a broader job placement program that also includes three weeks of work-readiness training. CUCS's internship program combines paid work experience with six to eight weeks of course work in soft skills and in such vocation-specific areas as office occupations, building maintenance, and social services.

Several organizations have started, or are about to open, computer training facilities and programs as part of their vocational services. They provide computers and staff to train residents in the basic computer applications such as word processing and the Internet. Staff at several supportive housing facilities reported that residents express interest in learning about computers, as did participants at two of the four resident focus groups. However, this interest is often quite general and does not necessarily translate into employment aspirations. Nevertheless, responding to this interest, 13 of the supportive housing groups have established computer-training programs. One of them, the Jericho Project, expects new residents to take at least four classes in its computer program. As of August 2001, 60 percent of all residents had taken at least one class. Another, the Institute for Community Living, offers a four-week course in computer skills aimed at people interested in clerical employment or just in learning about computers. Its goal is to help residents become comfortable working with computers.

Job Placement and Retention Support

Most of the supportive housing groups with vocational programs employ job developers to help residents find jobs with employers throughout New York City. Most graduates of the vocational programs run by supportive housing organizations tend to work in low paying service jobs, usually without benefits. While some agencies attempt to place people in jobs paying a few dollars more than the minimum wage, staff members admit that most participants lack the skills and work experience that would enable them to command higher pay. The best paying jobs are usually in social services. For example, "peer specialists" trained at one supportive housing organization's vocational program typically earn around $24,000 annually with benefits, or, for part-time positions, $10 an hour. Wages for building maintenance, food service, and other occupations targeted by vocational service programs tend to be considerably less. Most of the vocational providers feel that supportive housing residents are usually ill suited for retail and fast-food jobs. Customer relations can be stressful in retail environments, and middle-aged residents can find it demeaning to work alongside teenagers and young adults in fast-food establishments.

In general, the vocational programs place residents in full-time jobs. Although case managers and other supportive housing staff—as well as participants in the resident focus groups—tended to prefer part-time work, considering full-time work too stressful for most residents, most of the vocational staff felt that if a resident could succeed in part-time employment he or she could probably succeed in full-time work as well.

A few of the organizations have also created business ventures to employ their vocational clients. CUCS, for example, has started a jewelry-making business and is looking at the possibility of starting other micro businesses as well. The agency sees micro businesses as a way of providing flexible work for supportive housing residents. Such enterprises must require skills that residents already have or can develop in a short period of time. Residents can work at their own pace, either at home or at more central locations.

Housing Works, unlike all the other supportive housing and vocational service providers studied, guarantees a job at its parent organization for every Job Training Program (JTP) participant (most of whom are not residents of supportive housing) who passes both the JTP coursework and the core competency criteria for a particular position. Specifically, it places graduates in case management, clerical, building maintenance, food service, and retail jobs at its offices, residential facilities, and thrift stores. All graduates are guaranteed jobs with health insurance, paid vacation, and other benefits.

There was great diversity found among the organizations in the extent to which they hired residents of their own supportive housing facilities. Organizations identified benefits as well as drawbacks to employing residents within their housing programs. Benefits to employing residents within the agency include the feeling that by hiring residents they are able to fulfill both the need for residents to obtain employment and job experience and the need to fill certain positions in the organization. Also, by serving both as the residents' employer and as their service provider, the agency is able to offer residents valuable guidance in the transition to work. Since the roles of service provider and employer are combined, stress and problems can be noticed early and thus averted. On the other hand, some providers recognize that a conflict of interest can arise when attempting to provide housing and case management while also acting as the resident's employer. By the provider trying to be all of these things for a resident, the line between service provider and employer can become blurred, often making it difficult to provide comprehensive support services. Also, many feel that by providing residents employment inside the organization, those residents are not being encouraged to strive for greater independence.

In order to preserve the distinction between service provider and employer, organizations utilize a wide variety of strategies in the hiring of past and current residents. Some programs, like Jericho Project and Project Greenhope, will only hire former residents who have been out of the program for a length of time, usually at least one year. Jericho Project's staff is made up of 20 percent former residents, while Project Greenhope has a few former residents employed in security or porter internships. Other agencies, such as the Federation Employment and Guidance Service (FEGS)—recognizing the difficulties of employing one's own residents—will not hire its own residents; rather, it accepts referrals for employment from other supportive housing programs. Yet another way that agencies have resolved this conflict is by hiring residents to work in divisions of the agency besides the one in which they live. Both Project Return and Catholic Charities of Brooklyn and Queens follow this practice. Jobs that residents are most often hired for within the parent organization include maintenance, porter, front desk, and security; some are also hired for peer counseling and case management.

Most of the organizations try to help clients retain employment after initial placement. A few of the organizations employ job coaches to provide post-placement support. However, several respondents voiced concern about the difficulty of helping people keep their jobs. Some said that clients were not comfortable meeting with job coaches at the work site—that it was embarrassing for a client to have a coach while working alongside other workers who do not. Some also said it was unclear what the coaches could actually do at the work site. It was better, they said, for coaches to meet with clients elsewhere to discuss any issues they might be facing.

Most of the vocational programs include support groups for both trainees and graduates. These range from weekly meetings with vocational staff to monthly or quarterly dinners for program graduates. While support groups and other forms of group work are common elements of pre-employment and vocational training, they seem more difficult to implement for clients who have become employed or have otherwise graduated from a vocational program. Staff at several organizations said it was difficult to attract many program graduates to peer-group meetings. As a result they are experimenting with both the format of the meetings and the kinds of topics to be discussed. Some groups are making post-placement meetings more of a social event, combining a presentation or discussion with dinner. One group, the Bowery Residents' Committee, pays $200 to participants after six months of regular attendance at monthly meetings.

Partners, Referrals, and External Relationships

Most of the vocational programs operated by supportive housing providers are fairly insular, involving few if any partnerships with other organizations. While several are connected to VESID, none participate in programs operated by USDOL for vocational support, including the city's one-stop center. Only a few of the organizations—mostly those serving people who do not have a mental illness or HIV/AIDS—link up with New York City's Welfare to Work programs. Few groups contract with other organizations to provide vocational or related services for their residents. Likewise, few of the supportive housing providers have formal alliances with other organizations in the workforce development arena. And few involve private employers in the design or oversight of their vocational programs. For example, only two have employer advisory boards, although several others have expressed an interest in forming advisory boards. While some groups want to have closer connections to employers, others are more wary, partly out of fear of promising more than they can deliver.

Employment Outcomes

Few of the supportive housing groups have management information systems in place to track the employment outcomes of the participants in their vocational programs. Most are unable to provide comprehensive data on job placements, retention, wages, or advancement. The bulk of the employment outcome information collected for this study is based on the estimates of program staff. Most staff members say that vocational clients typically end up in low-paying jobs and often have trouble holding their jobs for extended periods of time. It was frequently remarked that clients often go through a rapid succession of jobs before one "sticks." In the case of persons with mental illness, clients often become unable to hold a job during acute phases of their disease but then return to work once their condition stabilizes.

The Jericho Project, serving formerly homeless individuals with histories of substance abuse but typically without mental illness or HIV/AIDS, is one of the few groups to systematically track employment outcomes. It reports that the average starting salary of residents it has helped to place is $8.04 an hour. In addition, 70 percent of residents placed in the past two years retained their jobs for at least six months, and 51 percent did so for at least one year. Of those who did not retain their jobs, two-thirds found new jobs within three months. Given the character of its target population, the Jericho Project probably achieves greater success than most vocational programs serving residents of supportive housing.

CONCLUSIONS AND RECOMMENDATIONS

Although supportive housing groups have created numerous vocational programs for their residents and other formerly homeless and disabled individuals, many residents in supportive housing are not employed or participating in vocational programs. The Corporation for Supportive Housing, in its recently completed *Next Step: Jobs Initiative* report, encouraged participating groups to promote employment in all aspects of their supportive housing programs—or, as coined by one author, to "vocationalize the homefront" (Parkhill 2000). While most of the groups in *Next Step: Jobs Initiative* continue to stress employment in multiple ways, the 20 supportive housing providers covered in this study, with one or two exceptions, show little sign of doing so. Despite program development and innovation, the supportive housing groups studied here do not seem to be reaching a very large segment of their target population. This raises a double-edged question: Are supportive housing organizations failing to reach their target population, or is the need for vocational services among formerly homeless residents of supportive housing less than service providers and their supporters have assumed?

Most residents of supportive housing confront formidable obstacles to employment, including poor basic skills, minimal work experience, and in many cases mental illness, HIV/AIDS, and other health problems. Many have not held a steady job in years, if ever, and do not always grasp the norms of workplace behavior. As one vocational service provider explained, formerly homeless individuals have had very little structure and support in their lives that would have prepared them for employment.

Two sets of issues emerge from the staff interviews and resident focus groups. One concerns the ability of vocational programs to attract supportive housing residents; the other relates to the programs' effectiveness in helping residents succeed in the labor market. The supportive housing industry needs a better grasp of the size of the pool of viable vocational clients and how it can reach them. The industry also needs a better sense of the vocational potential of supportive housing residents and the best way of realizing that potential.

Accessing the Market

Given the character of the supportive housing population and its multitude of employment barriers, it is critical to have realistic expectations of its employment potential. While some residents have the potential to become economically self sufficient within the labor force, others, most likely the majority, do not. Most of the latter are not likely to earn substantially more than the minimum wage or to hold jobs for extended periods of time. This is not to say, however, that competitive employment is unsuitable for residents with mental illness, HIV/AIDS, and other disabilities. It does suggest, though, that their vocational needs and expectations will differ from supportive housing residents that do not have these disabilities, and that they are not likely to achieve sustained economic independence through employment.

Supportive housing most likely does not offer a very large pool of individuals with the potential to benefit from mainstream employment services geared to long-term economic advancement. The most promising candidates for these programs probably come from two groups of supportive housing residents—individuals supported by the Department of Homeless Services (DHS), and residents whose rents are not subsidized by state or local programs (although some receive federal Section 8 rental vouchers). Termed "community" residents, the latter group is not limited to the formerly homeless or the disabled and includes the original residents of single-room occupancy hotels (SROs) that were acquired by nonprofit supportive housing providers, as well as individuals willing to pay market rents for apartments in supportive housing facilities.

A first priority should be to assess the employment status and work readiness of DHS and community residents—as opposed to residents with diagnosed mental illness and HIV/AIDS whose vocational potential is usually more limited. According to data provided by the Supportive Housing Network of New York, these two groups collectively account for 54 percent of New York's 12,000 units of supportive housing (22 percent DHS, 34 percent community).

The experience at Common Ground's two largest supportive housing facilities, if at all typical of the larger population, suggests that demand for vocational services among community and DHS residents is quite limited, especially if the goal is sustainable, self-supporting employment. At both the Times Square and the Prince George, the vast majority of community residents under age 60 are already employed and thus probably do not need vocational assistance. A much smaller fraction of the residents under 60 supported by DHS are employed—47 percent at the Times Square and 34 percent at the Prince George. Many of the unemployed DHS residents at the Times Square and Prince George, however, are disabled, either receiving SSI or SSDI or with pending applications. At the Times Square, only 4 of 29 unemployed DHS residents under age 60 do not receive SSI or SSDI or have pending applications for these benefits. At the Prince George, half of 42 unemployed DHS residents under age 60 do not receive SSI or SSDI or have pending applications. In sum, the demand for mainstream vocational services at these large supportive housing residences is quite limited.

If supportive housing residents do not constitute a large source of demand for mainstream employment programs designed to help people become economically self-sufficient, a potentially larger segment of the supportive-housing population, including residents supported by DHS as well as those with mental illness and HIV/AIDS, might be interested in other types of programs to help them obtain regular jobs in the private and public sectors. Although it may not be reasonable to expect them to become economically self-reliant, many of these residents could still benefit from competitive employment given the opportunity and necessary support. It is therefore critical to have realistic expectations about residents' true vocational potential. This is particularly important with regard to residents with mental illness.

One barrier to the employment of persons with mental illness may be the tendency of mental health professionals to underestimate their ability to work outside of a sheltered environment (McReynolds, Garske, and Turpin 2002; Nemec, Spaniol, and Dell Orto 2001). Psychiatrists, psychologists, social workers, case managers, and other staff, perhaps because they receive little training in vocational rehabilitation, may not always understand the extent to which mental illness impairs employment potential.[6] The vocational rehabilitation literature shows that it is extremely difficult to predict the employment outcomes of people with schizophrenia and other severe mental illnesses. Research also shows that there is no relationship between the clinical symptomatology of mental illness and the patient's ability to hold a job (Anthony and Jansen 1984). The only way of predicting employment outcomes for a person with mental illness is that person's previous work history. Yet despite these research findings, mental health practitioners are typically concerned that employment can induce too much stress for clients, risking a worsening of their condition. Our interviews with case managers and residents frequently elicited these concerns.

With regard to supportive housing residents with HIV/AIDS, a key employment barrier is the availability of employment opportunities that provide sufficient flexibility to accommodate the need to make frequent medical appointments and to take time off when not feeling well. This is not just a matter of employers providing flexible work schedules, but also of them having the ability to deal with last minute absences and other deviations from the schedule. Most employers, of course, have little tolerance for unplanned absences from the workplace. Housing Works, as discussed above, has addressed this issue by creating jobs for its trainees within its own organization.

If one priority for supportive housing providers should be to better gauge the number of residents potentially able to benefit from vocational services, another should be to improve how residents with vocational potential are steered toward vocational services and employment. The pool of potential vocational clients may be smaller than originally expected, but more can likely be done to help these residents succeed in the labor force.

One of the most straightforward ways of involving more supportive housing residents in employment and vocational services is to educate residents and staff about their ability to retain Medicaid and other benefits while employed. It is striking how few residents or staff members were aware of recent employment incentives designed to encourage employment among recipients of SSI and SSDI. For example, few were aware that recipients of SSI could retain Medicaid coverage so long as their annual earnings did not exceed approximately $33,000. Clearly, supportive housing staff and residents need to be better informed about these work incentives. A better understanding of how employment affects benefits eligibility should alleviate some residents' anxiety about working. Worries over the loss of government benefits should not be as big a barrier to employment as they appeared to be in our interviews.

Another, more difficult way of stimulating interest in employment is for case managers and other direct service providers to offer more encouragement and assistance. As noted above, vocational staff felt that case managers—at supportive housing facilities and at the day treatment and other programs that residents participate in—do not actively promote employment. Partly because they are often responding to emergencies and other urgent matters, case managers are viewed as not taking the time and effort to stress the benefits of employment to their clients. Moreover, many staff members report that case managers are not often aware of the different types of vocational support that are available for their clients. Part of the problem stems from the high turnover of case managers and the fact that many are new to the job and not well versed in vocational rehabilitation. As noted above, the problem is further aggravated by the lack of training case managers and other mental health professionals receive in the area of vocational rehabilitation. Social workers, psychologists, and other mental health workers receive little if any training in vocational rehabilitation in their professional education (Nemec, Spaniol, and Dell Orto 2001; McReynolds, Garske, and Turpin 2002).

Additional training of case managers could help "vocationalize" the supportive housing homefront. Indeed, given the number of vocational programs in New York City, not to mention the services provided by VESID, it may be a wiser use of resources for supportive housing organizations to put more emphasis on making case managers more effective advocates of employment than to invest in their own vocational training (hard skills) programs.

Increasing Effectiveness

The vocational programs offered by supportive housing organizations include a wide range of services, such as soft skills training, supported employment, occupational skills training, job placement assistance, and retention support. This study did not attempt to evaluate these programs but rather to gather information on the range of services provided and how they are delivered. Nevertheless, two issues stand out with regard to program effectiveness. One concerns the tracking of employment outcomes. The other relates to the emphasis on supported employment and long-term pre-vocational training.

Few of the groups could provide up to date data on attrition during training, job placement rates, wages, job retention, or wage progression. Some organizations track employment outcomes but do not compile the data so that it can be readily analyzed; instead the information is confined to individual client files. Other organizations do not collect outcome information on a systematic basis. As a result, much of the information on employment outcomes is based on the impressions of program staff. In order to provide stronger vocational services it is essential to know the outcomes of current programs. Since few supportive housing organizations possess the budgetary resources to invest in the management information systems necessary for improved tracking and analysis of employment outcomes, this is an area that will require support from government, foundations, and other institutions interested in promoting employment for supportive housing residents.

Among other benefits, better outcome data would help address a key question about many of the vocational programs offered by supportive housing providers. As discussed above, a number of these organizations operate supportive or transitional programs and in some cases extensive pre-employment programs such as psycho-social clubs and continuing day treatment. It would be useful to know the extent to which participants in these programs eventually move into competitive employment. To what extent do residents in intensive psychiatric rehabilitation programs, day treatment programs, and clubhouses transition to other types of vocational programs that lead to competitive employment? To what extent do people in supported employment and internships make the transition to competitive employment? Questions about the efficacy of these approaches were raised at two resident focus groups and in some of the interviews with vocational providers. The two resident focus groups had participants who had worked in internship or supported work programs but then became idle once their assignments came to a close; they seemed to make little effort to find permanent jobs afterwards. One cannot generalize from the experiences of a few former clients, but their stories do underscore the need to better understand the multiple pathways that can lead from supported to competitive employment. They are also consistent with research documenting that supported or sheltered employment is not an effective stepping stone to competitive employment (Bond et al. 2001). Also supporting the focus groups' concerns is that at least one vocational director was reorganizing his organization's supported employment program because what was supposed to be a temporary work experience had become one without end for most participants. With better information on program outcomes, supportive housing organizations will be better able to help residents make the most of their vocational potential.

Notes

1. This chapter uses the terms "homeless" and "formerly homeless" interchangeably to refer to once-homeless individuals now residing in supportive housing.
2. Weak soft skills are also considered a major impediment to employment among

other disadvantaged job seekers without mental illness or a history of homelessness (Houghton and Proscio 2001).

3. For details on work incentives for SSDI and SSI beneficiaries, go to the following Web site: http://www.ssa.gov/work/ResourcesToolkit/workincentives.html.
4. This concern is not without merit. Several focus group participants and case managers described situations in which the Social Security Administration erroneously terminated disability benefits, requiring residents to go through a lengthy application process to verify their disability and reestablish their eligibility.
5. For more background on psychosocial clubs see Bond and Resnick (2000) and Beard, Propst, and Malamud (1982).
6. For example, a national survey found that 2.9 percent of staff in psychiatric rehabilitation programs have backgrounds in vocational rehabilitation counseling (Fabian and Coppola 2001).

References

Anthony, William A., and Mary A. Jansen. 1984. "Predicting the Vocational Capacity of the Chronically Mentally Ill: Research and Policy Implications." *American Psychologist* 39(5): 537–544.

Beard, John H., Rudyard N. Propst, and Thomas J. Malamud. 1982. "The Fountain House Model of Rehabilitation." *Psychosocial Rehabilitation Journal* 5(1): 47–53.

Bond, Gary R., Deborah R. Becker, Robert E. Drake, Charles A. Rapp, Neil Meisler, Anthony F. Lehman, Morris D. Bell, and Crystal R. Blyler. 2001. "Implementing Supported Employment as an Evidence-Based Practice." *Psychiatric Services* 52(3): 313–322.

Bond, Gary R., and Sandra G. Resnick. 2000. "Psychiatric Rehabilitation." In *Handbook of Rehabilitation Psychology,* Robert G. Frank and Timothy R. Elliott, eds. Washington, DC: American Psychological Association, pp. 235–258.

Corporation for Supportive Housing. 1997. *Work in Progress...An Interim Report from the Next Step: Jobs Initiative.* New York: Corporation for Supportive Housing.

Culhane, Dennis P., Stephen Metraux, and Trevor Hadley. 2002. "Public Service Reductions Associated with Placement of Homeless Persons with Severe Mental Illness in Supportive Housing." *Housing Policy Debate* 13(1): 107–163.

Fabian, Ellen S., and John Coppola. 2001. "Vocational Rehabilitation Competencies in Psychiatric Rehabilitation Education." *Rehabilitation Education* 15(2): 133–142.

Fleischer, Wendy, and Kay E. Sherwood. 2000. *The Next Wave: Employing People with Multiple Barriers to Work: Policy Lessons from the Next Step: Jobs Initiative.* New York: Corporation for Supportive Housing.

Houghton, Ted, and Tony Proscio. 2001. *Hard Work on Soft Skills: Creating a "Culture of Work" in Workforce Development.* Philadelphia: Public/Private Ventures.

McReynolds, Connie J., Gregory G. Garske, and Joseph O. Turpin. 2002. "Psychiatric Rehabilitation: A Survey of Rehabilitation Counseling Education Programs." *Journal of Rehabilitation* 65(4): 45–49.

Nemec, Patricia B., LeRoy Spaniol, and Arthur E. Dell Orto. 2001. "Psychiatric Rehabilitation Education." *Rehabilitation Education* 15(2): 115–118.

Parkhill, Paul. 2000. *Vocationalizing the Homefront: Promising Practices in Place-Based Employment.* New York: Corporation for Supportive Housing.

Proscio, Tony. 1998. *Work in Progress 2: An Interim Report on Next Step: Jobs.* New York: Corporation for Supportive Housing.

U.S. Department of Labor (USDOL). 1998. *Employment and Training for America's Homeless: Final Report on the Job Training for the Homeless Demonstration Program.* Washington, DC: U.S. Department of Labor, Employment and Training Administration.

Part 2

Community-Based Workforce Development Initiatives for the Information Technology Sector

6
Workforce Development in the Information Technology Age

Michael A. Stoll
University of California, Los Angeles

Over the latter half of the twentieth century, workforce development policy in the United States aimed at enhancing the employment and earnings of low-income and less-educated workers.[1] Although these efforts have met with mixed success, the rise of new information technologies in the economy presents new challenges and opportunities for workforce development policy.

The expansion of the knowledge-based economy in the late 1990s increased demand for labor in all sectors, but the skill sets required for these jobs also increased, leaving many low-skill workers on the outside of the "new economy" (Autor, Katz, and Krueger 1998). In the information technology (IT) world of today, job skill requirements seem to change much more rapidly than in the past, which adds to the difficulty of getting low-skill job seekers into employment. Thus, the ability of workforce development institutions to link disadvantaged workers to jobs in the IT sector is likely to rest on their ability to adapt to and train for the changing skill dynamics of IT jobs.

Is there a demand for workers in IT jobs? If so, can past and current workforce development practice successfully connect low-skill workers to growing employment opportunities in IT? And if it cannot, what are the "best practices" found in workforce development that can accomplish this? This chapter seeks to answer these questions by examining the demand for workers and the rising skill requirements in IT jobs, by evaluating whether current workforce policy is positioned to meet the growing labor market needs in the IT sector, and by investigating how workforce development policy can help low-skill workers overcome barriers in the new economy labor market.

The need for workforce development institutions to successfully place low-skill workers in IT jobs cannot be overstated. For too long, workforce development has been viewed as part of social welfare policy or as programs of last resort for disadvantaged workers. This view has probably influenced or reinforced employer perceptions that workforce development programs are poverty programs, and as such are irrelevant to their labor supply needs. To the extent such policy and programs can successfully integrate low-skill workers into the IT sector, they will be seen as a key part of national economic development policy. Lessons drawn from the successes should prove particularly useful during continued implementation of the Workforce Investment Act (WIA) of 1998.

THE DEMAND FOR WORKERS AND SKILL IN IT JOBS

In order to analyze the demand for IT workers, it is necessary to first define IT. Although IT is a broad term, the U.S. Department of Commerce aptly defines it as "the infrastructure and knowledge that [are] necessary to market information [that is] readily available" (U.S. Department of Commerce 1999a, p. 3). IT positions include technical support, network administration, Web page design, software development, 3-D animation, digital video editing and mapping, hardware repair and maintenance, and database management and design. While IT jobs are heavily concentrated in high-tech sectors such as the computer industry, they have become integrated into most sectors of the economy, most notably the financial and health industries. It is estimated that by 2006 almost half of the nation's workforce will be employed by industries and in jobs that are either major producers or users of information technology products and services (U.S. Department of Commerce 1999b).

Growth in IT Jobs, Shortage of IT Workers

Jobs in the IT sector are growing rapidly. According to reports from the Commerce Department (2000) and the Information Technology Association of America (2000), between 1998 and 2000 the number of people working in IT-producing industries, or in IT occupations in non-high-tech industries, increased from 7.4 million to about 10 million (a

35 percent increase). At the end of 2000, such workers accounted for between 7 and 8 percent of the nation's workforce, up from between 4 and 5 percent in the mid 1990s.[2]

But many jobs in IT sectors and occupations are left unfilled at any given time. According to the 2000 Information Technology Association of America (ITAA) study, it was expected that about 840,000 of the anticipated 1.6 million newly created jobs in IT would go unfilled.[3] The overall vacancy rate for IT jobs was 8.4 percent, notably higher than the rate of 5 or 6 percent for the general economy during a typical economic expansion (Holzer 1994). This shortage hurts the prosperity of companies and of the economy as a whole. Recent studies on the crisis in filling IT service and support positions indicate that the shortage of IT workers has cost companies money through increased expenses such as overtime, lost revenue, and lowered profits, to the amount of $33.4 billion in 1999 (Computer Technology Industry Association 1999; U.S. Department of Commerce 2000; ITAA 2000). These results suggest that there is substantial unmet demand for IT jobs and a strong incentive for companies to connect with workforce development organizations and institutions to meet their labor supply needs.

The difficulty in filling IT jobs is in part related to the economic expansion of the late 1990s, which generated some of the lowest unemployment rates in 30 years. Though the labor market has loosened somewhat during the past three years, its earlier tightness, with unemployment rates hovering between 4.1 and 4.5 percent in 2000 and 2001, left few workers available to fill vacant IT jobs (U.S. Bureau of Labor Statistics 2000, 2001). However, even in a robust economy, there are demographic groups that experience labor market difficulties. The unemployment rate of African Americans (8.6 percent) and Latinos (6.3 percent) in March 2001 was still two to three times as high as that of whites (3.7 percent) (U.S. Bureau of Labor Statistics 2001). Yet it is precisely these groups that, if properly trained, can fill a significant percentage of vacant jobs in the IT sector. Indeed, the National Science Foundation (NSF) Commission for the Advancement of Women and Minorities in Science, Engineering and Technology Development reports that the shortage of high-tech workers could halt sustained economic growth unless more minorities and women are trained for these positions (NSF 2000). Community-based organizations (CBOs) and many community colleges are in an advantageous position to play an intermediary role of helping these workers acquire IT jobs because they have strong connections to inner city and minority communities.

The Skill Requirements of IT Jobs

The need for skills, on both the demand and the supply side of the labor market, challenges workforce development institutions trying to match disadvantaged workers with IT jobs. On the demand side, skill requirements for IT employment tend to be higher than for the overall job market. The U.S. Commerce Department (1999a) estimates that about 60 percent of core IT jobs require at least a college degree, while only 25 percent of jobs outside of this sector require a college degree.[4] Moreover, the skill requirements of jobs, in particular regarding the use of computers, are changing rapidly. Research indicates that in 1984, 25.1 percent of all workers in the United States used a computer at work (Autor, Katz, and Krueger 1998). By 2000, this figure had risen to 68 percent, representing a 170 percent increase since 1984 (Heldrich Center for Workforce Development 2000).[5]

Although skill requirements do appear to be higher in IT jobs, about 40 percent of IT employment does not require a college degree. These non-four-year-college jobs (e.g., telecommunications installer) often require a certificate of training but are positions that workforce development institutions could realistically and successfully train low-skill workers to fill. In order to capitalize on such training opportunities, workforce development institutions must become more strategic in their efforts by researching IT jobs to determine their skill requirements and by orienting training toward those jobs that are a good fit with the interests and abilities of low-income, low-skill workers.

On the supply side, the ability of workforce development institutions to groom disadvantaged workers for IT jobs is hampered by their lack of access to technology. The U.S. Commerce Department (1995) reports that individuals have unequal access to computer technologies according to their income, race, and education. For example, from 1994 to 1998, the gap in computer ownership between whites and African Americans grew by 39.3 percent.[6] Similarly increasing gaps in computer ownership and Internet access are found between rich and poor and between those with college degrees and those without high school diplomas (U.S. Department of Commerce 1999a). These data indicate that historical inequities dividing the nation, characterized by race and poverty, are the very ones along which the digital divide has opened.

THE RECORD OF WORKFORCE DEVELOPMENT POLICY

Can workforce development policy and institutions meet the challenges of placing low-skill workers in a growing number of IT jobs? To answer this question, we must examine the record of past workforce development policies and programs. Over the past 25 years, three programs have largely governed workforce development policy. First came the Comprehensive Employment and Training Act (CETA), from 1973 to 1982, then the Job Training Partnership Act (JTPA), from 1982 to 1998, and, most recently, the Workforce Investment Act of 1998, which took effect in July 2000. The primary objective of these statutes has been to increase the employment, earnings, and retention of disadvantaged and dislocated workers. Although a diverse array of programs has been implemented under these policy regimes, a closer look reveals that there are two broad employment and training models that have been tried: stand-alone basic education, and quick employment—or work first.[7]

The Basic Education Approach

Basic education was the dominant approach to employment and training under CETA and during the early years of JTPA. In this model, programs sought to remedy the lack of basic skills of disadvantaged workers by providing classroom training in basic subjects such as reading, writing, and math. With an objective of enhancing skills, many programs focused on helping program participants achieve their high school diploma or equivalency degree (the GED). The underlying philosophy of this training model is that education and skills are the chief determinants of an individual's future employment and earnings.[8]

Although this approach seemed sound in labor economic theory, evaluations of these basic education and training programs, such as the Work Incentive (WIN) program, indicated only a small impact on participants' employment, wages, or job retention. Where significant wage increases were found for program participants, few of the wage gains were attributable to enhanced skills development; most were due to longer hours worked by program participants (Strawn 1998; U.S. Department of Labor 1995).

There are several reasons basic education programs of the past failed to improve the employment, earnings, and retention of disadvantaged workers. These include the stigmatization of program participants by employers, the short duration of training programs, the lack of relevant skills training, and a disconnect between training programs and employers. Many employers were unwilling to hire program graduates because they viewed these programs as poverty—not training—programs. They were skeptical of the skills and productivity of program graduates and therefore viewed them as irrelevant to their labor needs (Harrison and Weiss 1998; Blank 1997; LaLonde 1995; Manski and Garfinkel 1992). Still, some training programs that used the basic education model were successful in connecting disadvantaged workers to jobs. Successful programs often had close ties to employers. As a result, on-the-job training and job search assistance were based on relevant and up-to-date information from employers (U.S. Department of Labor 1995).

The Work First Approach

During the last 10 years of the JTPA program, following the passage of the Family Support Act in 1988 (which included implementation of the Job Opportunities and Basic Skills [JOBS] program), there was a shift in employment training from centering on basic education and training to focusing more on job search assistance, work experience, and other employment related services. This approach, reinforced and expanded upon after welfare reform in 1996, has become known as the "work first" model. The work first model concentrates on giving participants rapid entry into the labor market by providing short-term training in employment enhancing activities and direct job search assistance, such as help with finding work, writing resumes, and training for interviews. The philosophy supporting the work first strategy is that social or "soft" skills (i.e., punctuality, dress, speech, workplace norms, etc.), knowledge of successful job search strategies, and quick entry into employment are important for obtaining a job and gaining work experience and on-the-job training to find better employment.

The evaluation evidence on work first training programs indicates that in the short term (i.e., one to two years) such programs have a greater impact on participants' employment and wages than the stand-alone basic education efforts. As was found with the basic education models, these work first programs increased earnings through more hours worked, rather than through higher wages (Friedlander and Burtless 1995; Kempel and Haimson 1994). However, the initial increase in the employment and earnings of participants in work first programs disappeared in subsequent years. How quickly and to what extent these program effects fade seems to depend on program design. The effects seem to fade most quickly in low-cost, job-search-only programs, called quick employment programs. However, work first programs that use a mixed approach to training by treating program participants to a full range of employment and training services, including skill development and basic education, in addition to sponsoring job search and soft skills training, have larger and longer-lasting program impacts (Strawn 1998; U.S. Department of Labor 1995). For example, Greater Avenues to Independence (GAIN) programs in Riverside and San Diego, which used a mixed approach to training that included work first and basic education components, sustained employment and wage increases for participants over a five-year period, whereas the employment and earnings of their control group peers who only received job search assistance diminished quickly after the first year of treatment (Strawn 1998; U.S. Department of Labor 1995).

While the mixed approach to work first training had longer lasting employment and wage effects than did quick employment programs, most programs failed to raise job retention rates of participants very much. The few exceptions are programs that combine employer-based training in relevant job skills with basic education, soft skills training and post-employment assistance (Strawn 1998). The evaluation literature clearly indicates that work first programs that focus only on quick employment strategies fail to increase the employment, earnings and retention of participants over the long run. This can be partly attributed to placements in mostly low-wage jobs that are unlikely to provide on-the-job training and advancement potential (Osterman 1995).

Implications for IT: Lessons Learned from the Basic Education and Work First Training Models

Workforce development experience offers some lessons about the potential applicability of basic education and work first training models to workforce development efforts geared toward IT jobs. Given the heightened skill requirements for IT jobs, programs that rely on work first models, which move low-skill workers quickly to work without first providing hard skills training, may have limited worth. Likewise, programs that use a basic education approach are disconnected from employers and lack relevant skills training, so they also may have limited success in linking low-skill workers to IT jobs. However, programs that provide training in concrete and relevant skills, that make connections to employers, and that give attention to post-employment assistance stand a chance of being much more successful. Moreover, job search assistance and soft skills training exercises seem to be effective workforce development practices when, and only when, they are used as complementary activities to hard skills training.

BEST PRACTICES IN WORKFORCE DEVELOPMENT

In response to the limited success of previous workforce development programs, a number of organizations have begun to experiment with different strategies and practices to improve the employment and earnings of low-skill workers. What are these practices, and do they promise to be successful in training low-skill workers for the dynamic IT sector?[9] An examination of the workforce development literature revealed best practices that often can accomplish this. These include employer links, relevant and timely skills training, a mixed approach to training, community colleges, flexibility and responsiveness, networking and collaboration among training providers, and post-employment assistance. We shall look at each of them in turn.

Employer Links

Not surprisingly, programs with links to employers have more success in placing program participants, in raising their wages, and in increasing their job retention than programs without connections to employers. In one example, CBOs contracted with San Francisco Works, a Welfare-to-Work, public-private partnership, to train welfare recipients for employment in the health and financial technologies areas. These CBOs had more success in placing program participants when employers were involved in the training process than when they were not involved (Bliss 2000). Beyond that, organizations in the IT sector that have shown large program impacts on participants' labor market outcomes, such as the Center for Employment and Training in San José, California, have employer involvement as a central component of their training design (Meléndez and Harrison 1998).

A number of factors explain the increased success of training programs that rely on employer involvement. First, training providers who deal with employers are more likely to have current information on work standards, skill requirements, and state-of-the-art technologies. Second, these relationships often lead to employer buy-in. Thus, training agencies with which employers are involved find themselves in the enviable position of being able to negotiate with employers over placing program participants, assisting them after employment, and altering training approaches. The Denver Workforce Initiative (one of the Annie E. Casey Foundation's Jobs Initiative sites), created a workplace curriculum for managers of companies involved with training providers. The curriculum helped managers understand workplace issues from the perspective of disadvantaged workers. This insight has led them to institute workplace policies such as transit assistance and to change cultural norms at work in ways that help low-skill workers stay employed at the firm longer, such as by supporting English as a Second Language (ESL) courses (Annie E. Casey Foundation 2000).

Third, such programs provide employers with incentives to hire program participants. Employers involved in training programs typically reduce their search and training costs because of greater access to an appropriately trained labor supply.[10] Thus, all of these factors tend to lead to greater placement and employment rates, wages, and retention for participants trained in programs with employer involvement. At the same time, firms that participate in external training programs also benefit through increased productivity, increased profits because of lower search and training costs, and greater retention of employees (U.S. Department of Labor 1996).

Employer involvement is accomplished in a variety of ways. The Bay Area Video Coalition (BAVC), a media arts center in San Francisco that successfully trains participants in multimedia and Web design, strategically uses its advisory board—made up of elected officials, members of community organizations, and industry executives—to gain access to employers (Chapple et al. 2000). Some local governments, such as the cities of Berkeley and Portland, use "first source hiring" strategies to bring employment opportunities to disadvantaged workers. They negotiate with businesses for access to job opportunities in exchange for development incentives (such as loans and tax abatements) (Molina 1998). Some organizations use sectoral strategies to target training at a cluster of jobs and employers in growth occupations and industries in the region (Annie E. Casey Foundation 2000). Others target IT jobs specifically. (Project Quest, a successful training program in San Antonio created by the Industrial Areas Foundation and two CBOs, focuses on specialized occupations in environmental technologies, financial services, and health care [Lautsch and Osterman 1998].) To achieve a narrow focus, some organizations conduct analyses of growth industries using labor market data on the region, and some hire job developers to directly approach firms to discuss the benefits of involvement with external training organizations (Annie E. Casey Foundation 2000).

Employer involvement is also uneven. Larger firms and firms with more resources are much more likely to participate than smaller and resource-poor firms, in part because of economies of scale: the former usually have personnel or expertise available to help facilitate their participation in external training programs (U.S. Department of Labor 1996). In addition, firms with unmet labor needs are much more likely to participate than those with fewer labor supply problems, for obvious reasons (Holzer 1999). Tucker Technology, a national, minority-owned telecommunications installation and maintenance company based in Oakland, California, faced severe labor shortages as a result of the explosive growth in fax machines, cellular phones, and Internet hookups. To satisfy its labor needs, the company formed links with CBOs throughout the country. They in turn designed and customized telecommunications installation training curricula for low-income community participants (Caggiano 1999).

Relevant and Timely Skills Training

Given the pace at which required skills and tasks in IT jobs change, relevant and timely skills training seems mandatory to successfully place and keep low-skill workers in IT jobs. But actual training in relevant skills has been absent from previous employment and training models, especially those that follow work first strategies. In large part, employer involvement in training will help agencies fill this absence and accomplish relevant and timely training. Another way to accomplish it is to contract with other agencies that have track records of successfully training workers in relevant skills. In the Casey Foundation's St. Louis Jobs Initiative, the Better Family Life (BFL) organization, which was responsible for coordinating training efforts as part of this initiative, asked St. Louis Community College to conduct its training because of the college's success at leading training in the past and its larger facilities and better equipment. This led to the creation of WorkLink, a program whereby BFL concentrates on soft skill and other pre-employment training while the community college trains the hard skill set (Annie E. Casey Foundation 2000).

The establishment of standardized curricula for various skill sets is another way to effectively train workers in relevant skills. Mature occupations are usually defined by skills standards, which are used to establish consistent information about the set of skills required for a particular job. The National Skills Standards Board defines these standards as "performance specifications that identify the knowledge, skills and abilities an individual needs to succeed in the workplace" (Northwest Center for Emerging Technologies 1999, p. 4). Hence, standards allow employers, trainers, and educational institutes to determine the exact skill requirements of jobs. Once established, standards allow job trainers to develop curricula to train workers in specific skills, and by definition such training should produce somewhat consistent skill outcomes across different training sites. This consistency of training allows programs to certify their program graduates, which plays two roles: it provides employers certainty about the bundle of skills that the potential worker possesses, and it also provides the potential worker with a marketable credential.

Job trainers in IT need to become familiar with IT skill standards, and standards must be updated regularly to keep up with the rapidly changing skill requirements of IT professions. There are a number of organizations that are establishing these standards. A national leader in creating standards in IT is the Northwest Center for Emerging Technologies (NWCET). Many institutions offer general or vendor-specific programs that lead to certification in an array of IT skills. For example, the Computer Technology Industry Association (CompTIA) offers a program on computer repair and maintenance that leads to an A+ certification. It has trained nearly 180,000 workers worldwide (CompTIA 1999).

The timing of skills training also matters to success. The literature indicates that training in hard as well as soft skills *before* job placement produces the greatest positive effect on job retention. San Francisco Works found that instruction in hard skills such as computer training for jobs in the financial and banking sector before employment or internship placements produced longer job retention rates for participants than when it occurred simultaneously with work (Bliss 2000). Presumably, training before placement led to greater familiarity with the computer skills and components, which in turn fostered greater confidence and ability on the subsequent job. This lesson contrasts sharply with the philosophy of work first, which attempts to move participants quickly into jobs and to rely on on-the-job training and job experience to train them.

Mixed Approach to Training

Work first employment programs clearly show that assistance in job search and training in workplace norms and customs is an important component of training, particularly for those participants who have been out of the labor force for long periods of time. A 1995 study by the U.S. Department of Labor (USDOL) indicates that successful training programs are ones that include soft skills training in addition to job-specific hard skills. The Casey Foundation's New Orleans Jobs Initiative (NOJI) has followed this strategy and gotten positive preliminary program results. Participants receive technical skills training and pre-employment and soft skills training, which teaches workplace codes (Annie E. Casey Foundation 2000). Welfare-to-Work programs such as Riverside's GAIN program, Florida's Family Transition Program and the Baltimore Options program also follow this balanced approach with signs of success (Strawn 1998).

Community Colleges: Flexibility and Responsiveness

Partnerships with community colleges will be increasingly important in workforce development, particularly in IT jobs. Community colleges have more capacity and resources than smaller job training sites or CBOs, which have traditionally served the disadvantaged. In fact, under the WIA there are great incentives for community colleges to play this role. To what extent they do so will be determined by a number of factors. It will depend on how far such institutions succeed in streamlining their policies and procedures with regard to changes in curricula, programs, and degrees or certificates; in increasing their funding base for training equipment; in connecting with industry to determine the appropriate and skill sets for which they should train; and in reaching out to CBOs to increase their potential client or student base (Lerman, Riegg, and Salzman 2000; Brewer and Gray 1997; Grubb 1996).

Community colleges can also play a big role in providing hard skills training for IT jobs. However, in order for this to occur, changes must be made both at the administrative level to streamline the bureaucratic process and bolster funding, and at the practical level by reaching out to industry. For example, NOJI is a collaboration of CBOs (such as the Citywide Tenement Group and All Congregations Together, a faith-based group), a local community college, businesses, and foundations. The community college is responsible for the technical skills training. To design the best training curriculum, the college worked closely with employers to determine industry standards. In addition, NOJI convinced policymakers and community college administrators to invest $65,000 in state-of-the-art machinery for its enrollees to use in training (Annie E. Casey Foundation 2000). These changes in responsiveness by the administration at the community college are illustrative of the kind of flexibility colleges must exhibit in order to make themselves part of the engine of economic growth in local economies.

Networking and Collaboration among Training Providers

No single organization usually has the internal capacity (size, resources, equipment, facilities, access to clients, and expertise) to complete the training process from beginning to end; thus, collaboration is necessary for success. Even when organizations appear to be encroaching on one another's "territory," either in geographic or program areas; collaboration may be effective (Harrison and Weiss 1998).

There are a number of examples that illustrate this. In both the St. Louis and the New Orleans jobs initiatives, CBOs and community colleges partner to accomplish their training goals. In both cases, community colleges conduct the hard skills training because oftentimes the CBOs do not have the expertise, the capacity or the resources and equipment to conduct the training themselves. However, the community colleges gain from these partnerships as well. They benefit from the additional participants referred to them from these CBOs, which usually have deep roots in disadvantaged communities, and from the additional soft skill training that CBOs conduct (Annie E. Casey Foundation 2000).

Such partnerships are also likely to benefit community technology centers (CTCs). Many CTCs are publicly funded organizations designed to close the digital divide by making computers and the Internet accessible to individuals in low-income and minority communities. Although their primary purpose is to provide access to technology, many CTCs, such as the Community Technology and Training Centers (CTTC) in Austin, Texas, are moving into more formal technical training for IT jobs (Chapple et al. 2000). To do this, they are partnering with larger training institutions, such as community colleges, because of their size and expertise. As these programs evolve, and as their training goals grow to include soft skills training, many CTCs presumably will look to partner with CBOs that have expertise in conducting such training.

These evolutions suggest the need for more regionally based coordinating agencies, which can facilitate networking and partnering among workforce development institutions. For example, Workplace Incorporated provides workforce development by coordinating job training, employment, and education services in the Bridgeport-Stamford region of Connecticut. It brings together community colleges, technical institutes and CBOs to train workers in computer repair and in computer-related design and drafting (U.S. Department of Commerce 1999a). Some CBOs are also playing this role, though perhaps not explicitly. The New Community Corporation in Newark, New Jersey, one of the largest community development corporations in the United States, brings together a variety of interests including corporate, education, and trade union representatives from throughout the region who help one another accomplish their employment and training goals (Harrison and Weiss 1998).

Post-Employment Assistance

Post-employment assistance can help participants learn new skills quickly and continuously, so as to keep pace with the rapid changes in task requirements in IT jobs. Post-employment programs can be located either at the worksite or at an external training institution. Research indicates that such programs are particularly effective when developed in conjunction with employers and that they are sensitive to specific workplace dynamics (Bliss 2000). In post-employment assistance, whether it takes the form of on-the-job training or formal apprenticeship programs, employers provide continued instruction in job skills. The Cooperative Health Care Network offers both in-service training and career upgrading programs to its graduates, with the objective of strengthening or updating skills for the current job or facilitating career advancement (Strawn 1998).

Post-employment assistance is most effective when it addresses the entire range of issues that confront disadvantaged workers. Indeed, this form of assistance is particularly important for reducing absenteeism and increasing job retention. Recent research indicates that 64 percent of the absenteeism problems of welfare recipients stem from child care and transportation problems (Holzer and Stoll 2001). To address these kinds of issues, the Chicago Commons Employment and Training Center provides comprehensive on-site support services, transportation assistance, and child care for its program graduates (Strawn 1998).

Another post-employment service some programs offer is the provision of mentors. Mentors give program graduates a point of contact for raising concerns, seeking advice, asking questions, and resolving conflicts at work. Though no studies have been conducted to assess whether such programs improve job retention and mobility, anecdotal evidence from San Francisco Works strongly suggests that such an approach is effective at lengthening participants' job tenure (Bliss 2000). One strategy is to use senior program graduates as mentors for recent graduates. In the St. Louis Jobs Initiative, program graduates who have stayed in a job for at least six months are asked to become program alumni, which entails assuming mentoring responsibility for current or recent program graduates (Annie E. Casey Foundation 2000). Some programs approach personnel in firms where graduates are placed and ask them to become mentors to the graduates. Many of the businesses that partnered with San Francisco Works matched employee volunteer mentors with San Francisco Works' program graduates.

CONCLUSION

The growth in demand for IT workers and the rise of innovative workforce development practices suggests there is great hope that new training institutions can play a large role in linking low-skill disadvantaged workers to IT jobs. But the rising and changing skill requirements of IT jobs present challenges in doing so.

This analysis reveals a number of lessons for workforce development practice. To be successful at placing low-skill workers in IT jobs, workforce development institutions must first move away from ineffective employment training models. Neither basic education training programs, which are disconnected from employers and lack relevant skill training, nor work first models, which move workers quickly to work without skills training, are likely to work in this new, skills-driven economy. Instead, workforce development institutions must become more focused on a mixed training approach that blends hard and soft skills. But in order to do so effectively, such institutions must be able to identify relevant jobs and skills in the IT sector for which they can realistically and effectively train low-skill workers. And, to the extent possible, they must include lifelong learning components to continuously upgrade the skills of participants. They must also be sufficiently connected to the IT sector to gain information quickly about the changing skills required for jobs and adapt in a reasonable amount of time to satisfy those new skill demands.

Likewise, workforce development systems must be dynamic and flexible in order to quickly respond to technology and changing skill characteristics of IT jobs. This includes adopting innovative practices such as establishing employer links, providing relevant and timely skills training, using a mixed approach to training, strategically networking with other training institutions, and instituting post-employment assistance. To the extent that institutions can bring about these changes, they should have success at continuing their mission of providing labor market opportunities for low-skill workers and should become key and valued players in the IT sector.

There is great hope that such practices can be promoted and instituted on a national scale under WIA. When it replaced JTPA as the main federal policy guiding workforce development, it mandated integration of national and state job training programs, reduced the number of funding streams from 70 to 3, and consolidated a patchwork of some 60 federal job training programs that had been generated over the past six decades. WIA is an ambitious attempt to rewrite and make sense of a wide variety of federal job training programs. In concept, it provides considerable flexibility in the provision of training services by creating a set of performance standards and by providing opportunities for trainers to understand the needs of industry in the local labor market. Such policy and program characteristics hold promise, since they promote flexibility and industry responsiveness. To what extent that promise can be realized under WIA would seem to depend on WIA's capacity to do three things: avoid undue influence by work first training models, obtain sufficient federal and state funding for training providers to offer relevant skills training, and foster a sharing of information and resources between business and training providers. Successful models exist to point the way.

Notes

The author would like to thank PolicyLink for its generous support of this project.

1. The term *workforce development* is used to describe those public policies (such as contained in the federal government's Job Training and Partnership Act) and nonprofit institutions (such as community-based organizations, other not-for-profits, and community colleges) that aim to improve the skills and therefore the labor market outcomes of disadvantaged workers in the United States, including the less educated, welfare recipients, dislocated workers, and disadvantaged youth. Although much of the coordination of workforce development has historically emanated from the federal government, increasingly state and local governments and private foundations, among others, are helping to shape workforce development in the United States.
2. Reports from the U.S. Department of Housing and Urban Development (2000) and the U.S. Department of Labor (1999) also confirm this trend. In fact, the U.S. Department of Housing and Urban Development estimates that in the largest 101 metropolitan areas in the United States from 1992 to 1997, high-tech jobs grew at a much faster pace (31.2 percent) than overall job growth (13.6 percent).
3. This estimate compares favorably to earlier studies of more limited IT occupations, which indicate that about 346,000 vacancies are anticipated, using a sample of for-profit companies with more than 100 employees (ITAA 1998).
4. This estimate of the percentage of jobs in the general economy that require a college degree is fairly consistent with recent data from other representative employer surveys, which show that about 20 percent of all jobs in the economy require at least a college degree (see Holzer 1996).
5. Both studies rely on Current Population Survey data from the National Bureau of Economic Research, collected in response to the same survey question.
6. This widening gap occurred even though computer ownership by African Americans grew at a faster rate, more than doubling from 10.3 percent in 1994 to 23.2 percent in 1998. Ownership among whites grew from 27.1 to 46.6 percent during that period.
7. The division of workforce development models into basic education and work first has also been noted in other studies (see, for example, Strawn 1998; U.S. Department of Labor 1995; Grubb 1995).
8. These ideas were in part influenced by the development of human capital theory in economics (see, for example, Becker [1964] for a discussion of these ideas).
9. In reviewing this literature, a broad base of training organizations was examined. It included, among others, CBOs, community technology centers, community colleges, and public and private initiatives and training intermediaries. This discussion highlights a number of promising practices. However, the coverage of these practices should not be viewed as exhaustive, but rather as representative of some of the more important practices that are likely to be particularly useful to agencies as they train workers for the dynamic IT sector. Moreover, these

practices should not be viewed as mutually exclusive: some practices may serve dual purposes, and many organizations incorporate more than one practice into their training programs and strategies.

10. Employers spend a nontrivial amount of money to keep any one low-skill job filled, particularly when one factors in the high turnover rates that are characteristic of these jobs. Research indicates that employers' search costs for low to semiskilled workers average between $300 and $1,500, depending on how difficult it is to find appropriate labor, and that training costs for these workers range from $700 to $3,000, depending on the type of training required (Frazis et al. 1998; Bishop 1994).

References

Annie E. Casey Foundation. 2000. *Stronger Links: New Ways to Connect Low-Skill Workers to Better Jobs.* Baltimore: Annie E. Casey Foundation.

Autor, David, Lawrence Katz, and Alan Krueger 1998. "Computing Inequality: Have Computers Changed the Labor Market?" *Quarterly Journal of Economics* 113(4): 1169–1214.

Becker, Gary. 1964. *Human Capital: A Theoretical and Empirical Analysis with Special Reference to Education.* Chicago: University of Chicago Press.

Bishop, John. 1994. "The Incidence of and Payoff to Employer Training." Faculty Working Paper 94–17, Center for Advanced Human Resource Studies, Cornell University.

Blank, Rebecca M. 1997. *It Takes a Nation: A New Agenda for Fighting Poverty.* New York and Princeton, NJ: Russell Sage Foundation and Princeton University Press.

Bliss, Steven. 2000. *San Francisco Works: Toward an Employer-Led Approach to Welfare Reform and Workforce Development.* New York: Manpower Demonstration Research Corporation.

Brewer, Dominic, and Maryann Gray. 1997. *Connecting College and Community in the New Economy? An Analysis of Community College Faculty–Labor Market Linkages.* Berkeley, CA: Rand Education.

Caggiano, Christopher. 1999. "Insider Training." Part of a special section on *Inc.* magazine's Inner City 100. *Inc.* 21(6): 63–64.

Chapple, Karen, Matthew Zook, Radhika Kunamneni, AnnaLee Saxenian, Steven Weber, and Beverly Crawford. 2000. *From Promising Practices to Promising Futures: Job Training in Information Technology.* New York and Oakland, CA: Ford Foundation and PolicyLink.

Computer Technology Industry Association. 1999. *CompTIA Workforce Study: The Crisis in IT Service & Support.* Lombard, IL: Computer Technology

Industry Association.

Frazis, Harley, Maury Gittleman, Michael Horrigan, and Mary Joyce. 1998. "Results from the 1995 Survey of Employer-Provided Training." *Monthly Labor Review* 121(6): 3–13.

Friedlander, Daniel, and Gary Burtless. 1995. *Five Years After: The Long-Term Effects of Welfare-to-Work Programs.* New York: Russell Sage Foundation.

Grubb, W. Norton. 1995. *Evaluating Job Training Programs in the United States: Evidence and Explanations.* Training policy study no. 17. Geneva: International Labor Organization.

———. 1996. *Learning to Work: The Case for Reintegrating Job Training and Education.* New York: Russell Sage Foundation.

Harrison, Bennett, and Marcus Weiss. 1998. *Workforce Development Networks: Community-Based Organizations and Regional Alliances.* Thousands Oaks, CA: Sage Publications.

Heldrich Center for Workforce Development at Rutgers University and Center for Survey Research and Analysis at the University of Connecticut. 2000. *Nothing But Net: American Workers and the Information Economy.* Work Trends V: Americans' Attitudes about Work, Employers and Government, vol. 2, no. 1. New Brunswick, NJ: Rutgers University.

Holzer, Harry J. 1994. "Job Vacancy Rates in the Firm: An Empirical Analysis." *Economica* 61(241): 17–36.

———. 1996. *What Employers Want.* New York: Russell Sage Foundation.

———. 1999. "Employer Demand for Welfare Recipients and the Business Cycle." In *Economic Conditions and Welfare Reform,* Sheldon Danziger, ed. Kalamazoo, MI: W.E. Upjohn Institute for Employment Research, pp.187–218.

Holzer, Harry J., and Michael A. Stoll. 2001. *Employers and Welfare Recipients: The Effect of Welfare Reform in the Workplace.* San Francisco: Public Policy Institute of California.

Information Technology Association of America. 1998. *Help Wanted 98.* Arlington, VA: Information Technology Association of America.

———. 2000. *Bridging the Gap: Information Technology Skills for a New Millennium.* Arlington, VA: Information Technology Association of America.

Kemple, James J., and Joshua Haimson. 1994. *Florida's Project Independence: Program Implementation, Participation Patterns, and First-Year Impacts.* New York: Manpower Demonstration Research Corporation.

LaLonde, Robert J. 1995. "The Promise of Public Sector-Sponsored Training Programs." *Journal of Economic Perspectives* 9(Spring): 149–168.

Lautsch, Brenda A., and Paul Osterman. 1998. "Changing the Constraints: A Successful Employment and Training Strategy." In *Jobs and Economic De-*

velopment: Strategies and Practice, Robert P. Giloth, ed. Thousand Oaks, CA: Sage Publications, pp. 214–233.

Lerman, Robert I., Stephanie K. Riegg, and Harold Salzman. 2000. *The Role of Community Colleges in Expanding the Supply of Information Technology Workers.* Washington, DC: Urban Institute.

Manski, Charles F., and Irwin Garfinkel, eds. 1992. *Evaluating Welfare and Training Programs.* Cambridge, MA: Harvard University Press.

Meléndez, Edwin, and Bennett Harrison. 1998. "Matching the Disadvantaged to Job Opportunities: Structural Explanations for the Past Successes of the Center for Employment Training." *Economic Development Quarterly* 12(1): 3–11.

Molina, Frieda. 1998. *Making Connections: A Study of Employment Linkage Programs.* Washington, DC: Center for Community Change.

National Science Foundation. 2000. *Land of Plenty: Diversity as America's Competitive Edge in Science, Engineering and Technology.* Washington, DC: National Science Foundation.

Northwest Center for Emerging Technologies. 1999. *Building a Foundation for Tomorrow: Skill Standards for Information Technology.* Bellevue, WA: Northwest Center for Emerging Technologies.

Osterman, Paul. 1995. "Skill, Training, and Work Organization in American Establishments." *Industrial Relations* 34(2): 125–146.

Strawn, Julie. 1998. *Beyond Job Search or Basic Education: Rethinking the Role of Skills in Welfare Reform.* Washington, DC: Center for Law and Social Policy.

U.S. Bureau of Labor Statistics. 2000. *Employment and Earnings.* Washington, DC: U.S. Bureau of Labor Statistics.

———. 2001. *Employment and Earnings.* Washington, DC: U.S. Bureau of Labor Statistics.

U.S. Department of Commerce. 1999a. *The Digital Workforce: Building Infotech Skill at the Speed of Innovation.* Washington, DC: U.S. Department of Commerce.

———. 1999b. *The Emerging Digital Economy II.* Washington, DC: U.S. Department of Commerce.

———. 2000. *Digital Economy 2000.* Washington, DC: U.S. Department of Commerce.

U.S. Department of Housing and Urban Development. 2000. *State of the Cities 2000.* Washington, DC: U.S. Department of Housing and Urban Development.

U.S. Department of Labor. 1995. *What's Working (and What's Not): A Summary of Research in the Economic Impacts of Employment Training Programs.* Washington, DC: U.S. Department of Labor.

———. 1996. *Involving Employers in Training: Best Practices.* Washington, DC: U.S. Department of Labor.

———. 1999. *Futurework: Trends and Challenges for Work in the 21st Century.* Washington, DC: U.S. Department of Labor.

7
Community Technology Centers

Training Disadvantaged Workers for Information Technology Jobs[1]

Lisa J. Servon
New School University

Information technology (IT) has wrought fundamental changes throughout society. IT has been instrumental in the shift from an industrial age to a network age. We now live in a society in which the production, acquisition, and flow of knowledge drive the economy and in which global information networks represent key infrastructure. These changes have had a profound effect on the labor market; workforce development intersects in important ways with the digital divide. Workers who do not have IT skills have access to much less opportunity in the labor market than those who do. Importantly, the area of workforce development allows for relatively straightforward intervention. This chapter focuses on the labor market for IT workers and how innovative programs and policies can be used to benefit both employers, who cannot fill available jobs, and disadvantaged workers, who cannot find good jobs. The focus here is primarily on entry-level IT jobs and workers because of this book's overarching concern for disadvantaged workers. "Disadvantaged" refers to those workers who have been largely detached from the labor force, who lack requisite skills, who may face discrimination in the labor market, and who are currently unemployed or employed in jobs that fail to pay a living wage.

This chapter makes two primary arguments. The first is that the shift to an information-driven economy involves a concomitant shift in the perception of workforce development activity. Rather than viewing these programs as social welfare—which is how they have traditionally been viewed—we must now see them as legitimate components of larger economic development strategies. The second is that the current economy—in which there is a high demand for entry-level IT workers—presents a unique opportunity for moving disadvantaged people into good jobs. IT jobs tend to be good jobs. Many require less than two years of training and, as the economy continues to shift in ways that require more IT skills from workers, these opportunities will continue to open up.

ECONOMIC SHIFTS AND THE IT LABOR MARKET

The shift from a manufacturing to a service and information-based economy has been described in great detail elsewhere; this section touches only on the issues most relevant to this chapter (Castells 1996; Bluestone and Harrison 1982). First, information plays a different and larger role in the current economy than in previous economic incarnations—information is now both a product of the new economy and an increasingly important input to production processes (Castells 1996). These structural shifts in the economy have impacted the sectoral composition of regions and the way in which production processes are organized across space. Regions that were dominant in manufacturing have declined unless they have been able to remake themselves.[2] New cities and regions in which IT plays a large role—Silicon Valley, Seattle, and Austin, for example—have grown substantially and have become leaders in the new economy. Internationally, a few cities—New York, London, and Tokyo—have achieved an uber-status as megacities (Sassen 1991). And less developed countries have become important as places in which to locate parts of the production process that can benefit from low-skilled labor and loose environmental regulations.

How have these changes affected the labor market in terms of entry-level jobs? The effects can be described in terms of a "skills mismatch" and a "spatial mismatch" (Servon and Nelson 1999). First, there has been a significant decrease in the availability of low-skilled, stable manufacturing jobs. These jobs used to offer relatively dependable work at living wages and with benefits. The shift from a manufacturing to a more service-oriented economy has changed the kinds of jobs available. Low-end service sector jobs tend to be lower quality jobs: they are often unstable or temporary, pay low wages, and offer few if any benefits. Although many cities have carved out new roles as service centers, the service sector tends to be highly polarized in occupation and wage structure between skilled and unskilled workers (Bluestone and Harrison 1982; Sassen 1991). As a result, the shift away from manufacturing has tended to benefit college-educated professionals and high-end service workers (Kasarda 1985). Many inner-city residents displaced by structural changes in the economy have found new jobs in the service sector, but these jobs tend to be low-wage, unstable, and without benefits. "As a result" Atkinson says, "cities face the challenge of bridging a growing gap between the skills required for employment in advanced services concentrated in urban cores and the limited skills that many entry-level big city residents bring to the job market" (Atkinson 1998, pp. 157–158). As technological literacy is added to the skill set needed to join the information economy, IT exacerbates the skills mismatch between higher end jobs in central cities and the low-skilled urban labor force living there (Atkinson 1998). Even low skilled tasks require proficiency in the use of telephones, fax machines, and computer equipment (U.S. Department of Commerce 1999). The result is that inequality persists, and many jobs in IT fields go unfilled.

The spatial mismatch has to do with economic and spatial restructuring that has resulted in a loss of stable, well-paid employment opportunities for urban residents. Advances in IT have lessened locational constraints, enabling firms offering low-skill jobs, particularly in manufacturing and routine services, to leave the inner city for the suburbs and, in some cases, overseas locations where production costs are lower. Meanwhile, segregation and discrimination have prohibited the poor and minority populations from following these jobs to the periphery, creating a spatial mismatch between low-income urban residents and employment opportunities (Teitz and Chapple 1998). IT will likely facilitate the further decentralization of economic activity, heightening the spatial mismatch, particularly as teleworking becomes more common and firms develop new ways of transmitting producer and personal services electronically (Graham and Marvin 1996). Some fear that the continued reconfiguration of spatial patterns, made possible by IT, will further cluster the affluent while leaving the poor trapped in places with few good jobs and services (Mitchell 1999).

The rise of the IT sector, however, has opened a unique window of opportunity. The Information Technology Association of America

(ITAA) estimates that the demand for IT workers in 2002 was 1,148,639, and that 578,711 of these positions would go unfilled. Many of these positions are entry level. For example, technical support people, who constitute 18 percent of the IT workforce (and who are entry level workers) are the most in demand, making up one quarter of all new positions in the field (ITAA 2001, 2002). These are relatively good jobs. According to a recent report issued by the U.S. Department of Labor (USDOL), "real average wages in the high-tech industries increased 19 percent since 1990, compared to a 5 percent average increase for the private sector as a whole. The average high-tech job pays 78 percent more than the average non-high-tech job—$53,000, compared to $30,000" (USDOL 1999, p. 3).

Many jobs experiencing high growth do not require a four-year college education. Harrison and Weiss cite research showing that for the period from 1992 to 2005, "only one of eight higher than average growth occupations will require a college degree, whereas fully two-thirds will require no more than a high school diploma" (1998, p. 10). A 1999 study put out by USDOL found that the majority of jobs currently being created require less than an associate's degree but often require other skills (USDOL 1999, p. 5). According to the USDOL researchers, "the alleged disappearance of low-skilled job opportunities in America has been exaggerated. There is, and will continue to be, considerable room in the economy for workers with modest formal schooling" (Harrison and Weiss 1998, p. 10).

Although not all of these high growth jobs are in IT or in well-paying sectors, many entry-level IT jobs also require less than a four-year college degree. At the same time, entry-level IT jobs do require specific skills, and the rapidly changing nature of the IT economy requires that IT workers continually upgrade their skills.

Furthermore, if we look at other occupational sectors we see that technology literacy is now viewed as part of the bundle of skills a worker must bring to the workforce. The Economic Policy Institute found that attainment of computer skills "tends to widen pay differences between educational groups more so than in the past" (Civille 1995, p. 202). In this new economy, "good jobs require analytical research skills, not simply the ability to read and write and follow instructions" (Civille 1995, p. 202). The Secretary of Labor's Commission on Acquiring Necessary Skills (SCANS) outlines the following set of five competencies for the high performance worker: using resources, dealing with interpersonal relationships, working with information, working with systems, and working with technology" (Civille 1995, p. 203).

THE DEMAND FOR IT WORKERS

The ITAA estimated that approximately 9.9 million people constituted the IT workforce in 2002, a 5 percent reduction from 2001 (ITAA 2001, 2002). The demand for IT workers has been experienced first in cities such as Seattle, Austin, Boston, and San Francisco, which have economies that are heavily dependent on technology industries. IT corporations deciding where to locate a new facility weight the quality of the workforce heavily in their decision matrices. For example, in a recent survey of industry leaders in San Francisco's Multimedia Gulch, access to "a qualified labor pool" was cited as the most important reason to locate in San Francisco. The multimedia industry's demand for a mix of technical and creative talent induces firms to locate in that city, even though the cost of doing business would be significantly lower in other areas. However, although survey participants stated that access to a qualified labor pool was the reason for doing business in San Francisco, these same firms still found it challenging to find qualified staff (including entry level employees).

But the demand for workers with IT skills is not isolated to traditional IT industries. Given the transformation of business practices that information technologies have brought about, universities, banks, hotels, and insurance corporations all need technical support workers, management information systems (MIS) managers, and system administrators. According to ITAA, of the 1,148,000 IT workers needed in 2002, 826,000, or 72 percent, were needed by non-IT companies. Non-IT companies are the largest employer of the IT workforce and have the highest unmet demand for skilled IT workers (ITAA 2001, 2002). A report issued by the Council on Competitiveness cites a 1997 survey in which nearly 70 percent of CEOs identified the skills shortage as the number one barrier to growth (Congressional Commission 2000). Non-IT firms also account for the majority of new demand for IT workers (ITAA 2001, p. 12). A 2000 survey conducted by the Employment Policy Foundation found that one-third of polled businesses said they

Table 7.1 IT Demand Gap, by Job Category

	All companies w/ 50+ employees	
IT career cluster	Demand	Gap
Technical support	218,238	107,624
Database development/administration	110,104	46,166
Programming/software engineer	134,637	69,292
Web development/administration	120,982	56,957
Network design/administration	186,613	85,534
Technical writing	17,461	8,526
Enterprise systems	75,177	32,026
Other	26,437	13,362
Digital media	11,940	5,871
Total	901,589	425,358

SOURCE: ITAA (2001).

would move operations overseas if qualified workers were not available in the United States.[3] The shortage of IT workers has spread from cities with economies heavily dependent on IT to other regions. Table 7.1 illustrates the gap in demand for IT workers by job category.

Interestingly, ITAA's estimates of the demand gap in IT workers are up from a year ago but still down from 2000 figures. The changes in demand, depicted in Table 7.1, reflect the corrections in the market that have been occurring over the past few years.

Industry spokespeople, like investors, were overly optimistic about the growth potential of very thin firms.[4] The drop in demand should be thought of as a correction, not as the beginning of a long-term decline in demand for workers with IT skills. An upward trend in this demand will likely continue (Foster-Bey, Rawlings, and Turner 2000). Although this sizable change clearly demands closer analysis, the fact remains that demand for IT workers is very strong and the gap is significant. The continued need for IT workers is evidence that a fundamental shift in the type of work being performed across sectors is under way (ITAA 2000, p. 11). Programs to train disadvantaged workers for IT jobs, then, need not be thought of as social welfare, but rather as a way to fuel an economy hungry for skilled workers. According to Bruce Bernstein, president of the New York Software Industry Association (NYSIA), the need to train low-skilled workers for available jobs is "an economic necessity, not a social prerogative." This shift in thinking is important. The perception of workforce development programs—especially those that target public assistance recipients—is often that they are in essence social work rather than economic development. Framing the issue as an economic development issue rather than strictly as a social welfare one is more likely to generate bipartisan support in the public sector as well as key backing from the private sector.

The demand for IT workers is likely to increase as the new mode of production continues to be absorbed and assimilated across institutions and industries (Meares and Sargent 1999). According to Castells, "the generalization of knowledge-based production and management to the whole realm of economic processes on a global scale requires fundamental social, cultural, and institutional transformations that, if the historical record of other technological revolutions is considered, will take some time" (Castells 1996, p. 91). As this process of transformation continues, the demand for workers with IT skills will only grow. A Department of Commerce report projects that by 2006 nearly half of all workers will be employed in industries that produce or intensively use information technology, products, and services (USDOL 1999, p. 60).

WHAT IS DIFFERENT ABOUT THE IT LABOR MARKET?

Classifying IT workers

Attempting to define and describe the IT labor market is challenging given the diversity of ways in which digital technologies are utilized. The most narrow definition of the IT labor market would include only "core" IT occupations: computer scientists, computer engineers, systems analysts, and computer programmers. These professions constitute the high end of the IT labor market. Core IT jobs require the most education and skills and pay the most. Workers with these skills are in greatest demand.

This narrow definition of the IT labor market fails to reflect the fact that as the economy becomes more digitized, virtually all occupations involve some use of information technologies. Although this paper will not discuss the way in which traditional sectors of the economy (administrative, retail sales, etc.) have been transformed by the adoption of information technologies, it is important to note that the IT labor market is much broader than core IT occupations. There is a large gray area between computer scientists and salespeople who use computers, and this gray area is occupied by a broad range of emerging IT occupations.

Recognizing the breadth of IT-related occupations, the Northwest Center for Emerging Technologies (NWCET) has developed eight career clusters that both expand the frame to include a larger universe of IT jobs and make more precise distinctions between types of IT work. The NWCET clusters enable a finer-grained approach to research and program design for IT-based workforce development. Using these eight IT career clusters can help provide better answers to key questions such as these: What IT jobs are most in demand? What skills are required to perform these jobs? What are the best methods for providing and acquiring these skills? (ITAA 2000, p. 8)

According to the ITAA, the former, narrower scope, which is still used by other research organizations, misses "the dramatic impact that the Internet, e-commerce and other influences have had on the nature of jobs and work." The NWCET job categories are as follows:

Database Development and Administration. This is the creation and management of structures, tools, forms and reports that help companies understand their data. Work functions include needs analysis, database design, testing, and maintenance.

Digital Media. This is the process of bringing sound, video, graphics, animation, and text together to create digital media products. Delivery platforms include Web sites, videos, computer games, and CDs. Work functions include needs analysis, visual and functional design, media production and acquisition, and design implementation and testing.

Enterprise Systems Analysis and Integration. This is the integration of complex and numerous information technology systems to create comprehensive customer solutions. Work functions include defining customer requirements, determining systems solutions, providing strategic direction for systems configuration, managing technology, and implementing enterprise-wide systems.

Network Design and Administration. This entails the development of networks that connect users to computer systems via cable, fiber optics, and wireless communications. Work functions include design and analysis, configuration and implementation, and the testing, administering, monitoring, and management of networks.

Programming and Software Engineering. This involves the translation of business problems into codes a computer can understand through the use of various programming languages. Work functions include analyzing needs, developing structures, designing, developing, implementing, and testing computer programs.

Technical Support. This involves assisting customers in diagnosing and correcting computer systems problems. Work functions include troubleshooting, customer service, hardware and software installation, configuration, upgrades, and systems maintenance and monitoring.

Technical Writing. This encompasses documenting, explaining, translating, and interpreting technical information for a variety of audiences. Work functions include writing, editing, and publishing of technical documents for products, product training, internal systems, Web-based training, and more.

Web Development and Administration. The creation, maintenance, and development of Web sites. Work functions include content and technical analysis; development, implementation, and maintenance of Web applications and site design; and management of Web environments and enterprise-wide Web activities (NWCET 1999).

What Is an Entry-Level IT Worker?

An important aspect of the IT labor market has to do with changing requirements for entry-level jobs. As the technology required to do particular jobs becomes less complicated and as institutions other than four-year colleges increasingly demonstrate an ability to train people for these jobs, employers have changed or decreased what is required to obtain a job. For example, Chapple and Zook describe the process by which particular occupations, such as computer support specialist and

Web developer, have matured to the point that skill levels required for entry-level positions have been reduced (Chapple and Zook 2000).

The shortage of IT workers has clearly played some role in these shifts as well. Employers are willing to lower their requirements when they are desperate for workers. As these jobs become more institutionalized, it becomes easier to figure out how to train people for them.

At the same time, even entry-level IT workers require some training. The term "entry level" is used here to refer to those jobs that require a two-year associate's degree or less. The focus here is on jobs that disadvantaged workers could be moved into in a relatively short time, and relatively inexpensively.

The Education/Skills Distinction

The current economy clearly demands more and different skills from workers than did the manufacturing-driven economy. Qualifications for many IT jobs are measured not in terms of postsecondary degrees but rather in terms of specific skills and abilities. The distinction between skills and education has become more important (NWCET 1999). A skilled worker in 1950 was unlikely to require additional training throughout his career. Today, the skilled IT worker must constantly upgrade her skills in order to remain productive. Lifelong learning has become the norm, yet an infrastructure of policies and programs to support this norm is lacking.

Workers in many emerging occupations require specific training, but they do not necessarily need higher education. Although the three occupations projected by the Bureau of Labor Statistics to grow most quickly between 1996 and 2006 all require at least a bachelor's degree, many new IT jobs require less in the way of degrees (USDOL 1999, p. 20). Table 7.2 illustrates the salaries and training requirements for several emerging IT positions that demand two years or less of training.

According to several recent studies, hiring managers overwhelmingly focus on capability rather than on formal qualifications like degrees or certifications (Chapple and Zook 2000; ITAA 2000; Harrison and Weiss 1998). ITAA's survey of employers found that "a good knowledge base in relevant areas came out as the single most important high level qualification (62 percent), followed by hands-on experience (47 percent)" (ITAA 2000, p. 19). Responses of hiring managers to

Table 7.2 IT Salary and Training for Emerging IT Occupations

	Salary		Training		
Emerging occupation	Beginning ($)	Experienced ($)	Credential	Avg. time	Avg. cost ($)
Telecommunications installer	7–15/hr	15–22/hr	Certificate	9 months	400
Technical writer[a]	12–33/hr	20–65/hr	Certificate	1 year	200
Technical support rep.	8–15/hr	12–35/hr	AS degree	2 years	720
PC technician	8–18/hr	12–35/hr	Certificate	2 semesters	300
Network administrator	15–20/hr	18–35/hr	AS degree	2 years	720
Network technician	10–24/hr	11–35/hr	Certificate	1 year	200
Computer programmer	12–31/hr	20–60/hr	Certificate	3 semesters	250
Web designer[a]	12–40/hr	25–115/hr	Courses	4 months	400
Webmaster[a]	10–20/hr	15–40/hr	Certificate	3–9 months	300

[a] Indicates high-demand occupation.

SOURCE: 21st Century Workforce Commission (2000).

the ITAA survey indicate that "many routes lead to in-demand IT skill levels" (ITAA 2000, p. 18). Harrison and Weiss cite research showing that "what employers say they want is people with better, more reliable schooling in job-relevant skills, not necessarily people with more schooling, per se."[5] An important characteristic of the new economy is its ability to take on workers who have technical proficiency and computer skills regardless of whether they have formal degrees (Chapple and Zook 2000; Moss and Townsend 1999).

At the same time, employers responding to the ITAA survey expressed a preference for candidates with degrees from four-year colleges. Murnane and Levy (1996) suggest that employers tend to view a bachelor's degree as a warranty for "a set of advanced academic skills, a strong work ethic, and general analytical and teamwork skills required in the workplace" (21st Century Workforce Commission 2000, p. 50). Although employers responding to the ITAA survey preferred candidates with a four-year college degree, they also saw the value of shorter-term, targeted skills training. For example, some community colleges and community-based training programs can deliver applicants with solid skill packages in a relatively short amount of time. However, the extent to which employers will accept applicants coming through such community-oriented training systems remains to be seen.

IT Job Ladders

Just as there are multiple entry points into IT jobs, there are also multiple tracks within the IT sector. The traditional concept of a job ladder may not be as applicable in the information economy as it was in the manufacturing economy. The Center for an Urban Future (2000) declared that "the days of the gold watch are over: The average person can now expect to change jobs many times during the course of his or her life. Yet the current job training system doesn't serve the average person at all" (p. 4). At the same time, some training programs that focus on IT have identified routes leading from entry-level jobs to higher-paying, more advanced jobs. Patterns of advancement in IT careers differ for people working in IT versus non-IT firms. Workforce development institutions are beginning to play an important role in such patterns by identifying "entry-level occupations that pay well, offer opportunities for advancement, and require only short-term training" (Chapple and

Zook 2000, p. 5). Also, whereas traditional career ladders were set within a single firm, IT ladders can rely on a mix of firms and other organizations with, for example, a worker coming back to a training program between positions in order to acquire additional skills.

MOVING WORKERS INTO JOBS

The IT sector is characterized by rapid change. This rapid change carries with it three primary implications. First, workforce development programs must be responsive to industry needs and constantly update curricula to provide the skills demanded by employers.[6] Second, the traditional concept of job ladders is called into question. Within the IT sector, many more people move from job to job quickly, which also makes traditional measures of job training effectiveness, such as job retention, potentially less appropriate. Obtaining and keeping a job for a long time is not necessarily a good measure of whether a job training program works. And third, workers must become lifelong learners. Training must be seen less as a one shot deal: graduates of training programs will likely continue to need training after placement in order to keep their skills current.

Four types of institutions offer relatively short term training (less than two years) in IT-related areas: community-based training programs (CBTs), community colleges, employer-led training programs, and proprietary schools.[7] These institutions offer a variety of programs and serve a wide range of populations. Although all of these training institutions occupy important niches in the landscape of IT training, community-based training programs and community colleges have placed the greatest emphasis on targeting, training, and placing disadvantaged workers in IT occupations.

Community-Based Training Programs

Community-based training (CBT) programs focus explicitly on helping disadvantaged populations to find employment. These organizations fall into two basic categories. One category consists of traditional workforce development organizations that have recently added IT training to their roster of services. Take, for example, Training Inc., based in Newark, New Jersey. Training Inc. has been providing workforce development training and services to low income communities since 1986. In 1995 this program began offering information technology training for the following jobs: personal computer (PC) technician, software applications specialist, and office support assistant.

The other category consists of organizations focused on creating access to technology. Such organizations moved into employment-oriented training to capitalize on the opportunity to help their constituents find employment. Playing2Win, a Harlem-based community technology center, is an example of a technology-oriented CBT program. Founded in 1983, Playing2Win was created with the goal of providing access to computers and the Internet for the underserved Harlem community. Over time this program added technology training to its menu of course offerings, and it has been successful in connecting low-income residents to jobs. The unifying thread in all CBT programs is a commitment to assisting low income and low skilled workers in finding employment (Chapple and Zook 2000).

CBT programs have demonstrated promise in training disadvantaged workers for entry-level jobs in the IT sector. Some of these programs work specifically with populations thought to have significant barriers to work. OpNet is one example. Founded in 1997, OpNet's mission is to create economic opportunities in the new media industry for low-income young adults, with an emphasis on women and people of color. OpNet maintains close connections with industry and has demonstrated success in training and placing low-income San Francisco Bay Area residents. OpNet works to forge strong business-community partnerships to benefit both the new media industry and low-income communities. For example, local businesses host internships for OpNet trainees, participate in professional development workshops, and help shape the program's curriculum. Their participation helps create a program that is reflective of industry needs and ultimately leads to the development of a skilled labor pool. This industry-community partnership also helps OpNet garner the resources and knowledge it needs to effectively connect low income communities to jobs.

Although CBT programs have demonstrated success in training disadvantaged communities, their ability to tackle the larger problem of moving large numbers of disadvantaged workers into stable IT jobs is somewhat restricted. First, these programs tend to operate on a relatively small scale. Second, like many community-based organizations, they tend to have exceptional, charismatic leaders. Both of these factors raise questions about whether these strategies can be replicated and brought to scale. At the same time, these programs serve an important function by creating pathways to IT employment for some of the most disadvantaged communities. At the very least, these programs must be studied more closely in order to determine what they do well, who specifically they serve best, and what happens to their graduates in the medium and long term.

Community Colleges

Community colleges offer several advantages as training institutions. They are economical, tend to be conveniently located, offer flexible schedules, and have a history of serving underrepresented minorities, adults, and immigrant populations. Research conducted thus far on community colleges that provide IT training has been largely exploratory, and the findings are mixed. In the ITAA's survey of IT employers, which asked them to rate four-year colleges, private schools, short courses, informal training, and community colleges, community colleges did not score as well as four-year colleges and private schools. The authors of the report recognize, however, that the relatively low score may reflect the fact that many community colleges do not offer specific IT degrees. Conversely, a study by the Urban Institute found that employers do not recruit at community colleges. The same study also found, though, that community college graduates "do not face any limits to their career mobility once they are hired" (Lerman, Riegg, and Salzman 2000, p. 23). Stoll posits that regulation and bureaucratization at many community colleges, coupled with the fact that many are disconnected from industry, has shaped employers' perceptions (Stoll 2000, p. 8).

It would be wrong, however, to label all community colleges in the same way; there are important exceptions. For example, in their excellent study of IT training programs, Chapple and Zook found several community colleges that appear to have effective programs. These colleges tended to have established computer science departments and committed faculty members. These community colleges have figured out ways to maneuver around the problems identified above. The Urban Institute study explored the issue of how community colleges find out what employers want and how they incorporate their findings into the curriculum (Lerman, Riegg, and Salzman 2000). The authors found that community colleges typically have an advisory board made up of industry representatives who advise the college on curriculum; suggested changes must be approved by a committee. The frequency with which this committee meets varies greatly and has much to do with how responsive course offerings are to industry needs. State regulations dictate some of this bureaucracy, so it would be useful to study more thoroughly differences in state regulations. However, some anecdotal information exists. Iowa Western Community College, for example, offers new classes on a temporary basis until they are approved. At Bellevue Community College in Washington State, administrators do not specify what software will be used for particular classes, giving instructors the opportunity to update or change what they will use without going through the approval process (Lerman, Riegg, and Salzman 2000, p. 16). Chapple and Zook (2000) cite De Anza Community College in California and the Borough of Manhattan Community College as examples of community colleges that have also overcome bureaucratization issues. Some community colleges—e.g., Seattle Central and Colorado community colleges—are members of workforce investment boards (WIBs). Their participation on these boards ensures that they maintain close connections with industry and local government.

A small number of community colleges have moved beyond industry advisory boards to create more formal connections with employers. Some of these partnerships have been initiated by particular corporations. In 1997, for example, Microsoft launched the Working Connections Program, committing $7 million to develop IT programs in community colleges. IBM created its S/390 University Program to enable colleges—both two- and four-year—to teach mainframe hardware and software. These programs tend to deliver high quality programs that produce a particular kind of graduate for a specific job. Some wonder, however, whether graduates will have mobility or whether their skill sets may lock them into one job. Some employers have taken a broader view of what is needed to increase the supply of appropriately skilled workers. For example, Sprint works with the Metropolitan Community Colleges and local agencies in Kansas City to increase the number of underrepresented students in IT careers. Sprint's program provides scholarships, tutoring, and other support to these students.

The Urban Institute study concludes that community colleges can potentially play an important role in training people for IT jobs. The authors cite high levels of enrollment, low graduation rates, and large numbers of older students to "suggest that community colleges are functioning as retraining institutions rather than primary training institutions" (Lerman, Riegg, and Salzman 2000, p. 26). In order to make more specific recommendations about how to use community colleges to address the IT labor market problem and the digital divide, we need first to gather best practices information from the group that seems to be successful and then determine whether and how such programs could be replicated at other community colleges.

Employer-Led Training Programs

Given the current shortage of IT workers, employers are faced with a choice either to "buy" workers away from other firms or to "build" them themselves through internal training. For the most part, employers rely on their employees' obtaining basic training from external sources; in-house training tends to focus on company-specific skills (Chapple and Zook 2000). Although many IT companies are reticent to invest in training because of the frequent job switching and poaching common to the industry, other forward thinking companies recognize that they must be part of the solution to the IT worker shortage by investing in training programs. Such an investment in training also serves longer-term strategic goals such as building a market for their technologies and capturing market share.

Perhaps the best known of these programs is Cisco Systems' Networking Academy program, which is available in all 50 U.S. states, Washington, D.C., and 121 countries. Launched in 1997, the Academy program is a partnership among Cisco Systems, education, business, government, and community organizations. The curriculum focuses on teaching students to design, build, and maintain computer networks. It is an eight semester (560 hour), Web-based, hands-on curriculum that is taught mainly in high schools and colleges, but also in some community organizations. As of this writing, Cisco Academy had enrolled 260,000 students at more than 9,800 Academies located in high schools, technical schools, colleges, universities, and community-based organizations.[8]

It should be noted that not all Networking Academies target low income or disadvantaged workers—like most employer-led programs, the Networking Academy was created because it positively impacts the company's bottom line. At the same time, the Cisco program has done more than most employer-led training programs to reach underrepresented communities. Cisco does this primarily through partnerships with community groups and international organizations. As of March 2001 there were 100 Networking Academies in 26 of the program's 34 Empowerment Zone communities. To encourage the development of Networking Academies in Empowerment Zone communities, Cisco donates all of the networking equipment necessary to educational institutions that establish centers in these neighborhoods.

The corporate sector appears to be recognizing the increased need for training. In a 1994 survey, 54 percent of establishments reported providing more formal training than they had in 1990; only 2 percent reported providing less (U.S. Department of Commerce et al. 1999, p. 15). Another study documented that business investment in education and training rose more than 33 percent between 1990 and 1998 (21st Century Workforce Commission 2000, p. 57). More than one-fifth of employer-based training focuses on computers (U.S. Department of Commerce et al. 1999, p. 16). However, most training efforts are not targeted at disadvantaged workers.

In addition, many corporate actors have chosen to focus their contribution to training on the K-12 school system. For example, 3Com's NetPrep GYRLS program provides network training to high school girls to encourage them to enter IT fields. The Dell Foundation launched a program in 2000 to help children prepare for the digital age. Although these efforts are clearly important, there must be a greater investment in workforce-oriented training programs. Employer-led training efforts are fragmented; there is a lack of coordination across companies, though they could achieve greater scale were they to collaborate.

The primary benefits of employer-led training programs are that private corporations tend to have the resources to invest in these programs and they can target the training very specifically to their needs. From the perspective of potential employees, this second benefit can be a limitation. Some believe that graduates of employer-led programs are trained too narrowly and that they face difficulty transferring the skills obtained to other work situations.

For-Profit Postsecondary Institutions, Proprietary Schools, and Private Technical Institutes

For-profit postsecondary institutions (which include private technical institutes and other proprietary schools) account for approximately 5 percent of enrollment in two-year institutions (Bailey, Badway, and Gumport 2001). Although many of these schools offer two-year associate degrees and certifications, for-profit secondary institutions cost more than community colleges. These institutions have been around for decades. For example, DeVry Institutes, one of the first and largest for-profit post secondary schools, was established in 1931. The focus of these institutions has been to provide career-oriented educational programs in business, technology, and other related services. These for-profit institutions operate close to the labor market, altering their course offerings with changing employment patterns and skills shifting. For example, when the DeVry Institutes first opened their doors the schools focused on radio, television, and sound systems. Now called DeVry University, this institution has expanded to include computer technology, electrical engineering technology, telecommunications management, and a host of other programmatic areas. The ITAA survey found that IT companies rated proprietary schools as an effective source of IT training because the perception is that these schools focus on specific skills and require few unnecessary classes. IT-related technical institutes have mushroomed in recent years. Although these institutions appear to be an effective source of short-term, specialized training, they are also very costly for participants, limiting their usefulness as a strategy to train disadvantaged populations.

Overall Advantages and Disadvantages

The four types of programs that train people for entry-level IT jobs have different advantages and disadvantages. Table 7.3 lays these out explicitly, along with some other descriptive information about each of these delivery mechanisms. Although IT training programs located in CTCs and community-based organizations have done some impressive

Table 7.3 IT Programs that Deliver Entry-Level Training

Program type	Relative cost	Target population	Length of program	Advantages	Disadvantages
Community-based training program	Free or low cost; training costs are usually covered by public or private sector grants	Low-income: disadvantaged or displaced workers	Various: programs range from a few sessions to several months of intensive training	Serves low-income people; strong connections to comunity; economical; little bureaucracy	Small-scale; replicability issues; charismatic leader syndrome
Community college	Low cost	Geographic focus, with open enrollment to the general population	2 years	Economical; many locations; flexible scheduling; history of underserved groups	Bureaucracy impedes flexibility
Employer-led program	Various: free to expensive, depending on the program	Wide ranging, depending on the goals of the program	Varies	Skills taught are relevant; eliminates the middleman; replicable	Narrow skill set; fragmentation across programs; questionable transferability of skills to other employers
For-profit post-secondary institutions/ proprietary schools	Relatively expensive	Various; general enrollment for those who can pay	1–2 years; longer for advanced degrees or certificate	Strong connections to industry; replicable	Expensive

work, it is unclear whether, in fact, they have "enormous potential for increasing the number of people who can participate in the knowledge-based economy" (Chapple and Zook 2000). Even the largest of these programs is operating on a relatively small scale. Further work needs to be done to determine whether and how these programs can achieve greater scale, who specifically they reach most effectively, and how dependent they are on "charismatic leaders" and "well-ingrained institutions" (Harrison and Weiss 1998, p. 7).

Many important questions remain unanswered because the data simply do not exist. How many people are trained each year through each of these types of programs? How many of these programs exist and where are they located? Can programs meet the demand for services? Are some programs more effective than others at placing graduates? Are some more effective at providing training that keeps a worker employable over the long term? These are questions that future studies would do well to consider.

Across the board, those programs that have thus far demonstrated success in producing graduates and placing them in jobs share the following characteristics:

- strong ties to industry
- after-placement services for graduates
- the ability to quickly modify curriculum

The primary challenge faced by all training programs is an acute shortage of faculty to do the actual teaching and training. The shortage of IT workers has created a situation in which those with the skills to teach these courses have little economic incentive to do so. Programs located in community-based organizations and CTCs also have difficulty sustaining funding and meeting demand for services (Servon and Nelson 1999; Chapple and Zook 2000).

RELEVANT POLICY EFFORTS

Policy also clearly affects the IT labor market. This section deals with those federal and state policies that relate most directly to the workforce development issue.

The H-1B Visa Program

One response to the IT labor shortage is the H-1B visa program. This program admits foreign skilled workers to the United States in order to fill jobs not being filled by U.S. workers. Although not all foreign workers who enter the country under the H-1B program are IT workers, estimates indicate that the program currently fills 70,000 IT jobs a year, roughly 28 percent of the average annual demand for IT workers (U.S. Department of Commerce 2000, p. 51). Approximately 460,000 H-1B visa recipients currently work in the United States. In 1990, Congress imposed a cap of 65,000 on the number of H-1B visas issued. In 1997, that cap was reached for the first time. The corporate sector has successfully pressured the federal government to increase the number of H-1B visas available for each of the past several years, and each year the new limit has been reached. In 2001, the cap was reached in March. Table 7.4 illustrates the annual increases in the number of H-1B visa holders allowed into the United States.

The primary accomplishment of the American Competitiveness in the Twenty-First Century Act of 2000 was that it raised to 195,000 the cap on the number of available H-1B visas, a type of temporary visa used to recruit established mid- and upper-level scientists (mainly information technology experts) from foreign countries. S 2045 was introduced on February 9, 2000, by Sen. Orrin G. Hatch (R-UT), and signed into

Table 7.4 Number of H-1B Visas, 1997–2004

Year	Number
1997	65,000
1998	65,000
1999	115,000
2000	115,000
2001	195,000
2002	195,000
2003	195,000
2004	65,000[a]

[a] This is the authorized level for 2004.

SOURCES: Tech Law Journal; U.S. Congress S 2045, American Competitiveness in the 21st Century Act; and the U.S. Citizenship and Immigration Services, Public Affairs Division.

law on October 17, 2000, by then-President Clinton. In 2004, the H-1B visa cap returned to 65,000, and as of this writing no new legislation has secured sufficient congressional and presidential support to raise this cap.

The Helping to Improve Technology Education and Achievement Act of 2000 (HR 3983, also known as the HI-TECH Act) was a related bill that sought to increase the caps on H-1B visas to 200,000 through 2003 and to increase funding for technology training and K-12 education. It also would have increased the H-1B application fee by $500 and would have earmarked the additional funds generated for education and training. HR 3983 was referred to the House Education and Workforce Committee, the House Judiciary Subcommittee on Immigration and Claims, and the House Science subcommittees on Basic Research and on Technology but failed to be moved out of committee for a vote of the House.

The H-1B visa program helps to fill demand for workers right now, but it is a stopgap measure. A longer term solution to filling these jobs with U.S. workers is needed. Even if annual increases continue in the number of H-1B visas allowed into the country, this solution is unlikely to meet the labor shortage in IT jobs by itself (Stoll 2000, p. 15). In addition, H-1B workers are likely to work in the most skilled jobs within the IT industry. These jobs create a complementary demand for lower-skilled IT workers, and that demand is currently going unmet.

Labor is often thought of as a relatively immobile input to production, especially as compared with inputs such as capital and raw materials. But labor does not necessarily need to be mobile in order to be globalized. This globalization of the labor force occurs either by moving parts of the production process offshore or by bringing foreign workers to the United States to work. First, firms can and do locate all over the world in order to take advantage of specific skills or the particular cost structure of a local labor market. One reason for the relative decrease in manufacturing jobs in the United States is the relocation offshore of a great deal of manufacturing activity to places in which labor is cheaper. Clearly, it is not that we have stopped making things. This aspect of globalization of the labor force has to do with multinational corporations expanding abroad to capture the lower cost of unskilled labor in other countries. Technology abets this disintegration of the Taylorist production process; for example, it is now easy for designers in one country to communicate quickly with those who produce the designs in another.[9]

Second, employers' demand for increases in the H-1B visa program show that firms are soliciting and obtaining labor from other countries: thus far the United States has had no trouble filling all of the allowed H-1B slots. This aspect of globalization involves fewer but more highly educated workers—the "core" IT workers discussed at the beginning of this paper. Castells points out that only "a tiny fraction of the labor force, concerning the highest-skilled professionals" is globalized, while "the overwhelming proportion of labor…remains largely nation-bound" (Castells 1996, p. 234). Raising the H-1B visa quota means generating more jobs for the second tier of IT workers—those who have particular skills but are not as highly educated as the first tier workers—which requires figuring out how to train the current workforce for these jobs.

Workforce Development and Welfare Policy

Workforce development policy has long been identified as a form of social welfare policy. This perception arises because workforce development programs are often targeted at the unemployed and at welfare recipients, creating the commonly held belief that these people either need remedial training in "soft" skills or need to be cajoled into working.[10] Workforce development proponents argue that these programs should instead be viewed as part of economic development policy because they help to maintain an available and appropriately trained workforce.

Several factors currently combine to make the link between workforce development policy and economic development stronger (Gruber and Roberts 2000). First, the labor shortage in IT fields has engendered a useful sense of urgency among employers. A report issued by the Center for an Urban Future maintains that "job training can no longer be dismissed as a feel-good favor to the downtrodden. It is now, at every level, a business necessity" (Center for an Urban Future 2000, p. 1) Second, the Clinton administration passed the Workforce Investment Act (WIA) in 1998 with the goal of coordinating more than 163 job training programs funded through a variety of government agencies. WIA emphasizes the importance of skills training and is characterized by the following goals: coordination of services, universal access, work first, consumer choice, and employer participation (Center for an

Urban Future 2000). Third, 1996 welfare reform that replaced Aid to Families with Dependent Children (AFDC) with Temporary Assistance for Needy Families (TANF) makes getting welfare recipients into the workforce a much higher priority than it was previously.

Both TANF and WIA share another important characteristic: they give much of the control of the programs to the states. Job training and welfare policy have nearly always been federal issues, which makes these recent changes significant. In effect, then, there are currently 50 different ongoing experiments in each of these policy areas. This devolution allows states to tailor their policy responses to their particular economies and workforces. Some states have responded to the changes in legislation more creatively and entrepreneurially than have others. Some have thought about these two programs together rather than dealing with them in separate policy categories.

Washington State, for example, has a booming high tech sector and declining core industries such as lumber and aerospace. Most workers who have been laid off do not have the skills they need for available IT jobs. In response, Governor Gary Locke created two programs. The first, Worker Retraining, guarantees 18 months of training to anyone who has been laid off. The training is designed to move workers from declining industries to those experiencing fast growth. The second program, Pre-Employment Training (PET) is delivered through the state's community college system, which works with employers to identify jobs for graduates. Community colleges have focused on delivering a 12-week program which provides free job training to welfare recipients and low income families, primarily at night and on the weekends. As soon as they are able, participants enter the workforce, but they continue to attend college to strengthen their skills foundation. According to the 2003 WorkFirst Study from the University of Washington, people "who received welfare in 2001 and participated in WorkFirst activities…were more likely to be employed and had higher wages than those who did not" (Klawitter 2001). However, state officials continue to modify the program, including Governor Locke's set-aside of $10 million for job coaches to raise the wages of PET participants and other low-wage workers and to help with the issue of job retention. Locke also shut down an underused training program operating through unemployment offices, thereby demonstrating a willingness to experiment with a mix of initiatives.[11] Other states, such as Texas and Indiana, have also launched creative initiatives based on their particular issues.

Nebraska's Applied Information Management (AIM) Institute is another example of an innovative IT workforce development program. The AIM Institute is a nonprofit membership organization created by a consortium of business, education and government entities to support and promote business growth related to information technology. Recognizing that a skilled IT workforce is critical to Nebraska's competitiveness, a critical focus of AIM's work is on information technology training. Through independent training modules and partnerships with high schools, universities, and colleges, AIM develops model technology curriculum and training opportunities for residents of Nebraska. Funding for AIM comes from a variety of sources including commitments from corporate members, subscriptions to AIM's CareerLink, and funding from state, federal and private granting agencies.

Some states, having also recognized the importance of a basic competence with technology for welfare recipients who are being moved to the workforce, are creating programs that provide these people with IT skills.

National Science Foundation: ATE and ITWC

The National Science Foundation (NSF) funds the Advanced Technology Education (ATE) program, which promotes improvement in technological education at the undergraduate and secondary school levels.[12] ATE works toward this goal by supporting curriculum development, facilitating professional development of college faculty and secondary school teachers, and creating internships and field experiences for faculty, teachers, and students. ATE also brokers relationships and partnerships between two-year and four-year colleges and funds a granting program called Centers of Excellence in Advanced Technology which supports projects that develop educational material, disseminate information, and engage in professional development for educators. The Northwest Center for Emerging Technologies (NWCET), previously mentioned, is a Center of Excellence and has received over $5 million in grants from the ATE program since 1995. ATE specifically targets women, underrepresented minorities, and persons with disabilities (Congressional Commission 2000, p. 33). In FY 2005, ATE will distribute an estimated 65 awards totaling $38 million.[13]

NSF also initiated the Information Technology Workforce Program (ITWS), a research program that focuses on projects addressing research questions related to the under-representation of women and people of color in the IT workforce. The genesis of this program was the recognition that, in order for the United States to maintain its global leadership in IT, there would need to be a continuous supply of well-trained engineering and computer science professionals. ITWS targets women and people of color as key populations that can help to increase the supply. In 2004, the program will issue approximately $5 million in funds for research in three primary areas: environment and culture, the IT educational continuum, and the IT workplace.[14]

IT Training Tax Credits

The Technology Education and Training Act (TETA) was proposed at the federal level in 2001. This legislation would provide tax credits to employers who provide training to their employees. The Technology Workforce Coalition argues that IT training tax credits will do several things: increase personal income tax revenue from new employees, increase local sales tax revenue from new employee spending, increase corporate tax revenue from increased employee productivity, and develop necessary skills in non-IT businesses.[15] In the meantime, some states have begun to move ahead with their own legislation in this area. Arizona was the first state to pass such legislation. It currently offers $5 million in Information Technology Training Tax Credits in a dollar-for-dollar match for training up to 20 employees per company in IT skills. The per employee credit cannot exceed $1,500.[16] Similar legislation is pending in other states, and at least two states, Ohio and Rhode Island, have implemented similar training tax credit programs.

RECOMMENDATIONS

What can be done to take advantage of the current window of opportunity? Moving disadvantaged workers into IT jobs requires action on the part of many stakeholders. This section lays out recommendations directed at training programs and at the public and private sectors.

For Training Programs

Work with employers. Existing research shows that workforce development initiatives work best when they include strong ties to employers (Harrison and Weiss 1998; Stoll 2000; Chapple and Zook 2000). These arrangements are most likely to create the kind of workforce development policy and institutions that are sufficiently flexible to modify training to the specific demand for skills" (Stoll 2000, p. 2). Flexibility and the ability to quickly respond to changes in the skills demanded are clearly characteristics that any IT training program must have. It is not surprising, then, that ITAA found that hiring managers value on-the-job training more highly than any other training.

For the Private Sector

Invest in training. The private sector has a great deal to gain by investing in training. The high value employers place on on-the-job training (OJT) means that the workplace is a primary site for the design and location of programs. Research on the effects of employer-based training show that firms providing formal OJT raise their productivity by roughly 10 to 15 percent, on average (U.S. Department of Commerce et al. 1999, p. 7). Another study found that employers get more bang for the buck by investing in education than by investing in capital stock. Firms whose workforce had a 10 percent higher than average educational attainment level had an 8.6 percent higher than average productivity level, while firms with a 10 percent higher than average level of capital investment had only a 3.4 percent higher than average payoff (U.S. Department of Commerce et al. 1999, p. 23). Folding training into the workplace also makes sense from the perspective of workers. Focus groups of workers interested in continuing education cited lack of time and high cost as two of the biggest barriers to taking courses outside of work. Many high tech companies have begun to invest in training, particularly at the K-12 level.

Create and participate in regional consortia. Another response involves regional consortia of firms joining forces to provide training. Some literature uses the term "coop-etition" to describe how rival companies cooperate when it is in their mutual interest (21st Century Workforce Commission 2000, p. 29).[17] An example is the Alliance for Employee Growth and Development, a joint training trust to which AT&T, Lucent Technologies, the Communications Workers of America, and the International Brotherhood of Electrical Workers (IBEW) belong. The Alliance consists of more than 200 labor/management committees that "help identify educational needs, coordinate training, and build enrollment" (U.S. Department of Commerce et al. 1999, p. 23). The Alliance also offers a range of training and learning opportunities that are tailored to local and individual needs. For example, participants can get involved in Alliance-sponsored on-site, off-site, and distance learning training programs. The Alliance offers tuition assistance and special services for dislocated workers. In addition to technical skills training, the Alliance also offers support services such as financial planning, career planning, test preparation, and certifications.

For the Public Sector

Support entry-level IT worker training. Public investment will be critical to maximizing the potential of the new economy. The rationale for public investment in training is that we cannot remain competitive as a nation without an educated and appropriately skilled workforce. Investment in human capital is needed in order to fuel the economy and create opportunities for historically disadvantaged groups to take advantage of the current demand for workers. This kind of investment in training will also assist workers who lose their jobs in adjusting to labor market changes caused by increased trade and globalization (USDOL 1999, p. 75). The federal government has some programs in place, but these need to be expanded and updated. The employer fee for H-1B visa petitions is currently $500, much of which goes to training. Given that demand for these workers has thus far been relatively inelastic, that fee should be increased as a way to increase funding for effective programs.

Create specific incentives for small firms. It is clearly more difficult for smaller firms to take on the added cost and burden of in-house training. Government incentives could help remedy this problem. For example, Section 127 of the IRS tax code, which makes employer-provided educational assistance tax-free to both the employer and the employee, is temporary. Section 127 should be permanently extended. State government can also create incentives for private corporations to invest in IT training.

Change regulations around education and training. The labor market has changed, but many government programs and policies have not changed along with it. For example, traditional government loans and grants can only be used toward degree programs. Lifelong Learning Tax Credits provide some assistance, and their expansion should be explored. Further, unemployment insurance (UI) recipients lose their benefits if they enroll in training that has not been approved by the state. Given that more people are receiving valuable training through alternative programs, there needs to be some shift in policy in this area. Current policy does not reflect and work with the current reality.

Target women and minorities for IT training. The ITAA points to "the under-representation of women and other minorities in the IT workforce" as a key factor contributing to the shortage of IT workers. Table 7.5 illustrates the racial/ethnic distribution of the science, engineering, and technology (SET) workforce in 1997, showing that relatively few women, African Americans, and Hispanics work in these fields.

By 2050, "the U.S. population is expected to increase by 50 percent, and minority groups will make up nearly half the population" (USDOL

Table 7.5 1997 Gender and Racial/Ethnic Distribution of U.S. and SET[a] Workforces (%)

	U.S. workforce	U.S. SET workforce
White male	41.7	67.9
White female	34.7	15.4
Black	10.3	3.2
Hispanic	9.2	3.0
Asian and other	4.0	10.2
American Indian	—	0.3

[a] SET stands for science, engineering, and technology. — = not available.
SOURCE: Congressional Commission on the Advancement of Women and Minorities in Science, Engineering and Technology Development (2000).

1999, p. 2). Given that these groups represent an increasing proportion of the labor force, it makes sense to take action to prepare them for the requirements of the current economy. The need for skilled workers is so great that employers literally cannot afford to discriminate. Moving minority and women workers into these fields now will also create the positive spillover effect of creating networks and ties that will have long-lasting effects.

The percentage of women earning computer science degrees has dropped steadily since 1984, when women made up 37 percent of degree recipients. By 1994, that figure had fallen to only 28 percent. According to the Department of Commerce, only 1.1 percent of undergraduate women choose IT-related disciplines, compared to 3.3 percent of male undergraduates (Cuny and Aspray 2000). If we follow the IT workforce pipeline, we see that the underrepresentation of women continues, from those pursuing computer science degrees through all levels of the workforce. Table 7.6 illustrates the drop-off rate as women move from college through postbaccalaureate degrees in computer science. According to Catalyst Associates, a nonprofit research organization based in New York, only 8.1 percent of women occupy executive positions (senior vice president and higher) at major technology companies, compared to approximately 12 percent in other sectors of the economy (Congressional Commission 2000, p. 40). Women also make up nearly 60 percent of the working poor in this country, and minority women are more than twice as likely to be poor as white women (USDOL 1999, p. 4).

A report issued by the Commission on the Advancement of Women and Minorities in Science, Engineering, and Technology Development identified several barriers that exist for women, underrepresented minorities, and persons with disabilities at various places along the SET pipeline. These include inadequacies in pre-college education; lack of access to higher education; a narrow and inflexible workplace environment; and a poor public image of the science, engineering, and technology fields (Congressional Commission 2000). According to this report, "the lack of diversity in SET education and careers is an old dilemma, but economic necessity and workforce deficiencies bring a new urgency to the nation's strategic need to achieve parity in its SET workforce" (Congressional Commission 2000, p. 5). Policies that address these barriers must be developed in order to move women and underrepresented minorities into the IT workforce. Such policies would range from im-

Table 7.6 Computer Science Degrees Awarded to Women, by Level

Academic year	PhDs awarded	% women	MSs awarded	% women	BA/BSs awarded	% women
1992–93	997	13.3	4,523	—	8,218	—
1993–94	1,005	15.6	5,179	19.1	8,216	17.9
1994–95	1,006	16.2	4,425	19.7	7,561	18.1
1995–96	915	11.7	4,260	20.0	8,411	15.9
1996–97	894	14.4	4,430	22.3	8,063	15.7

NOTE: — = not available.
SOURCE: Cuny and Aspray (2000).

proved elementary education to creating mentor relationships between IT professionals and college students majoring in related fields to providing members of these groups with early work opportunities in IT fields. The private sector can certainly share some of the burden for this work. In fact, were the number of women in the IT workforce increased to equal the number of men, the gap in supply vs. demand for IT workers would close entirely (Freeman and Aspray 1999).

Increase attention to and funding for K–12 education. This chapter is geared primarily toward understanding and solving the current shortage of IT workers. However, this issue is unlikely to go away anytime soon. In order to mitigate future problems, there must be greater investment in primary and secondary education, particularly for underrepresented minorities who often attend poorly performing schools. Three recent initiatives may provide some assistance in this area. First, the International Society for Technology in Education (ISTE) developed the National Educational Technology Standards (NETS), which outline technology skills that can be incorporated throughout the K–12 curriculum. Second, the Techforce Initiative, developed through a partnership between the Education Development Center, ITAA, and the National Alliance of Business, created an IT Pathway Pipeline Model, which integrates technology into students' learning beginning in primary school (Education Development Center 2000). Third, Intel, Hewlett-Packard, and Microsoft have joined forces on a project called Teach to the Future, which will train 100,000 U.S. classroom teachers to integrate computer technology into existing curricula. These three initiatives, although welcome, do not address the more basic problem of schools that deliver chronically poor performances in basic subjects such as math and reading. Also, pedagogy must be changed to reflect the needs of the current economy.

Partnerships

In addition to the measures outlined above, it will be critical for existing training programs, the public sector, and the private sector to partner with one another in order to devise effective ways of addressing the IT labor shortage and moving available workers into existing jobs. Promising examples of such partnerships already exist.

California's Employment Training Panel. The Employment Training Panel (ETP) is a California state agency created in 1982 as a cooperative business-labor program to retrain workers.[18] ETP's purpose has been to fund training that 1) meets the needs of employers for skilled workers, and 2) meets the needs of workers for good jobs. Since its inception, ETP has trained over 336,000 workers using over $645 million in funds. ETP is funded through the Employment Training Fund, which takes one-tenth of 1 percent of subjects' unemployment insurance wages paid by every private, for-profit employer in the state and by some nonprofits also. This fund generates between $70 and $100 million each year. Companies are eligible to apply for ETP funding if they are paying into the state's Employment Training Fund (ETF) and

- are hiring and training unemployed workers who are receiving unemployment insurance benefits (UI);
- face out-of-state competition and need to retrain current employees;
- need to upgrade workers in areas where there are demonstrable skill shortages;
- have special training programs in areas such as defense conversion, entrepreneurial training, and new industries.

ITAA partnerships. ITAA has initiated a variety of partnerships with industry, academia, and community groups in order to increase the number of IT workers. Several of these partnerships focus specifically on populations that are underrepresented in the IT industries. Recruiting for the Information Technology Age (RITA), a joint venture with Women Work!, is executing a plan to help women in transition achieve self-sufficiency through IT job training and placement. ITAA works with a group called Community Options to train and place people with disabilities. And the National School-to-Work Office has funded ITAA's work with the National Alliance of Business (NAB) and the Education Development Center (EDC) to facilitate, support, and promote IT employer participation in school-to-work efforts.

CONCLUSIONS

The current high level of demand for entry-level IT workers, from both IT and non-IT firms, presents a unique opportunity for integrating workforce development and welfare initiatives into economic development goals. Collaboration will clearly be key to solving the current shortage of IT workers. Creative partnerships among industry, government, educational institutions, and the private nonprofit sector have the potential to help industry fill jobs that will fuel the economy while at the same time creating new opportunities for groups that have historically experienced labor market discrimination. These partnerships can operate to increase and improve the flow of information about employers to job seekers, and vice versa.[19] If it is true that disadvantaged workers do not lack employment opportunities, two challenges remain. The first involves training the available pool of workers for these jobs. Doing so requires figuring out the best mechanism for delivering this training, and determining what subset of workers can be easily trained. The second challenge concerns ensuring that these jobs pay a living wage.

If history is any guide, the status (and pay and benefits) of jobs often decreases once they are occupied by disadvantaged workers, a group that consists disproportionately of women and people of color. Policy, therefore, plays a large and important role. Yet policy innovation has not kept pace with technological innovation. Policy directed at moving disadvantaged workers into stable, well-paying jobs must shift toward an investment focus. Only then can it help rectify current patterns of inequality.

Notes

1. This is a revised version of a chapter of my book, *Bridging the Digital Divide: Technology, Community, and Public Policy* (Malden, MA: Blackwell, 2002). It is reproduced in similar form here by permission.
2. Pittsburgh serves as one instance. Formerly a steel town, it has encouraged and fostered the growth of IT activities, with some success.
3. Center for an Urban Future (2000, p. 4). Chapple and Zook (2000) argue convincingly that the likelihood of massive movement of jobs overseas has been exaggerated, but that the issue of a shortage of workers with the necessary skills to fill available IT jobs remains important.

4. “Thin” firms are skeletal in organization, without many assets, resources, or personnel. Investors thought these firms would grow, flourish, and get fat.
5. Zemsky, cited in Harrison and Weiss (1998, p. 12).
6. I use Harrison and Weiss’s (1998, p. 5) inclusive definition of workforce development as consisting of “a constellation of activities, from orientation to the work world, recruiting, placement, and mentoring, to follow-up counseling and crisis intervention.”
7. Although four-year colleges offer a range of IT training, this chapter focuses on shorter term training programs, as these are the ones likely to be accessed by disadvantaged and transitioning workers.
8. More information on the program can be found at http://cisco.netacad.net/public/academy/About.html (accessed August 20, 2004).
9. Frederick Taylor wrote The Principles of Scientific Management in 1911; these principles became known as Taylorism. Taylorism involves vertical integration of the production process, with most aspects of production being concentrated in one place and in one firm.
10. This is not to say that soft skills are not important. In fact, Chapple and Zook (2000) show how critical it is to package soft skills training into larger IT training programs. Many programs—e.g., DeVry—market their inclusion of soft skills as a selling point.
11. This description of Washington State programs came from the Center for an Urban Future (2000).
12. The NSF is an independent U.S. government agency. Its mission is to promote the progress of science; to advance the national health, prosperity, and welfare; and to secure the national defense.
13. This information comes from the ATE Program Solicitation NSF 04-541 (replaces NSF 03-523).
14. Taken from the ATE Program Solicitation NSF 03-609 (replaces NSF 02-170).
15. The House bill (HR 1769 in the 107th Congress) was referred to the House Committee on Ways and Means on May 9, 2001, and nothing seems to have happened to it since then. The companion bill in the Senate (S 762) was read twice and then referred to the Senate Committee on Finance, where it seems to have remained.
16. Taken from the Information Technology Tax Credit Guidelines, Arizona Department of Commerce. http://www.azcommerce.com/doclib/WRKFORCE/IT%20Tax%20Credit%20Guidelines.pdf (accessed March 2001).
17. In addition, Harrison and Weiss (1998) maintain that “an important theme that has emerged from [the workforce development field] during the past 12 years is that firms must learn to strategically cooperate as well as compete with rivals (pp. 7–8).
18. This description of ETP comes from www.etp.ca.gov/program/program.cfm (accessed March 2001).
19. Holzer, cited in Harrison and Weiss (1998, p. 34), asserts that job seekers and employers lack sufficient information about each other, leading to the current state in which certain groups experience more unemployment and underemployment than others.

References

Atkinson, Robert D. 1998. "Technological Change and Cities." *Cityscape* 3(3): 129–70.

Bailey, Thomas, Norena Badway, and Patricia J. Gumport. 2001. *For-Profit Higher Education and Community Colleges.* Palo Alto, CA: Stanford University, National Center for Postsecondary Improvement.

Bluestone, Barry, and Bennett Harrison. 1982. *The Deindustrialization of America: Plant Closings, Community Abandonment, and the Dismantling of Basic Industry.* New York: Basic Books.

Castells, Manuel. 1996. *The Information Age: Economy, Society, and Culture.* Vol. 1, *The Rise of the Network Society.* Malden, MA: Blackwell Publishers.

Center for an Urban Future. 2000. *The Skills Crisis: Building a Jobs System that Works.* New York: Center for an Urban Future. http://www.nycfuture.org/images_pdfs/pdfs/The%20Skills%20Crisis.pdf (accessed January 4, 2005).

Chapple, Karen, and Matthew A. Zook. 2000. "Promising Futures: Promising Practices in Information Technology Training for Disadvantaged Adults." Paper presented at the Association of Collegiate Schools of Planning conference, held in Atlanta, November 1–5.

Civille, Richard. 1995. "The Internet and the Poor." In *Public Access to the Internet,* Brian Kahin and James Keller, eds. Cambridge, MA: MIT Press, pp. 175–207.

Congressional Commission on the Advancement of Women and Minorities in Science, Engineering and Technology Development (Congressional Commission). 2000. *Land of Plenty: Diversity as America's Competitive Edge in Science, Engineering, and Technology.* Washington, DC: Congressional Commission on the Advancement of Women and Minorities in Science, Engineering and Technology.

Cuny, Janice, and William Aspray. 2000. *Recruitment and Retention of Women Graduate Students in Computer Science and Engineering: Report of a Workshop June 20–21, 2000.* Washington, DC: Computing Research Association.

Educational Development Center. 2000. *IT Pathway Pipeline Model: Rethinking Information Technology Learning in Schools.* Washington, DC: Educational Development Center.

Foster-Bey, John, Lynette Rawlings, and Mark Turner. 2000. *Has the Rise of the Digital Economy Reduced Employment Opportunities for Less Educated Adults?* Urban Institute Working Paper on Regional Economic Opportuni-

ties. Washington, DC: Urban Institute Press.
Freeman, Peter, and William Aspray. 1999. *The Supply of Information Technology Workers in the United States.* Washington, DC: Computing Research Association.
Graham, Stephen, and Simon Marvin. 1996. *Telecommunications and the City: Electronic Spaces, Urban Places.* New York: Routledge.
Gruber, David, and Brandon Roberts. 2000. *Workforce Development Opportunities and Challenges: A report to the James Irvine Foundation.* San Francisco: James Irvine Foundation.
Harrison, Bennett, and Marcus Weiss. 1998. *Workforce Development Networks: Community-Based Organizations and Regional Alliances.* Thousand Oaks, CA: Sage Publications.
Information Technology Association of America (ITAA). 2000. *Bridging the Gap: Information Technology Skills for a New Millennium.* Arlington, VA: ITAA.
———. 2001. *When Can You Start? Building Better Information Technology Skills and Careers.* Arlington, VA: ITAA.
———. 2002. *Bouncing Back: Jobs, Skills and the Continuing Demand for IT Workers.* Arlington, VA: ITAA.
Kasarda, John D. 1985. "Urban Change and Minority Opportunities." In *The New Urban Reality,* Paul E. Peterson, ed. Washington, DC: Brookings Institution Press, pp. 33–67.
Klawitter, Marieka M. 2001. *WorkFirst Study: Employment.* Seattle: University of Washington, Daniel J. Evans School of Public Affairs.
Lerman, Robert I., Stephanie K. Riegg, and Harold Salzman. 2000. *The Role of Community Colleges in Expanding the Supply of Information Technology Workers.* Washington, DC: Urban Institute Press.
Meares, Carol Ann, and John F. Sargent Jr. 1999. *The Digital Workforce: Building Infotech Skills at the Speed of Innovation.* Washington, DC: U.S. Department of Commerce, Technology Administration, Office of Technology Policy.
Mitchell, William J. 1999. "Equitable Access to the Online World." In *High Technology and Low-Income Communities: Prospects for the Positive Use of Advanced Information Technology,* Donald Schön, Bish Sanyal, and William J. Mitchell, eds. Cambridge, MA: MIT Press, pp. 135–161.
Moss, Mitchell L., and Anthony M. Townsend. 1999. "How Telecommunications Systems are Transforming Urban Spaces." In *Fractured Geographies: Cities in the Telecommunications Age,* James O. Wheeler and Yuko Aoyama, eds. New York: Routledge.
Murnane, Richard J., and Frank Levy. 1996. *Teaching the New Basic Skills: Principles for Educating Children to Thrive in a Changing Economy.* New

York: Free Press.

Northwest Center for Emerging Technologies (NWCET). 1999. *Building a Foundation for Tomorrow: Skill Standards for Information Technology.* Bellevue, WA: Northwest Center for Emerging Technologies.

Sassen, Saskia. 1991. *The Global City: New York, London, Tokyo.* Princeton, NJ: Princeton University Press.

Servon, Lisa J., and Marla K. Nelson. 1999. *Creating an Information Democracy: The Role of Community Technology Programs and their Relationship to Public Policy.* Washington, DC: Aspen Institute Nonprofit Sector Research Fund.

Stoll, Michael A. 2000. *Workforce Development Policy and the New Economy: Challenges, Tensions and Opportunities in Connecting Low-Skill Workers to IT Jobs.* Los Angeles: University of California, Los Angeles, Center for the Study of Urban Poverty.

Teitz, Michael B., and Karen Chapple. 1998. "The Causes of Inner-City Poverty: Eight Hypotheses in Search of Reality." *Cityscape* 3(3), pp. 33–70.

21st Century Workforce Commission. 2000. *A Nation of Opportunity: Building America's 21st Century Workforce.* Washington, DC: U.S. Department of Labor, Office of Policy.

U.S. Department of Commerce. 1999. *Falling Through the Net: Defining the Digital Divide. A Report on the Telecommunications and Information Technology Gap in America.* Washington, DC: National Telecommunications and Information Administration.

———. 2000. *Falling Through the Net: Toward Digital Inclusion. A Report on Americans' Access to Technology Tools.* Washington, DC: National Telecommunications and Information Administration; Economic and Statistics Administration.

U.S. Department of Commerce, U.S. Department of Education, U.S. Department of Labor, National Institute of Literacy, and the Small Business Administration. 1999. *21st Century Skills for 21st Century Jobs.* Washington, DC: U.S. Government Printing Office.

U.S. Department of Labor. 1999. *Futurework: Trends and Challenges for Work in the 21st Century.* Washington, DC: U.S. Department of Labor.

8
Beyond the First Job

Career Ladder Initiatives in Information Technology Industries

Laura Wolf-Powers
Pratt Institute

In the past two decades, major growth drivers in the U.S. economy have included computers and software, information "content" such as broadcast entertainment, and advanced services and manufacturing that rely on information technology. This is particularly true in leading metropolitan agglomerations, where synergies between the global reach of communications systems and the local intensity of face-to-face communication are crucial to getting the most out of talent, entrepreneurial creativity, and productivity (Graham and Marvin 1996; Hall 1999; Sassen 2001). The polarity between information haves and have-nots in the most dynamic urban centers is stark, however. The digital divide creates or reinforces cultural distance among people who are geographically within a few miles of one another (Mitchell 1999; Servon 2002). Significantly, since it has as much to do with earning power as with access to information, the divide also reinforces income disparities among urbanites (Schön 1999; Hall 1999; National Telecommunications and Information Administration 2000).

In response, policymakers have recently begun to experiment with initiatives that train low-income urbanites for jobs associated with maintaining communications infrastructure. The ability to understand complex information technology, and to translate that knowledge into hands-on use and maintenance of the infrastructure through which people exchange information, greatly increases the chances of a non-college-educated person's earning a livable wage in today's urban labor market (Chapple et al. 2000a). Jobs installing and maintaining voice and data networks and their associated terminal equipment hold out the possibility of well-paying, blue-collar employment with advancement potential, much as semiskilled manufacturing jobs did in an earlier era.

Organizations such as the Bay Area Video Coalition in Oakland, California, and Per Scholas in the Bronx, New York, offer non-college-educated workers training in computer repair, data network configuration, web development and other skills (Chapple et al. 2000a). But the increase in information technology (IT) training options has done little to counter trends in corporate organization that limit mobility for non-college-educated employees in today's workplace. Changes in the contours of the employment relationship over the past several decades have affected employees at all levels of education and social status, but they have been particularly hard on the less educated. Employment practices that pose challenges for entry-level IT workers seeking security and mobility are varied. They include the following:

- Employer reliance on temporary workers or contractors rather than full-time employees
- The outsourcing of functions like data processing and computer support by large corporations[1]
- The growing tendency of firms both large and small not to conduct in-house training or maintain internal job ladders by which non-college-educated workers might gain skills and income over time[2]

These practices depart from the internal labor market norms that characterized large industrial and service firms for much of the twentieth century. Bridges formerly prevalent between basic, entry-level positions and more advanced jobs in IT-intensive sectors such as banking, insurance, and telecommunications have diminished or disappeared. As a result, workers find not only that access to entry-level jobs requires previous training where it did not in the past, but also that, once employed, they must undertake further skill development on their own in order to advance.

This chapter examines three community-based initiatives whose sponsors have identified what might be termed the "IT career ladder problem" and tailored their workforce development strategies accordingly. The initiatives focus on helping their low-income, non-college-educated clients to win good entry-level jobs installing and maintaining communications infrastructure. The jobs in which they strive to place their clients are good jobs in two senses. First, they pay family-supporting wages—cabling infrastructure installers typically make $10–$12 an hour. Second, there are relatively well-defined career ladders by which people in these entry-level jobs can move into higher-paying, higher-skilled positions over time (see Figure 8.1). All of the organizations profiled here are dedicated to enabling their clients to access the ongoing training necessary for career mobility in the information infrastructure industry.

The initiatives are also distinct in crucial ways. They are housed in different types of institutions. They rely on different sets of external collaborations to achieve a functioning mix of social services and client support, cutting-edge technical training, and the maintenance of ties to the demand side of the labor market. They have had different levels of success in terms of client placement and retention (though all have seen placement numbers drop during the recent downturn). Finally, each of the programs has a distinct relationship with the workforce development system emerging in its region under the 1998 Workforce Investment Act, or WIA.

STRUCTURE OF THE STUDY

Telecommunications services is a rich sector to study because unlike, for example, software or Internet commerce, it was once a bureaucratically organized, heavily regulated industry, virtually all of whose workers were represented by labor unions. Stable, predictable job and earnings progression was common, as was in-house training that enabled employees to qualify for advancement. As the industry has undergone gradual deregulation since the mid-1970s, and as technological advances such as fiber optics and new high-speed data-transmission protocols have blurred the distinctions between telecommunications, computing, and broadcast media, employment patterns have altered significantly. At the same time, as will be explained in further detail below, these very technological changes have opened career paths between traditional telecommunications technical work and IT occupations. And, despite the industry's general devolution, jobs all along the career continuum are relatively high-paying.

Figure 8.1 Career Pathways in Information Infrastructure

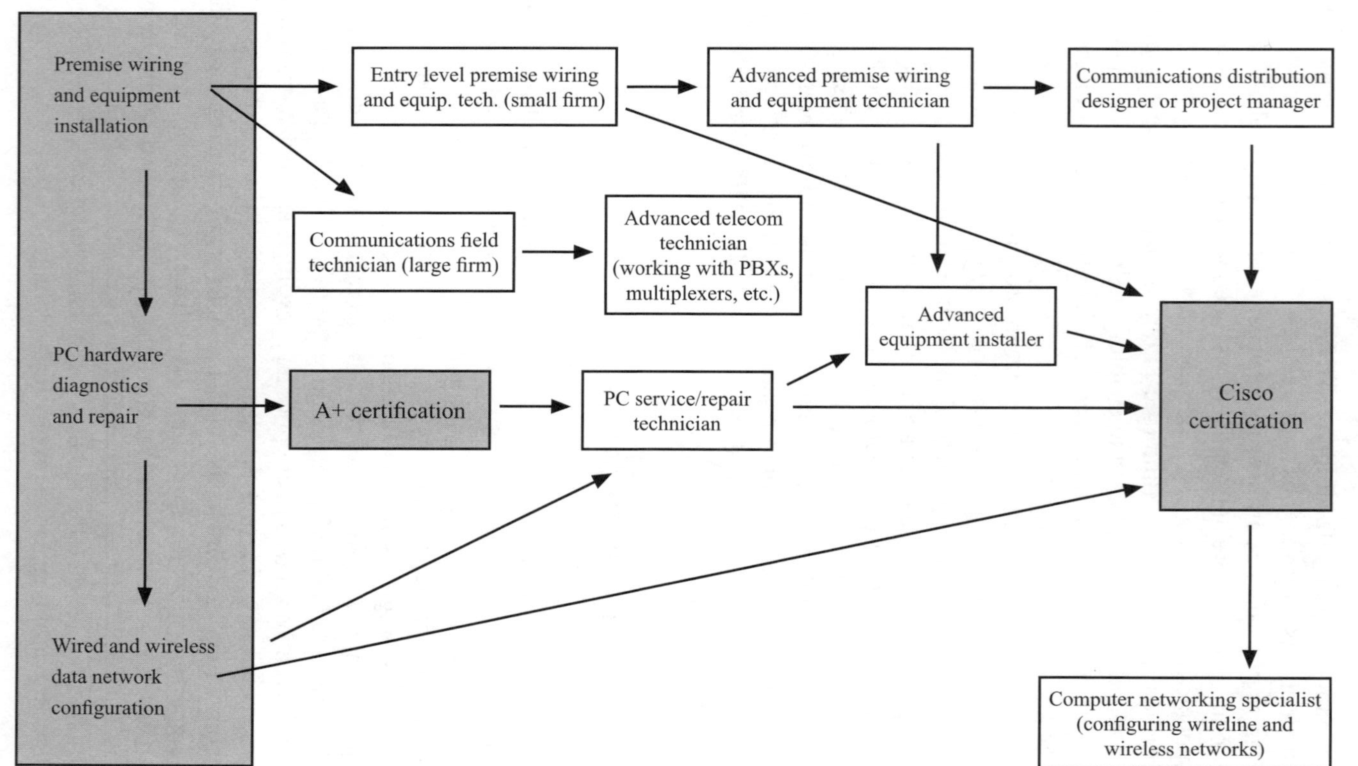

The three organizations profiled are located in Los Angeles and Oakland, California, and in Brooklyn, New York. The three focus regions (Los Angeles, San Francisco/San José, and New York City) were selected because they are identified in the literature as metropolitan agglomerations where high-speed bandwidth is densely concentrated to serve the needs of producer services and media firms with national and international markets, and where a concentration of Internet domain name registrations denotes the existence of technology-related enterprises that demand specialized telecommunications capacity (see Graham and Marvin 1996; Zook 2000). In these regions, entry-level opportunities in telecommunications and IT infrastructure maintenance are substantial and, if not (in the recent economic downturn) growing, stable enough to command the attention and curiosity of workforce development professionals.

INDUSTRY CONTEXT

The communications services industry in the United States in 2004 is the product of a series of judicial decisions and legislative acts which over the past thirty years have dismantled the AT&T-Bell telecommunications monopoly and created a convergence of telecommunications, computing, and broadcast media. In the late 1960s, AT&T, with its 22 regional Bell affiliates, was the sole provider of local and long distance telephone services. Western Electric, a Bell subsidiary, was the sole manufacturer of telecommunications network and customer premise equipment. The Bell System was the largest employer in the United States, with more than a million employees (Temin and Galambos 1987). Over several decades, federal judges, FCC commissioners, and congressional leaders curbed AT&T's market power and lowered barriers to entry for competing firms, gradually transforming telecommunications from a one-firm industry into a fiercely competitive sector with multiple players. Two regulatory developments are particularly significant:

- After the breakup of the Bell System in 1984, ownership of telecommunications facilities (wiring and terminal equipment) inside buildings was taken away from phone companies and given to end users. End users could hire the local Bell company to perform installation and maintenance work but were not required to do so. This created roles for independent "structured cabling" firms and installers of customer premise equipment such as call distribution systems and, eventually, data routers and servers.

- The Telecommunications Act of 1996 established guidelines for competition in local telephone markets and allowed long distance carriers, cable television companies, wireless service operators, and gas and electric utilities to offer local voice and data services over their systems. This dramatically increased the number of players seeking to provide commercial and residential end users with voice and data access. New entrants undercut established firms in part through lower labor costs, forcing the former Bell companies to become leaner.

Beyond these changes in regulation and market structure, the explosive growth of the Internet and of private data networks (local area networks and wide area networks) has transformed the communications industry technologically in the past decade.

Regulatory and technological changes have contributed to a volatile environment for workers. In the monopolistic Bell System, stable demand and regulated profits permitted extensive employee training, predictable career ladders, high pay, and relative employment security for technicians. In the aftermath of deregulation, however, AT&T and the regional Bells changed their labor practices with an eye toward competing with new, largely nonunion market entrants (Keefe and Batt 1997; Batt and Strausser 1997; Batt and Keefe 1999). Though telecommunications workers, on average, still earn more than the U.S. median, the gap is narrowing. Union coverage in the industry is down, real wages have fallen, and wage dispersion has risen (Table 8.1). Company-provided training and internal advancement is less common for technical workers in core firms. Additionally, cable television companies, which tend to have less generous employment policies than telephone communications firms, are growing much faster than their telecom counterparts (see Table 8.2).

Besides prompting changes within large enterprises, deregulation and technological change have created telecommunications-related technical work in firms that are not typically considered part of the communications services industry. Thousands of firms have emerged or

Table 8.1 Changes for Technical Workers in the Telecommunications Services Industry (Standard Industrial Classification 4810)[a] 1983–96

	1983	1996	% change 1983–96
Union density	67.5%	51.7%	−23.6
Median real weekly earnings	$489	$473	−3.3[b]
Wage dispersion among union workers (90/10) ratio[c]	1.71	2.25	31.6
Wage dispersion among nonunion workers (90/10) ratio[c]	3.13	3.13	0.0

[a] This SIC is roughly comparable to North American Industry Classification System code 5133.

[b] This cumulative 3.3 percent decline conceals great diversity between high-paid union workers, low-paid union workers and nonunion workers with respect to wages. Union employees in the 90th percentile, largely because of bargaining trends and growing seniority, saw their wages increase 14.5 percent between 1983 and 1996. Union workers in the 10th percentile experienced a 13 percent decline, and nonunion employees' wages declined 7 percent.

[c] Ratio of earnings of workers in the 90th percentile to earnings of workers in the 10th percentile. The highest-paid union technical workers earned 71 percent more than the lowest-paid union technical workers in 1983, for example.

SOURCE: Batt and Strausser 1997.

Table 8.2 Employees in Communications Infrastructure and Services Industries in the United States, mid-March, 1988 and 1997

Standard Industrial Classification	1988	1997	% change 1988–97
SIC 481—Telephone and radio communications	824,252	999,954	21.3
SIC 4841—Cable and other pay television broadcasting	104,614	174,351	66.7
SIC 1731—Electrical work (special trade contractors)	518,989	641,985	23.7
Total nonfarm private employment	110,873,900	131,381,200	18.5

SOURCE: Economic Census; Regional Economic Information System.

expanded in the past few decades to conduct inside wiring and equipment installation work that has arisen because of industry outsourcing trends and the broadband revolution. As technical work in the communications industry changes, both in skills and organization, it has more and more in common with the work done by IT technicians. Competencies and job profiles in some parts of the telecommunications sector are quite similar to those in IT, reflecting the increasing digitalization of telecommunications and the system's increasing connections to computers. While they are not conventionally considered communications industry employees, sought-after computer network administrators and technical support specialists have skills that increasingly overlap with those of communications technicians. Moreover, firm-specific training is being overshadowed in importance by external, industry-wide certifications. Examples include BICSI certification, which accredits people as structured cabling technicians; A+, which certifies a person's ability to diagnose and repair computer hardware; and Cisco, a manufacturer-sponsored series of accreditations that can be obtained by people with proficiency in data network configuration and administration. External certifications have become important mechanisms by which applicants, particularly the non-college educated, convey their qualifications to employers (Chapple and Zook 2000).

Another issue facing workforce development innovators is the communications industry's long-term patterns of sex segregation by occupation and of racial discrimination. Gender and race segmentation improved somewhat in the 1970s, particularly for women, as the AT&T Bell System became the target of federal efforts to enforce equal employment statutes (Noyelle 1987; Batt and Keefe 1999), but patterns of occupational dominance remain. In many smaller communications firms, hiring and promotion practices approximate those of the construction trades, which, although improving, have been notoriously closed to women and minorities (see Allen 1994). Thus, while female and minority applicants may now be more favorably received by hiring managers at core firms, access to smaller firms still requires a personal "bridge"—a contact with someone already employed at the firm. Helping low-income urbanites obtain entry-level jobs in this industry therefore demands that an organization be prepared to do more than train.

Technological convergence, the growing role of external certifications (particularly for applicants without college degrees), and the patterns of labor market discrimination described above have important implications for workforce development organizations. In urban areas rich with communications infrastructure, training that confers 1) baseline knowledge of the so-called physical layer of voice and data transmission systems, 2) familiarity with the workings of customer premise terminal devices such as personal computers (PCs), phone handsets and call distribution systems, and 3) working knowledge of the transmission devices (switches and routers) that allow telephones and computers to communicate with one another is valuable in and of itself in the labor market. It positions entrants for a number of different career paths (see Figure 8.1).[3] Whether they can access those paths depends on their own initiative and also on the inventiveness of workforce development organizations and those who fund them.

INNOVATIVE LABOR MARKET INTERMEDIARIES

We turn now to three urban labor market intermediaries whose sponsors have identified this multifaceted career ladder problem in communications and IT and created workforce development initiatives that help low-income, non-college-educated job seekers to respond to its challenges (Table 8.3). These institutions are actually tackling two problems simultaneously. The first is the dilemma described above—the decline of within-firm training and career pathways. The second problem is the failure of the primary education system in many urban areas to adequately prepare individuals (particularly those from low-income households) for the labor market. Surveys of employers demonstrate that literacy, basic math proficiency and soft skills are crucial prerequisites even for relatively low-paying employment, but many job seekers have difficulty reaching this bar (see Holzer 1996; Harrison and Weiss 1998). Planners and program principals at intermediaries striving to serve low-income urban populations must at once be conscious of industry dynamics and of the multiple needs of their clientele—needs that may require aggressive case management and intervention.

Table 8.3 Case Study Organizations

	Sponsoring organization	First year of operation	Main funding source	Organizational partner/s	First step/s on career ladder[a]	Subsequent steps
East Los Angeles Skills Center telephone installation & repair program and information technology academy Los Angeles, CA	East Los Angeles Skills Center (part of Los Angeles Unified School District—LAUSD)	1985 (telephone program) 2001 (information technology academy)	Los Angeles Unified School District (LAUSD)	Los Angeles Community Technology and Education Center/on-site ESL, daycare, counseling, basic education	LAUSD Division of Adult and Continuing Education curricula—computer literacy and telephone installation/repair	C-Tech computer cabling certification; CompTIA A+; Microsoft Certified Systems Engineer (MCSE); Network Administration
Brooklyn Networks Brooklyn, NY	Brooklyn Workforce Innovations (a subsidiary of the Fifth Avenue Committee)	2001	New York State Department of Labor InVest Program	New York City Technical College; Communications Workers of America (CWA) District 1	BICSI Installer Level 1 curriculum	Individual development accounts for further training of participants' choice—BICSI Level II or Cisco Network Administration
Communications Workers of America H-1B Technical Training Project Fremont, CA San Jose, CA	Communications Workers of America National Education and Training Trust	2000	U.S. Department of Labor H-1B Visa Grant	Oakland Private Industry Council (now part of East Bay Works)	Basic introductory communications curriculum—BICSI installer concepts, DSL, introduction to PC technology	CompTIA A+; Cisco Network Administration

[a] For detailed explanations of curricula and their acronyms, see Appendix 8A.

The East Los Angeles Skills Center Telephone Installation and Repair Program

The East Los Angeles Skills Center (ELASC), part of the Adult and Continuing Education Division of the Los Angeles Unified School District, is a community-based learning center that contains an alternative high school, adult basic education resources, and numerous vocational programs. In early 2001, ELASC added a fourth and a fifth stage to a standard three-stage progression of courses in microcomputer keyboarding and operations. The first addition is computer network cabling, which teaches students the cabling and software configuration skills necessary to link computers to the telecommunications system; the second is computer diagnostics and repair, which teaches students how to troubleshoot hardware problems within the computers. The network cabling and computer repair courses build the knowledge needed to study computer internetworking using both Cisco and Microsoft software. Two networking courses represent the final steps on the career ladder (Figure 8.2). For these courses, ELASC students attend the Community Technology and Education Center (CTEC), a new facility at the Los Angeles River Center building which receives funding both from the City of Los Angeles and through the Workforce Investment Act.

The IT career ladder developed by ELASC and CTEC articulates with the basic keyboarding and software applications courses that people seeking clerical jobs often elect to take. Thus, some students get off the ladder and use their keyboarding and word processing skills to get jobs, but those who develop an interest in how computers work have a chance to switch to a technical field. The ladder also articulates with one of ELASC's strongest blue-collar-oriented programs, Raul Macias' course in telephone and local area network installation and repair.[4] Macias, a former Pacific Telephone and General Telephone and Electric (GTE) employee and himself a graduate of ELASC, helps about 200 students per year complete a curriculum that includes instruction in voice and data cabling installation, cable splicing, and troubleshooting (on fiber optic and copper cable) and the basics of programming electronic telephones and private branch exchange switches. Most students in his course go directly into jobs with southern California telecommunications firms (either major local exchange carriers like GTE or "interconnect" firms), often building on Macias' personal contacts in these

Figure 8.2 ELASC/CTEC Information Technology Career Ladder

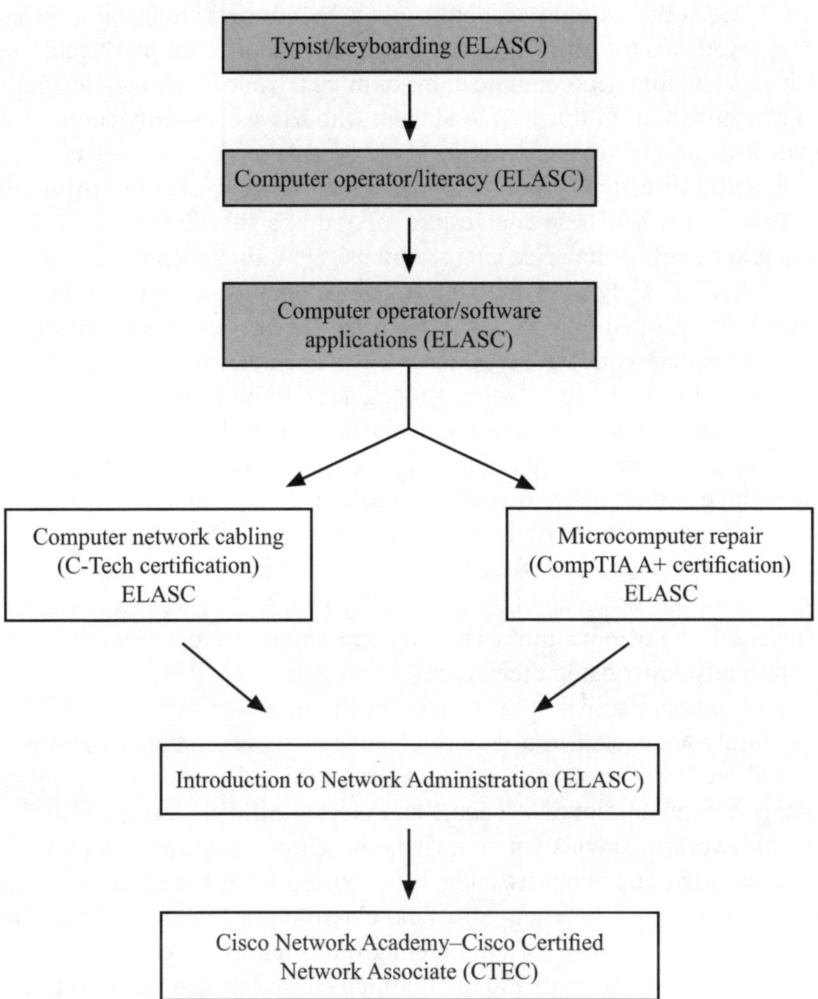

firms or on relationships that ELASC's principal, Peter Fernandez, has built through an industry advisory board. But many of them turn to the ELASC/CTEC training academy, either before seeking a job or once employed, for the skill upgrades that make them more marketable in either standard telecommunications or more advanced network technology occupations (Table 8.4). A student who has successfully completed Macias' communications course would be able to skip network cabling and enroll directly in microcomputer repair or network administration (see Figure 8.2). These courses are offered at a subsidized cost of $70 each, well below the price charged by private training vendors.

ELASC emphasizes short-term, competency-based training on the "open entry, open exit" model, which has proven successful for other programs that work with a disadvantaged clientele, such as San José's Center for Employment Training (Meléndez 1996; Harrison and Weiss 1998). Courses do not have fixed starting and ending dates. Students can start a course at any point and proceed at their own pace. The atmosphere approximates that of a workplace rather than that of a school, not only because most of the instruction is hands-on but because people enter and move on at different times depending on their readiness. In the classroom, advanced trainees solidify their knowledge and practice their skills by demonstrating tasks for new entrants to the program or by informally supervising their work.

In another parallel to the Center for Employment Training, ELASC is closely connected to a variety of indigenous organizations and political leaders.[5] These relationships prove critical in two ways. First, support from community leaders and elected officials has enabled the center, working on its own, to raise funding from state and federal government that augments its budget. Resources from the school district alone would only be enough to fund classroom teachers, but with the extra funding ELASC is able, among other things, to employ an 11-member counseling staff and to offer financial assistance to telecommunications graduates to help them purchase tools and work boots, which many employers require them to own. Second, the center shares its site on Selig Place in East Los Angeles with a mental health care provider, a community-based English as a Second Language (ESL) provider, and a daycare center, all of which help students overcome barriers to completing their training. It also maintains close relationships with neighborhood groups that are not located at its site. According to Harrison

Table 8.4 Success Rate of Information Technology Academy—East Los Angeles Skills Center and Community Technology Education Center, September 2001–February 2002

Students completed/ enrolled in computer network cabling course	Students completed/ enrolled in microcomputer repair (A+ certification)	Students completed/enrolled in introductory network administration	Students completed/ enrolled in network administration (CCNA)	Graduates placed in pertinent employment	Average wage at placement
30/40 (75%)[a]	5/20 (25%)	25/100 (25%)	20/50 (40%)	50/80 (62.5%)	$15.00/hr

[a] Program administrators provided estimates to the nearest 5%.
SOURCE: East Los Angeles Skills Center.

and Weiss, residents of low-income areas seeking skills and jobs often turn to community-based organizations (CBOs), which act as agents to "break paths, open doors, insist on quality services, and negotiate collectively with employers and governments" (1998, p. 39). ELASC clearly serves this function for many of its clients.

In part because of ELASC's commitment to short-term vocational training that immediately puts people into the labor force, advanced training in information technology did not initially seem to fit within its mission. But as ELASC and CTEC leaders began working together, the idea of an external career ladder that students could climb onto and off of eventually took shape. According to an ELASC project coordinator who helped develop the relationship with CTEC, "My fear was that somebody would have to be here four years to go to work. The commitment we make to vocational students here is that after six months you'll get a job. So we had to make sure that at every point, after every class we [sponsored], people would be able to go to work if they wanted." According to their needs and resources, some students choose to go straight through the entire progression of courses in the career ladder and then seek employment, while some take one or two modules, go to work, and return in the evening to upgrade their skills. Others choose to step off the ladder at a certain point and hold steady in a particular job or rely on informal on-the-job training to advance.

The Adult Division of the Los Angeles Unified School District has supported ELASC with no-strings-attached funding to hire instructors and provide training of whatever duration participants require to become competent. But the school district has also given administrators the leeway to develop external partnerships, raise funding independently, and co-locate with other local organizations. The East Los Angeles Skills Center has used this flexibility to great advantage and manages to combine a CBO-like atmosphere with the resources and wherewithal to design curricula and impart technical skills. Staff at ELASC have drawn on this strong base as they have worked with CTEC.

Brooklyn Networks

Whereas the East Los Angeles Skills Center worked with a community technology center to build additional rungs onto a communications career ladder whose basic skills components already existed in the institution, Brooklyn Networks (BN) sought to develop a training program that would get people onto a viable "first step." In order to do this, staff employed a sectoral strategy, an approach that has gained currency in both economic and workforce development in the past several years (Clark and Dawson 1995; Bosworth 1998; Fitzgerald 2000). One staff member describes how the organization settled on a sector: "We were looking around for career ladder jobs in what was then being called the "new economy." We had three criteria: 1) we wanted a growing sector where demand was high all along the career ladder; 2) we wanted the entry-level, first-rung jobs to pay wages that were enough to support a family, so that people could make a living wage right away; 3) we wanted the jobs to be accessible, so that people could get started in the career with relatively short-term training. We hit upon communications cabling and discovered that it met our criteria."

As part of their sectoral approach, staff members at Brooklyn Workforce Innovations (BWI), the community group that initiated the program, did extensive research on New York City's communications sector, surveying employers about their labor force needs and employment practices.[6] They learned that while some of the larger firms (including Verizon, the region's local exchange carrier) trained their own employees and had well-defined promotion systems, many of the newer employers in the industry had very little human resource infrastructure. However, these very employers had great need for entry-level workers at the time and expressed interest in hiring graduates of a cabling training program. Having gotten a basic picture of the industry (and, not incidentally, having built initial bridges to employers), BWI's staff created a program that prepares people to become entry-level communications cabling installers and then positions those who land at firms without internal career ladders to get additional training in communications equipment and network installation.

One product of BWI's research was the decision to use the Building Industry Consulting Services International (BICSI) Installer Level I curriculum. In addition to being known and respected by employers, the curriculum has a built-in career ladder, consisting of three separate certifications meant to be earned over a five-year period. Thus, BICSI Level I graduates can continue with the curriculum over time, either with employers' assistance or through Brooklyn Networks' Individual Development Account option (discussed below). Becoming licensed to teach the BICSI curriculum is expensive—an organization must outfit a laboratory with high priced equipment, send its instructors for training and certification and buy costly materials. (Through a partnership arrangement with New York City Technical College, BWI conducts classes in a room at the college which it has outfitted with state-of-the-art equipment as specified by BICSI.) BWI decision makers judge this outlay to be worthwhile, however, because BICSI's defined career path jibes with the likely career experience of the program participants.

A supportive learning environment, with dedicated teachers and a team atmosphere, is perhaps the key to the success that Brooklyn Networks participants have had in passing the difficult BICSI certification exam.[7] The instructors have many years of industry experience, having worked at New York Telephone and its successor, Verizon, in technical and managerial positions. It is important to the program's success, however, that the instructors also see themselves as educators (one, Rose Fahey, holds a masters degree in education). They worked at the beginning of the program to break the BICSI curriculum into what staffer Josh Wallack calls "manageable chunks" so that the students would be able to understand its concepts more easily.[8] Instruction includes two days of team-building activity in which students get to know program staff (two instructors, a vocational counselor and a job developer) and work with one another to develop the sense of teamwork they will need to get through the course material and pass the BICSI certification exam. Students are paired through a buddy system during the training, encouraged to practice in groups in the hands-on lab on their own time, and offered a "job club" option during the placement phase so that they can support one another in their bids to find jobs. The extensive experience that BWI and its parent organization, the Fifth Avenue Committee, have in providing social support and advocacy to low-income clients has served the organization well here, since a variety of resources are readily at hand to help participants meet the challenges inherent in this rigorous curriculum.

Another element of BWI's career ladder strategy is a relationship between Brooklyn Networks and local leaders of the Communications Workers of America (CWA), which represents most employees at Verizon and many employees of the area's smaller cabling firms. In contrast to the way it is in other cities, much of the telecommunications cabling work done by small firms within New York City's five boroughs is handled by unionized firms, and a working relationship with a union was thus a critical precondition for success. Additionally, BWI staff recognized that CWA leaders were well acquainted with the concept of skill and wage mobility, having incorporated career ladders into collective bargaining agreements with Verizon and its predecessors for decades. CWA officials have helped BWI develop contacts at small cabling infrastructure firms. CWA leaders have also visited the Brooklyn Networks classroom to talk about the communications industry and have offered to help prepare BN graduates for the Verizon entry-level installer exam.[9] Additional opportunities for cooperation may arise if CWA locals in the New York area become more involved in designing and administering training for telecommunications employees.[10] These efforts on CWA's part tie in with the union's commitment to become more inclusive of minorities and to be more active as a force for economic development in the city's low-income communities; BWI has provided an opportunity for the union to work in a concrete way toward these objectives.

In light of the economic downturn affecting New York City for the past several quarters, Brooklyn Networks has achieved a relatively high placement rate for graduates, even those who did not pass the BICSI certification exam (Table 8.5). Making resources available to graduates who want to advance further along the career path has now become a matter of concern. To that end, BWI has received a grant from the Robin Hood Foundation to help Brooklyn Networks graduates set up Individual Development Accounts (IDAs). IDAs are matched savings accounts similar to Individual Retirement Accounts (IRAs); graduates contribute monthly, BWI matches their contributions, and the money that accumulates finances additional training. Program staff encourage BN graduates to use IDA proceeds either for BICSI Level 2 training or for Cisco Network Administration training and couple career counseling efforts with financial literacy seminars.

While its CWA partnership is central to BN's success, notably absent is a strong relationship with the city's Workforce Investment Board (WIB). Advocacy groups in New York City have expressed concerns about the city's workforce development system since the inception of the WIB in 2000, voicing anxiety that the organization is mired in controversy among city and state agencies and that badly needed efforts to link workforce development to economic development are not going

Table 8.5 Success Rate of Brooklyn Networks (Brooklyn Workforce Innovations), July 2001–December 2003

Total students enrolled	Students completing 5-week course	Students placed in pertinent employment	Average wage at placement	% who receive benefits with job
89	78 (87.6%)	57 (73.1%)[a]	$10.25/hr.	71[b]

[a] Indicates percentage of those completing course who were placed in telecommunications jobs.
[b] Includes 2003 participants only.
SOURCE: Brooklyn Networks.

forward. Under Mayor Rudolph Giuliani, the city's Human Resources Administration spent only a fraction of the federal funds available for workforce development in the city (National Employment Law Project 2000; Fischer 2001). Thus, BWI has had to pursue its sector-based workforce development strategy on its own, without broader city support or technical assistance.

CWA National Education and Training Trust (CWA/NETT) H-1B Technical Training Project

In addition to collaborating with community-based organizations such as Brooklyn Networks, the Communications Workers of America acts as a labor market intermediary in its own right. Local union chapters in northern California and Cleveland offer apprenticeship training to employees of CWA-represented firms that do not have the economies of scale needed to mount internal training efforts (the employers pay into a joint apprenticeship training trust fund similar to those that exist in the building trades). Collaborations with telecommunications equipment enterprises such as Cisco Systems make it possible for CWA members nationwide to take online courses leading to advanced technical certifications (such as the Cisco Certified Network Associate curriculum, or CCNA) at reduced cost.

CWA's contracts with large communications companies have traditionally defined career and wage progression for employees of those firms but left the measures up to the companies to implement; the idea of union involvement in training is new. CWA officials first articulated it in the late 1980s as they monitored trends in the industry and saw the explosion of small telecommunications wiring contractors who were being hired (in place of large phone companies) to install voice and data infrastructure in commercial buildings. According to Cleveland-area leader Ed Phillips, an early proponent of broad-based training, "If you have basic training in voice and data cabling, you can then go on to become proficient in any number of other skills, like data network configuration, systems integration, etc. It's like fingers leading off a hand. You can stick with cabling and go in that direction, or you can get more involved on the computer side or the router side. Once they have the basics, people can learn in a number of directions."

The H-1B Technical Training Project, so named because it is funded by the fees paid to the federal government by applicants for H-1B alien work visas, provided career ladder training not for union members, but rather for unemployed and underemployed northern California residents who have sought assistance from a public sector workforce development agency. In getting involved in a more community-oriented workforce development effort in northern California and elsewhere, CWA signaled its interest in becoming more engaged in the communities around its local offices. This mirrors efforts in the labor movement as a whole to leverage education and training to help redefine organized labor as a "social movement" with deep roots in communities (see Parker and Rogers 2000; Swinney 2001; Takahashi and Meléndez 2002).[11]

The project, funded by the U.S. Department of Labor through its H-1B Skills Training Grant Program, was a partnership with the Oakland Private Industry Council, which runs a WIA-designated One-Stop Career Center in downtown Oakland under the terms of the Workforce Investment Act.[12] In 2000 and 2001, the Private Industry Council (PIC) recruited and oriented 126 participants in Oakland, and students traveled to the CWA/NETT site (originally located 30 miles south in Fremont, but eventually housed at CWA Local 9423 in San José). There they took a two-week, 60-hour training course that covered the basics of structured voice and data cabling, direct subscriber line (DSL) technology, and personal computer technology. They then had the option of continuing: CWA and PIC staff encouraged students who had completed the foundation training to return to CWA's facility for upgrade training as computer technicians (known as A+) or as internetworking technicians (using the CCNA curriculum). Although the program no longer is in operation, it showed promise: by December 2001, 38 percent of the graduates of the two-week course had registered for upgrading (Table 8.6). Some of the participants treated A+ and CCNA training as direct continuations of their initial training and continued to be full-time "learners," while others got jobs and returned to CWA in their spare time to gain the skills necessary for advancement.

The career ladder component of the northern California H-1B program was accessed primarily through distance learning. Though most program graduates were physically present in CWA's Cisco training lab for A+ and CCNA instruction, the courses themselves were taught online through an arrangement between the CWA and Stanly Community

Table 8.6 Success Rate of CWA/NETT and Oakland Private Industry Council H-1B Technical Skills Training Program, July 2000–November 2001

Students enrolled	Students completing 2-week course	Total students employed as of March 2002	Students in pertinent employment[a]	Average wage at placement[b]	Completing students who have enrolled in A+ or CCNA
126	105 (83%)	68 (65%)	21 (20%)	$12.76/hr.	40 (38%)

[a] Indicates percentage of those who completed course who were placed in telecommunications jobs as of March 2002.
[b] Wages are for the 18 students in pertinent employment whose starting wages could be verified.
SOURCE: CWA/NETT.

College in Albemarle, North Carolina.[13] Staff members of CWA/NETT served as proctors, helping students in the lab as necessary, but there were no formal class sessions. This aspect enabled students to come to the training lab when it was convenient for them and to learn at their own pace, echoing ELASC's open entry/open exit approach. It reduced students' sense of being part of an organized effort, however, since although they had online mentors from the community college and proctors in the lab, they did not have classmates in the traditional sense and their primary interaction was with a computer program. This flexibility and independence was better suited to some learners than to others, according to program director Jim Landers.

A challenge that faced the CWA/NETT H-1B program was its distance—in many senses—from its workforce development partners in Oakland. The Fremont site where the training classes were first held was a 40-minute drive from Oakland (where most participants live), and the facility later moved farther south to San Jose. Although the PIC worked with local community groups to arrange transportation from Oakland to the CWA training site, the physical distance from the city posed problems for participants, particularly in the skill-upgrading phase. The division of labor between the union education center and the Private Industry Council, an arrangement in which participants trained at a CWA site but remain tied to the PIC for social support and job placement, created distance of a less tangible sort. CWA/NETT concluded that a union entity was less well suited than the PIC to handle case management and job placement. Yet the union's less involved stance, particularly with regard to placement, arguably reduced students' informal contact with union members and employers and thus canceled out some of the advantages that a union might have been expected to have in the workforce development arena.

CWA/NETT's experiment with providing training to the largely economically disadvantaged population served by WIA one-stop centers in the East Bay concluded at the end of 2002 after eight two-week telecommunications overview courses. The computer laboratory continued to be available through 2002 to graduates of these classes, as well as to others referred by the one-stop. CWA/NETT staff conducted classroom instruction leading to A+ and CCNA certification—four A+ courses and three CCNA trainings through December of that year. After that, however, CWA staff began to direct their efforts entirely toward skill upgrading for people who were already members of the union.

The reasons behind this shift—or, rather, this step back from an arena the union had been tentatively exploring—are various. First, the economic picture had clouded since CWA/NETT was founded, and there are fewer technical jobs in the information infrastructure industry available at entry level to people with short-term training, or even with A+ and Cisco certification. Second, and perhaps more importantly, CWA as an institution is pulled in several directions by the changing economy. On one hand, union leaders are motivated by a desire to represent a greater proportion of the increasingly diverse (and increasingly contingent) communications and information workforce. Technological transformations such as the move toward broadband connectivity, combined with the trend away from company-provided training, make skill development a strategic area for the union.[14] In this view, the union's implementation of public sector grants to train underemployed and unemployed workers is an opportunity to help build a pool of skilled workers and to stimulate enthusiasm for the union. It is also a way for the union to fulfill an expansive social mission rather than taking the bread and butter approach which many believe has contributed to union decline in recent decades (Takahashi and Meléndez 2002).

At the same time, CWA remains a membership organization. In the communications sector, local leaders and their national counterparts represent the interests of existing members, most of whom work for the still heavily regulated former Bell companies. Locals representing these members are often focused on preserving employment security, high wages, and traditional job ladders within firms whose employment practices, although in flux, remain based on internal labor markets. In this view, the union's efforts to train underemployed and unemployed workers are superfluous, since training has traditionally been, and should continue to be, the province of employers. Tension between these two points of view has affected the CWA in recent years and was likely a contributing factor in the union's decision not to seek federal funding to continue the H-1B project in its initial form after 2002. The union has, however, rededicated itself to promoting skill upgrading among existing members, both to help them achieve mobility within their companies and to make job transition easier in the event they are laid off.

TOWARD A SET OF GENERAL PRINCIPLES FOR CAREER LADDER STRATEGIES IN THE INFORMATION INFRASTRUCTURE INDUSTRY

The three programs profiled in this report are dedicated to helping their clients achieve basic proficiency in telecommunications infrastructure installation. They are also striving to provide resources that those clients who are not placed in workplaces with internal career ladders can use to move beyond their first jobs. Culled from a larger sample of eleven intermediaries in the field, they represent the diversity—in terms of both sponsoring organizations and program components—of programs that exist to support people on this particular career path.

While one must always qualify an attempt to generalize from a small sample, the case studies that underlie these profiles yield some principles that policymakers and funders can apply to future initiatives. Examined together, the three cases impart important lessons about how to organize and replicate viable career ladder–oriented training for low-income job seekers. The lessons are most applicable in the communications and IT sectors, but they have implications for other sectors in which career and wage progression exist and in which living-wage jobs are both identifiable at entry level and attainable by non-college-educated applicants. The following principles can be gleaned.

1) Research that identifies articulation points between telecommunications and IT skill sets, and that develops a picture of how access to the industry is structured in a particular labor market, enables organizations to develop interventions that help their clients progress along external career ladders.

The convergence of voice, data, audio, and video technologies in offices and homes, together with profound structural change in the regulated telecommunications industry, calls for a revised understanding of occupations, certification practices and career ladders in both telecommunications and IT. The organizations profiled in this chapter have taken up that challenge, recognizing that the skill sets of telecommunications technicians exist on a continuum with those of computer network administrators and that external certifications (rather than within-firm training) are often the key to advancement. Beyond this recognition lies a pedagogical issue: that it is crucial not only to identify these articulation points between skill sets but also to shape the curriculum materials associated with external certifications, targeting them to learners with a high school education or less.

It is also important that intermediaries understand the structure of access to information infrastructure jobs in their local labor markets. Brooklyn Networks' assessment of the sources of labor market demand for telecommunications technicians in the New York area informed its choices of curriculum and organizational partners, which have been key elements in its success. The other two organizations (ELASC/CTEC and CWA/Oakland One-Stop) have not conducted as thorough and explicit an analysis of local labor markets: here the research is more informal, based in Los Angeles on an industry advisory board and in the East Bay area on unions' familiarity with local employers.

2) Successful IT career ladder systems for low-income individuals have three components: links to organizations and social institutions in their communities, technical expertise in training for the sector, and strong relationships with employers.

Workforce development research consistently shows that social supports, high quality training, and access to employers are the three keys to helping low-income job seekers move from unemployment or underemployment into living-wage labor markets. The case studies here demonstrate that this is, unsurprisingly, equally true for programs that have career mobility as an objective. They also demonstrate, however, that in creating a program with these components, a variety of combinations of internal resources and external partnerships are viable. Some of the necessary strengths come from within the sponsoring organizations, while others are achieved through collaboration with organizational partners and cosponsors. To echo the findings of another recent study of technology training programs, "Regional partnerships and coordination maximize the impact of training efforts, allowing programs to focus on their strengths" (Chapple et al. 2000b, p. 20).

3) The participation of community-based service and advocacy organizations in information infrastructure training consortia contributes to programs' success.

Training low-income individuals for occupations where technical expertise and certification are involved requires the participation of institutions (whether firms, colleges, or labor unions) that are not strictly neighborhood-based. But this study also confirms the logical precept that such training is rarely effective without the participation of community-based organizations (Harrison and Weiss 1998; Glasmeier, Nelson, and Thompson 2000; Fleischer 2001). The level of trust that community-based service and advocacy groups can achieve among participants enables them to do effective case management, helping trainees to cope with family issues, transportation, and child care and helping to guide them toward educational support when needed. The involvement of CBOs' leaders as mentors and advocates also helps participants to challenge traditional patterns of gender and racial segmentation in technology-intensive industries. ELASC instructor Raul Macias welcomes women into the telephone repair course, for example, and his encouragement builds their confidence in their technical abilities. Brooklyn Networks staff members, in their pursuit of strategic partnerships, assume a role that might be described as a combination of job development and client advocacy. They have successfully engaged New York area CWA locals (whose leadership is primarily white and male) in promoting Brooklyn Networks graduates (who are primarily black and Hispanic) to CWA-represented contractors as potential hires.

4) Institutional and financial support from the public sector, especially at the local level, could improve and expand career ladder initiatives for information infrastructure occupations.

In the cases profiled here, organizations have tailored training to career pathways they have identified. In doing so, they have developed partnerships and funding streams. But their efforts are not systematically tied, financially or organizationally, into broader regional sectoral strategies for workforce development. The exception here is ELASC/CTEC, where Los Angeles officials have dedicated Workforce Investment Act dollars to the latter part of the IT skills continuum. In general, however, decision makers at local Workforce Investment Boards could do more to strengthen career ladder programs in the information infrastructure industry. In particular, they could support efforts to provide upgrade training to technology workers at small firms that lack formal training programs. This would be a promising investment because incumbent workers, with relatively short training courses, could advance to fill higher-level openings and make room at entry level for other trainees.

5) Labor unions help to structure entry-level access to the telecommunications and IT sectors, but their role is an ambivalent one.

Effective labor intermediaries, according to Fitzgerald, have the capacity not only to connect supply with demand, but also to influence demand (2000, p. 29). Although community colleges, Community Development Corporations (CDCs), and other training providers have successfully persuaded employers to train more intensively and to take high-skill, high-wage paths to profitability, unions, by virtue of collective bargaining agreements, are in a unique position to wield such influence. The industry's history of unionization is a partial explanation for why most telecommunications technicians earn high wages, even in nonunion firms. Thus, one might expect best practice approaches to career ladder–oriented training in this field to routinely involve unions.

As the profile of the CWA's H-1B program demonstrates, however, the reality is more complicated. Unions in telecommunications are pulled in many directions by the changing structure of their industry. They are motivated both to expand the scope of their membership and activities in concert with a rapidly changing industry and to fulfill the expectations of members still operating under the rules of the old industry. Unions are also inexperienced at being workforce development organizations and at dealing with the requirements of public funding sources. As a result, models such as Brooklyn Networks, which rely on close relationships with unions but do not involve them as primary program sponsors, may ultimately be the most effective way of drawing on unions' strengths.

CONCLUSION

The information infrastructure industry is one of a small number of sectors in which living-wage entry-level jobs are accessible with brief training, and in which a career ladder is evident. In this sector, industry analysis suggests, some individuals will be fortunate enough to obtain first jobs with employers that have internal career tracks (such as the former Bell local exchange carriers). Some will learn enough on the job that they will be able to advance across firm boundaries on their own. Some will, because of time constraints, educational limitations, or preference, remain in an entry-level job by choice (see Fitzgerald 2000;

Fitzgerald and Carlson 2000). But many will be involuntarily stuck on the first rung of the job ladder.

The organizations described here are working to position low-income clients to take fuller advantage of career ladders that exist in the information infrastructure industry. This entails putting people on track—i.e., introducing them to a sector in which they may not have considered becoming employed—then, helping them to get entry-level positions, and, finally, creating infrastructure within which they can access skill upgrading and career counseling and move to higher-skilled, more remunerative jobs. Their training job has been made more straightforward by the existence of external certifications such as BICSI and Cisco, and all three programs identified the need for certain basic components: links to organizations and social institutions in their communities, technical expertise in training for the sector, and close relationships with employers.

Organizations whose leaders are thinking beyond the standard workforce development outcomes of job placement and retention are unusual. A push from federal and state funding sources could catalyze change in this area, as could more concerted interest from local Workforce Investment Boards. The U.S. Department of Labor has shown a promising interest in training for incumbent workers in recent years (Fitzgerald 2000). The high-growth information infrastructure sector would be an excellent candidate for investment in incumbent worker training, because if such training succeeded, it would create more entry-level, relatively high-wage opportunities in urban areas for workers with short-term training.

Notes

1. While large firms often provide training, pensions, and health insurance and pay efficiency wages, outside contractors to which functions are outsourced tend to forego these practices and tolerate low quality and high turnover.
2. For discussions of all three trends, see Cappelli et al. 1997; Herzenberg, Alic, and Wial 1998; Osterman 1999.
3. The career paths conception outlined in Figure 8.1 is a result of the author's interviews with training providers, employers, and academic specialists in workforce development in the three focus regions—northern and southern California and New York City.

4. Since word processing and other clerical work on computers have traditionally been female-dominated, most of the participants who enter the career path from this direction are women, whereas most of the people who enter from the telephone class are men. In the computer support and networking courses, then, there is a more equal gender mix.
5. While officially part of the school district, ELASC's original parent was a War on Poverty-funded community learning center started in the mid-1960s, and the institution has clearly been intent on keeping what one leader referred to as its "personal touch, its ability to work with people individually."
6. Brooklyn Networks is a project of Brooklyn Workforce Innovations, which is the workforce development subsidiary of the Fifth Avenue Committee, a community development and advocacy organization serving South Brooklyn.
7. Instruction for an initial class of 18 students began in July 2001, and in May 2004 the program completed its fourteenth five-week cycle. Participants attend class six hours a day, five days a week, with part of each day devoted to employability skills and workplace professionalism.
8. The BICSI curriculum is designed for learners with higher educational levels than most of the low-income job seekers participating in Brooklyn Networks, despite the fact that participants are required to be at only an eighth grade reading level.
9. However, Verizon has not hired new employees at entry level since 2001.
10. CWA and Verizon considered forming a hiring hall–type structure through which Verizon installation and repair workers would be employed on an as-needed basis but were unable to come to agreement on how it would be structured.
11. The Takahashi and Meléndez paper appears as a chapter in this volume.
12. Under the same Department of Labor grant, CWA/NETT works in the Washington, DC, area with students referred through the Workforce Investment Board of Prince George's County, Maryland.
13. If they wish, individuals can take the community college–sponsored courses using their home computers, but most of the participants in this program do not have Internet connections in their homes.
14. One local leader in northern California commented, "We feel we have to become a training ground for the worker. In this age the Bells are moving away from the old 'we train you, we know it all' model. Especially in an economic downturn, training costs are scrutinized. Training is an area that is pushed away."

Appendix 8A

Telecommunications and Networking Technician Certification Models

BICSI INSTALLER CERTIFICATION

Building Industry Consulting Services International (BICSI), is a professional association for telecommunications infrastructure design and installation firms. It has been in existence since 1974, mainly as a trade association for cable plant designers and engineers. In 1997 it began a program to train and certify cable installers and technicians. Installer training is offered at BICSI conferences and seminars held in different parts of the country and is also licensed to proprietary schools and to local groups (such as Brooklyn Networks). BICSI's training teaches basic knowledge of premise cabling standards and cabling media, as well as techniques for "pulling" cable, splicing it, terminating it, testing networks, and troubleshooting problems. Its more advanced levels introduce LAN hardware and software. Certification is awarded to people who pass BICSI exams regardless of whether they have been through the training. The unsubsidized cost of each level of BICSI training is $950, plus exam fees.

C-TECH ASSOCIATES NETWORK CABLING SPECIALIST CERTIFICATION

C-Tech Associates Incorporated is a New Jersey–based training company that has developed short-term job training curricula to prepare people for entry-level network cabling jobs. C-Tech courses are taught using equipment that is stored in small cases, which means that the sponsoring institution does not have to build out an expensive lab and can use space flexibly. C-Tech designs, develops, and manufactures the classroom equipment. Since its founding in 1995, C-Tech has expanded to more than 260 certified training facilities (CTFs) throughout the United States. C-Tech training materials are used by community colleges, high schools, U.S. Job Corps centers, correctional facilities, and trade unions. The East Los Angeles Skills Center is one such facility.

A+ COMPUTER TECHNICIAN CERTIFICATION

The A+ certification is sponsored by the Computing Technology Industry Association (CompTIA), a trade association made up of computing and communications companies. A+ certified students can demonstrate competency in troubleshooting hardware for IBM compatibles and/or Macintosh computers using MS-DOS, MS Windows, or Mac OS software. A+ is a vendor-neutral standard, which means that holders of the certification can be assumed to know how to troubleshoot and repair hardware problems with all PCs. A+ is chiefly an exam, not a curriculum, though it is possible to buy from CompTIA a job task analysis which outlines the competencies covered on the exam (some training organizations have used this as the basis for developing a curriculum). According to CompTIA, the A+ exam is "targeted for entry-level computer service technicians with at least six months' on-the-job experience," but it may also be useful for helping telecom technician trainees gain basic proficiency with computing hardware. A San Francisco–based effort to train disadvantaged adults as network administrators has used A+ certification as a beginning step in that process—helping the trainees gain basic familiarity with PCs through A+, then moving them into Cisco Certified Network Associate training (described below).

MANUFACTURER CERTIFICATIONS

This type of certification is issued by manufacturers of cabling and network equipment as a marketing tool and distribution strategy. A manufacturer offers an installation contractor free or inexpensive training for the contractor's employees in the installation and maintenance of a particular kind of cabling or network switch; when the designers and installers employed by the contractor complete the vendor-specific course, the contractor becomes authorized to install and maintain that manufacturer's equipment. Installation contractors use manufacturer certifications to promote their services to potential customers. They may also act as value added resellers, marketing and reselling the equipment of the manufacturers with which they are affiliated.

THE CISCO CERTIFIED NETWORK ASSOCIATE (CCNA) CERTIFICATION

The CCNA is a manufacturer certification focused on LANs and WANs powered by Cisco switches and routers. Unlike other manufacturers, Cisco has made its exams—along with an extensive training program—available through training partner locations (where instructor-led training is offered) and through remote learning labs, where students learn by means of a Web-based curriculum. Trade schools, community colleges, unions and even CBOs have become training partners and lab locations; they essentially resell Cisco training to students (in the case of nonprofits, they provide it at cost or at a subsidized price). Cisco training is said to be about 20 percent specific to Cisco products and 80 percent generic, so many people take the Cisco route to becoming familiar with the installation, configuration, and operation of LANs, WANs, and dial-up access services. CCNA training has been suggested as a follow-on to A+ training and to basic cabling training.[1] The CWA has negotiated a special arrangement with Cisco and has set up several Cisco remote labs with the goal of providing union members with skills upgrading opportunities.

Appendix Note

1. Cisco also offers two additional levels of training: CCNP (network professional) and CCIE (internetworking expert).

References

Allen, Steven G. 1994. "Developments in Collective Bargaining in Construction in the 1980s and 1990s." In *Contemporary Collective Bargaining in the Private Sector*, Paula B. Voos, ed. Madison, WI: Industrial Relations Research Association, pp. 411–445.

Batt, Rosemary, and Jeffrey Keefe. 1999. "Human Resource and Employment Practices in Telecommunications Services, 1980-1998." In *Employment Practices and Business Strategy*, Peter Cappelli, ed. New York: Oxford University Press, pp. 107–152.

Batt, Rosemary, and Michael Strausser. 1997. "Labor Market Outcomes of Deregulation in Telecommunications Services." Paper presented at the 50th annual meeting of the Industrial Relations Research Association, held in Chicago, January 3–5, 1998.

Bosworth, Brian. 1998. "Regional Economic Analysis to Support Job Development Strategies." In *Jobs and Economic Development: Strategies and Practice*, Robert Gilroth, ed. Thousand Oaks, CA: Sage Publications, pp. 85–104.

Cappelli, Peter, Laurie Bassi, Harry Katz, David Knoke, Paul Osterman, and Michael Useem. 1997. *Change At Work.* New York: Oxford University Press.

Chapple, Karen, and Matthew Zook. 2000. "Why IT Jobs Stay." Paper presented at the annual conference of the Association of Collegiate Schools of Planning, November 2–5, Atlanta.

Chapple, Karen, Matthew Zook, Radhika Kunamneni, AnnaLee Saxenian, Steven Weber, and Beverly Crawford. 2000a. *From Promising Practices to Promising Futures: Job Training in Information Technology for Disadvantaged Adults.* New York: Ford Foundation.

———. 2000b. *From Promising Practices to Promising Futures: Job Training in Information Technology for Disadvantaged Adults: Synthesis of Key Findings.* Oakland, CA: PolicyLink.

Clark, Peggy, and Steven Dawson. 1995. *Jobs and the Urban Poor: Privately Initiated Sectoral Strategies*. Washington DC: Aspen Institute.

Fischer, David. 2001. *Under the Mattress: Why NYC's Jobs System Remains a Work in Progress.* New York: Center for an Urban Future.

Fitzgerald, Joan. 2000. *Community Colleges as Labor Market Intermediaries: Building Career Ladders for Low-Wage Workers.* New York: Ford Foundation.

Fitzgerald, Joan, and Virginia Carlson. 2000. "Ladders to a Better Life." *The American Prospect* 11(15): 54–60.

Fleischer, Wendy. 2001. *Extending Ladders: Findings from the Annie E. Casey Foundation's Jobs Initiative.* Baltimore: Annie E. Casey Foundation.

Glasmeier, Amy, Candace Nelson, and Jeffrey W. Thompson. 2000. *Jane Addams Resource Corporation: A Case Study of A Sectoral Employment Development Approach.* Washington DC: Aspen Institute.

Graham, Steven, and Simon Marvin. 1996. *Telecommunications and the City: Electronic Spaces, Urban Places.* London: Routledge.

Hall, Peter. 1999. "Changing Geographies: Technology and Income." In *High Technology and Low-Income Communities: Prospects for the Positive Use of Advanced Information Technology,* Donald Schön, Bish Sanyal, and William J. Mitchell, eds. Cambridge, MA: MIT Press, pp. 45–68.

Harrison, Bennett, and Marcus Weiss. 1998. *Workforce Development Networks: Community-Based Organizations and Regional Alliances.* Thousand Oaks, CA: Sage Publications.

Herzenberg, Stephen A., John A. Alic, and Howard Wial. 1998. *New Rules for a New Economy: Employment and Opportunity in Postindustrial America.* Ithaca, NY: ILR Press.

Holzer, Harry. 1996. *What Employers Want: Job Prospects for Less Educated Workers.* Thousand Oaks, CA: Sage Publications.

Keefe, Jeffrey, and Rosemary Batt. 1997. "Technology and Market-Driven Restructuring: United States." In *Telecommunications: Restructuring Work and Employment Relations Worldwide*, Harry C. Katz, ed. Ithaca, NY: ILR Press, pp. 31–88.

Meléndez, Edwin. 1996. *Working on Jobs: The Center for Employment Training*. Boston: Mauricio Gaston Institute for Latino Community Development and Public Policy.

Mitchell, William J. 1999. "Equitable Access to the Online World." In *High Technology and Low-Income Communities: Prospects for the Positive Use of Advanced Information Technology,* Donald Schön, Bish Sanyal, and William J. Mitchell, eds. Cambridge, MA: MIT Press, pp. 135–161.

National Employment Law Project. 2000. *Workforce Investment Board Support Letter.* New York: National Employment Law Project. http://www.nelp.org/docUploads/letter1%2Epdf (accessed February 28, 2002).

National Telecommunications and Information Administration (NTIA). 2000. *Falling Through the Net: Toward Digital Inclusion.* Washington, DC: National Telecommunications and Information Administration. http://search.ntia.doc.gov/pdf/fttn00.pdf (accessed January 3, 2002).

Noyelle, Thierry. 1987. *Beyond Industrial Dualism: Market and Job Segmentation in the New Economy*. Boulder, CO: Westview Press.

Osterman, Paul. 1999. *Securing Prosperity: The American Labor Market: How It Has Changed and What to Do about It.* Princeton, NJ: Princeton

University Press.
Parker, Eric, and Joel Rogers. 2000. "Sectoral Training Initiatives in the U.S.: Building Blocks of a New Workforce Preparation System?" In *The German Skills Machine: Sustaining Comparative Advantage in a Global Economy,* Pepper D. Culpepper and David Finegold, eds. *Policies and Institutions*, Vol 3. New York: Berghahn Books, pp. 326–362.
Sassen, Saskia. 2001. *The Global City.* 2nd ed. Princeton, NJ: Princeton University Press.
Schön, Donald A. 1999. "Introduction." In *High Technology and Low-Income Communities: Prospects for the Positive Use of Advanced Information Technology,* Donald Schön, Bish Sanyal and William J. Mitchell, eds. Cambridge, MA: MIT Press, pp. 1–23.
Servon, Lisa J. 2002. *Bridging the Digital Divide: Technology, Community, and Public Policy.* Malden, MA: Blackwell Publishing.
Swinney, Dan. 2001. "A Labor-Led Workforce Training and Education System: Practical Opportunities and Strategic Challenges." A report on the work of the Manufacturing Workforce Development Project of the Chicago Federation of Labor. *Social Policy*, 31(3): pp. 23–32.
Takahashi, Beverly, and Edwin Meléndez. 2002. *Union-Sponsored Workforce Development Initiatives.* New York: Community Development Research Center, Milano Graduate School, New School University.
Temin, Peter, and Louis Galambos. 1987. *The Fall of the Bell System: A Study in Prices and Politics.* Cambridge: Cambridge University Press.
Zook, Matthew A. 2000. "The Web of Production: The Economic Geography of Commercial Internet Content Production in the United States." *Environment and Planning A* 32(3): 411–426.

Part 3

Recasting the Role of Community Colleges

9
Community Colleges, Welfare Reform, and Workforce Development

Edwin Meléndez
New School University

Luis M. Falcón
Northeastern University

Carlos Suárez-Boulangger
Hyde Square Task Force

Lynn McCormick
City University of New York

Alexandra de Montrichard
New School University

Federal policies in employment training and assistance for the nation's low-income population have changed dramatically since welfare reform was officially launched with the enactment of the Personal Responsibility and Work Opportunity Reconciliation Act of 1996 (PRWORA). A major component of federal welfare reform has been the Welfare-to-Work (WtW) grant to states to facilitate the transition of welfare recipients into the workplace. These grants target the Temporary Assistance to Needy Families (TANF) participants who are considered least employable: those without a high school education and those with low reading or math skills, substance abuse problems, or poor work histories. In addition, WtW grants focus on participants about to reach their time limit on TANF. These major changes in federal welfare have resulted in a policy shock to the federally assisted employment training system at the state and local levels. The employment training system is now oriented towards serving the most disadvantaged populations and emphasizing job placement over training and education.[1]

The objective of this paper is to ascertain how community colleges have responded to the WtW initiative and to assess the implications of their participation in these programs for local workforce development systems. Community colleges serve as key institutions in the restructuring of local labor markets. With a long history as sponsors of employment and training programs targeting both disadvantaged populations and specific local industry needs, community colleges are well positioned to occupy a central role as local and regional labor market intermediaries. Whether they can take advantage of welfare reform to maintain or advance their position as labor market intermediaries will depend on the ever-changing local policies governing work requirements for TANF participants and the internal dynamics of the colleges themselves.

Overall, we found that community colleges responded effectively and creatively to the challenges posed to them by welfare reform, and they have shown that they are capable of playing a major role in regional labor markets. They have benefited from favorable state regulations regarding welfare programs, but beyond that, the extent to which community colleges have responded successfully to welfare reform initiatives at the local level has been determined largely by internal factors. These factors include the college leadership's commitment to a comprehensive mission for the college, the existence of programs and prior experiences serving the disadvantaged at the college, favorable faculty and staff attitudes toward non-degree programs, and a proactive leadership promoting and articulating ongoing relations and collaborations with local labor, businesses, industries, and social service agencies.

We adopted a two-step method for the study. First, we conducted a survey of 251 community colleges in the United States. This sample was drawn from a sampling frame of more than a thousand community colleges throughout the country, compiled from various lists including the membership rolls of the American Association of Community Colleges (AACC), the Hispanic Association of Colleges and Universities (HACU), and the Historically Black Colleges and Universities (HBCU).[2] In the survey, we asked administrators about their involvement in WtW programs as well as other programs serving socially disadvantaged students. In particular, we collected information on the level of staff dedication, support services, and case management in programs targeting welfare recipients; on the linkages between TANF and degree programs; and on the extent of employer participation in the programs.

The survey of community colleges indicates that about 80 percent of community colleges nationwide offer some kind of TANF program. Most of these are spinoffs of programs that existed prior to the enactment of PRWORA, although a large proportion of the colleges surveyed designed completely new programs to meet the stricter requirements of WtW regulations. TANF programs were designed to respond directly to policy regulations emphasizing job placement and work experience. Almost all TANF programs that we surveyed offered short-term training and internships with employers. In general, we found that student outcomes from these programs were comparable to outcomes for other training providers such as community-based organizations (CBOs) operating under the Job Training Partnership Act (JTPA). Administrators at community colleges interviewed for the study estimate that two-thirds of students complete the programs in which they enroll and slightly more than three-quarters find jobs in the areas in which they train. However, our most interesting finding is that, contrary to JTPA-like classroom-based skills training, nearly all of these programs (90.4 percent) also offer college preparatory courses and most of the short-term training (71.2 percent) is articulated to degree programs, so that academic work is conducive to one's long-term educational goals. This makes community colleges important regional labor force intermediaries because they can train the unemployed for entry-level jobs and provide a stepping stone for academic and career advancement.

The survey data provided a general picture, based on quantitative indicators, of how much relative progress community colleges had made in responding to local WtW initiatives. We used this information to rank the colleges in terms of their degree of institutional involvement with WtW initiatives. We categorized community colleges according to whether each one 1) had already implemented WtW programs and was actively developing new ones; 2) had some relatively small WtW programs or was in the initial stages of program development; or 3) indicated that it was not actively engaged in adapting existing programs or designing new programs targeting WtW participants.

In the second phase of the study, based on findings from the survey data, we selected seven community colleges to visit for in-depth case studies. The seven campuses selected represent the first group, those who have pursued the development of WtW programs more aggressively. These campuses are examples of what we classified as the "most advanced" community colleges in terms of their involvement with WtW programs. In general, they also offered multiple employment services and programs and were integral participants in local workforce development networks. The selected colleges are not representative of all community colleges, either in the survey sample or nationwide, but rather represent community colleges' "best practice" in the workforce development field. We selected colleges for the case studies from each of the three size clusters identified in the study. We chose two community colleges each from two large urban areas (Los Angeles and New York), two from medium-sized cities (Fresno, California, and Denver), and one from a small city (Valencia, New Mexico).

A listing of the case studies involving these seven colleges is presented in an appendix to this chapter. The case studies provide an in-depth look at the patterns identified by the survey data, and we present our findings in more detail in subsequent sections.[3] The comparative analysis of the case studies is based on the assessment of four critical areas for programs that specialize in meeting the job training needs of disadvantaged populations. Based on prior research, these four important functions of programs serving the disadvantaged include 1) case management and social support services, 2) instruction and academic support services, 3) overall program design and integration with other academic units, and 4) links to industry and employers.[4] Serving welfare participants requires significant resources and changes in all four of these institutional functions. The institutional functions facilitate training by taking into account participants' social and educational needs and barriers, by making program participation easier, and by providing students with necessary support and connections to employers and entry-level jobs.

The next section of the paper begins with an overview of the potential of community colleges in the current realignment of employment and training systems. Like other institutions, community colleges have responded with several strategies, including adapting existing programs and courses to comply with WtW regulations. Many community colleges have also begun to design and develop entirely new programs. The section ends by explaining why, in our opinion, community colleges have the potential to become premier regional workforce development intermediaries. The potential role of community colleges depends on the colleges' ability to convert WtW programs from a short-term option into the first rung of a longer-term career ladder for disadvantaged workers. In this context, community colleges are in a unique position to benefit from the new Workforce Investment Act (WIA) and federally sponsored training programs.

In the section after that, we present the findings from the seven case studies conducted in five cities, summarizing key lessons from the field. The intent of this discussion is to provide concrete examples of how community colleges have implemented WtW programs and to discuss how these examples illustrate the institutional dynamics affecting community colleges and their emerging role as local labor market intermediaries. In the last section we discuss how welfare reform has strengthened the position of community colleges as regional labor force intermediaries. Their innovation in response to the WtW policy shock has expanded their opportunities to engage in long-term partnerships with local labor and social agencies, employers, and community groups.

COMMUNITY COLLEGES AND WORKFORCE DEVELOPMENT

The workforce development field has evolved tremendously since the enactment of PRWORA. An early study by Public/Private Ventures, a social policy demonstration and evaluation organization, that examined how WtW policy affected the employment training system in 13 states concludes that welfare reform "overwhelmed" the system (Elliott, Spangler, and Yorkievitz 1998). However, the authors recognize that even within the context of the limitations imposed by the work first approach, which emphasizes short-term placement goals for participants, community-based organizations and other service providers have explored programmatic directions that are now leading the way to a more comprehensive restructuring of the local employment training system. It is generally acknowledged that employment training programs are not typically synchronized with job-specific demand for workers; instead they focus primarily on general skills acquisition for participants regardless of relevancy (Grubb 1996). The study indicates that employers are taking a more proactive role in designing and supporting training programs targeting welfare recipients. Job training programs' proactive coordination of WtW initiatives with the private sector has encouraged employer participation.

Other evidence suggests that employment training administrators have redesigned programs to take into account best practices in workforce development, specifically the simultaneous provision of skill acquisition, job-readiness processes, and industry-specific skills (Greenberg, Strawn, and Plimpton 1999a; Grubb 1999; Meléndez and Suárez 2001). Among the practices incorporated in the redesign of old programs and the design of new ones are the targeting of specific industry sectors and occupations (sectoral strategies) and the simulation of workplace dynamics in job training programs (Elliot and King 1999). Researchers have also identified a significant number of programs providing post-placement support for inexperienced workers (Golonka and Matus-Grossman 2001). These reports confirm the findings from an earlier survey of effective CBO-based programs that assist welfare recipients with the transition to work. Stokes (1996) and the U.S. General Accounting Office (USGAO) (1996) found that effective programs provide case management to participants, offer job-readiness training that includes life management skills, and serve as a reliable connection to employers. When necessary, vocational training is part of the program and targets the identified needs of local employers. These programs screen participants for the appropriate skills and match them to the most suitable jobs given their profiles and experiences.

Within this context of policy changes and responses from employers and other service providers, community colleges have become key players in the system of delivery of training services to the population targeted by WtW grants (Bosworth 1997; Carnevale and Desrochers 1997, 2001; Falcone 1994; Fitzgerald 2000; Fitzgerald and Jenkins 1997; Gennett, Johnstone, and Wilson 2001; Golonka and Matus-Grossman 2001; Gooden and Matus-Grossman 2001; Grubb, 1999a,b, 2001; Grubb et al. 1999; Meléndez and Suárez 2001; McCabe 1997; Strawn 1998). Traditionally, community colleges have served different populations than four-year colleges, in both socioeconomic status and level of academic preparation. In addition, some of the training programs offered by community colleges' short-term programs are consistent with PRWORA demands for an accelerated transition into the workplace. Still, for many community colleges, the necessity of participating in the training activities flowing from the new legislation has prompted them to develop new programs and structures to meet a stringent set of program requirements (Katsinas et al. 1999).

Community colleges typically offer a mix of academic programs to TANF participants. Most liberal arts programs in community colleges, along with social sciences and business, have so-called articulation agreements with four-year colleges where credits taken as part of an associate's degree program are transferable to a bachelor's degree program. In some states, like Florida, the state mandates the transferability of credits for the higher education system as a whole, rendering such articulation agreements unnecessary. However, not all of the vocational courses taken as part of an associate's degree are transferable to programs in four-year colleges. In our study we paid particular attention to the articulation of non-degree programs to degree programs. Most new programs designed to serve welfare recipients have a significant component of continuing education or noncredit courses. These courses, such as General Equivalency Degree (GED) preparation and English as a Second Language, are helpful in advancing participants' basic skills to the level required by basic academic courses. Most programs enacted prior to PRWORA that serve the disadvantaged or engage in contract-based employee training have a strong component of noncredit courses. In particular, job readiness and life skills courses and workshops, which are so essential to the design of WtW programs, are not generally college level courses. So, not all courses are transferable to more advanced degree programs; however, the importance of articulation, where work in preparatory training courses is counted as a prerequisite for more advanced courses and awarded college credits, cannot be overstated. Short-term vocational training programs that are designed to feed participants into certificate and degree programs create, by definition, an opportunity for advancement.

Providing the opportunity for academic and career advancement is, theoretically, the greatest advantage of community colleges over other employment training institutions, such as community-based job-training organizations and employer-based training. In a survey of the research on work-oriented programs for welfare recipients, which included the National Supported Work Demonstration, Work Incentive Program (WIN), and Job Opportunities and Basic Skills (JOBS), Gueron (1990) concludes that these programs offer valuable lessons about the potential for large-scale and effective transformation of the welfare system. However, she also warns that the evidence suggests that program impacts have been modest, that many trainees remain dependent on some form of assistance or work-related support, and that poverty is not significantly reduced. Community colleges that link short-term vocational and job readiness training to long-term education and structured advancement opportunities can overcome some of the most critical limitations of past efforts at work-based welfare reform (Greenberg, Strawn, and Plimpton 1999).[5] As such, community colleges offer the best opportunity for disadvantaged workers to advance their skill level and training.

Community colleges have shown employers in many parts of the country that their programs can become reliable sources for well-trained workers. And many state labor and social service agencies have seen that community colleges have the capacity and experience to serve a large number of disadvantaged students by creating specialized support programs and adapting their existing infrastructure to meet these students' needs. Community colleges have demonstrated that they can engage in mutually beneficial collaborations with community-based and church-based organizations as well as with business and industry groups. Above all, community colleges can provide numerous educational programs for any partnership and can connect short-term vocational training with long-term education.

WIA has established a framework for long-term reform of the system in which community colleges are positioned to benefit as much from the new policy framework as any other type of service provider. In a policy briefing to its membership, the American Association of Community Colleges (1998) noted that WIA provides the conditions for community colleges to become the workforce development intermediary of choice, a concept endorsed by Raymond Bramucci (1999), then Assistant Secretary of Labor for the Employment and Training Administration. Among other advantages granted by WIA, the law mandates that community colleges have representatives on state and local workforce development boards. Community colleges have positioned themselves to become One-Stop Career Center (OSCC) administrators or designated satellite offices for other OSCCs. Among other functions, OSCCs serve as an entry point for employment and training services. Many community colleges now also provide Individual Training Accounts (ITAs) and customized training services (Gutierrez 1997). The favorable policy climate and the recent success of community colleges in serving low-income and disadvantaged populations as well as local industry have led many experts in the field to propose a more central role for colleges in regional workforce development systems (Barnett 1995; Carnevale and Desrochers 1997; Grubb 2001; Grubb et al. 1999; Jenkins and Fitzgerald 1998).

In this section we have provided a brief overview of the literature assessing the role of community colleges in workforce development, particularly their experience and potential as employment service providers for welfare recipients. The challenge of welfare reform has induced community organizations to improve delivery systems and employers to become more active in WtW programs. Community college programs are often articulated with degree programs, facilitating students' transfer from short-term vocational training to long-term education. By creating this organic link between programs, colleges are setting in place a mechanism to close the gap between education and training, as has been proposed by Grubb (1996), Bailey (1998), and others. Given the existing network of community colleges throughout the nation, community colleges have the potential to make the greatest impact on workforce development efforts of any type of service provider. In the next section, we present evidence of community college participation in programs targeting welfare recipients and the implication of this participation for the workforce development field.

LESSONS FROM THE FIELD

In our fieldwork, we identify a cluster of factors that have influenced community colleges' responses to WtW legislation. Some factors, like federal and state laws and regulations, are external to the colleges and, therefore, out of their control. However, the community colleges included as case studies are among the many around the country that have implemented proactive strategies to participate in WtW programs.[6] They have designed and implemented programs that consider the special circumstances of welfare recipients as prospective students. Such factors as prior experience with programs serving the disadvantaged, the college leadership's beliefs about the mission of the college and its role in the local economy, the availability of an adequate infrastructure of social and educational services to support disadvantaged students, and ongoing collaborations with local state agencies and employers, all have been instrumental in the rapid response of community colleges to WtW policy initiatives.[7]

This discussion details key aspects of the colleges' responses to welfare reform legislation and their experiences in implementing new programs. Their experiences may encourage federal and state policymakers to adjust regulations to better serve the needs of welfare recipients. At the same time, these lessons can also help program managers reflect on their practices and share their experiences with colleagues who struggle with similar issues.

Case Management and Support Services

Conventional wisdom would suggest that community colleges are far from the ideal institutional setting to house programs targeting the disadvantaged. In contrast to community-based organizations that provide more focused and individualized attention in a smaller setting, community colleges are often large institutions with programs that serve hundreds or thousands of students with widely divergent needs and circumstances. Community colleges of this type may remind some students of the indifference that they may have experienced in large inner city high schools, which ultimately may have reinforced their decision not to continue their education. Traditionally, social and academic support services have been embedded in systems geared to serve hundreds of students. As a result, there is not enough time, nor are there enough resources, to provide individual attention. The question of whether community colleges are the most appropriate institution to provide employment and training services to disadvantaged populations hinges upon whether these mass gateways of education can create an effective support system for needy students, one that is similar to those provided by community-based organizations.

The evidence gathered in this study suggests that community colleges have implemented many successful programs over the years and that this prior experience allowed them to respond relatively quickly to the WtW initiative. WtW grants motivated community colleges to design programs that field a strong case management component. Through these programs, counselors can devote personal attention to participants and organize group sessions for life management and job readiness workshops. Counselors report that group sessions and collective discussions are usually more effective than individual counseling for helping students move from understanding their problems to finding solutions. In group sessions, students share experiences of coping with particular problems and their knowledge of what resources are available to them. Meléndez and Suárez (2001) write that dedicated programs that structure the student's experience within the college tend to promote solidarity among students and create peer support groups. These programs create an enabling environment in which students help each other and do not necessarily have to rely on staff for instruction or advice.

In addition to a strong case management system and group activities, students are formally organized into cohorts and assigned a shared "block" schedule. The combined effect of this type of program structure is to provide a smaller and more manageable environment within the larger community college infrastructure. A "small school" environment is particularly important when students begin attending the program. Over time, students are referred to different services and resources on campus in order to become familiar with the institution and develop an understanding of how to solve an array of problems.

Although students are occasionally referred to outside resources, for the most part community colleges have the necessary infrastructure in place to deal with students' social and academic problems. For example, the colleges included in the case studies provided a variety of support services, from special programs for women and the disabled to referrals for housing or substance abuse counseling and treatment. Almost all provided day care facilities or made arrangements with outside providers to serve students. The Valencia, New Mexico, campus created a specialized program to respond to the reality of domestic violence as a critical problem for program participants. A CBO sent a representative to each student orientation to provide literature and general information. As a result, the CBO relates that a large percentage of women—as high as 12–15 percent of the student body, which numbers 1,700—have contacted it through a confidential telephone number provided during orientation for women to discuss their problems or those of a friend.

Despite all the similarities among the programs highlighted in the case studies, each campus adopted a unique strategy and program structure to provide support services appropriate for its student body. In Fresno, for example, Fresno City College adopted a "community job center" strategy modeled after two existing programs: a successful center targeting the needs of immigrant workers and a program serving disabled students. The flagship community job center, located in a Manchester, California, shopping center, provides job counseling and offers a range of job readiness classes and workshops. The center has adopted the structure of a one-stop center in partnership with the local Private Industry Council. To facilitate mentoring of WtW participants experiencing multiple barriers to employment, the two organizations developed a "coach" model, in which community volunteers and part-time workers devote intensive individual attention to a small number of program participants.

Alternatively, the Community College of Denver has adopted a "track" model, where the counselor serves as case manager for a small cohort of program participants who have chosen a vocational training track, such as bank teller. The case managers also serve as job readiness instructors—administrative coordinators who monitor internships and relations with employers, job developers, and post-placement support staff. The core idea of this model is that a single mentor simultaneously establishes relationships with employers, targeting a particular industry or sector, and serves as an all-purpose case manager for program participants. The college's partnership with Norwest Bank is a textbook case of a successful sectoral model: almost all students that go through the program find employment at the bank or at other financial institutions in the city. Retention rates for Winning Independence Nurtures Greater Strength (WINGS) participants after six months were similar (53 percent for the first cohort and 65 percent for the second cohort) to those of regular hires—an impressive achievement considering the work experience and educational differences of the two groups.

What lessons can be drawn from the experiences of community colleges that have implemented WtW programs? Experiences with the provision of case management and support services point to a set of common strategies. First, community colleges can create a manageable small school environment by forming student cohorts and assigning case managers to work closely with them. Many colleges have structured programs this way in the past. In particular, they have established grant-based projects targeting a diverse, disadvantaged population. Their new programs stand out because of the rapid deployment of resources and the magnitude of the effort in response to the WtW initiative—an effort that is particularly intriguing since community colleges are not generally perceived as having programmatic flexibility and the capacity for innovation. These colleges have responded with much determination and have adapted existing programs to a design that fits the needs of a hard-to-serve population.

Second, the effort to serve a large group of students with specific needs seems to have been made possible by the network of existing resources supporting adult learners in community colleges. The key is that the network of resources leveraged to support the WtW initiative is both internal and external to the college. On campus, community colleges have numerous specialized service centers and offices. At the same time, partnerships with community-based organizations and local social service agencies play a pivotal role in sustaining programs.

Instruction and Academic Support

In comparing the job readiness of the initial waves of program participants with the more recent ones, practitioners supervising WtW programs in community colleges observe that participants in recent cohorts are in greater need of extensive remedial education and have had fewer workplace experiences than earlier participants. Regardless of whether prospective students have completed high school, the functional English literacy of most new intakes is below the ninth grade level. Determining the literacy level of prospective students is essential for community colleges since state regulations require that students test at a minimum level before they are allowed to enroll in college level courses and receive tuition reimbursement. How well a student tests determines the amount of remedial education he or she must complete before enrolling in vocational skill training and basic academic courses.

One might argue that the rigorous assessment of students' basic academic proficiency level is a bureaucratic exercise by community colleges. After all, how much education is required for an entry-level job? But from a practical point of view, the restructuring of the economy means that more education is likely to be required of future students than has previously been the case. The economic sectors that are growing—particularly those industries generating the bulk of new entry-level positions—are creating jobs in which cognitive and functional literacy is necessary.

Consider two sectors targeted by most WtW programs: office assistants and bank tellers. Office assistants need to know basic keyboarding, filing systems, business correspondence, and communication with customers and supervisors; bank tellers need a minimum understanding of computerized accounting and financial systems. In a competitive job market, not only do WtW students need a minimum literacy level to understand core job competencies, they need to master this knowledge at a performance standard set by other workers competing for the same jobs. Expectations for the success of welfare reform must consider that an increasing number of program participants are in need of remedial education to attain basic skills and that, as more people are trained, the job market becomes more competitive for entry-level positions. In an economic downturn, the task of training and placing disadvantaged students in entry-level jobs becomes even more challenging.

If practitioners are correct in their assessment of incoming students and the challenges of the workplace, the current focus of community college programs on basic skills remediation for WtW participants is both appropriate and necessary. To the extent that community colleges are in a better position to provide basic skills instruction more effectively than community- or employer-based training programs, the enrollment of welfare recipients in community college programs should continue to increase in the near future. Community colleges are well positioned to provide basic skills instruction for adult and non-traditional students (Martin 1999). Most colleges have basic skills learning centers and labs that specialize in remedial education for incoming students. Special programs adapt basic academic skills instruction to vocational contexts, either as separate modules or integrated into vocational skills courses. In many cases, GED preparation is offered to prospective students as a part of short-term vocational training programs. Typically, funding for these programs is a permanent appropriation through the state's education department.

Some of the colleges selected for this study are good examples of innovators in providing academic support services for welfare recipients and other disadvantaged populations. For example, Los Angeles Trade Technical College (LATTC) utilized state funding for WtW programs to create a new Learning Skills Center. Prior to the creation of the center, LATTC offered basic literacy and computer instruction as separate programs scattered across the campus. The new center consolidated academic improvement programs already in existence into one location, added computer-aided, self-paced instruction, lab monitors, and additional instructors, scheduled workshops and discussion sessions on a regular basis, and extended its hours of operation. All services are open to the full student body, not just to WtW program participants, but WtW students have priority for one-on-one tutoring and other activities at the center. In addition, Los Angeles City College (LACC, not to be confused with LATTC) has operated a learning skills center for over a decade and now offers special sessions for students enrolled in the WtW program.

In Denver and New Mexico, GED preparation was incorporated into the basic program curriculum. Denver's sectoral strategy is based on vocational tracks and requires students to have a high school diploma, which is a prerequisite for entry-level positions in targeted occupations such as banking and health technologies. The Valencia campus of the University of New Mexico, primarily a two year institution, faced a particularly challenging situation because of the relatively low literacy of students coming into the WtW program. The college served as the local social agency, receiving more than 2,000 WtW participants from 1997 to 1999. Eighty percent of the participants did not have a high school degree. Eighty-five percent tested below the ninth grade level in English and more than half tested below the sixth grade level. With such low literacy levels, basic education was central to the college's employment training program. At the same time, 40 percent of the population had never held a job and the majority of trainees had been out of a job for many years. In response to this reality, the University of New Mexico created several centers to assist students with their education and employment needs. The Student Enrichment Center provides one-on-one tutoring and study groups in math and English. The Adult Education Center covers GED preparation, basic education, English as a Second Language, employability skills, and time management and study skills. The college also operates a leadership skills center, Building Leadership through Adult Student Training (BLAST), of whose clients about 30 percent are WtW program participants.

Like the other colleges reviewed above, Fresno Community College offers a comprehensive package of academic support services. One of the most innovative services is the Vocational Training Center, which aims for highly adaptive responsiveness to local job market conditions. Having been in operation for more than a decade, this center is modeled after best practices in community-based employment training.[8] During any given year, the center offers over a dozen training modules on occupations in high demand in the local job market; the modules last from seven to 30 weeks. The center offers an open entry–open exit format so students can enroll at the start of every week after a brief orientation and proceed through the training modules at their own pace. Training consists of hands-on, contextual learning so students start practicing and modeling the occupation from the beginning of the module. In addition to the job training that the center offers, the college has 13 additional short-term vocational skills certificate programs designed for WtW program participants. Free tuition encourages enrollment from the target group of WtW students, among others. The results of this approach are strong: the center has a job placement rate of 97 percent.

Perin (1998) suggests that instructional practices make up the hardest area to change in community colleges, particularly in the context of integrated academic and vocational education. However, there are some qualitative indicators that point to the potential effect of WtW initiatives on improving instructional practices in community colleges. For example, the human services department at LACC offers two certificates (general, and drug and alcohol rehabilitation) designed to incorporate pedagogy that has proven effective with disadvantaged students. Courses are student-focused and participatory, and experiential learning is integral to the program. Students rotate through internships with three employers in a program that takes from one and a half to two years to complete.

For community college programs serving WtW participants, the focus on remedial basic education and GED preparation appears to be determined by the academic profile of the student population. These activities are complementary to components of existing programs and are not exclusively intended for WtW program participants, as may have been the case in the past. As related earlier, one common lesson from these case study experiences is that community colleges are using the academic support infrastructure already in place to accommodate the needs of a new type of student in WtW programs. The new LATTC Learning Skills Center, for example, consolidated operations from mainstreamed services to target a population presumed to be more difficult to serve.

Some programs complemented instruction in existing support centers with new staff or arranged for special attention and resources to be assigned to program students. In some cases, special measures were taken, but for the most part, existing academic support services are used to provide services to the WtW program. Making changes in instruction methods beyond offering basic remedial education courses is a relatively slower process and more difficult to track and monitor. However, early signs indicate that some departments are beginning to implement pedagogy that better fits the WtW student profile (Martin 1999; Dirkx 1999). The institutional response of community colleges to the challenge of serving educationally disadvantaged students suggests that they have the infrastructure and the experience to continue to develop and establish appropriate and effective programs.

Program Design and Development

Program design and development is one area in which state policies and the views of state officials affect the role of community colleges. For example, the state of California designated $66 million to help colleges assimilate WtW programs. As a result, the community colleges in this state had the most dramatic response to the WtW initiative of any state. Virtually all staff interviewed as part of the survey sample in California stated that their college was undertaking the redesign of old programs and the design of new ones. That initial impression was confirmed by in-depth research undertaken during the site visits at the three California campuses.

Two factors have been most important in shaping California's state policies regarding community college participation in welfare initiatives. First, the governor's office and community colleges reached an agreement regarding the appropriate framework for the colleges' participation in reform efforts and assigned the necessary financial resources to facilitate policy implementation. Second, college administrators reported that the state political leadership sent a clear message to all campuses: "Your involvement is important. We will support your efforts, and we will reward those who take the task seriously." The combination of assigning substantive funding and sending a strong political message to relevant bureaucracies, such as the state social and labor agencies and the community college system, was very effective. State funding allowed department heads to pay faculty and staff additional compensation to develop new courses and file necessary paperwork. Colleges were able to hire additional staff to coordinate program activities with employers and local social agencies. Also, during the initial implementation phase the colleges took a risky approach to getting their programs under way: they offered some courses without meeting the state's minimum enrollment standard, which determines state reimbursement to the college for the costs associated with the course. However, the risk paid off as the WtW grant reimbursed the colleges for salaries and other uncovered expenses.

The California cases document the extent to which departments have adapted existing programs to meet WtW program requirements. The basic restructuring of these courses involved grouping existing introductory vocational courses (for jobs like office assistant) with remedial courses in basic education, life management skills, and job readiness. To accommodate the minimum work hours required by the state, these courses were offered for more hours during the week, often based on a nine-week schedule that corresponded to about half a semester. Almost all programs placed students in internships that qualified as a work-related activity or in work-study jobs. The end result of such a packet was to achieve the state mandated total of 32–35 hours per week of work-related activities. Whether the credits for vocational or basic math and English courses could be transferred to a certificate or degree program depended on a host of factors that varied from campus to campus. Typically, at least some credits were transferable. New programs served as an extension of existing departmental programs, often starting at a lower level of basic academic skill requirements.

The initial phase of program development was followed by an effort by community colleges to replicate their successful programs. The new programs often targeted segments of the job market not previously served by the college. They expanded departmental programs targeting welfare program participants and replicated the model of short-term training developed during the initial phase of program development. The California Work Opportunity and Responsibility to Kids (CalWORK) office at LACC organized an advisory board comprising the department chairs of the largest and most active departments, such as business, human services, and dietetics, as well as representatives from the president's office and other government offices on campus. The strategy paid off handsomely.

The departments began to assess what job market areas they could target for the development of new short-term training (about six months) that could be designed as part of one-year certificate and two-year degree programs. In developing these programs, the departments used some of the same elements of program design previously employed, including more contact hours per week and internships to satisfy WtW program requirements. However, in this second round of program design, the college leadership began to use block scheduling to combine new program courses with other departmental programs. The business department's marketing stresses that students can take "back to back" courses and go "back to work." Courses are offered in sequence so that students who attend "2 afternoons + 2 evenings" can get their degree in "2 years." By design, the new programs targeted fast growing occupations and depended on already existing relationships with industry partners for internships, curriculum design, and recruitment of adjunct faculty to teach new courses. LATTC followed a similar strategy in the expansion of the programs targeting WtW participants.

In Denver, the second phase response to the WtW initiative involved the replication of short-term training with new occupational tracks. The tracks have two basic design characteristics. The first is the targeting of particular entry-level positions within an expanding industry, such as bank teller or health technician. The sectoral focus is intended to establish long-term relations with key industry groups and employers. Through those consultations, the program determines the job-specific training preferred by employers. The second aspect of the program is to train candidates specifically for anticipated job openings in the region. At the Community College of Denver, training is organized into three stages that combine classroom discussions with a workplace internship. During the first month, training focuses on job readiness workshops and a minimum of work with participating employers. Over the next three months, students spend 18 hours in basic and vocational education at the college and 22 hours at work each week.

In conjunction with employers, the program trains supervisors in effective supervision strategies for program participants and maintains regular communication with them about how the trainees are performing at work. In these sessions, any problems with work performance or attendance are discussed with the supervisors. Students are also assigned a workplace mentor, a more experienced worker who can answer work-related questions and help solve everyday problems. During the last stage of the program, students work full time but attend weekly sessions with the track coordinator, who continues to monitor their progress for the next three months. The staggered training design of the track model seems to work well for introducing inexperienced workers to the rigors of the workplace and has produced very high placement and retention rates. Of the 99 participants in the first training cohort, 90 percent were placed in internships and 66 percent in unsubsidized employment.

These examples suggest that community colleges are pursuing two somewhat different strategies in taking WtW programs to scale. The Los Angeles experience portrays the colleges as "widening" the number of programs that comply with WtW requirements and articulating short-term training with certificate and degree programs. They have focused on working within academic departments to create new programs to accommodate an increasing number of students. In Denver and to some extent in New Mexico, the colleges are pursuing a "deepening" strategy which replicates the sectoral short-term vocational training modules that target new occupations. Fresno follows a blended model: its Vocational Training Center pursues a sectoral strategy similar to the Denver example, while the academic departments' strategy resembles more closely the Los Angeles experience.

Both strategies have proven successful in different contexts. The key is to apply the correct strategy in the appropriate situation. Sectoral strategies are more commonly associated with dedicated (or self-standing) programs and short-term training modules. The academic departments' strategy is appropriate for short-term vocational training programs that are more closely related to, and serve as feeders to, established certificate and degree programs. This also involves the redesign and expansion of existing certificate and degree programs.

Links to Industry

Labor market intermediaries have a dual responsibility to simultaneously serve workers in need of training and employment and employers who prefer to hire the best available candidates in the job market. This is a balancing act indeed. The previous sections detailed how community colleges have served the needs of disadvantaged populations by providing short-term vocational training and educational programs in a variety of occupations with market demand. This section expands on the experiences of the community colleges and employers interviewed in site visits regarding their working relationship for the implementation of WtW programs.

One of the salient characteristics of the colleges included in the study is the maintenance of long-term, well-established relationships with employers and local social and labor agencies. These ongoing relations contribute to the ability of community colleges to respond in an effective and timely way to WtW initiatives. In particular, community colleges in California established relations with industry through the different academic departments as part of their regular program operations. As a technical school with a focus on training for trade industries, LATTC naturally established relations with industry. For decades, LATTC has invited industry leaders to become advisors to its programs and help the college design internships, projects, and curricula. Departments also hire adjunct faculty from industry to teach vocational courses on a regular basis.

A similar process is in place at LACC. There, the human services department requires not one but three internship rotations of about ten hours a week, with each rotation lasting a semester. This regime is part of the student's socialization to a profession, through which practitioners learn many of the core competencies from experience. The implication is that departments must constantly coordinate activities with industry and foster a vast set of relationships to satisfy student demand for internships and placements. Similarly, Fresno Community College has an aggressive policy of work-study internships implemented through different departments. The college's vocational skills training relies on cooperative work agreements with all the trades. In addition, the college subsidizes up to 75 percent of work-study internships.

The Denver Community College sectoral strategy is built on the concept of a progressive transition of interns to the workplace. In some cases, employers fully absorb the internship cost. Norwest Bank's WINGS program absorbs the cost of the internship in compliance with local banking industry regulations and pays its interns wages that are above the federal minimum. The bank promotes almost all participants to full-time employees after four months of training. After six months of employment, the retention rates of WtW program participants compare very favorably with those of regular hires.

The WINGS program's success is explained by some of the factors that define effective practices for labor market intermediaries. The program trains interns for the specific teller position that the bank needs to fill at the moment. The training module is designed in collaboration with the bank so that the skills that trainees learn are specific to bank operations. The program then recommends interns for "on-time" interviews for openings in the different branches—that is, when the branches have an opening, not before or after. The program only sends candidates on interviews when they are "job ready" and a good match for a particular position at the bank branch. Aside from technical qualifications, a good match is also determined by assessing subjective factors such as personalities (of both workers and supervisors) and objective factors such as the availability of public transportation to work and commute length.

A key factor boosting retention rates in the WINGS program is the post placement support offered to participants and employers. Personal problems experienced by participants are addressed away from the attention of supervisors. Absenteeism is dealt with promptly and is a major impetus for rotating students from one site to another to accommodate transportation needs or family responsibilities. Appropriate corrective measures to support students in overcoming the particular issues behind a problem or unexpected behavior are also provided. When difficult situations arise, the track coordinator meets with the line supervisor and the participant to evaluate the situation and discuss solutions to the problem. Supervisors are trained in strategies that have proven effective in motivating program participants and in methods to teach trainees appropriate procedures and techniques.

The simplest formula for job retention, we were told, is to ensure that employees are effective and happy in their jobs. One of the most interesting observations about the benefits of the college-employer partnership is that, in addition to all the factors already mentioned, collaboration with the college has simplified the bank's relations with government agencies and reduced the paperwork associated with the WtW initiative. The more the program functions like other business operations, the more satisfied the bank is with the community college partnership.

Holzer (1999), examining data from an employer survey in Michigan, suggests that employers hiring welfare recipients are concerned with issues of job readiness and basic skills preparation before they hire and with issues of absenteeism and attitude in the workplace after they hire. Given what we know of employers' concern about participating in WtW initiatives, how do community colleges design programs, operations, and practices to respond to these concerns? The examples presented above illustrate some of the strategies employed by specific programs to respond to industry concerns. All programs share a design that places emphasis on the various issues identified by employers. Substance abuse and absenteeism are detected early on by requiring participants to follow a full-time schedule during training. Students benefit routinely from counseling services and participate in life management skills workshops. Workplace attitudes are identified and adjusted by a combination of job readiness workshops and practice during internships before participants are referred to jobs. These activities socialize students to the routines and cultures of the workplace.

The degree to which WtW programs provide basic and job-specific skills instruction varies by program, but all the programs visited for this study offer a combination of basic and vocational instruction at a level sufficient to be competitive in the job market. One of the key functions of the programs is to screen candidates for job readiness, work attitudes, and functional basic and vocational skills required by the job. Students are referred to employment interviews only when the program staff determines that they are ready for a permanent job. Once the students are successfully placed with an employer, most programs offer at least minimum post-placement services. Some programs, such as Norwest Bank and Community College of Denver, offer more comprehensive post-placement follow-up for participants.

The appropriateness of the community colleges' responses to the WtW initiative is ultimately defined by how well they are serving the needs of both students and employers. One aspect of the program is incomplete without the other. The disconnect between training and post-training employment opportunities is well documented (Grubb 1996). However, the programs reviewed in this study have helped us understand how to close the gap between the education and training needs of disadvantaged populations and the needs of employers for a well-trained and job-ready supply of entry-level workers. The cases presented here provide evidence that programs designed to incorporate both aspects of the job matching process are more effective than other training programs in terms of placement rates, starting wages, and retention rates. Colleges have implemented several strategies to remove barriers to employment, improve skills, and connect students to jobs. Academic departments tend to engage many employers and to design programs that offer more generic training that can be adapted to different contexts. Self-standing, short-term vocational training programs that follow more focused sectoral strategies create programs that target the specific needs of one or a few employers and engage industry leaders more intensively in the design and implementation of the program.

Leadership in a People Business

Workforce development is by nature a people business. It is about improving the education and experience of entry-level workers and about providing a reliable supply of ready workers to the job market. Workforce development is also labor-intensive, as it requires program staff and instructors to engage actively in the provision of services. And, it is a people business in a final, important dimension—leadership within institutions is crucial for developing ideas, structuring resources, and designing and operating programs. On each campus, we found that it took a combination of leaders to get new programs off the ground. We identified at least three levels of leadership that play specific, key roles in the design and implementation of WtW programs: presidents or other senior level executives, deans, and program directors.

Program and departmental directors play the role of social entrepreneurs. For the most part they are responsible for putting all the pieces together. In many cases, they are already heading ongoing programs, and new WtW funding represents an opportunity to renew, consolidate, or expand existing programs. All of the directors we talked to had shown themselves to be creative in combining funding streams, designing programs to meet state regulations for participant work, mobilizing the college's internal resources to provide support services to students, and developing links to employers.

A few examples of effective practices are worth mentioning as illustrative of directors' creativity. At LACC, Mark Gunderson, the CalWORK director, created an advisory board consisting of the department chairs of programs with the greatest potential for development. The board also included representatives from the labor department on campus and from the president's office. It was instrumental in mobilizing college resources and in setting priorities for how to use the state's grant to the college. In Denver, Elaine Baker, the program director, used her experience in the design and operation of a workplace learning project to design a model that incorporates contextual learning and practical work experience from the very beginning of the program. The track model has proven to be very successful and appealing to industry leaders.

College presidents and other executives in campus administration played a critical role in crafting external partnerships with community groups and mediating relations with the political establishment. In New Mexico, for example, Alice V. Letteney, the college executive, saw WtW as one more step toward building a comprehensive education and training campus. She actively sought designation of the Valencia campus as the administrator on behalf of the state government of the region's welfare program. As a result, the program operates as a social agency housed within the college and is responsible for the intake, assessment, referral, and monitoring of clients in a three county region. The campus also houses the regional office for the state labor department.

In Fresno we observed a similar pattern in a much larger metropolitan area. The college president was instrumental in assembling an impressive partnership with local social service and labor agencies. The local welfare department has field offices located on campus and actively participates in the design and implementation of programs serving welfare recipients. In partnership with the Fresno Private Industry Council, it has opened a community job center that combines the job readiness activities of the campus with the intake, referrals, and monitoring functions of an OSCC. At the time of the study, the partnership was planning to expand the number of community job centers from three to eight, in collaboration with a church-based coalition and the social services and labor departments. In all of these partnerships, the college functions as the managing partner and administrator of a multi-sectoral partnership.

Deans are the administrators of the academic system. No program can be implemented without their support, whether that support is enthusiastic or not. Behind every successful departmental program there is an administrative team taking responsibility for its implementation. At LATTC, Bobby McNeel, the dean in charge of designing programs, insisted on starting a program to train women for non-traditional occupations in the trades. His purpose was to create opportunities for women in occupations with significantly higher starting salaries and more structured advancement opportunities than those in traditional female occupations. The idea is based on the principle that it will take more than entry-level jobs for female-headed families to achieve financial self-sufficiency.

A final story ends this discussion of lessons learned from the case studies. It encompasses the dynamics of institutional change, social entrepreneurship, and leadership. At the request of college leadership, the real names of characters and the college are not identified in this example.

At one of the colleges, we were most impressed with the political astuteness of the dean in charge of designing and developing new courses and programs in one of the most important college divisions. At first, full-time faculty in this division resisted participating in the new WtW program. Some professors questioned the work first approach and honestly believed that any short-term training program did a disservice to students over the long term. However, most professors were simply indifferent. They did not want to accommodate a new schedule, nor did they want to spend time developing a new course syllabus.

Despite faculty objections, the dean designed very successful certificate programs in "hot" occupations where most students have job offers before they graduate from the program. The new certificate programs, all staffed with adjunct faculty, offer a compact schedule and a state-of-the-art curriculum. The success of the student-friendly certificates quickly attracted the attention of regular students, who began to enroll in the program along with the targeted welfare recipients. As students shifted their demand in favor of more certificate courses, enrollment in regular courses declined and even forced the closing of some sessions (courses require a minimum enrollment for state reimbursement of student tuition).

Soon after, full-time faculty began inquiring about participating in the new certificate programs. The dean understood faculty dynamics and never criticized faculty for lack of interest in the certificate program or mandated that they teach sessions they did not want to. As he explained in an interview, the dean reasoned, "What is the point of trying to recruit full-time professors that do not want to teach in the program? I'd rather have enthusiastic adjuncts who empathize with students and share the goals of the program than reluctant faculty who may not give the students their best efforts." Eventually, when the department was able to add permanent positions as a result of the increase in enrollment, this dean hired some of the more dedicated adjunct faculty. The dean also attracted dedicated full-time faculty to teach in the program as they changed their views about the value of the certificates. In the end, all students benefited from the new certificate programs. A major lesson derived from this example is that the enrollment of "regular" students in new certificate programs almost guarantees that the certificates will become an integral and permanent part of the college program.

CONCLUSIONS: IMPLICATION FOR THE WORKFORCE DEVELOPMENT FIELD

Federal Welfare-to-Work policies transformed the role of the primary federal assistance program from providing income maintenance to the poor to providing work transition services along with time-limited income maintenance. Similarly, WtW policies have shaken the nation's employment training system. The emphasis has shifted from offering training and education programs to providing job readiness training and placement. The special federal grants for Welfare-to-Work initiatives, and the immensity of the task of placing so many people in entry-level jobs, have attracted numerous actors to the employment training field. Our study was designed to assess how community colleges, the primary educational institutions serving the educational needs of disadvantaged adult populations, have responded to the challenge posed by the welfare policy changes.

Based on our the findings from a national survey of community colleges, we selected seven colleges to study in depth in terms of how they serve the social and educational needs of welfare recipients and other disadvantaged students. We selected these case study sites from among those colleges that were more experienced and involved with Aid to Families with Dependent Children (AFDC) recipients and other disadvantaged populations. Our intent was to provide examples of community colleges that engage in effective WtW practices and to examine their program components. Although the findings from a limited and (by design) biased sample of colleges cannot be generalized to apply to all colleges nationwide, case study research illustrates the institutional dynamics behind the intriguing trends revealed by the survey data.

We found that the implementation of successful TANF programs was not an isolated or random phenomenon but an outgrowth of community colleges' historical, institutional commitment to serving the educational needs of disadvantaged populations. The community colleges that offer effective job training have developed an internal infrastructure of social and academic support services and external partnerships with government and community groups that enabled them to respond rapidly and effectively to the Welfare-to-Work initiative. Our data analysis and comparison of programs revealed some common patterns of program design that can be attributed to state policy regulations. These common elements include individualized case management, provision of child care and other social services, on-the-job internships, job readiness and soft skill courses, remedial courses in basic academic skills, and short-term vocational training. Beyond these common elements, we found great variation in how colleges combined these program elements.

Some colleges began self-standing (not directly affiliated with departments) short-term vocational training focusing on a specific occupational sector within an industry. Others adapted their certificate and degree programs to short-term certificate programs that complied with state welfare policy guidelines. The evidence from our case studies suggests that sectoral strategies are very effective at engaging employers and supporting the participants' transition to work, whereas academic department initiatives are more effective in articulating short-term training to certificate and degree programs. Welfare reform has served to strengthen community colleges' role as regional labor force intermediaries. It has induced them to examine and redesign existing programs, seek partnerships more proactively with regional businesses and industry, and to engage employers more rigorously in the design and operation of their programs.

Community colleges are well positioned to capitalize on a favorable political environment and establish themselves as leading regional labor market intermediaries. Regional workforce development systems integrate a diverse group of institutions and actors that mediate the training and development of workers and connect them to employers. Some of these institutions, such as temporary employment agencies and headhunters, specialize in screening and matching workers to specific positions. Others, like community-based organizations, provide disadvantaged workers with training and support systems necessary for the transition to work. In general, community colleges are perceived as educational institutions with limited resources, which they devote to serving disadvantaged populations or to responding to employers' specific job training needs. The results of our survey and the site visits conducted as part of this study suggest that community colleges are more actively engaged in workforce development than we anticipated.

If welfare reform has provided the spark to engage community colleges more proactively in workforce development, WIA provides a favorable policy framework for community colleges to become the anchors of the emerging workforce development system. Community colleges' efforts in designing and redesigning programs to reach "backwards" to accommodate students who might not be ready to participate in certificate and degree programs have given them the ideal opportunity to compete effectively in the market for WIA-sponsored training. Programs may include adult short-term vocational training, out-of-school youth vocational and educational programs, and contracts for job-specific and work-placed training in partnership with employers. Based on the data from our case studies, it is evident that various community college programs targeting welfare recipients provide effective training and meet the standards of WIA.

The community colleges' effective and creative responses to the challenges posed to them by the new WtW policy have demonstrated that they are capable of playing a major role in regional labor markets. Community colleges have shown employers and community organizations that they can design mutually beneficial collaborations and that their programs can reliably provide well-trained workers. To social service agencies, community colleges have demonstrated that they have the capacity and experience to serve a large number of disadvantaged students by creating specialized support programs and by adapting their existing infrastructure to meet these students' needs. Community colleges, in fact, can provide educational programs for any partnership. They are positioned to adapt short-term training to long-term education, and to help students climb career ladders and achieve occupational advancement. Of all the service providers engaged in WtW training, community colleges are the best-positioned institutions to design programs that aim beyond entry-level jobs. Finally, from a national perspective, community colleges have campuses in all cities and regions of the country. Their active engagement in workforce development provides a tremendous infrastructure to serve disadvantaged populations.

Notes

1. See Hayes (1999) for a general review of federal legislation affecting employment services, and Fisher (1999) for a more specific review of the empirical research on WtW programs.
2. Three different samples were drawn from the national list we compiled. The first sample, referred to as the general sample, includes 116 colleges selected randomly. In addition to the general sample, two further samples were gathered for Hispanic serving and African American serving community colleges. These were defined as institutions with a minimum of 10 percent of the student body classified as Hispanics or African Americans, respectively. We surveyed 83 Hispanic serving community colleges and 52 African American serving community colleges.
3. The cases are taken from Meléndez et al. (2002).
4. See for instance Grubb et al. (1999) on the critical role of teaching methods and course design, and Meléndez and Suárez (2001) on effective programs serving disadvantaged Hispanics. Recent research has addressed the specific needs of welfare recipients as they participate in community college programs. Ganzglass (1996) offers an early assessment of the challenge to community colleges in redesigning programs and financial systems to take advantage of TANF funding, while Strawn (1998) and Greenberg, Strawn, and Plimpton (1999) offer an analysis and review of the policies that affect welfare recipients' participation in colleges programs. Grubb et al. (1999) and Golonka and Matus-Grossman (2001) offer a comprehensive analysis of the interaction of program design, support services, and policies in community college programs serving welfare recipients.

5. Fitzgerald (1999) identifies a major limitation of past WtW reform programs: these programs focus almost entirely on welfare participants and do not pay enough attention to the quality of jobs available to them once they get training. She suggests that jobs that provide high wages, benefits, and the opportunity for advancement benefit recipients most, reduce employee turnover, and help workers develop lifelong changes in attitudes toward work and work habits. To attain better paying jobs, welfare recipients must improve their skills beyond the minimum level required for entry-level jobs.
6. The reader should bear in mind that the colleges selected for case study are not intended to be representative of all colleges. On the contrary, the intent is to portray select examples of colleges that have implemented effective WtW programs and reflect regional labor market variability. It should be noted that there are many other community colleges that have proactively implemented WtW programs but could not be included in this study. The experiences related in the case studies are not unique nor do they apply to all community colleges. However, it is our hope that the good practices discussed below will become more common among community colleges in the near future.
7. In part, the availability of a support services infrastructure is the direct result of the many programs before TANF supporting such infrastructure in community colleges and other community settings. See Bell and Douglas (2000) for a full discussion of work-related programs under Aid to Families with Dependent Children (AFDC), and other federal funding streams. For a general discussion on how partnerships with community, school, and employer groups facilitate reform efforts in colleges see Golonka and Matus-Grossman (2001), Liebowitz, Haynes, and Milley (2001), and Roberts (2002).
8. See Meléndez (1996) for a detailed case study of the San José-based Center for Employment and Training.

Appendix 9A

Case Studies

1) *Welfare-to-Work Initiatives in Los Angeles: Los Angeles City College and Los Angeles Technical College*
   Alexandra de Montrichard and Edwin Meléndez
2) *Community Colleges as Primary Skill Developers and Labor Market Intermediaries: Fresno City College*
   Carlos Suárez and Edwin Meléndez
3) *Making Connections to Jobs, Education and Training: The Essential Skills Program of the Community College of Denver*
   Carlos Suárez and Edwin Meléndez
4) *The SU PARTE Welfare-to-Work Initiative of the University of New Mexico, Valencia Campus*
   Alexandra de Montrichard and Edwin Meléndez
5) *Innovators Under Duress: Community College Initiatives in "Workfare" Settings*
   Lynn McCormick

References

American Association of Community Colleges. 1998. *The Workforce Investment Act: Implications for Community Colleges.* An AACC white paper. Washington, DC: American Association of Community Colleges.

Bailey, Thomas. 1998. "Integrating Vocational and Academic Education," In *High School Mathematics at Work: Essays and Examples for the Education of All Students.* Washington, DC: National Academy Press, pp. 24–29.

Barnett, Lynn. 1995. *Community Colleges and Workforce Investment: A TEAMS Community College Capacity Building Project.* Washington, DC: American Association of Community Colleges.

Bell, Stephen H., and Toby Douglas. 2000. *Making Sure of Where We Started: State Employment and Training Systems for Welfare Recipients on the Eve of Federal Reform.* Assessing the New Federalism series. Washington, DC: Urban Institute.

Bosworth, Brian. 1997. "Economic Development, Workforce Development, and the Urban Community College." *Community College Journal* 67(6): 8–13.

Bramucci, Raymond L. 1999. "Community Colleges and the Workforce Investment Act, An Interview with Raymond L. Bramucci, Assistant Secretary of Labor for the Employment and Training Association." *Community College Journal* 69(6): 40–43.

Carnevale, Anthony P., and Donna M. Desrochers. 1997. "The Role of Community Colleges in the New Economy," *Community College Journal* 67(5): 26–33.

———. 2001. *Help Wanted . . . Credentials Required: Community Colleges in the Knowledge Economy.* Washington, DC: Educational Testing Service and American Association of Community Colleges.

Dirkx, John M. 1999. "New Skills for Literacy Educators." In *The Welfare-to-Work Challenge for Adult Literacy Educators,* Larry G. Martin and James C. Fisher, eds. New Directions for Adult and Continuing Education No. 83. San Francisco: Jossey-Bass, pp. 83–94.

Elliott, Mark, and Elizabeth King. 1999. *Labor Market Leverage: Sectoral Employment Field Report.* Field Report Series. New York: Public/Private Ventures.

Elliot, Mark, Don Spangler, and Kathy Yorkievitz. 1998. *What's Next After Work First: Workforce Development Report to the Field.* Field Report Series. Philadelphia: Public/Private Ventures.

Falcone, Lisa, ed. 1994. *The Critical Link: Community Colleges and the Workforce.* Washington, DC: American Association of Community Colleges.

Fisher, James C. 1999, "Research on Adult Literacy Education in the Welfare-to-Work Transition," In *The Welfare-to-Work Challenge for Adult Literacy Educators,* Larry G. Martin and James C. Fisher, eds. New Directions for Adult and Continuing Education No. 83. San Francisco: Jossey-Bass, pp. 29–41.

Fitzgerald, Joan. 1999. "Welfare-to-Work: What are the Realities for Employment Retention and Advancement?" Unpublished manuscript. Center for Urban and Regional Policy, Northeastern University, Boston.

———. 2000. *Community Colleges as Labor Market Intermediaries: Building Career Ladders for Low Wage Workers.* Boston: Center for Urban and Regional Policy, Northeastern University.

Fitzgerald, Joan, and Davis Jenkins. 1997. *Making Connections: Community College Best Practice in Connecting the Urban Poor to Education and Employment.* Report No. GCP-97-1 prepared for the Annie E. Casey Foundation. Chicago: University of Illinois at Chicago, Great Cities Institute.

Ganzglass, Evelyn. 1996. "Workforce Development and Welfare Block Grants: Implications for Community Colleges." *Community College Journal* 66(4): 21–23.

Gennett, N., C. Johnstone, and M. Wilson. 2001. "The Shift to Workforce Development." *Community College Journal* 71(5): 60–63.

Golonka, Susan and Lisa Matus-Grossman. 2001. *Opening Doors: Expanding Educational Opportunities for Low-Income Workers.* New York and Washington, DC: Manpower Demonstration Research Corporation (MDRC) and National Governors Association Center for Best Practices.

Gooden, Susan, and Lisa Matus-Grossman. 2001. *Opening Doors to Earning Credentials: Impressions of Community College Access and Retention from Low-Wage Workers.* New York: Manpower Demonstration Research Corporation.

Greenberg, Mark, Julie Strawn, and Lisa Plimpton. 1999. *State Opportunities to Provide Access to Postsecondary Education Under TANF.* Washington, DC: Center for Law and Social Policy.

Grubb, W. Norton. 1996. *Learning to Work: The Case for Reintegrating Job Training and Education.* New York: Russell Sage Foundation.

———. 1999a. *From Isolation to Integration: Occupational Education and the Emerging Systems of Workforce Development.* Centerpoint Series No. 3. Berkeley, CA: National Center for Research in Vocational Education.

———, ed. 1999b. *Honored but Invisible: An Inside Look at Teaching in Community Colleges.* New York: Routledge.

———. 2001. "Second Chances in Changing Times: The Roles of Community Colleges in Advancing Low-Skilled Workers." In *Low Wage Workers in the New Economy: Strategies for Productivity and Opportunity,* Richard

Kazis and Marc S. Miller, eds. Washington, DC: Urban Institute Press, pp. 283–306.

Grubb, W. Norton, Norena Badway, Denise Bell, and Marisa Castellano. 1999. "Community Colleges and Welfare Reform: Emerging Practices, Enduring Problems." *Community College Journal* 69(6): 30–36.

Gueron, Judith M. 1990. "Work and Welfare: Lessons on Employment Programs." *Journal of Economic Perspectives* 4(1): 79–98.

Gutierrez, Michael. 1997. *The Role of Community Colleges in the One-Stop Career Center System: Four Case Studies*. National Coalition of Advanced Technology Centers Report Series, Vol. 1, No. 5. Waco, TX: Center for Occupational Research and Development.

Hayes, Elizabeth. 1999. "Policy Issues that Drive the Transformation of Adult Literacy," In *The Welfare-to-Work Challenge for Adult Literacy Educators,* Larry G. Martin and James C. Fisher, eds. New Directions for Adult and Continuing Education No. 83, San Francisco: Jossey-Bass, pp. 3–14.

Holzer, Harry J. 1999. "Will Employers Hire Welfare Recipients? Recent Survey Evidence from Michigan." *Journal of Policy Analysis and Management* 18(3): 449–472.

Jenkins, Davis, and Joan Fitzgerald. 1998. *Community Colleges: Connecting the Poor to Good Jobs.* Policy paper for the Education Commission of the States' Critical Roles for Community Colleges project. Denver: Center for Community College Policy.

Katsinas, Stephen G., Grace Banachowski, Tim J. Bliss, and J. Matthew Short. 1999. "Community College Involvement in Welfare-to-Work Programs." *Community College Journal of Research and Practice* 23(4): 401–421.

Liebowitz, Marty, Leslie Haynes, and Jane Milley. 2001. *Driving Change in Community Colleges.* Vol. 1, *Building Systems for Advancement to Self-Sufficiency.* Boston: Jobs for the Future.

Martin, Larry G. 1999. "Continuum of Literacy Program Models: Alternative Approaches for Low-Literate Welfare Recipients." In *The Welfare-to-Work Challenge for Adult Literacy Educators,* Larry G. Martin and James C. Fisher, eds. New Directions for Adult and Continuing Education No. 83. San Francisco: Jossey-Bass, pp. 43–57.

McCabe, Robert H. 1997. *The American Community College: Nexus for Workforce Development.* Mission Viejo, CA: League for Innovation in the Community College.

Meléndez, Edwin. 1996. *Working on Jobs: The Center for Employment Training.* Boston: Mauricio Gastón Institute for Latino Community Development and Public Policy, University of Massachusetts Boston.

Meléndez, Edwin, Luis M. Falcón, Carlos Suárez, Lynn McCormick, and Alexandra de Montrichard. 2002. *The Welfare-to-Work Policy Shock: How*

Community Colleges Are Addressing the Challenge. New York: Community Development Research Center, Milano Graduate School of Management and Urban Policy, New School University.

Meléndez, Edwin, and Carlos Suárez. 2001. "Opening College Doors for Disadvantaged Hispanics: An Assessment of Effective Programs and Practices." In *Low-Wage Workers in the New Economy: Strategies for Productivity and Opportunity*, Richard Kazis and Marc Miller, eds. Washington, DC: Urban Institute Press, pp. 307–325.

Roberts, Brandon. 2002. *The Best of Both: Community Colleges and Community-Based Organizations Partner to Better Serve Low-Income Workers and Employers.* New York: Public/Private Ventures.

Strawn, Julie. 1998. *Beyond Job Search or Basic Education: Rethinking the Role of Skills in Welfare Reform.* Washington, DC: Center for Law and Social Policy.

Perin, Dolores. 1998. *Curriculum and Pedagogy to Integrate Occupational and Academic Instruction in the Community College: Implications for Faculty Development.* New York: Community College Research Center, Institute on Education and the Economy, Teachers College, Columbia University.

Stokes, Robert S. 1996. *Model Welfare-to-Work Initiatives in the United States: Effective Strategies for Moving TANF Recipients from Public Assistance to Self-Sufficiency.* Report prepared for the Connecticut Business and Industry Association by RSS Associates. Hartford, CT: Connecticut Business and Industry Association.

U.S. General Accounting Office (USGAO). 1996. *Employment and Training: Successful Projects Share Common Strategy.* Report to the Chairman, Subcommittee on Human Resources and Intergovernmental Relations, Committee on Government Reform and Oversight, House of Representatives, by Carlotta C. Joyner, director, Education and Employment Issues, GAO. GAO/HEHS–96–108. Washington, DC: U.S. General Accounting Office.

10
Innovators Under Duress

Community Colleges in New York's Workfare Setting

Lynn McCormick
Hunter College, City University of New York

Welfare reform, initiated with the passage of the Personal Responsibility and Work Opportunity Reconciliation Act (PRWORA) of 1996, has been one of several initiatives at the federal level that aims to devolve policymaking to the state and local governmental levels. Other initiatives have come in the areas of federal job service and training, health care, and other social services (Watson and Gold 1997). Proponents argue that devolution makes state and local governments more attuned to the specific needs of their local constituencies than they would be under a single, large, and distant federal bureaucracy. The literature on reinventing government frames a debate on the extent to which state and local governments can act as policy "entrepreneurs" in shaping the behavior of others. This article offers a view of how this specifically has been done by New York City with community colleges that train welfare recipients.

Those who promote greater governmental effectiveness through the reinvention process argue that local governmental systems can become more responsive and efficient if exposed to market pressures and competition (Osborne and Gaebler 1992; Watson and Gold 1997; Besharov and Samari 1999; Kazis and Seltzer 2000). The federal government creates such pressures through "fiscal federalism," a process by which states are given greater responsibilities for program outcomes, accompanied by smaller amounts in block grant funding (Steuerle and Mermin 1997). This places incentives on state and local governments to become more efficient in service delivery. One way to achieve greater efficiency and citizen responsiveness is to begin contracting out service provision to non- or for-profit enterprises. In this way, governments become entrepreneurial, argue Osborne and Gaebler (1992) and achieve desired policy outcomes through "steering," or shaping the performance of outside service providers, rather than through "rowing," or providing direct services. Governments steer by setting policy goals and then designing rewards and sanctions to push service providers to achieve the goals. Contractors receive program funding only upon achieving stipulated benchmark goals, regardless of the level of service provided. In this way, a local government can become "a skillful buyer, leveraging the activities of multiple service providers to meet public policy objectives" (Kazis and Seltzer 2000, p. 10).

In the area of welfare reform, in addition to becoming entrepreneurial, governments also must stimulate a significant cultural change, argue some scholars, among all who participate in local welfare systems—bureaucrats, outside service providers, and welfare recipients. Cultural change is needed to bring about a wholesale reorientation in the purpose of welfare—away from the idea of entitlement and toward a culture of work and a system that is more attentive to the needs of employers (Hercik 1998; Kazis and Seltzer 2000). PRWORA shifted federal welfare policy to a work first approach. It did so by limiting the training benefits of welfare recipients (now called TANF, or Temporary Assistance for Needy Families) and emphasizing instead quick placement in private sector jobs or government workfare (in the latter, individuals carry out work assignments, often in government positions, for their welfare benefits). The work first school of thought holds that welfare recipients benefit more over the long run through immediate employment than from formal education. Jobs teach individuals how to show up on time, balance work and family responsibilities, and other so-called soft skills, as well as hard skills such as typing and filing, through on-the-job training. The debate in work first circles today is over the extent to which state welfare systems should also offer TANF recipients opportunities for education as a companion to working (Elliott, Spangler, and Yorkievitz 1998; Strawn 1999; Golonka and Matus-Grossman 2001).

Regardless of a state's position toward education's role in welfare reform, the literature on reinventing government assumes that the state (or local) government almost exclusively will become the policy entrepreneur and do all the steering of everyone else—both service providers and TANF recipients. What I have found, however, by investigating the welfare reform environment in New York City is that, although the state and local governments have dominated in shaping the practices of employment and training providers in the city, they are not the only ones doing the steering. In addition, there are strong policy entrepreneurs outside of government who are pushing back. With this resistance, they influence government policies as well. The significance of this finding is that we should not assume that only governments do the steering in devolved states—an assumption of the literature to date. Instead, an interplay of government versus grass-roots entrepreneurs makes reinventing government a nonlinear process. It also complicates our predictions and future evaluations of various localities' welfare reform outcomes.

This chapter sheds light on the reinventing government debate by studying community colleges in New York City's strong workfare environment—one which puts most of its faith in the power of work to alter welfare recipients' future earnings. Through detailed case studies of two such colleges in New York—Hostos and LaGuardia community colleges—I aim to answer two questions: 1) How specifically have the state and city's workfare-oriented policies affected existing education programming for welfare recipients at these institutions? and 2) Have curricular innovations come to a complete halt, or have community colleges found ways to innovate in spite of this policy setting? What follows is, first, a description of New York's workfare policies and, second, the strategic response of two community colleges that have continued innovating in the educational area in spite of the state and city's relative lack of support for training.[1]

WELFARE REFORM, WORKFARE, AND TRAINING

Devolution of programmatic responsibility for welfare reform could result in 50 different state experiments on the best way to move individuals from welfare dependency to self-sufficiency. Both George Pataki, governor of New York, and Rudolph Giuliani, former mayor of New York City, have seen themselves as taking the lead in workfare in the country. The state and the city both enacted workfare programs before Congress passed PRWORA in 1996. Under its workfare provisions,

New York City has put to work the largest number of welfare recipients of any metropolitan area in the United States.

Although the federal law stipulates that vocational training may substitute for only 12 months of a TANF recipient's work activities, each of the states has flexibility in determining the balance between school and work by identifying what constitutes "school" or "work" and through various supports provided for these activities. Hence, each state can steer the actors in its welfare system either toward workfare exclusively or toward a system in which opportunities for more schooling are integrated. Observers classify the state systems as follows: 1) those that do not encourage schooling but only promote workfare among TANF recipients (13 states), 2) those that moderately encourage schooling (allowing postsecondary education to meet 12 months of work activity—12 states), and 3) those that strongly do so (allowing postsecondary education to meet more than 12 months of work activity—22 states) (Greenberg, Strawn, and Plimpton 2000). Four states, including New York, allow their counties to determine such welfare rules within a broad state law. In New York State's case, New York City has amplified the state's leaning toward workfare over education.

Many see the Family Support Act, which President Reagan endorsed and Congress passed in 1988, as the inspiration for states to begin experimenting heavily with workfare programs (Albelda and Tilly 1997; Casey 1998; Leon 1995).[2] New York State ran workfare programs in the early 1990s under this act, primarily for its Home Relief (HR), or general assistance, population. With Pataki's entrance as governor in 1995, he and the legislature worked together to broaden the workfare program to include all public assistance recipients while limiting education and training benefits. Because New York is one of the few states in which local governments maintain responsibility for designing, implementing, and partially funding public assistance programs, local governments decide the extent to which they want to make a tradeoff of training for workfare.

Giuliani was equally enthusiastic about emphasizing work. New York City policy formally allows TANF recipients to count 12 months of postsecondary education as a work activity. Moreover, through various initiatives, including luring Wisconsin's Jason Turner (the workfare guru who drew headlines for his state policy of not counting education as a work activity) to run its Welfare-to-Work program, New York

City has also fashioned a strong workfare environment for its welfare recipients. The city started the NYC Way program in 1995, which combined workfare with a more rigorous eligibility and address verification program. This helped cut city welfare rolls and related financial obligations. New York City, housing about 70 percent of the state's welfare population (but only 40 percent of the state's overall population), must, under state regulations, shoulder approximately 70 percent of the total local governmental share in welfare payments (Leon 1995; Weir 1997; Casey 1998).[3] In the first program year, the city cut the number of public assistance cases by 60 percent (Leon 1995).

In 1997, the state legislature formalized its workfare initiative with the Welfare Reform Act (Mannix et al. 1998). New York City's revised workfare program under the state legislation is called the Work Experience Program (WEP). WEP, administered by the city's Human Resources Administration (HRA), places the highest priority on workfare, which averaged about 35,000 participants monthly in 1998, rather than on facilitating education and training (Casey 1998).[4] Casey states that "while the City does not publish the number of welfare recipients in education and training activities, education and training providers say that the City's policies have caused sharp declines in activities such as English as a Second Language (ESL), basic literacy, GED, and vocational training. City University (CUNY) reports that the number of welfare parents in the CUNY system has declined from about 26,000 to about 13,000" (1998, p. 14).

The drop in CUNY enrollments, due to the HRA's practice of channeling TANF recipients into workfare versus education and training, is confirmed by other sources including many of the respondents interviewed for this research. HRA intake staff discouraged schooling in two ways: 1) by placing welfare recipients into workfare without mentioning their right to some college and vocational training, and 2) by showing an unwillingness to designate WEP sites near college campuses, which would aid those wanting to combine workfare and college (Mannix et al. 1998; Casey 1998).

POLICY IMPACTS ON NEW YORK CITY'S COMMUNITY COLLEGES

How has this workfare policy environment influenced training offerings within the city's community colleges and other two-year institutions? Citywide, New York's community colleges and other two-year postsecondary institutions offer less programming and support services for TANF recipients than their counterparts nationwide. One could conclude that the overly rigid workfare policy environment that New York City and State present have caused this outcome. However, we also find that a subset of New York colleges have developed TANF programming in spite of this environment. In a survey of all postsecondary institutions in New York City, which we report on elsewhere (see Meléndez et al. 2002), we found that, as a group, these institutions are less likely to undertake special programming for TANF recipients, compared to similar schools nationally.[5] New York City institutions also are much less likely to offer TANF and other non-traditional students alternatives to full-time study, like non-degree or certificate programs (Table 10.1).

The survey findings lend support to an argument that this lag in institutional innovation for TANF students is due to the relative lack of city and state support for TANF training in the strict workfare policy environment of New York City. Hence, local governments in the city are effectively steering the behavior of service providers in this policy environment. A subset of the New York colleges, however, shows a different pattern. These two-year colleges—all belonging to the City University of New York (CUNY) system—show a high rate of involvement

Table 10.1 Community Colleges Offering Programs or Services for Students with Special Needs (%)

Type of program or service	US[a]	NYC	CUNY
Low reading or math skills	80.9	70.6	100.0
Lack of high school diploma or GED	70.4	52.9	83.3
Poor work history	50.0	35.3	66.7
Students with young children	60.5	52.9	83.3
Substance abuse problems	29.4	17.6	16.7

[a] From general sample in Meléndez et al. 2002.
SOURCE: Meléndez et al. 2002; author's calculations.

Table 10.2 Program Offerings for TANF Students by Institutions with TANF-Specific Programs (%)

Type of program colleges offer	US[a]	NYC[b]
Degree programs	71.2	100.0
Nondegree programs	82.7	60.0
Coursework to develop soft skills	96.2	100.0
Preparatory courses	90.4	60.0
Short-term training programs	84.9	60.0
Tutorial programs	81.1	80.0
Internships with employers	77.4	80.0

[a] From general sample in Meléndez et al. 1999.
[b] TANF programs are only in CUNY schools and one other institution.
SOURCE: Meléndez et al. 1999; author's calculations.

in programming for TANF students, other non-traditional students, and students with special learning needs (Tables 10.1 and 10.2). How have the CUNY colleges developed programming for TANF recipients? What tactics and features characterize those that have been the most innovative? Answers to these questions come from studies of the two CUNY community colleges, Hostos and LaGuardia. CUNY is a network of 11 senior (or four-year) and six community colleges. LaGuardia, with 11,000 students, and Hostos, with 4,200, represent the third largest and the smallest of the community colleges in this system (CUNY 1997). These cases show that TANF programming can result in workfare-oriented policy environments when institutions pursue innovative means, pedagogies, or institutional structures to work around a workfare system.

Innovative Means

Educational opportunities for welfare recipients have expanded in some New York institutions because of the activities of different institutional activists. These activists are also policy entrepreneurs but are lodged outside of local government. Although they "row," by taking direction from government agencies, they also "steer." The activists believe that for the work first philosophy to succeed, TANF recipients require access to training so they can build a long-term career path that will move them out of poverty. Key activists have included welfare rights organizations, CUNY "Central" as the umbrella administration for multiple colleges, and staff activists within individual colleges that serve TANF recipients directly.

Welfare rights activists

After continued protests by New York's highly organized welfare rights organizations, the HRA modified its practices that discouraged TANF recipients from seeking training. Litigation, trying to reform workfare, took an early lead in New York. Issues that the Welfare Law Center, the Legal Aid Society, and others in the city's welfare-rights movement have contested include the following: 1) illegal diversion of welfare recipients from benefits, 2) low-quality child care placements for TANF-covered children, 3) lack of workplace safety for workfare participants, 4) unwillingness of nonprofit organizations to become WEP sites, 5) illegal denial of food stamp and Medicaid assistance, and 6) payment of below prevailing wages for workfare placements, contrary to a New York State Supreme Court decision (Abramovitz 1997; Mannix et al. 1998; Laarman 1998; Casey 1998; NASW 1999; WLC 1999).

In regard to educational rights, the Welfare Law Center and the Legal Aid Society brought a class-action suit on behalf of all TANF recipients against the HRA over its policy of assigning recipients to WEP activities regardless of their desire for education or training. The plaintiffs in this case, single parents on welfare who were enrolled in education or training programs, charged that the city's policy violated the state law requiring that individualized assessments and employability plans be made for each TANF recipient and that assignments be made according to recipient preferences when possible (Mannix et al. 1998).[6]

The original plaintiff, Evelyn Davila, for example, was enrolled in an 11-month medical technician program but was told by the city to give this up and take a WEP assignment in order to continue receiving her welfare payments.[7] In July 2003, the TANF recipients won the case on appeal in the Supreme Court of the State of New York. Fisher reports that "under the agreement, the city must assess the needs of welfare recipients and come up with 'employability plans' which may include job training or additional schooling. Recipients can appeal those plans if they disagree with them. The settlement also allows attorneys from the Welfare Law Center to monitor the city's efforts" (2003, p. 1).

Hence, broad-based organizing and protests have been key mechanisms by which New York City's welfare reform laws and agency practices, including those related to postsecondary education, have been modified to encourage education and training alongside work. Activism by CUNY's central administration—as I will describe next—has also been crucial to the educational offerings that do exist today for TANF recipients.

CUNY Central

In the 1980s and early 1990s, CUNY's central offices worked closely with the City's HRA under Mayor Dinkin's administration to develop educational programming and services for the poor. This early institutional support helped set up several programs and services for welfare-receiving students. Although some of the programs have ceased to exist under the current climate of welfare reform, these earlier efforts have stimulated the individual CUNY colleges to begin thinking of programming for welfare recipients.

In the early period, the central CUNY office established the Center for College Options, which played a support and liaison role for public assistance recipients wanting to enter CUNY by helping them with financial aid, testing, remedial work and other hurdles. In addition, in 1993, CUNY created the College Opportunity to Prepare for Employment (COPE) program, its brainchild to encourage AFDC recipients to gain college credits and skills as a means to achieve eventual financial independence. HRA intake staff readily referred appropriate welfare recipients to CUNY colleges for enrollment in this program.

CUNY and the City's HRA initially designed the COPE program to move single, welfare-receiving parents through at least two years of college and an associate degree program. These credentials offer career-focused skills, entry to semi-skilled jobs, and a foothold in a potential lifetime career that could involve further education. With this as their goal, COPE program staff focused on the retention and graduation of students. Prior to welfare reform, the COPE program consisted of three components. First, the program targeted only a subset of welfare-receiving students. For instance, the first year's COPE cohort represented only 11 percent and 14 percent of all eligible students at Hostos and LaGuardia, respectively.[8] Staff selected these first COPE participants according to their potential for future employability and their college readiness.

A second component of this early COPE program was to move each incoming cohort of students through as much of the academic experience together as possible. Staff arranged block scheduling of classes so that all COPE students attended classes only with one another; this facilitated peer studying, joint use of tutors, and peer counseling. The third program component involved support services offered to students, which included everything from personal and academic counseling to specialized workshops and job placement.

Before welfare reform, COPE students could attend college full or part time and receive welfare stipends and other training related expenses (TREs) for up to three years. This meant that an early COPE program participant's day would be composed exclusively of classes, studying, and time spent receiving counseling and other support services until she finished a two-year degree. Child care responsibilities were balanced against this academic work. Controlling for entering characteristics and skill levels, researchers who compared COPE students with other welfare-receiving CUNY students found that COPE students made faster progress toward a degree compared with similar non-COPE students at the same colleges (Gittell et al. 1996).[9] Hence, COPE, which had been put in place because of CUNY Central's support, offered a subset of welfare-receiving students the services they needed to gain skills and credentials.

Staff activists

After PRWORA, COPE underwent significant changes.At first, the city reduced TREs to two years and initiated workfare requirements of 20 hours a week for all TANF recipients. Then, in 1998, it reduced TREs to 12 months and increased the work requirement to 35 hours (ten more than the state's mandate). Now, an incoming TANF-receiving COPE student can obtain a year's exemption from WEP to take occupationally oriented classes (TREs can no longer be used for academic classes that lead to transfer to a four-year college), but often also must work. Typically, she will take a full load of 12–15 class credits (up from 5 allowable class credits before the settlement of the Davila lawsuit in 2003). The remaining 20–23 hours to meet the full work requirement must be spent in an internship, work study, WEP assignment, or job. The second and remaining years in school are not covered by TREs, so the student must work 35 hours weekly along with attending school.

At the same time the COPE program moved to the performance-based payment system instituted by the HRA, CUNY also expanded the COPE program rolls. This has watered down programmatic support for each participant. Under the new HRA guidelines, student retention and graduation are no longer compensable program goals. Currently, COPE staff secure program funding if, and only if, they place TANF recipients in jobs. The city will even pay colleges for placing TANF recipients in jobs who have never enrolled in classes. After welfare reform, CUNY increased the number of campuses offering COPE (from an initial four community college campuses to 10) and opened it to all welfare-receiving students without increasing the overall COPE budget. This has tripled the size of the COPE programs at Hostos and LaGuardia in numbers of participants while cutting individual program budgets. These changes, therefore, have placed significant financial pressures on the ability of staff to assist individual TANF students.

Because of the program's expansion, as well as an explosion in the HRA's workfare-related reporting requirements, COPE counselors now help students negotiate the HRA and WEP assignments rather than deal with personal or financial issues as they had before. They have also successfully intervened to make their TANF students' days logistically possible. Initially, workfare job placements were mostly in Brooklyn—a significant distance to travel from Hostos, LaGuardia, and some other CUNY campuses. This made the logistics of getting back and forth to work, school, and the HRA office for reporting requirements impossible as a daily regimen, prompting various staff responses to find a solution. Initially, CUNY colleges joined with TANF recipients to protest this arrangement. This led the state legislature in 1997 to mandate that college students be placed in workfare jobs at or near their colleges. Even after this mandate, however, the city was slow in complying, taking more than two years to register the CUNY colleges as legitimate workfare settings and excluding two from ever getting this designation (Arenson 1998; New York Times 1998). The two left out were Hostos and the Borough of Manhattan Community College. Since those two are situated in Democratic strongholds, some observers attribute this to politics.

As a result, Hostos' staff had to find a different solution to help its welfare-receiving students stay in school under workfare. Because the city did not designate Hostos as a WEP site, its TANF students must either travel to an external WEP assignment or be involved in an internship or federal work study assignment. Since work study funding can be used for on-campus work assignments, Hostos' financial aid office has aggressively pursued this funding. It led all of CUNY's community colleges in the use of the work study assignments for its students, covering 61 percent of its welfare-receiving students in 1998. In fact, in early 1998, more than half (57 percent) of all CUNY COPE students who utilized work study positions in lieu of WEP assignments were at Hostos (Table 10.3). This share declined later in the year, simply because other CUNY colleges followed Hostos' lead and began utilizing work study more fully.

COPE staff at both colleges have been remarkably resilient. The COPE programs at Hostos and LaGuardia now represent the largest and most successful (in terms of job placements) within the CUNY system. Each has grown threefold since its first year of operation; currently 800–900 students receive services at each campus. The two colleges make the highest job placements among all CUNY COPE programs. For example, during the 1997–1998 school year, each of these two programs placed about 100 students in jobs, representing about half the placements made by COPE staff at CUNY's six community colleges and one-third the number made at its 11 senior colleges.[10] Furthermore, Hostos and LaGuardia have dealt successfully with budget cutbacks. They have devised different, but equally successful, mechanisms that help students carry out their WEP assignments on-site and negotiate the often burdensome HRA bureaucracy. In addition, the staff at each college try to link students with work experiences that employ degree-related skills, both at their WEP placements and, later, on their first jobs.

What we see here, then, is that the overly restrictive workfare policies that New York City's HRA has put in place have become less so through the innovative tactics of a variety of actors. The actors have successfully litigated or pressured policymakers to ensure that TANF recipients can claim their educational rights. Unique pedagogical philosophies, as discussed below, also facilitate recipients' learning.

Table 10.3 Use of WEP Exemptions and Nontraditional Programming in CUNY (%)

Type of program or service	All CUNY colleges	Community colleges	Hostos C.C.	LaGuardia C.C.
WEP exemptions within COPE				
Work study (Spring 1998)	100	81	57	18
Work study (Fall 1998)	100	87	36	9
Internships (Spring 1998)	100	96	20	75
Internships (Fall 1998)	100	87	38	24
Welfare recipient enrollment (1998)	100	53	9	8
Nontraditional programming				
Continuing ed. enrollment (Fall 1997)	100	45	1	19
Certificate prog. enrollment (Fall 1997)	100	43	2	6
Total enrollment (1997)	100	37	2	6

SOURCE: CUNY COPE statistics, 1999; CUNY Student Data Book, Fall 1997.

Innovative Pedagogies

Within CUNY, Hostos and LaGuardia take innovative pedagogical approaches to their students. Hostos' mission is to provide "educational opportunities leading to socio-economic mobility for first and second generation Hispanics, African Americans, and other residents of New York City who have encountered significant barriers to higher education."[11] LaGuardia has a similar mission to that of Hostos but carries it out differently.

Bilingual college

Since its founding, Hostos has followed a bilingual educational model, one that focuses on Hispanic adult learners with limited English proficiency. Since more than two-thirds of Hostos students claim a Caribbean ancestry and list Spanish as their native language, the college offers a Spanish-English learning environment. Furthermore, Hostos students are more likely than other community college students at CUNY to have an out-of-state or foreign high school degree (31 percent versus 15 percent for the system as a whole), a GED (31 percent versus 24 percent), and difficulties passing the CUNY skills assessment tests (55 percent did not pass any tests at Hostos versus 35 percent CUNY-wide). Hostos students, in general, also require much more support than those in the rest of CUNY. This is because they are more likely than students in any of CUNY's other community colleges to be poor (two-thirds came from households making less than $15,000 in 1997 versus 42 percent from the system as a whole) and supporting children (61 percent versus 36 percent, respectively) or functioning as a single parent (43 percent versus 17 percent) (CUNY 1997).

The bilingual component includes these special services: bilingual administrative functions, college orientation, counseling and advising, tutoring and instruction, cultural activities, and library materials. Although Hostos has been lauded in the past for its bilingual approach, more recently it has come under increasing criticism for failure to move its graduates into an English environment. When a significant number of its graduating class failed a writing exam that CUNY's trustees imposed university-wide as a belated requirement for graduation, the college's president was asked to resign (Arenson 1998). Today, the college is working on improving test scores among its student body, according to its special needs (Varro 2004).

Co-op model

LaGuardia is the only cooperative education college within CUNY. The co-op model allows the college to create a stronger link between the classroom and the workplace. The college views this approach "as a particularly effective learning strategy for a New York City open enrollment institution; [the students of which are] essentially minority, low income and recent or first generation immigrants."[12] This approach helps students explore different career options and apply classroom concepts to work situations. Hence, it makes the transition from education to employment more successful for them. The co-op program accomplishes this through the use of internships: full-time students must complete a related introductory course and two internships as part of their degree programs. LaGuardia had wanted to go further with the co-op experience and boost the number of required internships but has been restrained by CUNY so that it does not stray too far from a traditional academic model. Even so, because of its philosophy LaGuardia outpaces all other CUNY institutions in the use of internships; in early 1998, 75 percent of all CUNY COPE students gaining a WEP exemption to fulfill an internship were enrolled at LaGuardia (Table 10.3). This amount declined as other COPE programs began to learn from LaGuardia and use internships more to avoid unrelated WEP assignments for their students.

Cluster learning

Another key educational innovation at LaGuardia is the widespread use of "learning communities" or "clusters" throughout the College. Clusters involve combining two or more courses for a group of students to take together. LaGuardia staff started pairing ESL students together in their non-language courses in the 1980s. Since then, the idea has spread to the whole college. Staff have found that students in clusters get better grades than if they were to take the course alone, because students who take the same classes can study together as well as offer peer support and advice on personal issues. Faculty members in cluster courses also plan their courses together and integrate what they are teaching so that information offered in one class supports that in another. The staff (faculty and counselors) form clusters by combining students with similar educational interests into a human resources cluster, an accounting cluster, and so forth.

Hence, both of these "best practice" organizations have developed innovative pedagogies that are intended to facilitate learning among non-traditional adult learners. Even so, limits have been placed on these pedagogical innovations by the wider CUNY administration, which is resisting pushing these innovative models to the extreme. A final set of innovations in the colleges' structure has also taken place, in part to circumvent other CUNY restrictions which limit the ability of college staff to fit into the new workfare regulations.

Innovative Structures

One hurdle that CUNY presents to college staff wanting to develop new programming for their TANF students is the lengthy time it takes for the bureaucracy to approve new credit-bearing degrees or programs. For example, staff at Hostos estimate it took four years to get the final approval needed from CUNY to begin operating a new LPN certificate program. This delay becomes particularly problematic given that the HRA will only allow for a year of training to take place, yet the associate degrees offered by CUNY's community colleges take at least two years to finish. LaGuardia has been especially innovative here. By building up a substantial adult education division, it has provided an alternative academic structure—albeit one that does not confer credit—for developing short-term training programs for TANF recipients and others. LaGuardia is clearly the leader here; of the almost 28,000 people enrolled in adult continuing education classes among all 17 colleges within the CUNY system, almost 20 percent attend LaGuardia (Table 10.3). In addition, LaGuardia utilizes this division to house a development corporation that can make more direct ties with business, facilitating placement of its students in internships and jobs beyond what a traditional college can offer. These specific initiatives include LaGuardia's Project Enable and its HRA-funded Vocational Work Study (VOWS) program, its Adult Career Counseling and Resource Center's job search and training components, and its Urban Center for Economic Development—all located within the college's Adult and Continuing Education Division (ACE).

Project Enable and VOWS

Project Enable runs several training programs for homeless heads-of-household, other public assistance recipients, and the low-income unemployed. It operates programs on-site in shelters, in transitional housing, and on campus. Recently, it began an HRA-funded pilot project for TANF recipients, the Vocational Work Study (VOWS) project. VOWS offers training in computerized office skills to participants who concurrently carry out workfare assignments within the New York City Housing Authority (NYCHA). Participants work at NYCHA three days a week and come to LaGuardia for all-day training on the fourth and fifth days in skills related to their work assignment. The training program follows an "open entry–open exit" model; welfare recipients enter training whenever they are ready. Staff run the training in short modules that offer novel instructional techniques such as peer and small group instruction to better meet participants' needs. The project's staff is trying to convince the HRA and the city that short-term training can be effective and also be integrated into workfare settings. The NYCHA has hired several trainees as full-time staff, indicating the project's success as a training program.

Adult Career Counseling and Resource Center

Another way that LaGuardia works with welfare recipients is through the Adult Career Counseling and Resource Center (ACCRC), housed in Adult and Continuing Education. The center serves "all adult students enrolled in noncredit continuing education classes and community residents who want to explore career changes and enter or re-enter the job market."[13] ACCRC assists welfare recipients through several programs, including its Job Search Skills Program, its Work First Center, and the InVEST Pilot Program.

The Job Search Skills Program helps single individuals find jobs—people who have applied for public assistance and have waited several months for benefits. ACCRC staff teach participants job seeking skills (e.g., interviewing techniques, how to identify likely employers) and offer access to computers, phones, and a job placement specialist.

Also housed under ACCRC is one of the HRA's Work First centers—an unusual partnership since most Work First centers are located in community-based organizations. As a Work First Center, ACCRC receives referrals from the HRA; it teaches these TANF recipients job seeking skills and provides help in finding jobs.

The ACCRC also offers New York State's pilot program InVEST, as do three other organizations throughout the state. The Individual Vocational Education and Skills Training Program (InVEST) involves a collaboration of four agencies: the state Department of Employment, the Higher Education Service Corporation, CUNY, and the HRA. This program offers training vouchers to public assistance recipients who are working but earn so little that they still depend on welfare. The goal is to enhance their skills so they can obtain a job that will take them off welfare. HRA offers the client six months of TREs to take a course that can lead to better employment. The Family Institute, a component within LaGuardia's ACE that operates programs to promote schooling among the poor and educationally disadvantaged, designed six-month programs in computer information systems and computer repair for the pilot.[14] Since ACE houses both Work First and the InVEST training program, it can identify those applicants who are eligible for six months of training when they come in for job seeking assistance. HRA pays for this noncredit bearing short-term training.

Regardless of these innovations, however, no source finances continuing education that may lead to certificates or degrees for those who are working. As the ACCRC director explains, "What is missing from this system is a middle ground, where people can obtain financial aid for more vocational training,…funds that can support training for low income individuals who want to continue their education and training but do not have sufficient resources to pay for these programs. An example would be those individuals who leave public assistance but are still in low level jobs."

Although LaGuardia has excelled at providing short-term, noncredit training through its continuing education division and two-year associate degrees through its other programs, it has done relatively little in the way of offering certificate programs. For instance, whereas 9,576 of its students enrolled in continuing education courses in 1997, only 44 were enrolled in one-year certificate programs (CUNY 1997). Even so, the college's 6 percent share of CUNY enrollment in certificate programs mirrors its share of overall enrollment (Table 10.3). One-year certificate programs earn credit that the student can later apply toward an associate or a bachelor's degree. The creation of certificate programs has been underutilized in much of CUNY because of the overly lengthy approval process, which discourages the establishment of shorter but credit-bearing programs.

As with other COPE Programs at CUNY, LaGuardia has on staff its own job placement specialist who nurtures contacts with local employers. However, since she also works out of LaGuardia's ACCRC, she is well integrated with the range of job development activities for all of the College's TANF recipients, not just those who are full-time students. Therefore she has the ability to make linkages among LaGuardia's programs for TANF recipients in order to set up longer-term career ladders. At the same time, employers are regularly involved in the college's economic development activities, which further strengthens job linkages. Even though the activities have not been formally coordinated, the pieces are all there at LaGuardia, which should, over time, facilitate formal career ladder planning for welfare recipients. These economic development activities are substantial and involve the efforts of the LaGuardia Urban Center for Economic Development (LUCED) and its participation in CUNY's Quality Consortium, its Taxi and Limousine Institute, and its partnership, along with other educational institutions, in the Communications Managers Association. Each is briefly profiled below.

LaGuardia's economic development corporation, LUCED, was created within the college's Adult and Continuing Education Division in the mid-1980s to offer education and training programs to private, public, and nonprofit sector organizations. The center designs and holds customized training sessions, offers workshops for businesses (one is "Government Contracting for Minority and Women Entrepreneurs"), links these firms to the college's co-op program and its student interns, and provides technical assistance and training to entrepreneurs and small businesses. LUCED's Preparing for Profit (PREP) Program and Entrepreneurial Assistance Center specifically target minorities, women, and small businesses. Each year LaGuardia places more than 2,000 interns in 600 local companies, in part through LUCED contacts.[15]

LUCED's total quality management component conducts programs for businesses wanting to improve the quality of their products and services through worker training programs and technical assistance. In the early 1990s, LUCED held its first conference on quality management for small business, after which it developed a program to offer affordable consulting on this issue to local small businesses. In 1998, funds from the Alfred P. Sloan Foundation allowed LUCED to expand these services. The college's Industrial Management Resource Program (IMRP) now conducts the program and offers services jointly with the Long Island City Business Development Corporation.[16]

LaGuardia's Taxi and Limousine Institute was cofounded and is funded by the city's Taxi and Limousine Commission. The Institute offers continuing education courses to all drivers in accordance with the commission's training requirements and to date has prepared over 45,000 people to qualify for a taxi license.[17] Another way for LaGuardia to connect with New York companies and help serve both company and student interests is through membership in industry associations and partnerships, like the regional Communications Managers Association, for which it offers educational advice. These connections also help the college run a successful co-op program, making important employment links for its students.

CONCLUSION

The findings of this work indicate that workfare settings, and the incentives or disincentives that states and cities provide, can hamper employment and training innovations developed for TANF recipients. However, in such settings, as in New York City, other actors in the policy environment also play a significant steering function. As Brettschneider (2001) notes, actors can counter top-down planning that does not meet their needs through a variety of mechanisms such as litigation, adversarial tactics, or interorganizational collaboration. Some of New York's community colleges, in league with other nonprofits and TANF recipients, have used these tactics and others to try to increase employment and training opportunities in a strong workfare regime. Hence, colleges like Hostos and LaGuardia that are the "rowers" are also steering the work first debate from their position of influence. They are resisting a "race to the bottom" that some scholars (Lynch 1994) argue may occur in devolved governmental systems that are more interested in cutting the costs of service provision than in solving intractable social problems like persistent poverty and welfare dependency.

Both colleges needed an alternative vision to carry out a successful "welfare-to-school-to-work" policy. They developed this vision, in part, through the efforts of CUNY Central and the HRA in previous educationally oriented city administrations. This alternative policy also received substantial support and definition from New York's "workfare reform" legal and activist community. Both colleges have also been able to innovate TANF-specific programming through various staff efforts to make training accessible in spite of the limitations inherent in the broader policy environment. Both colleges encourage staff innovation through an active mission for serving the poor and through pedagogical philosophies that aim to motivate nontraditional students. In addition, LaGuardia's Adult Education Division offers an organizational structure that is more flexible for creating new and unusual programming. Because of these features, both colleges have been able to reshape New York's rigid workfare regime to incorporate skill training for TANF recipients. Their efforts are particularly important as states now work to move the remaining TANF recipients off welfare—those that are least educated and skilled (Besharov 2004). Through such efforts, they, along with local government, are reinventing welfare.

Notes

Portions of this chapter appeared previously in the *Community College Journal of Research and Practice*, Vol. 27, No. 6, July 2003, and are republished by permission.

1. These colleges were chosen from a larger national survey because each offered programming targeted specifically at welfare recipients. See Meléndez et al. (2002) for results of the national survey.
2. Leon (1995) and Casey (1998) also describe earlier federal efforts to stimulate workfare programming (e.g., President Johnson's WIN program for AFDC recipients in 1967) and state workfare provisions (e.g., the New York State Work Relief Program in 1959, which required that employable Home Relief clients work on Work Relief projects to secure their benefits).
3. For instance, in December 1997, New York City housed 817,000 welfare recipients out of a total of 1.16 million in the state (Casey 1998).
4. White (1997) states that although the City reported 38,000 WEP participants in early 1997, it placed 166,683 people into WEP from July 1995 through October

1996, or about 126,000 annually.

5. *Peterson's Guide to Two-Year Colleges* (1999) lists 20 community colleges in New York City. Each of these was contacted for a telephone interview; 17 agreed to be interviewed. The full results of the survey are reported in Meléndez et al. (2002).
6. In a case originally filed in 1996 as *Davila v. Hammons,* the plaintiffs won a preliminary injunction against the city in March 1997 in the Supreme Court of New York County. The city appealed this decision—in what was now the case of *Davila v. Eggelston*—and agreed to a settlement favoring the plaintiffs in 2003 (Fisher 2003; Poverty Law Center n.d.).
7. Initial critiques of New York City's WEP program contend that it seldom led to skills enhancement or permanent jobs for the TANF recipients (Finder 1998; White 1997).
8. These figures come from 1995 administrative records of the COPE programs at Hostos Community College and LaGuardia Community College.
9. Characteristics included a student's age, gender, welfare status, ethnicity, college of attendance, and high school group (i.e., whether high school degree was from a school in the New York City public, New York City private, New York State, or foreign/out-of-state system, or from a GED program).
10. Taken from 1999 administrative records of the COPE programs at Hostos Community College and LaGuardia Community College.
11. See "Hostos Community College," http://www.hostos.cuny.edu/about/hostos01.htm (accessed August 10, 2004).
12. Taken from information on LaGuardia Community College's Cooperative Education Program at the college's Web site, http://lagcc.cuny.edu (accessed May 28, 1999).
13. See "Adult and Continuing Education," Programs, Adult Career Counseling and Resource Center, http://www.lagcc.cuny.edu/ace/new.htm (accessed August 10, 2004).
14. For more details on the programs of the Family Institute, see the United Way Web page, http://caresdb.uwnyc.org/cares/AgyRslt_45.cfm?AgyRec=2940 (accessed August 11, 2004).
15. Taken from information on LaGuardia Community College's Cooperative Education Program and LUCED at the college's Web site, http://www.lagcc.cuny.edu (accessed May 28, 1999).
16. See "Industrial Management Resource Program," http://www.lagcc.cuny.edu/ace/imrp/index.html (accessed August 11, 2004).
17. See "Adult and Continuing Education," Programs, The New York City Taxi Driver Institute, http://www.lagcc.cuny.edu/ace/new.htm (accessed August 11, 2004).

References

Abramovitz, Mimi. 1997. *Workfare and the Non-Profits? Myths and Realities.* Report for the Task Force on Welfare Reform, New York City Chapter, National Association of Social Workers. http://www.naswnyc.org/w2.html (accessed April 1, 1999).

Albelda, Randy, and Chris Tilly. 1997. *Glass Ceilings and Bottomless Pits: Women's Work, Women's Poverty*. Boston: South End Press.

Arenson, Karen W. 1998. "CUNY Wins Ruling in a Dispute Over Graduation Requirements." *New York Times,* December 10, B:25. http://www.nytimes.com/archive (accessed April 1, 1999).

Besharov, Douglas. 2004. "There's More Welfare to Reform." *New York Times,* March 6, A:15. http://www.welfareacademy.org/pubs/welfare/theresmore welfaretoreform.pdf (accessed August 11, 2004).

Besharov, Douglas, and Nazanin Samari. 1999. "The *Other* Wisconsin Miracle: How Wisconsin Foundations are Helping Create a Responsive Market for Child Care." *Philanthropy* 13(3): 30–33. http://www.philanthropyroundtable.org/magazines/1999/may/besharov.html (accessed August 10, 2001).

Brettschneider, Eric B. 2001. "Bottom-Up Planning in a Top-Down World." In *Social Work in the Era of Devolution: Toward a Just Practice,* Rosa Perez-Koenig and Barry Rock, eds. New York: Fordham University Press, pp. 211–222.

Casey, Timothy J. 1998. *Welfare Reform and its Impact in the Nation and in New York.* Report of the Policy, Advocacy and Research Department, Federation of Protestant Welfare Agencies. New York: Federation of Protestant Welfare Agencies. http://www.welfarelaw.org/CaseyPaper.htm (accessed May 5, 1999).

City University of New York (CUNY). 1997. *CUNY Student Data Book, Fall 1997.* Vol. 1. New York: CUNY. http://www.cuny.edu/abtcuny/facts/databook97/tocvol1.html (accessed May 13, 1999).

———. 1999. CUNY COPE (College Opportunity to Prepare for Employment) statistics. http://www1.cuny.edu/portal_ur/content/studentjobs/cope.html (accessed October 27, 2004).

Elliott, Mark, Don Spangler, and Kathy Yorkievitz. 1998. *What's Next After Work First: Workforce Development Report to the Field.* Philadelphia: Public/Private Ventures.

Finder, Alan. 1998. "Evidence Is Scant That Workfare Leads to Full-Time Jobs." First article in series, Does Welfare Work? *New York Times,* April 12, A:1.

Fisher, Luchina. 2003. "New York City Agrees to Education for Welfare Recipients." *Women's Enews,* August 22, from the National Organization for

Women Web page, http://www.now.org/eNews/aug2003/082203welfare.html (accessed August 10, 2004).

Gittell, Marilyn, Kirk Vandersall, Jennifer Holdaway, and Kathe Newman. 1996. *Creating Social Capital at CUNY: A Comparison of Higher Education Programs for AFDC Recipients.* New York: Howard Samuels State Management and Policy Center, City University of New York.

Golonka, Susan, and Lisa Matus-Grossman. 2001. *Opening Doors: Expanding Educational Opportunities for Low-Income Workers.* Manpower Demonstration Research Corporation (MDRC) and National Governors Association Center for Best Practices.

Greenberg, Mark, Julie Strawn, and Lisa Plimpton. 2000. *State Opportunities to Provide Access to Postsecondary Education Under TANF.* Washington, DC: Center for Law and Social Policy. http://www.clasp.org/pubs/ (accessed September 21, 2001).

Hercik, Jeanette M. 1998. "Organizational Culture Change in Welfare Reform." *Welfare Information Network Issue Notes* 2(4). http://www.welfareinfo.org/Isseorganiza.htm (accessed August 11, 2004).

Hostos Community College. 1999. Various Web site materials. New York: Hostos Community College. http://www.hostos.cuny.edu (accessed April 1–May 28, 1999).

Kazis, Richard, and Marlene Seltzer. 2000. "Toward a Demand-Led Workforce Development System." Paper presented at the Welfare to Work: New Solutions for the New Economy UK/US Symposium. Boston: Jobs for the Future. http://www.jff.org/jff/kc/library/0114/index_html (accessed August 11, 2004).

Laarman, Peter. 1998. "An Insult to the Poor: Why New York Churches Are Resisting Workfare." *Sojourners* (September–October). http://sojourners.com/soj9809/980915.html (accessed April 1, 1999).

Leon, Rachel. 1995. *Workfare in NYS: Does It Work? A Study of the Impact of New Workfare Regulations and the Correlation Between Emphasis on Workfare and Job Entry.* Albany, New York: Hunger Action Network of NYS. http://www.crisny.org/not-for-profit/unions/hannys-1.htm (accessed April 1, 1999).

Lynch, Roberta. 1994. "Can Markets Govern?" *American Prospect* 5(16): 125–134. http://www.prospect.org/print/V5/16/lynch-r.html (accessed August 11, 2004).

Mannix, Mary R., Marc Cohan, Henry A. Freedman, Christopher Lamb, and Jim Williams. 1998. "Welfare Litigation Developments Since the Personal Responsibility and Work Opportunity Reconciliation Act of 1996." *Clearinghouse Review* 31(1): 435–453. http://www.welfarelaw.org/artcommw.html (accessed April 1, 1999).

Meléndez, Edwin, Luis M. Falcón, Carlos Suárez, Lynn McCormick, and Alexandra de Montrichard. 2002. *The Welfare-to-Work Policy Shock: How Community Colleges Are Addressing the Challenge.* New York: New School University, Community Development Research Center.

National Association of Social Work (NASW) 1999. "Job Centers: NYC's Diversion from Aid = Loss of Human Rights." *Currents* (January). First in a series of articles by New York City chapter, NASW Task Force on Welfare Reform. http://www.naswnyc.org/w7.html (accessed April 1, 1999).

New York Times. 1998. "Obstructing Local Welfare Reform." Editorial. *New York Times,* July 4, A:10. http://www.nytimes.com/archive (accessed April 1, 1999).

Osborne, David, and Ted Gaebler. 1992. *Reinventing Government: How the Entrepreneurial Spirit is Transforming the Public Sector.* Reading, MA: Addison-Wesley.

Peterson's Guides. *Peterson's Guide to Two-Year Colleges.* 1999. Princeton, NJ: Peterson's Guides Inc.

Poverty Law Center. n.d. "Settlement Requires New York City to Evaluate TANF Recipients for Education and Training Programs Before Assigning Them to Work Activities." http://www.povertylaw.org/legalresearch/cases/act_abstract_for_print.cfm?id=51713 (accessed August 10, 2004).

Steuerle, C. Eugene, and Gordon Mermin. 1997. *Devolution as Seen from the Budget.* No. A-2 in the series Assessing the New Federalism: Issues and Options for States. Washington, DC: Urban Institute. http://newfederalism.urban.org/html/anf_a2.htm (accessed August 15, 2001).

Strawn, Julie. 1999. *Welfare-to-Work Programs: The Critical Role of Skills.* Kellogg Devolution Initiative Paper. Washington, DC: Center for Law and Social Policy. http://www.clasp.org/pubs/jobseducation/skillspapere.htm (accessed May 18, 1999).

Varro, Barbara. 2004. "1 College, 2 Languages." *Chicago Tribune*, March 7. http://www.chicagotribune.com/business/custom/educationtoday/chi-0403060310mar07,0,3301021.story (accessed August 11, 2004).

Watson, Keith, and Steven D. Gold. 1997. *The Other Side of Devolution: Shifting Relationships Between State and Local Governments.* Assessing the New Federalism report. Washington, DC: Urban Institute. http://newfederalism.urban.org/html/other.htm (accessed August 15, 2001).

Weir, Margaret. 1997. "Is Anybody Listening? The Uncertain Future of Welfare Reform in the Cities." *Brookings Review* 15(1): 30–33. http://www.crisny.org/not-for-profit/unions/weirwi97.htm (accessed May 11, 1999).

Welfare Law Center (WLC). 1999. "Federal Court Finds New York City Illegally Deters and Denies Food Stamps, Medicaid, and Cash Assistance Applications and Bars Expansion of 'Job Centers.'" From *Welfare News*

(March). New York: Welfare Law Center. http://www.welfarelaw.org/wnreynolds.htm (accessed May 5, 1999).

White, Andrew. 1997. "WEP (Workers Expect Paychecks)." *City Limits* (69). http://www.citylimits.org/lores/archives/9703wep.htm (accessed April 1, 1999).

11
Community Colleges as Workforce Intermediaries

Building Career Ladders for Low-Wage Workers

Joan Fitzgerald
Northeastern University

OVERVIEW

When Temporary Assistance to Needy Families (TANF) was enacted in 1996, the country was experiencing a tight labor market, which created vacancies for many new workers. Yet even in this booming economy, the employment and earnings prospects for job seekers leaving welfare was dismal. Today, openings in the service-sector occupations that former TANF clients have been filling (e.g., retail clerk, lawn service technician, certified nursing assistant, child care provider) are once again growing, but pay in these low-skill jobs is still near the minimum wage and has not increased in real terms in more than two decades. Indeed, despite record economic growth in the five year period after TANF was passed, over one-fifth of male and almost one-third of female workers earned poverty-level wages (Mishel, Bernstein, and Schmitt 1999).

These figures are not merely a reflection of more people working part-time. Although more full-time jobs are available to help people make the transition from welfare to work, a report by the Conference Board found that the number of full-time workers who are poor increased from 1997 to 1998 (Barrington 2000, p. 4). This study estimates the number of working poor in the United States at between four and five million. The cause of this trend is an increase in the relative share

Table 11.1 Change in Employment (%), by Pay Category, 1963–98

Industry	% of Employment	
	1963	1998
High-paying	28	21
Middle-paying	37	16
Low-paying	35	63

SOURCE: The Conference Board.

of low-skill, low-wage employment, largely driven by the shift from manufacturing to services (Table 11.1).

Clearly, long-term economic independence will not be achieved simply by moving people off TANF and into dead-end jobs. Low-wage workers have to be able to advance into more highly skilled and better paying jobs. To do so, they need to continually upgrade their skills.

Community college vocational programs are uniquely poised to provide the training needed for low-wage workers to advance into these better paying jobs. Most of the nation's community colleges have developed short-term training programs, some specifically for TANF clients. A few community colleges are attempting to build on these programs by offering courses and programs for students after initial placement to prepare them to advance on the job. This report presents best practice in these programs.

My intent, however, is not simply to present best practice. Cumulatively, even best practice programs will have very limited impact if the economy is creating too many low-paying and dead-end jobs. Community colleges are uniquely positioned to succeed at creating career ladders and wage progression opportunities because they have the potential to influence the structure of employment. Many community colleges engage in economic development activities that provide technical assistance to businesses to help them become high performance work organizations.[1]

These programs seldom have any connection to the vocational programs community colleges offer for people moving off welfare. In both types of programs, however, community colleges act as labor market intermediaries that not only connect supply and demand but also attempt to influence demand. To the extent they are successful in these programs, community colleges can help to create better paying jobs as well as provide the training for people to fill them. Going to scale with career ladder and wage progression strategies means that community colleges have to convince employers to create more middle-paying jobs.

This chapter examines the extent to which community colleges play a more active role than in the past in encouraging employers to restructure jobs, given the proliferation of low-wage jobs. Three highly successful community college programs that focus on career ladders or wage progression are presented:

- Job Ladder Partnership, Shoreline Community College (Seattle metropolitan area)
- Essential Skills Partnership, Community College of Denver
- Environmental Health and Safety Program, South Seattle Community College

I highlight the elements of the programs that are behind their success and discuss more broadly the extent to which community colleges can be intermediaries that influence employers to create better jobs. The discussion focuses on the structure of employment, the policy environment, and how community colleges institutionalize programs with limited funding streams.

The sites were identified through informal interviews with community college administrators, membership organization representatives, and researchers. The three colleges chosen were mentioned repeatedly as ones trying to build career ladders into their certificate and degree programs, particularly those programs targeting Welfare-to-Work clients.

At each site, interviews were conducted with faculty and administrators, the college president, business partners, and social service agency and community organization partners. In addition to these sources, the cases are based on college documents and evaluation data.

COMMUNITY COLLEGES AS LABOR MARKET INTERMEDIARIES

About two-thirds of community colleges have short-term vocational programs geared to welfare recipients (Meléndez and Falcón 1999).

Most of these last from three to six months, are noncredit, and do not articulate with related degree programs. In 1997 I was part of a research team that identified best practice in these programs (see Fitzgerald and Jenkins 1997). In this project we identified teaching innovations such as creating learning communities and integrating literacy with vocational instruction. We examined how community colleges formed partnerships to provide the intensive support services needed by this population to finish programs and adjust to the world of work. We also noted the concern that many of the dedicated community college faculty and staff conveyed over how the forthcoming welfare reform would impact their programs. Staff at LaGuardia Community College's highly effective welfare reform program, the College Opportunity to Prepare for Employment (COPE), expressed pride in having moved many former welfare clients from basic literacy to an associate degree in three years. Yet they feared that the time limits and "work first" requirements of the recently passed welfare reform legislation would undercut their ability to continue the program.

Indeed, their fears proved justified. New York has not invested savings from the reduction in welfare caseloads into education and training (see Emsellem 2000). Since New York City's version of Welfare-to-Work, the Work Experience Program (WEP), gives workfare priority over education, funds for COPE have been reduced (see McCormick [1999] for details on state and city funding of public assistance in New York). Even as it cut COPE funds, the city expanded the program from 4 to 10 campuses. As a result, LaGuardia's COPE classes have tripled in size while funding has dwindled. The counseling and case management that made the program so successful have been reduced drastically. Staff have been forced to select students requiring less remediation. COPE students are now eligible only for certificate programs of one year or less, reducing the possibility that they will be able to obtain jobs that will move them out of poverty.

Community college Welfare-to-Work programs throughout the country have faced similar constraints. Work first has forced many community colleges to do more creaming and less training. But there has been another response. Some community colleges are developing a second generation of programs that still use short-term training to get people into jobs quickly but also have explicit steps for continuing training after students become employed. These programs provide real opportunities for wage progression and occupational upgrading that are not present in most Welfare-to-Work programs.

The three career ladder programs described in this report take different approaches to career ladders and focus on different industries. The Job Ladders program at Shoreline Community College has pathways (curricula) in manufacturing, customer relations, health services, and information technology. South Seattle Community College is experimenting with offering modules instead of courses in environmental health and safety. The Essential Skills Program at Community College of Denver has several job ladder career tracks but has been most successful in early childhood education and medical instrument technology.

Although relatively new, these programs are showing impressive results in both job placement and advancement. Their success is mostly a function of identifying a limited number of occupations that have relatively high starting wages, minimal entry-level requirements, and opportunities for advancement. Yet studies from the Economic Policy Institute and the Conference Board reveal there are few jobs with these characteristics. This is not simply a supply-side problem that can be solved by providing more education and training programs. It is a demand-side problem of an economy not creating enough jobs that allow entry-level workers to advance. Because of community colleges' economic development mission, a lot of hope has been placed in those institutions to be the intermediaries that not only link supply and demand but also influence employers to create better jobs (see Fitzgerald 1998a; Rosenfeld 2000; Rosenfeld and Kingslow 1995). Is this too much to expect of a community college? To answer this question, we need to have a better sense of what is meant by a labor market intermediary.

Labor market intermediaries connect people to jobs. Their varying roles can be placed on a continuum, based on the extent to which they try to influence factors of supply and demand. The most basic intermediaries don't add value to the supply; they simply make connections. Headhunters, for example, help employers find the most qualified people for specific jobs. They operate at the high end of the labor market, finding highly qualified people for top jobs in firms or organizations. The U.S. Employment Service, which helps unemployed workers find jobs, is also in the category of connector. The $80, on average, that it spends on each participant reduces that person's unemployment insurance payments by about two weeks (Osterman, 1999, p. 135). At both the high and the low end of the labor market, temporary agencies also connect people to jobs. Although many Welfare-to-Work programs are built on the concept of "temp to perm," there is increasingly a dark side to this type of intermediary. Proliferating temp agencies working through a network of hiring halls in Chicago's inner-city neighborhoods provide manual day labor for suburban employers. In the crudest sense they are intermediaries, but as Peck and Theodore (2001, p. 4) show, their actual function is to assist firms in exploiting workers "whose social and economic circumstances render them contingent." At best, connectors reduce the length of unemployment. At worst, they are exploitive.

Placement intermediaries provide some combination of job training, education, and social support services to prepare clients for the labor market. Since most middle-class people have access to education and social networks through which jobs are found, placement intermediaries work mostly with low-income groups. Many community-based organizations (CBOs) have become quite effective in this arena. A large literature identifies the specific program elements and documents how organizations network to provide the comprehensive set of services needed to move people from welfare to work, often into living-wage jobs (see Meléndez 1996; Harrison, Weiss, and Gant 1995; Meléndez and Harrison 1998; Harrison and Weiss 1996; Lautsch and Osterman 1998). Many community colleges also network with CBOs and social service agencies to provide support services, but some offer them on their own (see Fitzgerald and Jenkins 1997). Both CBOs and community colleges develop relationships with employers to ensure they are providing the right skills and to extract commitments to hire program graduates. There is seldom any attempt to influence employers to increase wages, add benefits, or improve the quality of jobs.

A progressive intermediary attempts to work on both the supply and the demand side of the labor market. Since community colleges provide education and training and many have an economic development mission, they have the potential to address both supply and demand side issues. Many community colleges assist firms not only in adopting new technology, but in upgrading the skills of their workers. Most states fund community colleges to do business outreach and technology transfer (see Fitzgerald 1998b). By providing technical assistance in manufacturing modernization and customized training, community colleges have the potential to maintain and even increase the number of high performance workplaces in the local economy. To the extent that providing these services to employers results in more employers taking a higher wage and skill path, community colleges can have some impact on local labor market demand. Yet there is little evidence to date that community colleges have the leverage needed to convince employers to change if the low road is profitable.

In the career ladder and wage progression programs presented below, community colleges are attempting to convince employers to increase pay, add benefits, create advancement opportunities, and consider internal promotions that would not have been considered before, as higher quality and more stable workers become available through their training. I present the cases individually before discussing the extent to which the programs allow the community colleges to act as progressive intermediaries.

THE THREE COMMUNITY COLLEGES

The programs included are not necessarily best practice since most of them are too new to have much data on long-term career progression. They were chosen because they illustrate innovation in focusing on career ladders or wage progression. The case study presentations do not provide comprehensive information on the entire community college or even on related programs. Rather, the details on the programs are used to frame the discussion on limitations imposed by the structure of the economy and by institutional factors, and on how state policy can support wage progression strategies. Each of these issues speaks to the capacity of community colleges to be labor market intermediaries.

Shoreline Community College Job Ladder Partnership Program

Shoreline Community College in Seattle is one of the few community colleges integrating career ladders into its Welfare-to-Work programs. The Job Ladder Partnership involves Shoreline and six other community or technical colleges with employers in creating work and learning pathways in four occupational clusters:

- manufacturing
- customer relations
- health services
- information technology

The areas were chosen because of local demand in occupations in these sectors which pay family wages and offer benefits. Further, these clusters have relatively low entry-level skill requirements yet offer opportunities for advancement with readily available training.

Funding for the program is the result of the commitment of Washington governor Gary Locke to focus welfare reform on moving people out of poverty, not just off welfare. Locke sees the state's community college system as essential to accomplishing this goal. To realize the necessary funding, in 1998 the State of Washington made an initial transfer of $17 million from the Department of Social and Health Services (DSHS) to the State Board for Community and Technical Colleges. The funds were earmarked for developing programs to promote job advancement and wage progression. In 1999 an additional $20 million was allocated for the programs.

Three programs were established at Shoreline with the funds:

1) A 12-week pre-employment training program that links to the needs of one employer or a group of employers.
2) A work-based learning program that provides tuition assistance to serve as a bridge between free tuition and eligibility for federal Pell Grants. Any parent under 175 percent of the poverty line and working 20 hours weekly is given free tuition to any community college technical program, usually for one or two quarters, until Pell eligibility kicks in.
3) Professional and technical education redesign and delivery. This program designates funds to community colleges for redesigning programs to make it easier for students to combine school and work (e.g., by offering evening and weekend courses), to shorten programs, and to add more certificate programs.

In 1999 another work-study program was added for TANF recipients. This program provides part-time employment, usually with CBOs, for students enrolled in college courses. Work-study jobs must be related to the student's course of study and can last no longer than two academic quarters. Students can work in the private sector or on campus.

By the time the funds were allocated, Shoreline's Workforce and Economic Development Division was already experimenting with welfare reform programs based on career ladders. One program prepared students to be billing specialists, then provided training for them to move up to medical reimbursement specialists, and from there into a nationally certified program in health care information technology. The program had tremendous success both in placing students in entry-level jobs and in stimulating students to return for more training. Building on this success, Dr. Holly Moore, vice president for workforce and economic development at Shoreline, called a meeting of area community and technical colleges to coordinate a response to the new workforce development funds. The six community colleges serving the suburban parts of the county agreed to collaborate in program planning and development. The goal of the partnership was to share resources and connections in order to serve employers and students better.

Each of the colleges had independent relationships with employers, maintained by "customer service representatives." Under the partnership, the customer service representative at any given college represents all of the colleges. Representatives with strong existing relationships with employers in one of the sectors serve all of the colleges in that sector. In other cases, representatives serve businesses in all four focus sectors in a geographic region. The point is to build on preexisting relationships. Sharing business partners allows the schools to fill job orders more efficiently. Since the schools are on different schedules, at least one of them is likely to have graduates at a time when an employer has hiring needs.

The business partners are essential to the program. Each college has one lead staff member in charge of employer outreach. Business partners are assigned to an outreach specialist based on which specialist has the best relationship with that employer, as opposed to by geography or industry. Of course, colleges with strong programs in a given occupational area tended to have the best employer connections. The partners work closely with staff on developing curricula and also provide instructors for some courses. Approximately one-third of job placements are with partner employers. Another third is with other employers in the same industry, and the remainder is with employers not in the industry for which training was provided.

Part of the work in developing partnerships with employers is adapting the programs to include specific skills employers need. Although some partner employers are committed to hiring program graduates, they have not all approved the curriculum of each program. This will be a long process, as many employers define the same job quite differently. A medical technician, for example, may have different job responsibilities in different hospitals. But through the partnership of colleges, each institution can tailor its program to the needs of a specific employer. Employers consistently emphasize good work habits and trainability over specific occupational skills. Thus, two-thirds of Shoreline's preemployment training (PET) curriculum focuses on life and employability skills, job search skills, world of work instruction, and basic skills.

The retention specialist shows the student diagrams of career pathways that identify many possibilities for advancement, then works with the student on choosing one of the paths. Shoreline first started testing the effectiveness of intensive retention services through the college's participation in a project sponsored by Public/Private Ventures (P/PV). The project funds community colleges in several states in efforts to help students understand the importance of getting and keeping a job and moving on to the next level. The next level may be a pay increase or a totally different career path. Shoreline started the intensive retention services with its Computer Numerical Control (CNC) program. After two quarters of instruction, most CNC graduates take entry-level jobs paying anywhere between $8.50 and $15.00 an hour, depending on how well they perform.

TANF recipients get authorization from their DSHS case manager before entering the program, then go through an assessment to determine barriers. Typical problems include lack of housing, transportation, or child care, dealings with the court system, and domestic violence. The case manager seeks to determine whether the timing is right for that individual, since the program has a strict attendance policy. If it seems that the applicant's problems can be managed while he or she is in the program, the student is referred to appropriate support services.

The Job Ladder Partnership

A guiding principle of Shoreline's Job Ladder Partnership is to combine education and work as much as possible. Students go through an initial assessment and are then placed into the pre-employment program, work, remedial classes, or English as a Second Language (ESL). As soon as students have enough skills to begin an entry-level job in one of the chosen sectors, they have to combine work and continuing education. Students develop a career plan early on and work with a counselor to keep moving ahead on their career goals.

The two steps in the program are described below.

Pre-employment training (PET)

In this 12-week program students acquire life and work skills. They develop a career plan and identify the education and training required to allow them to achieve it. Students select between evening (weekdays, 5:00–9:30 p.m.) or weekend (Friday–Sunday) sessions. They also select one of three pathways—manufacturing assembly, office occupations (information technology), or health services (basic caregiver). Students interested in non-office customer service positions are referred to other Job Ladder Partnership colleges for call center training. In addition to the 7.5 hours per week of occupational skills instruction, each student acquires 14.5 hours of basic and soft skills, taught through workshops in industrial safety/first aid and worker rights and responsibilities, and through classes in life/employability skills, job search skills, and basic computer skills. Syllabi for these courses are quite detailed, outlining the skill competencies, expectations, and weekly course material to be covered.

A computer laboratory offers supervised, self-paced instruction in keyboarding, computer software, and using the Internet. Students requiring basic skills remediation are referred to college Adult Basic Education/General Equivalency Degree (ABE/GED) or ESL programs, or to the college's English, math, or reading and writing learning laboratories. Students do not have to work during this part of the program, although 30–40 percent do.

When students complete the program, they receive a certificate. In many program areas, Shoreline is moving away from conferring degrees and toward bestowing skill-based credentials. This is part of a broader trend at both the community college and the high school level. In fact, both Washington and Oregon already have plans to require that students earn skill-based certificates of mastery in order to receive high school diplomas. To develop such certificates, Shoreline and other community colleges work with employers to identify a list of tasks workers must learn to perform for specific occupations. Programs are then redesigned to include these tasks, and performance criteria are developed for students to demonstrate their competence.

Placement and advancement through career ladders

After completing the PET comes the second step: students must work at least 20 hours a week to continue in the program. Upon entering the PET program students begin working with a retention specialist and the program's placement services manager, who refer them to one of the partner employers. Toward the end of the program the retention specialists begin working closely with the student and with the program's job developer. The retention specialists meet with students weekly to discuss job searches and to help them anticipate what their personal lives will be like once they are working. Students are placed based on their performance. Students are not graded, but they must have a 70 percent proficiency rating in all of their classes to earn a certificate. Students with high proficiency ratings are placed with partner companies, while those who do not perform as well are placed with other companies.

Shoreline has two staff members dedicated to retention. A third is provided for TANF students through TRAC (Training, Rehab, Assessment and Consultation), a for-profit organization contracted by DSHS. Either Nate Windle, manager for retention services, or TRAC retention specialist Johanna Hedge maintains weekly contact with new graduates during their first 30 days on the job. Depending on the student, contact is reduced to once every two weeks between 30 and 60 days on the job. During this period, any number of issues can arise. Windle offers several examples of how specialists work with recent graduates. When one man lost his transportation, Windle helped him to get a bus pass and to make a device to carry his tool box on the bus. Typically students need help with figuring out how to get around such barriers, but sometimes, Windle explains, it's other issues, such as how to budget money to last between paychecks. "One of the things I try to bring home," he says, "is that if you don't have a plan for yourself, someone will have it for you. Then you're stuck." Whether the issue is child care or transportation, staff help workers to see that they need to have backup plans. Hedge adds that she often provides moral support for students struggling to adjust to holding a full-time job. Sometimes children are resentful that their parent isn't available as much, and the student feels guilty. Others need help in selecting appropriate work clothes. Several students, now that they are earning more, seek assistance in moving their families to safer neighborhoods. Whatever the issue, Windle says, "the idea of the program is that they don't have to figure everything out for themselves."

After the 90-day probation period, staff ask participants to begin thinking about their future with the company. "If they don't like their jobs," Windle explains, "I ask them to visualize staying for three to six months so they can get their work portfolio together." If participants are unhappy with their work, Windle encourages them to think about going back to school or to talk to their employers about advancement possibilities. "As much as we want them to keep their jobs, we want them to be happy," he continues, "and they don't know what [particular jobs entail] if they've never worked. After all, we've all had time to do job exploration—I certainly did it in the military." For the most part, staff maintain contact by phone.

For participants who are dissatisfied in their jobs, Windle identifies courses they could take at Shoreline, such as CNC Programming, that would lead to a better position and a raise. This and other courses take only one quarter, so the participants can see a real connection between education and job advancement. "What's hard," Windle says, "is that they typically have to do it on their own time. Although some employers pay for courses, many do not."

A new computerized career-planning tool, the Career Pathway Passport, allows students, with the support and assistance of their retention specialist, to develop career plans and document their progress. Using the interactive program, students begin career planning with a counselor but can continue modifying their goals and charting their progress independently. The Passport has two databases—one listing available jobs in the four career pathways offered by the employer partners, and another containing the education programs offered by the six partner colleges in these fields. College and employer contacts are listed. The Shoreline Web site describes how students use the system:

"The career transcript portion of the passport works by using pull down menus and forms. Every time a student enters or completes a training program or job they get either an entry or exit "visa" as appropriate. Employment or training that is not already part of the database can also be entered and included in the list of visas. Any change in employment can lead to a new visa. The visa system provides a hook for maintaining contact with those workers who are in the system, since they will want to come in and get their passports updated periodically with new visas."

The career-planning portion of the passport demystifies for students how they can combine work and education to climb a job ladder. Using the pull down menus listing database options, the retention specialist and the student together select training programs and jobs in the career pathway that take the student from where he is to his long term employment goal. Contact information lets the student know whom to call to take advantage of the next employment or training opportunity on his customized career pathway. The system utilizes software technology to create a career-planning tool, at the core of which is a database of local opportunities.

Support Services

The retention specialist maintains contacts with community organizations that help poor people enter the labor market, and she refers students to these support services. Many students, for example, visit a community-run store that provides free business clothes. The retention specialist also refers students to Shoreline's manager for family support services, a support person provided through the state's WorkFirst program, who directs them to one of three DSHS offices in the area to ask about social services for which they might be eligible.

Students are responsible for making their own arrangements for transportation and child care. They are encouraged to inquire with DSHS to see if they are eligible for transportation and child care funds. Child care is provided at the college, and most students receive full or partial subsidies through DSHS. If partial, students are required to pay the difference between DSHS payments and the cost of services. Students sign an agreement that acknowledges their responsibility in this area. The agreement further stipulates that they will be expelled from the program and will not receive a certificate of completion if they miss more than four sessions (two sessions for weekend students) or fail to meet with their retention specialist.

Outcomes

The completion and placement rates of the program compare quite well to best-practice Welfare-to-Work programs throughout the country. The overall program completion rate is 74.3 percent, which is very high for a 12-week program. The rate varied from 56.6 percent for Winter 1999–2000 to 86.6 percent in the Genie program for Fall 1998 (Table 11.2).

Wages fell in the second year, and one reason for the drop was that more single women were enrolled for that period. For the most part,

Table 11.2 Pre-Employment Training Outcomes Summary 1998–2000

Cohort	Total enrolled	Total completers	Total employed	With benefits	Empl. rate (%)	Average wage ($)
Genie Fall 1998[a]	45	39	28	23	72	11.85
Genie Spring 1999[a]	15	11	9	6	82	11.40
Job Ladder Spring 1999	45	37	29	21	78	9.60
Job Ladder Fall 1999	60	45	35	19	78	9.18
Job Ladder 1999–2000	53	30	24	12	80	9.28
Job Ladder Spring 2000	60	—	—	—	—	—
Subtotal FY 1998–99	105	87	66	50	75	10.80
Subtotal FY 1999–2000	179	75	59	3	79	10.05
FY 1998–2000	284	162	125	80	77	10.50

[a] All students were enrolled in a customized training program for Genie Industries, a local supplier of hydraulic lifts. — = data not available.

SOURCE: Shoreline Community College.

staff have not been able to entice women into the higher paying manufacturing jobs. Another reason was that the second year students had more serious barriers to employment. It was harder to get them through the program in 12 weeks with the skills they needed to qualify for positions with employer partners. As a result, they were placed in less preferable, lower wage jobs at the start, with the hope of helping them move up after placement.

Retention and advancement data for the 41 students who got jobs in the Spring 1999 training cycle show that the average hourly entry wage for these students was $9.57. About half of all the students have received wage increases since starting. The current average wage for those who have experienced a wage or job change is $10.29, representing a 7.5 percent annual increase.

Funding

The program receives approximately $2,500 per student from the state's pre-employment training, tuition assistance, and program redesign funds. Retention services are partially funded by a grant from Public/Private Ventures ($50,000), and by DSHS (for a TRAC retention specialist). This funding covers the cost of training and retention services, but the current funding levels do not acknowledge that students need retention services for at least a year after placement. As new students enter, the caseloads of the two full-time staff members providing retention counseling continue to increase.

The college adds $55,000 in in-kind contributions for community college and employer sponsored training at the work site. DSHS provides $17,000 per year in child care subsidies.

The state of Washington allocated $28.8 million to 34 community colleges for fiscal year 2001. Community colleges still had to apply for each program, but overall there was more funding available. These funds broke down into seven line items:

- $7.1 million for short-term (12-week) customized pre-employment programs that are co-sponsored by an employer. Funds are allocated to applicants.
- $3.6 million for college work-study for TANF recipients and the working poor, allocated by a formula that apportions slots based

on the number of eligible students at the college.

- $6.6 million in work-based learning tuition for those working and going to school, allocated to colleges on a formula basis.
- $4.4 million for support staff with which to operate programs, including financial aid officers, advisors, and counselors, allocated on a formula basis with three different support levels.
- $1 million in workplace basic literacy or ESL programs that recipients take while working. Funded on a project basis, based on application.
- $5 million for Families that Work, a program combining literacy and parent education. Available to community colleges and CBOs based on application.
- $1.1 million for child care on campuses.

All of these funds were allocated from the state's TANF caseload savings. Expenditures on welfare cash grants have gone down by $250 million a year since TANF was introduced, although total expenditures have increased as the funds have been shifted to other services for the poor and working poor. Ken Miller, WorkFirst coordinator of the Office of Financial Management, says that the state is spending $50 million more on child care and $100 million more on training, job placement, and wage progression strategies as a result of the cash grant savings. Miller notes that the $28.8 million allocated to community colleges represents a new relationship between the old welfare system and community colleges.

Summary

Shoreline is out in front of most community colleges in creating career ladder programs for low-income populations. To get there has required significant rethinking of how and when courses are offered, what makes an effective business partnership, and how to provide pre- and post-placement counseling to students. Few of these changes could have been made if not for significant financial support from the state of Washington. Furthermore, a cooperative environment, both among community colleges and between employers and community colleges, facilitated the high placement and retention rates. But the colleges were unable to sustain the partnership because of lack of funding. Shoreline's program continues independently.

South Seattle Community College Environmental Health and Safety Program

Administrators and faculty at South Seattle Community College (SSCC) see curriculum modules as the wave of the future in technical education. Modules differ from regular courses in that they are not scheduled according to the fixed semester calendar; instead, they merely require that students demonstrate performance-based competencies to pass them. Two forces are driving the move to modules. First, the time limits and work first requirements of welfare reform mean that students need short-term training to prepare for work. Since TANF recipients are under pressure to find work quickly, they cannot wait for the next semester to start. Further, even a 12-week commitment can be difficult for someone not used to working or going to school. Modules offer a way to divide a longer course or program into manageable segments with job advancement connected to each of them. Second, many employers are looking for ways their employees can pick up specific skills quickly to perform their jobs. Modules allow busy people, many of whom already have degrees, to learn a specific skill without taking a semester-long course that may cover a lot of material they already know.

To be more responsive to the needs of students and business, South Seattle President David Mitchell wants to see the approach institutionalized. The enrollment statistics support him; less than half of enrollees are full-time day students. The late interim associate dean, Laura Parkins, was assigned to work with faculty and staff on developing more modular programs. It will take time to reach Mitchell's goal. It's a bigger task than taking an existing course and dividing it into segments. It involves working with individual employers and industry associations to identify skill standards and to establish performance-based criteria for mastering the skills. Programs are designed so that each module is connected to specific skill standards. Typically, short-term certificate courses do not provide credits toward a degree. A unique aspect of the modules being developed at South Seattle is that they cumulate credits toward both certificates and degrees.

The Environmental Health and Safety program highlighted in this case study illustrates how work and learning can be combined so that students can find jobs quickly and then take manageable steps to continue their education and increase their earnings. Further, it describes the role of business and community partners in developing a high-quality curriculum and supporting students as they make difficult life transitions. On the demand side, it reveals that as employers find better quality workers who stay on the job longer, they may be willing to turn temporary jobs into permanent ones, pay better wages, and provide benefits.

The Environmental Health and Safety Program

Three factors converged to motivate South Seattle administrators and faculty to create a new modular program in environmental health and safety. The first was declining enrollment. With enrollment diminishing, faculty and staff of the associate degree program in toxicology, chemistry and hazardous materials called a technical advisory board meeting in August of 1999 to ask board members how to improve the program. They learned that there was high demand for skilled technicians in the field but that the program was not meeting the needs of employers. The program covered theory, rules, and regulations but not hands-on experience or recognized certifications. The employers desperately needed people with the certifications required by the state of Washington to work with specific substances.

The second factor was a particularly motivated board member, Brad Schroeder, vice president and co-owner of TCB Industrial. TCB provides supplemental labor for environmental cleanups. The company's clients include construction and environmental cleanup firms and county, city, and state governments. Its typical jobs involve railroad accidents, Superfund site cleanup, household hazardous waste collection, and oil spills. The firm employs 107 people in Seattle and 60 in a Portland, Oregon, facility.

Three years ago, when Schroeder was having difficulty finding employees with the basic 40-hour hazardous materials certificate required for all cleanup jobs, he started a training program at TCB. Schroeder chose this route over working with South Seattle because of his experience teaching at another community college. In that job, he had quit in frustration when he was required to teach material to students working in the environmental cleanup field that both he and the students knew was not providing them with the skills they needed to do their jobs. Since the community college was not willing to change its curriculum, Schroeder decided to create a school that would offer all of the individual certifications required for brownfields certification. Once he had gotten that school going, the South Seattle initiative interested him because it would complement the school he had already created and enable him to expand his business to meet the growing demand for labor in the environmental cleanup field. Schroeder mobilized employers in the field to work with South Seattle in revamping its program.

The third factor for administrators was that redesigning the program into modules would allow the college to create wage progression opportunities for graduates of its pre-employment program in hazardous waste management. This program, funded by the Washington Community College Board, was designed for TANF recipients.

How the South Seattle program works

The program begins with a core of 10 modules that provide 14 college credits and certification in brownfields. The modules range from 8 to 24 hours of instruction.[2] Students must pass a performance-based examination to earn a certificate in each module. Then they can follow a path toward either a technician or a supervisor level certificate.

The HAZWOP (hazardous waste operator) module is considered the minimum requirement for employment, even for workers with advanced degrees. It provides 40 hours of instruction in hazardous waste handling. This module was already being offered as a TANF pre-employment course. It is offered from two to three times a year, usually to classes of 20 students. Once a person has the introductory and HAZWOP modules, they can pursue the other core requirement modules.When the program becomes fully operative, modules will be offered during evenings and weekends to accommodate work schedules.

As workers accumulate certifications, they become eligible for more types of jobs. Those certified for confined spaces can clean ship holds and machine pits for firms such as Boeing, a major employer in the Seattle area. Those with the blood borne pathogen certificate are often sent to the University of Washington to clean HVAC systems in medical research departments. Those with the lock out–tag out certificate work in many industrial settings, locking out all energy sources while they do cleanup or repairs. HAZWOP graduates start at $11.50 per hour and can go as high as $22.50 per hour for some certificates. Graduates of the first environmental cleanup module are qualified to work in disposal of hospital waste, cleaning of contaminated sites such as shipyards, and recycling of hazardous materials such as paint. TCB and several other firms, including Foss (an oil distributor and refinery) and Boeing, hire certificate holders.

The technician level certificate prepares individuals to conduct assessments for the presence of hazardous materials such as asbestos. The supervisor level certificate has been popular among technicians who were working as hazardous waste technicians for firms such as Boeing before many certification requirements were in effect. Boeing and many other companies are now requiring these workers to have degrees. This group has many of the specific skills but needs additional instruction in computers and in understanding the legislative environment and applying the legislation to workplace standards.

All of the 50–53 credits for these programs count toward the AAS degree in environmental health and safety. Associate degree graduates earn between $30,000 and $40,000 and in some cases considerably more. Flexible scheduling and modularization allow students to learn while working.

The increasing problem of brownfields assures continued labor market demand. Many banks now require that both commercial and residential properties have Phase I site assessments before they will approve a loan. The growing need for site assessment has created a certification for people able to do Phase I, II, and III assessments.[3] Further, many employers are required to have board certified industrial hygienists, safety professionals, and hazardous materials managers. People in these positions make sure companies stay within OSHA exposure limits, monitor compliance with health and safety procedures, develop emergency response plans, and establish company waste handling policies that meet legislative requirements. All three board certifications require students to pass a rigorous examination. People in these positions earn between $40,000 and $50,000 per year at the entry-level technician level.

Modules are taught by adjunct faculty, such as Schroeder, who have both field and teaching experience. Academic modules are taught by South Seattle faculty. Plans are under way to offer some of the more cut-and-dried modules, such as those dealing with the Clean Air Act and Clean Water Act, online. In these modules, students must become completely familiar with the legislative regulations that affect their work.

Support services

Before the brownfields curriculum, some students taking HAZWOP were referred from DSHS or from community organizations. Keith Marler, workforce coordinator at South Seattle, noticed that students from the King County Jobs Initiative (KCJI) and Seattle Jobs Initiatives (SJI), who had case managers and an array of social service supports, had higher completion rates.[4] Based on this discovery, the college has developed partnerships with several community and trade organizations to provide the resources students need to finish their courses. As the TCB school joins its program with South Seattle, KCJI will place clients at both places and provide case management and support services for them.[5]

Funding

Funding for developing the modularized curriculum comes from the state's TANF savings, which were reallocated to the State Board for Community and Technical Colleges (see Shoreline case for details). The late interim associate dean Parkins and TCB's Schroeder developed grant proposals for funding the development of the AAS degree in environmental health and safety.

Summary

The success of South Seattle's Environmental Health and Safety Program is a function of an industry characterized by occupations with clear requirements for advancement and a method of offering training that makes it easy for working people to build additional competencies. As with Shoreline, state funds are available for developing this and other programs to serve low-wage workers. It will be interesting to see if the programs being developed in other occupations obtain similar levels of employer involvement and willingness to work on career advancement.

Community College of Denver Essential Skills Program

While community college programs in Washington and Oregon have received considerable state funds to create career ladder programs, the Community College of Denver (CCD) has developed its career programs for TANF recipients through vocational certificates called Essential Skills. This program provides foundation skills in four separate career tracks (early childhood, financial services, manufacturing, and central supply technology). The college promotes the Essential Skills Program as a work first program since it requires internships, which count toward work-related activity. In developing this program, one of the college's goals is to serve as a model for other colleges in supporting both entry-level and incumbent workers. Five factors are behind the program's success: 1) vocational training in high-demand occupations, 2) a cohort approach that promotes group learning, 3) intensive career counseling, 4) internships, and 5) strong business partnerships.

Early childhood education and paraprofessional medical occupations are often considered low-wage, dead-end jobs. Indeed, few programs designed to move people up career ladders from entry-level positions have been successful (see Fitzgerald and Carlson 2000). Although limited in size and funding, The Essential Skills programs in early childhood and central supply technology have put students on a track to career advancement. Program Director Elaine Baker is especially proud of the college's success in early childhood education. "The research says that you can't take people on welfare and successfully place them in child care professions," she says. "Well we're doing it. It takes work, but our program has successfully prepared and placed 19 group leaders into the Denver child care community." Students who have completed the central supply certificate go on to try for national certification. Eight program graduates were expected to complete the tutorial for the October 2000 certification test (Meléndez and Suárez 1999).

The Essential Skills Program

The philosophy behind Essential Skills is as important as the curriculum in understanding the program's success. A guiding principle of the program is that all learning takes place in relationships. The relationships developed through the program bond students with counselors, employers, their families, and one another. This "whole life" approach is proving to be quite successful.

The student-counselor relationship begins as soon as a student enters the program. Coordinators work with groups of 12–15 students and see students daily. Baker points out that "Our folks require a lot of career planning. They don't project themselves into the future very well. They live in an interpersonal world driven by crisis, which does not lend itself to long-term planning. As their lives stabilize they need people to work with them on doing that."

Counseling includes more than helping students choose a career and an education plan: counselors help students undergo a shift from seeing themselves as being mostly incompetent to seeing themselves as learners capable of changing their lives.

The program creates an environment in which students can learn from one another. This is facilitated through group interaction and study sessions. Students can bring their children to dinner study sessions. Throughout the program students engage in classroom discussions, individual sessions with the transition coordinator, and facilitated group sessions to develop strategies for overcoming barriers to self sufficiency. Students focus on creating and maintaining circles of support to provide backup systems (e.g., for child care) to reduce the possibility of missing work. Further, as the relationships continue after employment, the group reinforces the individual's professional identity. This approach requires coordinators and faculty to develop relationships with students based on trust, rather than on authority.

Another emphasis of the program is on understanding the nature of work relationships. The internships lay out expectations for jobs, and the program offers mentoring and workshops in which students can discuss their reactions to and problems with work. The main vehicle for this information is a course developed specifically for the program, "Communication for the Workplace." One course topic is understanding performance appraisals and other types of feedback; another is managing conflict. The program views work as a culture where the newcomer doesn't necessarily understand the rules. Baker elaborates on the need to create a basic shift in how coworkers and supervisors are perceived: "Our students need to understand that work is a transactional environment—that personal circumstances do not change the fact that the work needs to be done. An employer who points this out is not being unsympathetic or discriminatory. They need to understand and not personalize that." The approach differs from most soft skills courses in both content and delivery. Content is blended with the everyday experiences that students are likely to encounter in their internships. Classroom exchanges are interactive, using problem solving and role playing. In addition to covering such basic skills such as writing a memo, students also go through exercises in listening, giving and receiving feedback, approaching superiors on the job, understanding learning styles, and accepting diversity in the workplace.

The Essential Skills Curriculum

Students are recruited through the Denver Department of Human Services (DHS). In the month before entering the program most students participate in a series of classes and workshops provided by DHS that offer career counseling and teach communication and other life skills. In the first month at CCD students attend classes 35 hours weekly, which includes GED prep for those who need it, group time, and workshops. During the next three months students work 24 hours a week in paid internships and attend vocational classes for 15 hours. All students take the core, which includes computer literacy, a workshop in reading, writing, and speaking, and communication for the workplace (Table 11.3). Students in the early childhood program take an introductory course and a lab. Central supply technician students take a class in medical terminology. Students complete two credits of work readiness and three credits in reading, writing, and speaking in workplace situations.

Those with limited English proficiency take ESL classes during the internship period as well. Students are not required to have a high school diploma or GED to enter the program. They must have a seventh grade or above reading level. Tutoring and GED preparation are available during the program. Students who fall below the minimum reading level are required to enroll in developmental courses or work in the developmental studies labs. Central supply technicians are required to have a high school diploma or GED.

Depending on what electives are taken, certificates require up to 16 credits. All courses earn college-level credits. The certificates articulate to other degrees, and almost 25 percent of certificate earners continue to take courses toward an associate's degree. Although Essential Skills classes are self-contained because of scheduling around internships, staff attempt to mainstream students into regular college activities and services.

Table 11.3 Essential Skills Certificate in Central Supply Technology

Course number	Class title	Credits
Workplace core		
CIS 105	Introduction to the PC	2
REA 015	Reading, Writing, Speaking	3
COM 113	Communication for the Workplace	2
	Co-op Experience (credits may vary)	4
Vocational core		
CST 100	Central Supply Technology	3
HWE 100	Medical Terminology	2

Since most of the certificate classes are separate from other degree programs, female students are mainstreamed into the college community by getting them involved in the campus Women's Center. The Center is an additional source of assistance in dealing with child care, transportation, domestic, or other issues that prevent students from attending or from performing well in the program. The Center replicates services offered by Essential Skills counselors, but the exposure is valuable because if students continue their education after completing the program, they are already acquainted with it should they need assistance.

Combining the internships with course work means that students understand the connection between what they are learning in class and what they do on the job. Further, students are evaluated on their performance in real situations during their vocational training.

Career Ladders

Although there are more job openings in financial services than in the other tracks, the progression from cashier to other rungs in banking is not clearly aligned to college course work, as in the other tracks. To address this, CCD has begun working with partner banks and the American Banking Institute to offer courses to program graduates. Although the child care and medical instrument technician positions do not have the highest number of job openings of the four tracks, they offer more opportunities for career advancement.

Graduates of the early childhood education program have experienced the most career advancement of the four tracks, probably because the educational component of the program is the most clearly articulated. Essential Skills requires six credits in early childhood education. Group leaders must have six more credits, in addition to 1,395 hours of contact with children. Upon completion of the Essential Skills certificate students have completed nine credit hours in early childhood education and 650 contact hours with children, putting them well on their way to group leader certification. Over half of those completing Essential Skills in early childhood go on to fulfill the additional course work for becoming group leaders. Several students have completed the Colorado certificate programs for director's associate and director, and three students were scheduled to receive associate degrees in 2000. Group leader, director and director's associate are positions in high demand in the Denver area.

Central supply technicians sterilize instruments for hospital surgeries. While there are only about 30 openings per year in Denver in central supply, it is a position that is often used for lateral moves within hospitals. Certification in central supply brings a pay increase of between $0.50 and $1.00 per hour. Starting hourly wages are around $9.00. The next rung on the ladder is surgical technology, a nine-month certificate course. Other possible moves are to certified nursing assistant or licensed practical nurse. Generally, people who go into the medical technician curriculum do not want to perform the type of hands on personal care required in these occupations.

Support Services

Helping clients learn how to negotiate the world of support services is an important part of the program. This includes communicating effectively with the city's Human Services case managers on how to access other community resources, including child care, transportation, medical care, dental care, financial planning, housing, mental health services, and domestic violence resources. Students receive help in working around the inconsistent ways that policies and incentives are often implemented. Many services are introduced as part of the transition skills curriculum, while students work through more complex individual issues with the individual track coordinators or the clinical social worker on staff. DHS career track coordinators and Welfare-to-Work industry managers work closely with CCD track coordinators on recruitment, assessment, job placement, and support services issues.

A track coordinator is assigned to each cohort. The track coordinator keeps tabs on student attendance and performance for the duration of the program. Students discuss problems that may be affecting attendance or performance with the coordinator, and they jointly work out solutions. The coordinators do job placement and also keep track of student performance on the job. Finally, the track coordinators are the liaison between the program and the students' DHS case managers.

Outcomes

The combined tracks of the Essential Skills program have a 70 percent completion rate and a 58 percent employment rate at completion. Six months after completion 77 percent of students are employed. The 1998 cohort had a 66 percent retention rate one year after completion. The average starting wage for the first year was $7.51, and for the second year it was $8.51.

Wages in child care increased during the same period. Early child care assistants started at $6.50 an hour and group leaders usually began at $8.00. Director's associates earned $11.00 an hour in the Head Start programs. Almost all of the child care sites working with the program have benefit packages.

Funding

All funding for program development and operation has come from the City of Denver's TANF and Welfare-to-Work dollars and from the U.S. Department of Labor (USDOL). As of 2000, the annual project budget included $422,261 in TANF dollars and $145,974 in Welfare-to-Work funds to serve 100–125 students per year.

Specific courses have been developed using various funding sources. The Communications for the Workplace course was funded by the U.S. Department of Education. The Colorado Community College Board provides funds for curriculum development. Only limited funds are available, however, so a large part of what the state office does is help colleges with finding funds and writing grants.

Summary

Essential Skills has taken the first steps in moving from a Welfare-to-Work to a career ladders program. The whole life approach, which emphasizes learning how to build relationships in addition to building job-specific skills, addresses many of the problems that make the transition from welfare to work so difficult. The career ladders in child care and central supply technology are short. But for many students, climbing one or two rungs is quite an accomplishment. The president has made a strong commitment to the faculty to develop more career ladder programs in occupations and sectors that have greater opportunities for advancement. The state's Community College Board has supported the certificate approval process and has provided technical support throughout the program's development. Even with this support, staff are continually involved in securing grants for present operations as well as working toward the institutionalization of the program once the Welfare-to-Work funding streams are eliminated.

DISCUSSION: WHAT WOULD IT TAKE TO INSTITUTIONALIZE WAGE PROGRESSION STRATEGIES?

The set of factors influencing the extent to which community colleges can be successful in delivering wage progression programs includes the priorities of individual colleges as well as the broader policy environment. Because of the level of commitment demanded and the need to secure external resources, wage progression strategies have to be a priority from the top down to succeed. Once the decision has been made to implement such strategies, community colleges can learn much from one another about what program features work. State policies in Welfare-to-Work, incumbent worker training, and economic development have to be in place to support wage progression. The structure of labor market demand, however, ultimately determines the extent to which career and wage progression strategies can expand. As labor market intermediaries, community colleges can influence the skill demand of local employers in a small number of cases. But it is difficult for any one organization or institution to act independently as a labor market intermediary, and certainly this is true if state policy does not support it. Labor market intermediaries—at least those with the goal of increasing access to and opportunities for better paying jobs—involve a network of organizations supported by state policy. These issues are discussed below, through seven principles gleaned from the experiences of the three colleges.

Community Colleges Need to Make Career Progression a Priority

Community colleges are being asked to be more things to more people than ever before. Their students range from those who don't have high school diplomas or proficiency in English to those who have college degrees. Knowing that a college cannot be all things to all people, presidents must choose the areas in which their institutions will specialize. Career progression programs are typically built from Welfare-to-Work programs, which are not as glamorous or profitable as customizing training for business or developing new technology centers. Given the high levels of investment and low levels of support for Welfare-to-Work, the job of a president who makes this area a top priority is not easy. A president must have, or create, a faculty and staff that embrace this mission.

The college presidents I spoke with have done this in different ways. Shoreline, rather than forcing new programs on faculty who are already teaching full-time loads, uses adjunct faculty from industry. President John Lederer explains that the college's Workforce and Economic Development Office has been more successful if it first demonstrates the effectiveness of new programs and new teaching approaches, then lets faculty decide for themselves how the new programs can complement or feed into existing offerings. This strategy allowed the college to get the program up and running quickly while generating faculty support. Funds for program redesign are now available to entice faculty to alter their classes along the lines of the program—including evening and weekend scheduling, offering credit for prior knowledge and learning, and structuring more intensive, short-term courses that lead to certificates. South Seattle's president, David C. Mitchell, has encouraged faculty to develop independent relationships with employers in order to make their programs more responsive to industry needs. An associate dean was assigned specifically to help faculty interested in developing modular curricula in collaboration with business.

The presidents have also given program staff considerable autonomy in developing programs. Elaine Baker, the Essential Skills program director at Community College of Denver, is able to hire faculty for the program. She emphasizes that this is important because the students have very different needs and learning styles than the mainstream student population. A previous study of the program found that some staff provided by the community college had low expectations for the students (see Meléndez and Suárez 2001). In hiring, Baker looks for faculty who don't have preconceived ideas of ability but are willing to provide more structure to and experiment with different teaching styles to facilitate learning.

Indeed, one of the most important factors in a program's success is a willingness to experiment with new approaches. President Windle explains that the Shoreline Job Ladders staff motivate one another to keep trying to improve how they do things. "We never say 'we've arrived.' We're always looking for ways to serve our folks better." This means the staff tries many things that don't work. "Failure is a learning tool here, not a reason to get your head cut off." This attitude is what it takes for administration and faculty to stay the course through years of program development, implementation, and continual fine-tuning.

Continuing Education Has to Be Flexible

An increasing number of community college students work while attending school. Colleges are trying several strategies to make course offerings more flexible. One is to offer classes at more convenient times. Several of the programs offer classes on evenings and weekends. All three have frequent start-ups for programs. This means not only that there is little wait time between deciding on the program and starting, but also that if students have to drop out, they can pick up again quickly when their life circumstances improve.

To become even more flexible, community colleges are offering more certificate programs. The certificate approach allows the college to meet local labor market needs and add or eliminate programs as demand dictates. Because certificates typically are noncredit, they do not require as many bureaucratic steps to get up and running. Some of the colleges offer credits with certificate courses that count toward associate's degrees. Although this strategy may mean that students without high school diplomas or GEDs are not eligible, credit accumulation toward degrees is essential for advancement in many fields.

South Seattle's modular programs provide another type of flexibility. The direct connection between completing modules and getting wage increases motivates workers to endure the hardship of working full-time while attending school. The late interim dean Laura Parkins and workforce coordinator Keith Marler suggested that modules are the wave of the future for community colleges. They noted, however, that the approach challenges how community colleges are organized. Modules are organized on demand, not by the regular academic calendar, and they often use adjunct faculty from industry. Indeed, modules are becoming standard for professional and technical training in many corporations. Some businesses have software to assess employee skills in multiple areas, and much of this assessment is done online. Employers like modules because an employee can attend classes to quickly learn the skills he needs for the job. Working with staff from the Washington State Board of Community Colleges, South Seattle is developing modularized, skill-based programs in electronics and emissions technology and has a grant to develop a program for the stevedore industry.

Denver's program is built less on flexibility than on replicating working life. Students spend a full day in a combination of classes, work-based instruction or internship, and negotiating social services. They are offered support and advice in managing the various aspects of their life, but they cannot avoid taking responsibility.

Another way institutions can make it easier to combine work and learning is to offer courses at the work site. But employers must make it easier as well by providing at least partial release time for employees to attend classes. Some union-sponsored skills upgrade programs, for example, offer classes that overlap shift changes (see Fitzgerald and Carlson 2000). Typically, employees quit one hour early or start one hour later to take a two-hour class. One hour is donated by the employer and one by the employee. Although none of the colleges have employer partners that are donating time for training, several staff suggested that they would request it at some point.

Continuing Education Has to Be Tied Directly to Job Advancement and Wage Progression

For new labor market entrants the whole concept of planning for one's future may be new. Even if one wants to move up, the connection between further education and job advancement is not always evident. This is especially true for people employed in sectors where there are no career ladders. Shoreline's Career Ladders information technology students, for example, would have little way of knowing that a job as a call center operator for a software company could lead to a job as a Web page designer.

The value of Shoreline's Passport system for developing career plans is that it shows students both how they can move up in one company and how they can advance by moving into related occupations in different industries. Shoreline's Career Ladders students are supported by retention specialists in developing career plans, and once Passport is running, they will be able to use it to mark their progress and find jobs. Retention specialists are committed to working with each student for a minimum of one year or until the family is out of poverty. Passport is more interactive and useful than most job listings available to TANF recipients in particular and to community college students in general.

Community College of Denver offers similar help in mapping out career ladders, though it is done through a series of career awareness activities combined with individual vocational counseling. The educational coordinator, a grant funded staff person who works exclusively with the program, prepares an individual education plan with each student at the beginning of the semester and, as the students become more aware of career options, helps them plan their future course of work and study. The process allows students to map out realistic career ladders and to understand what they have to do to achieve their goals.

Some industries are more suited to this approach than others. In the environmental health and safety field, incentives for entry-level workers are quite obvious. Workers know the exact wages associated with each certification. The more certifications they have, the higher paying jobs they can get. With the modular curriculum offered by South Seattle, students can develop a plan for combining work and education that would be unmanageable under the semester system. Furthermore, the modules add up to credits for degrees that are in demand by employers. Even environmental engineers with baccalaureate degrees take South Seattle's modular courses to fulfill requirements for continuing education.

In sectors or occupations where career ladders are not as obvious, employers and community colleges can work together to identify ways of structuring work that build in career progression. Community College of Denver is beginning to do this with its banking partners.

State Government Has to Support Career Progression Programs

Funding wage progression programs is a challenge. There are several funding issues that affect the ability of these programs to go full scale. One is how particular types of community college programs are funded. A second is how state welfare policy allocates funds for education and training, particularly savings realized through declining TANF rolls. Some states are reinvesting these funds into education and training, others are focusing on child care, and still others are letting them accumulate unspent. The third issue is how community colleges fit into overall state education reform.

Most community colleges receive funding from a combination of local property taxes, tuition, and state funds. States typically fund community colleges on a full-time equivalency (FTE) basis.[6] This means that the state allocates a set amount per full-time enrollment in credit-bearing courses. Since most of the Welfare-to-Work programs are non-credit courses (typically because they are less than college level), funding must be obtained from targeted programs.

Staff responsible for fundraising at all three colleges expressed frustration that there is no reward system in state funding formulas for their programs. Programs that rely on special funding pools are not sustainable in the long run. If the funds run out or an administration with different priorities comes in, funding can be cut abruptly, even if the program is highly successful. The three options programs are left with are to get very good at writing grant proposals, to lobby for more state funds, or to change the programs to credit courses.

For states such as Washington that have earmarked welfare savings for skills upgrading, at least a temporary source of funding is available for turning Welfare-to-Work into career progression programs. The State of Washington has facilitated the Job Ladder Partnership at Shoreline and the modular programs at South Seattle by designating funds specifically for developing job ladders for low-income workers. Washington is one of the few states that are spending all of their TANF caseload savings (the state's TANF savings have been spent by 2002) on training, placement, job retention and advancement, and child care.

South Seattle is using the TANF funds to design modular programs that earn college credits and thus fall under the FTE funding formula. This involved a complete revamping of every course and going through an approval process, both at the college level and before the State Board of Community Colleges. Program development for SSCC took approximately one year and cost $40,000 in taking staff from their regular assignments to do program development. The idea of credit-bearing modular courses may be easier to implement in Washington because of the state education reform of the 1990s. The secondary education system is moving from diplomas based on seat time to certificates of mastery based on skills, which will be accepted by all colleges and universities in the state. Community colleges in other states attempting to move to a system using proficiency-based certificates might have more difficulty in gaining employer and public acceptance of the idea. In Washington the preparations have already been laid, making implementation easier.

In Colorado the extent to which community colleges get TANF funds for education and training programs is determined at the county level. The Colorado legislature moved the responsibility for appropriating TANF funds to county commissions, which receive funds based on a formula and allocate them as they see fit. The city of Denver expanded eligibility for TANF training funds ($3.8 million annually) to the working poor (defined as being within 225 percent of the poverty line) and dedicated the remaining TANF savings to support services in housing, medical care, child care, mental health services, and other support services. Denver County is one of the few counties that allocated much funding for education and training.

The Colorado Community College and Occupational Education System is educating community college presidents on advocating for more education and training funds from the county commissions. Mary Crabbe Gershwin, director of systems planning, laments that obtaining state funding has become a retail sales game. "We're telling our presidents that it's not sufficient to know good programs," she says. "We need to know who is making key policy and funding decisions. We need to do more advocacy." But she cautions that this is not an easy task. "Presidents have faculty, capital construction, and other needs facing them. Low-wage workers aren't on their radar screen." For the State Community College Board, this means that Gershwin and her staff have to move the issue up on the agenda by aligning and integrating low-wage worker progression with other programs that presidents value. Her office works with presidents in connecting low-wage worker progression to a college's information technology strategy or its employer partnership strategy.

States differ on work first requirements. In Colorado, one hour a day of vocational training counts as work. Shoreline's 12-week program does not qualify under Washington's work first regulations as work activity. In Washington, only 30 percent of total participation in work first can be vocational training. What this means is that social service agencies are not likely to refer clients to three-month training programs, even though all evidence demonstrates that more extensive training (even three month's worth) increases wages and reduces dependence.

Even in states that have earmarked funds for wage progression, staff must be entrepreneurial in their search for funds. Providing support services is a challenge for the colleges. The directors and staff at all of the programs spend a considerable amount of time writing proposals for funding to government agencies, foundations, and employers. The Colorado Community College and Occupational Education System plays a key role by helping colleges identify foundation and government funding sources for program development and implementation.

Community Colleges Need Partners

Partnerships allow organizations to provide services together or invest resources to their mutual advantage. Because community colleges' primary mission is education, they need partners to ensure that they are providing the skills that employers need and the support services that students need. All of the colleges have effective partnerships with employers, social service agencies, and community organizations.

Employers are key partners in all three programs. Their contributions include helping with curriculum development, establishing performance competencies, teaching courses, offering scholarships, and providing internships. In return, employers get better prepared workers. While this relationship seems obvious, training programs can falter even when demand is high. In the late 1990s, when labor demand in hazardous waste management was growing rapidly, South Seattle and two other community colleges in the area witnessed declining enrollments. The other colleges closed their programs, either from the mistaken assumption that declining enrollments meant lack of demand, or because they did not want to commit resources to overhaul them. But the problem was that the programs were not preparing students for the certifications demanded by industry. President Mitchell chose to invest in building a new program from the ground up because he believed that it served two important audiences—those trying to get off TANF, and local employers. He built it by developing relationships with key employers.

Once employers trust the quality of workers hired through community college- or CBO-run training programs, they are more inclined to contribute funds for training. In Denver, Norwest Bank contributed approximately $40,000 in resources for each cohort in the financial services track of the Essential Skills program. The donated resources include one week of in-house training, mentoring, program supervision, and social and professional events. Other agencies subsidize internships. In Denver, Head Start agencies and Catholic Charities pay 15 percent of payroll costs for interns. Eight Denver hospitals provide on-site training for internships and have committed to offering paid internships (though at the time of this writing they are subsidized through either TANF funds or Welfare-to-Work wage subsidies). The community college–employer partnerships certainly are of the "win-win" variety.

Getting there has taken a lot of work. It takes awhile for each partner to figure out its expectations of the other. Educators often want to hold meetings that include employers while developing or revamping programs. Employers are typically more results oriented and get frustrated because they perceive that nothing is happening. They want to know from the start what's being offered and how it will benefit them. As one community college staff member stated, "They don't want partnerships, they want results."

It may even take awhile for community college outreach staff to figure out who is the right person to contact for a potential business partner. Often the person who needs to be convinced of the need for training is the supervisor who has to pull someone off the line for training. "You'll only make your case," Baker warns, "if you show them that training is going to make their lives easier and improve return on investment." Working with employers, the college does a literacy audit of competencies and develops a curriculum around needs.

An issue all of the colleges face in trying to be relevant to employers is balancing employers' need for customized training with students' need to have more general training applicable in multiple employment settings. The colleges find it difficult to generate sufficient demand for courses specific to any one employer. Yet even with cooperation from several employers, it is not easy to develop a program that meets the needs of a large group of small- to medium-sized employers.

The second set of partnerships community college programs need is for providing extensive support services. President Mitchell of South Seattle sees student services as the biggest problem for community colleges committed to serving low-income populations. He suggests that most colleges have rather rigid systems that will have to be restructured. Further, funding streams to support extensive services are usually temporary. Indeed, a large body of literature on community college programs points to the importance of support services in program completion for low-income students. These include transportation, child care, career counseling, life skills development, and case management (Fitzgerald 1993; Fitzgerald and Jenkins 1997; Harrison, Weiss, and Gant 1995; Harrison and Weiss 1996; Jenkins and Fitzgerald 1998; Meléndez and Falcón 1999). Community colleges do not have the funding or the infrastructure to provide all of the support services students need. While community colleges can provide some of these services, it may not be desirable for them to move too far away from their educational mission. Fitzgerald and Jenkins (1997) suggest that community colleges that offer too many social services are in danger of mission creep and that the most successful community colleges are those that establish partnerships to provide services. Common partners are social service agencies and CBOs.

Two of the programs have CBOs as partners. The CBOs mainly provide referrals, both to the college program and to support services. However, some CBOs provide the support services and soft skills training. Others work with graduates on job-keeping skills.

Another important partnership for all of the programs is with government agencies implementing state Welfare-to-Work and TANF programs. South Seattle has just remodeled a building that will be used as a One-Stop Career Center.[7] The Department of Social and Human Services will be located on campus, allowing students easy access to services. Staff estimate that the facility will bring several hundred students a week onto campus. While this may seem like an obvious choice, in some states one-stop services are located far from community college campuses, making it more difficult for these students to gain access to education (see McCormick 1999).

The Role of a Labor Market Intermediary Is More Complex than Connecting Supply and Demand

The three programs demonstrate that community colleges can be quite effective placement intermediaries. Community College of Denver has worked with firms on improving productivity through education and training. "Once supervisors understand that classes can impact their team's productivity," Baker notes, "their involvement with the program moves from accommodating to participating." In an internal document Baker elaborates on how the community college becomes more important to the employer:

> Looking back at the development of our partner relationships, we can see a shift in roles, from educational provider to a blend of educational provider/organizational consultant. This shift is the outgrowth of numerous factors. First, we are in a unique position to gain access to valuable information about the problems that employees experience in doing their jobs. Much of this information is seldom captured within normal channels of communication because of the hesitancy of employees and/or supervisors to call attention to situations that are inefficient or problematic. Some of what we learn has immediate relevance to our education and training concerns, while other information relates to broader organizational issues. Our skill is in capturing this information and sharing it with our partners in a constructive format.

Baker cites a number of instances where she has convinced companies to invest in worker upgrading by demonstrating that it can be justified by productivity increases. Community College of Denver contracted to teach a 12-hour basic math class to employees in the shipping department of a food processing plant. The company had shifted to a just-in-time delivery system, which brought an increasing number of clerical and accounting errors. Most of the employees had been with the company 20–25 years, and many did not have a high school diploma. Baker proposed that the company develop a pre- and post-test and asked that the company also monitor errors in the shipping department. The improvements were so dramatic that all plant employees were put through the course. Once management saw the evidence in return on investment data, it was willing to pay for instruction. The bottom line is that employers need evidence of return on investment if they are to invest in training.

Community colleges have little leverage, however, as progressive intermediaries. While outreach staff have been able to demonstrate returns on investment for training, there are few instances where employers were influenced to create better jobs because the community college provided them a stream of reliable workers.

Career advancement opportunities are not simply a function of industry structure, but also of choices particular employers make. Bank teller programs illustrate this.[8] To date, Community College of Denver has had little success in developing career ladders in the financial services area, Baker reports, although the program is very successful in placing graduates and Norwest Bank is an active partner. In 2001, CCD planned to address this by working with the American Institute of Banking and partner banks to identify appropriate courses for program graduates.

Banking is an interesting case for examining the potential for career ladder and wage progression strategies. It appears that the pendulum swung as far as it could go in the direction of deskilling entry-level jobs. Now, some banks, unable to keep up with the high turnover inherent to these high-stress jobs, are adding skills to existing jobs and creating advancement opportunities. The extent to which this marks a significant trend remains to be seen.

In the past 15 years, banking has been changed by direct depositing, telephone banking, the Internet, and, most significantly, automated teller machines (ATMs). The effect of ATMs has dramatically restructured the job of teller but for the most part has not upgraded it.[9] In some banks the use of ATMs for routine banking transactions has been accompanied by a shift toward more sophisticated teller jobs with greater skill requirements. More frequently, though, tellers still conduct only routine transactions while customer service representatives and officers—typically college graduates—open new accounts and sell bank products such as loans and CDs. The percentage of banking jobs accounted for by professional occupations (those requiring post-secondary education) has grown dramatically (see Gester 1999).

With the emphasis on sales, many banks changed telling from a predominantly full-time to a part- and peak-time job with even less opportunity for moving into better or full-time positions.[10] Seeing little growth opportunity, many tellers quit this high-stress job after a few months. Indeed, human resource directors at six large Chicago banks working with teller training programs revealed that their annual turnover rates were between 60 and 80 percent. Two directors mentioned that the increase in part-time and peak-time scheduling has reduced employee loyalty, particularly in the banks that make it clear to prospective employees that neither part- nor peak-time jobs are stepping stones to full-time positions. But treating tellers as casual labor seems more cost-effective to managers than making the teller position a permanent first rung on a career ladder.

Interviews with several human resource officers suggest this strategy is changing for some banks as they recognize that tellers are the front line for customer contact. Rather than treating these front-line workers as casual laborers, some banks are recognizing the value of investing more in their training, creating full-time opportunities, adding benefits, and offering better wages. These decisions are the result of seeing that customers are better served with front line staff who are knowledgeable. It may be the case that similar observations will be made by employers in other service industries, creating a window of opportunity for community colleges to expand entry-level training programs into career ladder programs.

Overall, these examples illustrate how community colleges are being proactive in responding to the needs of business. That community colleges have a limited capacity to affect skill demand is not a criticism but rather a reality. As one administrator put it, "When it happens, it's a bonus. When it doesn't, colleges can help students find ways to cumulate skills and move to other types of employment."

Wage Progression Strategies Won't Work for Everyone

Despite a supportive state government, a spirit of cooperation between employers and the community colleges, and a well-designed education or training program, it is not easy moving people into better jobs. Most of the programs are too new to have much data on career advancement. The most common comment I heard in talking with faculty and staff at these and other community colleges was, "It's hard."

Although some graduates are eager to continue their education while working, others find that the adjustment from not working to going to school, then to work, is enough of a life change. "When you're dealing with someone who is a single parent, and has been out of the labor force, going to school is very new, intensive, and stressful," Shoreline's Lederer explains. "Then they are placed in a job. They have a lot vested in that job. Several students have declined to go back to school right away, telling me that they need to focus on the job if they're going to succeed."

Furthermore, not everyone wants to advance, Shoreline's Windle points out. Career progression programs are great for students who are eager to move ahead and only need someone to help them figure out how to overcome obstacles. Others are not interested in working, let alone advancing, no matter how much help they are given. Windle sees these attitudinal differences in different classes. He notes that, in general, students in the evening class seem to have more life barriers and both less desire and less ability to overcome them. Many of these students are enrolled because they have been told they have to do something or they will be off TANF. In contrast, students in the weekend class are noticeably more ambitious. He attributes the difference to the fact that most of the weekend students are working and thus are better able to see possibilities for advancement.

It is these differences in attitude that concern employers. Many employers are not as concerned about specific skills as they are about attitude. This is why the five programs place a lot of emphasis on soft skills.

The issue is more complex, however, than learning the right attitude. Windle explains that students face a lot of dignity issues on their first jobs. He relates the story of one woman who had emotional issues that made it difficult for her to get along with people on the job. After several years, she had held no job for longer than four months, and always put the blame on the employer, who, she said, didn't treat her with respect. Only after she became open to exploring how her interaction style might alienate people was she able to stay with one job for over a year. Windle says he has to guide students through matters like "picking and choosing their battles, not quitting until they have another job, the right way and wrong way to quit a job, having a backup plan."

For those who do want to continue their education while working, a solution may be to incorporate learning into work time, but not too many employers pay for employees to go to school on company time, particularly if they are new. Some employers working with the Job Ladders program have realized that becoming a learning organization offers a good strategy for reducing turnover and maintaining a more committed and better qualified labor force. For the most part, however, employees must upgrade their skills on their own time.

These comments from staff are more realistic than pessimistic. There are people who can move from basic literacy to a college education. They are the exceptions. Programs cannot be built around the assumption that everyone will follow a path of lifelong learning that ends in college. This does not mean the opportunity should not be available. It does mean that other paths to living-wage employment are needed, such as the Earned Income Tax Credit and unionization of more service sector jobs (see Fitzgerald and Carlson 2000).

CONCLUSIONS: A STRATEGY FOR COMMUNITY COLLEGES TO BE LABOR MARKET INTERMEDIARIES

These successful career ladder programs are small in scale relative to the need (the Conference Board report estimates there are between four and five million full-time workers earning poverty-level wages). Increased state funding for skills upgrading would help community colleges expand these programs. But if community colleges are to act as progressive intermediaries, they cannot do it alone. This level of intervention requires a two-pronged policy agenda. First, states have to make skills upgrading—including training for those making the transition from welfare to work and incumbent worker training for low-wage workers—a priority. This requires funding to community colleges for career ladder programs and to businesses for training workers. Second, local labor market intermediaries are needed to make the connections between supply and demand. Local labor market intermediaries connect economic and workforce development in key sectors of the regional economy. This approach is known as a sectoral strategy. Sectoral strategies are receiving considerable attention in both economic and workforce development circles because of their focus on growth industries and their potential to create career advancement opportunities for low-wage workers. In sectoral strategies an intermediary provides solutions to industry problems and uses those solutions to improve training for incumbent workers and increase access to the industry for disadvantaged workers (Dresser and Rogers 1998, p. 71).

Clark and Dawson (1995) define sectoral initiatives as those that

- target a particular occupation within an industry,
- intervene by becoming a valued actor within the industry that employs the occupation,
- exist for the primary purpose of assisting low-income people to obtain decent employment, and
- eventually create systemic change within that occupation's labor market.

Shoreline Community College is a partner in a larger sectoral initiative, the Seattle Jobs Initiative (SJI).[11] Seattle is one of six cities that make up the Annie E. Casey Foundation's eight-year Jobs Initiative. Started in 1995, the $30 million Jobs Initiative supports local government, community organizations, and educational institutions in pursuing a systems reform agenda that places people from low-income communities in jobs that provide family-supporting benefits and have advancement potential.

As a labor market intermediary, SJI facilitates and coordinates a network of community organizations, community colleges, employers, unions, and government agencies to make all the links necessary to get people into jobs in targeted sectors of the regional economy. A targeted sector team—composed of a sector manager, a broker, CBOs, and community colleges—works to create better links between supply and demand. The sector managers and brokers are SJI staff, while the CBOs and community colleges are subcontracted to provide services. Brokers are people or organizations with strong ties to industry that market

SJI to employers and serve as the liaison among employers, training providers, and CBOs. The brokers help employers experiencing labor shortages or high turnover identify workforce and training needs and work with the CBOs that refer candidates for job openings. In addition, brokers engage employers by involving them with community colleges in curriculum development and by encouraging them to provide internships. As the brokers work with employers to learn their level of satisfaction with participants, they suggest curriculum changes to community colleges. This division of responsibilities allows each organization to focus on its core competencies. Brokers understand employer needs; community colleges provide education and training; CBOs provide recruitment, referrals to social support services, case management, soft skills, and post-employment follow-up.

With funds from the state incumbent worker training program (the Job Skills Program), Shoreline and SJI partnered in the Washington Incumbent Worker Training Demonstration Project. The project was started in 1997 to test whether state customized training programs could promote the development of job ladders for low-income workers by marketing incumbent worker training in targeted industries. The Shoreline-SJI demonstration launched separate initiatives in aerospace and cosmetology. Lederer, who worked with SJI at the time, found that the sector-based approach was successful in organizing employers around training in the aerospace industry (1998, p. 11). He writes that "this finding is supported by the fact that Shoreline Community College and hundreds of aerospace supplier firms represented by the Washington Aerospace Alliance were able to cooperatively develop and receive an industry-wide Jobs Skills Program Grant to fund upgrade machine operator training . . . [It] remains to be seen whether the development of these upgrade training opportunities will, in fact, result in job promotion and wage progression."

Yet Lederer says that neither the cosmetology nor the aerospace prototypes have achieved the scale and scope necessary to transform local labor markets in those sectors. This is partly because not enough time was allotted in the demonstration program to create that level of change in industry practice. But a big part of the failure is that employers are unwilling to make the high-skill, high-wage choice if they can be profitable following a low-skill, low-wage path. Indeed, while SJI has been successful overall in providing people in low-income communities with access to jobs paying at least $8.00 an hour, it has had little success in convincing employers to create more career ladders (Fitzgerald and Leigh 2002). Despite this, community colleges, acting independently, have the capacity to be effective placement intermediaries.

All three programs have been successful in connecting poor people to jobs to which they otherwise would not have had access. Yet Shoreline's collaboration with the state's incumbent worker training program and SJI illustrates that even when state training policy, community colleges, and local labor market intermediaries are acting in concert, it is difficult to affect the demand side.

We need to take the lessons derived from these initiatives and develop additional demonstration projects that have sufficient time to work. Further, we need to rethink how to provide incentives for employers to make the high-wage, high-skill choice. Community colleges are well positioned in current policy initiatives to become key providers of career ladder programs for incumbent workers. Most states have allocated funding for community colleges to develop new Welfare-to-Work programs and improve existing ones. It is likely community colleges will benefit from future federal incumbent worker funds as well. Thirteen cities received a total of $11.2 million in Incumbent Worker Training Demonstration grants from the U.S. Department of Labor for projects that improve the job retention and career advancement of incumbent workers in key industries. Community colleges are key actors in all 13 partnerships. These initiatives are already demonstrating success, suggesting that more permanent incumbent worker training funds will become available to community colleges.

Notes

This research was conducted while the author was visiting a faculty member at New School University's Community Development Research Center. The author expresses appreciation to the center's director, Edwin Meléndez, for generous support during this year. The project was funded by the Ford Foundation. The views expressed are solely those of the author. Special thanks are extended to community college staff, employers, government employees and others who were interviewed, particularly Elaine Baker, Community College of Denver; Mary Crabbe Gershwin, Colorado Community College and Occupational Education System; John Lederer and Holly Moore, Shoreline Community College; Brad Schroeder and the late Laura Parkins, South Seattle Community College.

1. Both federal and state programs fund community colleges to retrain workers for new jobs, provide technical assistance to local employers, and provide customized training (see Bakum 1991; Brint and Karabel 1989; Rosenfeld 1994). These business outreach programs usually focus on small and medium-sized enterprises. Some community colleges provide these services as partners in Manufacturing Technology Centers (MTCs) and Manufacturing Outreach Centers (MOCs), created in 1988 as part of the federal Manufacturing Technology Extension Center Act. The MTCs and MOCs provide modernization assessment, analysis of training needs, technical assistance in adopting new technology and modern management practices, workforce training, and advice on entering new markets (Shapira, Youtie, and Roessner 1996). Many states fund business outreach and technology transfer programs in all of their community colleges (Clark and Dobson 1991; Flynn and Forrant 1995).
2. One credit is earned for every 10–12 lecture hours, 22 lab hours, or 33 work experience hours.
3. A Phase I assessment establishes the potential for contamination by examining the deeds of the property and surrounding sites. If a strong likelihood is established, a Phase II study samples parts of the property for the presence of contaminants. A Phase III study is an even more complete analysis done by dividing the property into a grid and sampling segments in order to determine the extent of contamination.
4. These initiatives support local government, community organizations, and educational institutions in connecting people in low-income communities to training and living-wage jobs (at least $8 an hour) with benefits. Seattle is one of five cities that make up the Annie E. Casey Foundation's Jobs Initiative demonstration program. Started in 1995, the Jobs Initiative seeks to change how metropolitan labor markets work for low-income communities. Each site receives approximately $700,000 per year for planning and implementation and must provide matching funds from other sources. The King County Jobs Initiative has similar goals but does not receive funding from the foundation.
5. In addition, King County and the City of Seattle have received a $147,500 grant from the Environmental Protection Agency's Brownfields Job Training and Development Demonstration Pilots Program to train people in this field. The pilots "bring together community groups, job training organizations, educators, labor groups, investors, lenders, developers, and other affected parties to address the issue of providing environmental employment and training for residents in communities impacted by brownfields. The goals of the Pilots are to facilitate cleanup of [brownfield] sites contaminated with hazardous substances and prepare trainees for employment in the environmental field, including training in alternative or innovative treatment technologies." <http://www.epa.gov/brownfields/job.htm> (accessed 2000). The two-year grant pays for 50 students from low-income neighborhoods to complete programs in environmental assessment and cleanup techniques. The initiative targets the Duwamish Corridor of Seattle, an industrial area with more than 50 abandoned, contaminated sites needing cleanup and redevelopment. KCJI clients take the 40-hour HAZWOP module and after

employment continue taking modules to get more certifications. Training is provided by KCJI and TCB. The grant provides funding to expand the program and pay tuition for KCJI participants for up to 176 hours of credit. As the program expands at South Seattle, KCJI clients may take these credits there.

6. Several states are moving to performance-based funding. These states typically use some combination of completion and job placement rates in allocating funds (see Fitzgerald 1998 for more detail).
7. One-Stop Career Centers are at the core of the federal Workforce Investment Act of 1998, which consolidates federal job training, adult education and literacy, and vocational rehabilitation programs into a more streamlined and flexible workforce development system. The one-stops are the centralized point of access for all federally funded employment programs. The overriding goal of the One-Stop Employment Center approach is to place people in jobs as quickly as possible. Individuals use the one-stops to find jobs, to find out about and access occupational education programs and career development services. The majority of clients are eligible only for a core set of job search services. Eligible clients can access job training through the one-stops.
8. Bank Tellers and Beyond, offered by Wright College, one of Chicago's City Colleges, is a noteworthy program that could not be included in this study because staff were very involved in revamping the program. Although the program's director, Nancy Bellew, had envisioned career ladders as part of the program, it took almost five years to interest banks in anything but entry-level training. The case is interesting in that it reveals the role of persistence of program staff in working with business partners in moving from entry-level to skills upgrade training. From its inception, the program has had all the right stuff—good curriculum, employer involvement, support services, and post-placement follow up. Yet the retention rate of graduates at most banks was initially no higher than that of those hired "off the street." Few tellers advanced. Despite repeated efforts by Bellew, the banks expressed little interest in the college developing further courses to build skills for advancement. Five years later, two of the original bank partners are hiring almost all students as soon as they graduate. LaSalle Bank has reported a 68 percent retention rate of tellers since 1997. Almost half, 48 percent, have been retained longer than one year. Of all program graduates hired, 38 percent have been promoted to Teller 2 (see Fitzgerald and Carlson, 2000).
9. ATMs allow banks to serve customers better and to reduce transaction costs significantly. According to the American Bankers Association a teller transaction costs a bank about $1.07, while the same transaction conducted at an ATM costs 27 cents. In 1975, fewer than 10 million ATM transactions were initiated for a total of $1 billion in transactions. By 1995 that number had risen to 9.7 billion transactions processed at 123,000 ATM terminals and valued at $650 billion.
10. Peak-time workers are used to cover high traffic hours such as late afternoons and weekends. The key difference between part- and peak-time jobs is that peak time workers receive higher wages but are not eligible for benefits.
11. Of course, the majority of students who need such assistance at Shoreline and South Seattle are not affiliated with the Seattle Jobs Initiative. The colleges have to provide services for these students.

References

Bakum, John. 1991. "A New Training Role for Community Colleges." *Employment Relations Today* 18(Summer): 221–227.

Barrington, Linda. 2000. *Does A Rising Tide Lift All Boats? America's Full-Time Working Poor Reap Limited Gains in the New Economy.* New York: Conference Board.

Brint, Steven, and Jerome Karabel. 1989. *The Diverted Dream: Community Colleges and the Promise of Educational Opportunity in America, 1900–1985.* London: Oxford University Press.

Clark, Marianne, and Eric Dobson. 1991. *Increasing the Competitiveness of America's Manufacturers: A Review of State Industrial Extension Programs.* Washington, DC: National Governors' Association.

Clark, Peggy, and Steven Dawson. 1995. *Jobs and the Urban Poor: Privately Initiated Sectoral Strategies.* Washington, DC: Aspen Institute.

Dresser, Laura, and Joel Rogers. 1998. "Networks, Sectors, and Workforce Learning." In *Jobs and Economic Development: Strategies and Practice,* Robert Gilroth, ed. Thousand Oaks, CA: Sage Publications, pp. 42–63.

Emsellem, Maurice. 2000. *Implementing the Workforce Investment Act of 1998: Model Language for State Legislation, WIP Plans, and One-Stop Agreements. NELP Advocacy Series.* Paper prepared for the Working for America Institute 2000 national conference, "Good Jobs and Strong Communities: Tools for Building the High Road." Washington, DC: National Employment Law Project.

Fitzgerald, Joan. 1993. "Labor Force, Education and Work." In *Theories of Local Economic Development: Perspectives from Across the Disciplines,* Richard D. Bingham and Robert Mier, eds. Newbury Park, CA: Sage Publications pp. 125–146.

———. 1998a. "Is Networking Always the Answer? Networking Among Community Colleges to Increase Their Capacity in Business Outreach." *Economic Development Quarterly* 12(1): 30–40.

———. 1998b. "Principles and Practices for Creating Systems Reform in Urban Workforce Development." Discussion paper commissioned by the Brookings Institution for the Annie E. Casey Foundation Jobs Initiative Policy Retreat.

Fitzgerald, Joan, and Virginia Carlson. 2000. "Ladders To A Better Life." *American Prospect.* 11(15): 54–61.

Fitzgerald, Joan, and Davis Jenkins. 1997. *Making Connections: Community College Best Practice in Connecting the Urban Poor to Education and Employment.* Report no. GCP-91-1 prepared for the Annie E. Casey Foundation.

Fitzgerald, Joan, and Nancey Green Leigh. 2002. "Job-Centered Economic Development: An Approach for Linking Economic and Workforce Development." In *Economic Revitalization: Cases and Strategies for City and Suburb.* Thousand Oaks, CA: Sage Publications, pp. 194–222.

Flynn, Erin, and Robert Forrant. 1995. *Facilitating Firm-Level Change: The Role of Intermediary Organizations in the Manufacturing Modernization Process.* Boston: Jobs for the Future.

Gester, Kimberly. 1999. "Career Ladders in Banking: Implications for Welfare Reform." Master's project, University of Illinois at Chicago.

Harrison, Bennett, and Marcus Weiss. 1996. *Networking Across Boundaries: CDCs and CBOs in Regionally Engaged Workforce Development Alliances.* Thousand Oaks, CA: Sage Publications.

Harrison, Bennett, Marcus Weiss, and Jon Gant. 1995. *Building Bridges: Community Development Corporations and the World of Employment Training.* New York: Ford Foundation.

Jenkins, Davis, and Joan Fitzgerald. 1998. *Community Colleges: Connecting the Poor to Good Jobs.* Policy Brief commissioned by the Education Commission of the States as part of ECS's Critical Roles for Community Colleges project, funded by the Metropolitan Life Foundation.

Lautsch, Brenda, and Paul Osterman. 1998. "Changing the Constraints: A Successful Employment and Training Strategy." In *Jobs and Economic Development: Strategies and Practices,* Robert Gilroth, ed. Thousand Oaks, CA: Sage Publications, pp. 214–233.

Lederer, John. 1998. *Final Report: Washington State Incumbent Worker Training Demonstration Program.* Shoreline, WA: Shoreline Community College.

McCormick, Lynn. 1999. "Innovators Under Duress: Community College Initiatives in 'Work First' Settings." Paper presented at the 41st annual conference of the Association of Collegiate Schools of Planning, October 21–24, Chicago.

Meléndez, Edwin. 1996. *Working on Jobs: The Center for Employment Training.* Boston: Mauricio Gastón Institute for Latino Community Development and Public Policy, University of Massachusetts Boston.

Meléndez, Edwin, and Luis M. Falcón. 1999. *The Welfare-to-Work Policy Shock: How Community Colleges Are Addressing the Change.* Boston: University of Massachusetts, Boston Mauricio Gastón Institute.

Meléndez, Edwin, and Bennett Harrison. 1998. "Matching the Disadvantaged to Job Opportunities: Structural Explanations for the Past Successes of the Center for Employment Training." *Economic Development Quarterly* 12(1): 3–11.

Meléndez, Edwin and Carlos Suárez. 1999. *Making Connections to Jobs,*

Education, and Training: The Essential Skills Program of the Community College of Denver. Report submitted to the Employment and Training Administration, U.S. Department of Labor. Boston: Mauricio Gastón Institute, University of Massachusetts, Boston.

———. 2001. "Opening College Doors for Disadvantaged Hispanics: An Assessment of Effective Programs and Practices." In *Low-Wage Workers in the New Economy,* Richard Kazis and Marc Miller, eds. Washington, DC: Urban Institute Press, pp. 307–326.

Mishel, Lawrence, Jared Bernstein, and John Schmitt. 1999. *The State of Working America 1998–99.* Ithaca, NY: Cornell University Press, ILR Press.

Osterman, Paul. 1999. Securing Prosperity: *The American Labor Market: How It Has Changed and What to Do About It.* Princeton, NJ: Princeton University Press.

Peck, Jamie, and Nik Theodore. 2001. "Contingent Chicago: Restructuring the Spaces of Temporary Labor." *International Journal of Urban and Regional Research* 25(3): 471–496.

Rosenfeld, Stuart A. 1994. *Two-Year Colleges at the Forefront: The Consortium for Manufacturing Competitiveness.* Carrboro, NC: Regional Technology Strategies.

———. 2000. "Community College/Cluster Connections: Specialization and Competitiveness in the United States and Europe." *Economic Development Quarterly* 14(1): 51–62.

Rosenfeld, Stuart A., and Marcia E. Kingslow. 1995. *Advancing Opportunity in Advanced Manufacturing: The Potential of Predominantly Minority Two-Year Colleges.* Carrboro, NC: Regional Technology Strategies.

Shapira, Philip, Jan Youtie, and J. David Roessner. 1996. "Current Practices in the Evaluation of U.S. Industrial Modernization Programs." *Research Policy* 25(2): 185–214.

Part 4

New Directions in Community Collaborations and Partnerships

12
Interorganizational Networks among Community-Based Organizations

Héctor R. Cordero-Guzmán
Baruch College–CUNY

In recent years there has been growing interest among community-based organizations (CBOs), foundations, governments, and academics in examining the role and impact of CBO collaborations (or interorganizational networks) on organizational resources, on program capacity, and on the outcomes of participants in community-based workforce development programs.[1] Harrison and Weiss (1998a), for example, argue that network formation and maintenance are central to the development not only of successful organizations but also of employment training and workforce development programs. Their analysis focuses on organizational networks between programs and employers, community colleges, government agencies, and other CBOs, and it raises particular questions about the kinds of practices that lead to the formation of successful networks between CBOs.

This chapter examines the factors related to the development of interorganizational networks (or collaborations) among community-based organizations engaged in workforce development programs and initiatives.[2] Based on material from case studies and on a review of the literature, I discuss two questions:

- Why do CBOs enter into networks with one another? Here I focus on some of the internal and external reasons (mostly government- and funder-related) why CBOs seek to collaborate with one another on workforce development programs and on other service and program initiatives.

- What are some of the important factors associated with the formation and management of successful networks between community-based organizations engaged in workforce development and other community initiatives?[3]

The chapter begins with a review of the literature on what are variously called interorganizational relations (Galaskiewicz 1985), workforce development networks (Harrison and Weiss 1998a), alliances (Ferguson and Dickens 1999), or collaborations (Mattessich and Monsey 1992). The literature is quite fragmented (Ferguson and Dickens 1999; Galaskiewicz 1985), and in this chapter I discuss four related areas of research. The first is research on networks in formal organizations (Galaskiewicz 1985; Podolny and Page 1998); the second is research on collaborations (Mattessich and Monsey 1992; Winer and Ray 1997); and the third focuses more specifically on CBO collaborations (Keyes et al. 1996; Ferguson and Dickens 1999; Pitt, Brown, and Hirota 1999). Finally, I discuss research on workforce development networks (Bonavoglia 1999; Harrison and Weiss 1998a; Meléndez 1990; Meléndez and Harrison 1998).

Following the review of the literature, I use material from several case studies to discuss the most important factors in the formation and management of successful interorganizational networks. The case-study material comes from interviews with program managers and from an analysis of documents and reports on the Comprehensive Community Revitalization Program (CCRP) in the Bronx (OMG 1994, 1995; Spilka and Burns 1998a, 1998b; Sviridoff and Ryan 1996) and the Neighborhood Strategies Project (NSP) in New York City (Bonavoglia 1999; Pitt, Brown, and Hirota 1999). It also examines the efforts of the Center for Employment and Training (CET) in New York City to establish and develop networks with programs in both CCRP and NSP initiatives. These case studies exemplify recent attempts to build networks among CBOs engaged in workforce development, and they also illustrate some of the opportunities for and challenges to research, practice, and program development. The chapter concludes with some suggestions for future research on CBO networks and the role of organizational resources, practices, structures, and networks on the outcomes of participants in CBO programs.

THE LITERATURE ON WORKFORCE DEVELOPMENT, COMMUNITY-BASED ORGANIZATIONS, AND NETWORKS

In spite of a growing literature on the evaluation of employment and training programs (Friedlander, Greenberg, and Robins 1997; Gueron, Pauly, and Lougy 1991; Manski and Garfinkel 1992), there is relatively little research on the role of community-based organizations in general or on the characteristics, processes, resources, and practices of such organizations in particular. Few studies have looked at the outcomes experienced by participants in these kinds of community-based programs. It has only been in recent years, partly prompted by a trend toward devolution and by other changes in welfare and employment training and in workforce development policy, that researchers have focused attention on the role that community-based groups, organizations, and service providers play in the workforce development system (see Harrison and Weiss 1998a,b,c,d; Meléndez 1996, 1997).[4]

In their seminal work, Harrison and Weiss and their collaborators (1998a,b,c,d) argue that traditional research and program evaluation of workforce development programs focused overwhelmingly on the characteristics of participants in the programs and on supply side interventions. This came at the expense of a sophisticated analysis both of the demand (or employer) side of the labor market and of the institutional processes, practices, opportunities, and constraints encountered by community-based organizations. The CBOs were trying to adapt to, mediate, and respond both to the employment needs in their communities and to their institutional social, political, and economic environment. Harrison and Weiss and their collaborators (1998b,c,d) make the case that an analysis of the history and structure of community-based organizations and of the nature of their interventions was missing from labor market research. This limited our understanding of which kinds of interventions work, why they work, and the ways in which many CBOs help to match supply and demand by recruiting participants, training them, and placing them in jobs.

The three volumes of case studies reporting on their research (Harrison and Weiss 1998b,c,d) focus predominantly on the history and development of CBOs engaged in workforce development. They demonstrate how there are many organizations around the country that have created internal and external networks involving central institutions in the workforce development system. Through such networks, these organizations have been able to increase the employment of their clients and have themselves grown to become important actors in the local workforce development system. In the book summarizing their research, Harrison and Weiss (1998a) stress the importance of network formation and maintenance to the development of successful organizations and employment training programs. They assert that "the most effective CBOs—those that have shown themselves to be able to arrange skills training and placement for a nontrivial number of neighborhood residents into jobs paying above poverty-level wages, simultaneously enhancing both participants' sense of self-worth and the reputation of the CBO—are those that are good at, and assign a high priority to, networking across organizational and territorial boundaries" (p. 2). The main organizational workforce development networks that they study are those between CBOs and 1) employers, 2) other community-based and nongovernmental organizations, 3) educational institutions, and 4) public sector institutions and government.

Harrison and Weiss (1998a, p. 7) note that most of the theory that shapes their analysis of community-based workforce development networks and organizations is guided by the literature on corporate strategy and regional economic development. Podolny and Page (1998) find that the network form of organization has a number of advantages over purely hierarchical or purely market (i.e., competitively) arranged organizations. Their analysis of firms and of corporate networks suggests "that network forms of organization foster learning, represent a mechanism for the attainment of status or legitimacy, provide a variety of economic benefits, facilitate the management of resource dependencies, and provide considerable autonomy for employees" (p. 57).

Focusing more specifically on community-based organizations, Mattessich and Monsey (1992) have done the most extensive reviews of the literature on CBO networks built around social services.[5] They define a collaboration as "a mutually beneficial and well defined relationship entered into by two or more organizations to achieve common goals" (p. 7). Collaborations are "more durable and pervasive relationships," the authors suggest, and they "bring previously separated organizations into a new structure with full commitment to a common mission." The authors see three distinct types of relationships: collaboration (formal), coordination (informal), and cooperation (project-specific; see Note 1).

Mattessich and Monsey find 19 factors related to successful collaborations and group them into six categories: 1) factors related to the environment, 2) issues of membership, 3) matters of process and structure, 4) communications, 5) purpose, and 6) resources. Each category includes several subtopics. For each subtopic, I include in parentheses the number of studies in the authors' review that mentioned this as a factor. In terms of the *environment,* their review of the literature suggests that there are three important factors related to successful collaborations. The first is a history of collaboration in the community (6). In his review of the literature on interorganizational relations, which focuses on resource procurement and allocation, political advocacy, and organizational legitimization, Galaskiewicz (1985, p. 292) finds that coalition building around political advocacy is dependent on linkages to the community. The second factor given by Mattessich and Monsey is that groups involved in the collaboration are perceived as leaders in the community (3). The third factor is a favorable social and political climate (3).

In terms of *membership,* Mattessich and Monsey find that respect, understanding, and trust between the organizations and an appropriate cross section of members (11) were cited in a majority of the studies they reviewed as being important to the success of collaborations. The other two factors related to membership were that the members must see that it is in their self-interest to participate or perceive that their organization or their clients have something specific to gain from the collaboration (6) and that the organizations have an ability to compromise (3). In terms of *process and structure,* Mattessich and Monsey find several important factors mentioned in the literature. The first two are that the members share a stake in the process and the outcome (6) and that there are multiple layers of decision-making (6). They also find that flexibility (4), developing clear roles and policy guidelines (4), and adaptability (3) relate to process and structure in successful collaborations. In the area of *communications,* Mattessich and Monsey find that open and frequent communication (9) and established formal and informal communication links (5) are central to efficient and successful collaborations. With respect to *purpose* of activities, the literature suggests that in order to be successful a collaboration has to have concrete and attainable goals and objectives (5), and that the groups involved in the collaboration need to have a shared vision (4) and need to see it as achieving a unique purpose (3). Last, in terms of *resources,* Mattessich and Monsey find that sufficient funds (8) and a skilled convener (7) are important factors related to the success of collaborations.

In their study of community development corporations (CDCs), Keyes et al. (1996, p. 202) argue that nonprofit organizations do not exist in a vacuum; "they survive and prosper when they are part of a network of organizations that support and undergird their activities." These institutional support networks are crucial to the development of social capital and to the successful operation of these organizations, say the authors: social capital sharing networks among nonprofit organizations are more likely to be sustained (and therefore successful) when there is a long-term relationship of trust and reciprocity, a shared vision among the organizations, mutual interest in the network, and a financial nexus that ties the groups together. They also find several challenges confronting CBO support networks (p. 219), including 1) uneven development, 2) what they call the dangers of offering overly aggressive supports, 3) competition and conflict among networks that support different visions and types of organizations, and 4) the need to spend resources on the fiscal and managerial stabilization of more troubled programs.

In the conclusion to their book, *Urban Problems and Community Development*, Ferguson and Dickens (1999) recognize the lack of research on CBO networks, particularly in the areas of community economic development and workforce development, and state that the literature on alliances is scarce and fragmented. "Despite the importance of alliances," the authors say, "there are no standard frameworks in urban change or community development studies for guiding the analysis, design, implementation, or evaluation of alliance building processes" (p. 590). The essay attempts to organize the fragmented literature and suggests more research on CBO alliances (what I call interorganizational networks).

Following their sociological treatment of organizations, Ferguson and Dickens find that there are several stages in the development of CBO networks and that "trust is a factor at every stage of alliance development." They suggest that networks come into being only after organizations can affirmatively answer four questions:

1) Can I trust my allies' motives?
2) Can I trust their competency?
3) Can I trust their dependability?
4) Can I have confidence in their collegiality?

If the answers to all four of these questions are satisfactory, then the network has a chance to establish itself and begin to work on its goals. The conditions listed by Ferguson and Dickens could be seen as factors related to the formation of networks, but when it comes to networks' development, maturation, and renewal, other factors come into play.

The authors enumerate five dichotomies in the development of alliances: 1) trust versus mistrust, 2) compromise versus conflict or exit, 3) commitment versus ambivalence, 4) industriousness versus discouragement, and 5) transition versus stagnation. During the first stage participants get to know one another and build trust between their organizations at the various levels of leadership. In the second phase, the participating organizations search for agreement on the goals of the network and hold discussions on how the network will be structured and will operate. During the third phase, the participating organizations work on solidifying their roles, developing the set of tasks that they will carry out within the network, and resolving any conflicts and issues that might arise out of their initial participation in the network.

In the fourth phase, industriousness versus discouragement, the network goes through "growing pains." During this trying time, participants must experience some initial payoffs if the network is to succeed. Ferguson and Dickens (1999) suggest that at this stage several obstacles can arise which may affect the survival of the network: "unexpected lapses in funding, unsuccessful leadership transitions, malfeasance, incompetence, failure by some members to perform their responsibilities, unexpected delays, and uncontrollable events that destroy past progress" (p. 603). If the organizations in a network are able to negotiate and overcome these obstacles, then the network enters the final stage, transition versus stagnation. At this stage the network continues to work on its original goals and demonstrates (or fails to) its ability to adapt to a changing environment. The network must have the flexibility to transform itself to respond to the changing characteristics and needs of the various organizations involved and the communities and constituencies it serves.

The growing literature on CBO networks and workforce development presents us with a number of hypotheses and generalizations about why organizations enter into networks (Ferguson and Dickens 1999; Harrison and Weiss 1998a; Pitt, Brown, and Hirota 1999), the various stages in the development of networks (Ferguson and Dickens

1999), and the factors that are associated with successful collaborations (Mattessich and Monsey 1992). In the next section I draw on material from three New York City case studies—the Comprehensive Community Revitalization Program (CCRP) in the Bronx, the Neighborhood Strategies Project (NSP), and the Center for Employment and Training (CET)—to inform our reading of the literature and to examine and illustrate the main factors related to the formation, development, and management of successful interorganizational networks.

THE FORMATION AND MAINTENANCE OF INTERORGANIZATIONAL NETWORKS

In general terms, my analysis of CET and CCRP and my research on the activities of other organizations suggest that there are five key roles that CBOs (and broader, collaborative-based comprehensive community initiatives) have played, and can continue to play, in workforce and community economic development (Stone 1996). The first role is to serve as a source of program development, funding, and management. The second is to stimulate the creation of organizational networks between CDCs, CBOs, and other actors (within and outside of the community) in the workforce and community economic development system. These may include employers and corporations, foundations and other funders, educational and training institutions (schools, community colleges, universities), government agencies and officials, the nonprofit sector, and other CBOs or business groups. Third, they can stimulate the gathering, analysis, and use of information on program processes, interventions, and outcomes.

The fourth role of CBOs is to serve as a job matching service between employers and community residents. Organizations do this by seeking resources to develop programs that pair individuals from the community (according to their skills, interests, and experience) with employment opportunities received by the organization from direct employer requests or developed through formal and informal organizational and individual contacts. Finally, CBO networks serve as an advocate for community residents and an intermediary between them and their community-based organizations, other outside organizations, governmental and nongovernmental agencies, and other communities.

In the area of workforce development, community-based organizations are also involved directly in adult education, general skills and occupation-specific vocational training, career counseling and development, resume preparation, job interview skill development, job placement, and post-placement support services (including, in many instances, placing the same individual in another job).

These CBO activities contribute directly to the creation of jobs for residents in the community and also contribute to job creation and community economic development by managing and building connections and, ultimately, working networks between actors and institutions; by providing resources, information, and support services for community residents; by providing information and support for research and planning; by improving the social climate; and by building and maintaining the social and physical infrastructure and the human resources of low-income communities.

Why Do CBOs Enter into Interorganizational Networks?

In their volume on workforce development networks, Harrison and Weiss (1998a, p. 40) suggest that there are several reasons why CBOs network with one another. Groups seek to work together when 1) the projects involved are too risky for one organization, 2) no single organization has the internal capacity to provide an adequate service, 3) key information leading to success is located in other organizations and cannot be easily acquired or purchased, 4) they seek to expand their services and move into other areas for which they need access to local resources and knowledge of local conditions, 5) no single group is sufficiently large to attract a diverse pool of vendors and suppliers and to bring the project to scale, and 6) gaining legitimacy in the eyes of other actors in the system requires a structure wherein various stakeholders participate in the decision-making process.

Similarly, in their evaluation of the Neighborhood Strategies Project (NSP), a set of CBO networks in three New York City neighborhoods, Pitt, Brown, and Hirota (1999) discuss some of the reasons why organizations develop networks with one another. Their report lays out four concrete benefits to network formation. The first is that by putting organizations in contact with one another, networks help to stimulate new organizational perspectives on and approaches to community problems. Second, networks strengthen organizational capacity by giving individual organizations that are part of a collective access to resources and technical assistance they might otherwise not be able to secure. Third, organizations enter into networks to enhance and expand their contacts and opportunities. By working with other organizations, CBOs are able to develop strong ties to other groups and increase the number of connections, or weak ties, that they have with the various constituencies in the community. Finally, networks help organizations leverage resources, which enables them to be more efficient by combining their limited resources and assets with those of other organizations and using those ties to secure additional resources and funding.

Our case studies, review of reports, and reading of the literature suggest that there are three broad sets of reasons why community-based organizations seek to collaborate with one another: internal organizational reasons, funder-related reasons, and government-related reasons (see Table 12.1). Internal factors are mostly related to the evolving needs of the organization and its clients. Funder-driven reasons involve agencies collaborating to apply for funding, or a funder seeking a collaborative to develop a particular program or initiative. Similarly, organizations form a network in order to apply for funding from a government agency, or an agency seeks a collaborative to develop and carry out a particular program.

Internal reasons

Our interviews brought out several internal reasons why CBOs enter into networks with one another. The case study materials highlight these reasons. The first involves client driven pressure to expand the quality and number of services they provide, to expand their portfolio of activities and programs, or to expand their services into other geographical areas. Second, organizations collaborate as a way to acquire expertise from others (and share their own resources with others) facing similar circumstances and serving similar or related populations. Networks can provide more resources to fund staff and activities. Third, organizations collaborate as a way to reduce or share the costs of program management and related activities, or because they perceive that networks will give them access to a broader range of opportunities for program development and funding. And fourth, organizations collaborate in order to enhance their visibility and the reputation of their programs in the community.

Funder-related reasons

As we have noted, agencies sometimes collaborate to apply for funding, or a funder seeks a collaborative to develop a particular program. For funders, collaboration can be a way to bring scale to projects when there is no one agency with the capacity to provide the services. It can also be a means of creating affinities (or synergies) between groups and organizations working on common problems in similar communities (or in the same one). Funders also use collaborations as a way of disseminating contracts among a number of groups, organizations, and service providers, thereby spreading the scope and visibility of their interventions and enhancing organizational learning while also diffusing and minimizing the risk of failure. Foundations seek to work with collaboratives because they can help deliver programs and services to numerous constituencies, engaging a variety of sources of community-based knowledge, expertise, and experience.

In many of our interviews, when we asked organizations to give us examples of networks that were not working or were breaking down, we were told that when organizations are matched by an outside agency (like a foundation) because the outsider thinks that the organizations will be able to work well together, they often end up not working well. This does not mean that funders or intermediaries cannot come in and make good matches. The point is rather that outsiders should not assume that the matches they make are going to work well unless the organizations involved work hard at building a solid relationship and developing trust. When funding is the main factor that brings groups together, programs may languish (partly owing to lack of leadership or direction) and relations are likely to break down. In contrast, when organizations come together because they share goals, experiences, methods, perspectives, and sometimes practices, the network is more likely to work better and the programs are more likely to be sustained. Rather than trying to match specific agencies, intermediaries and funders should focus on creating the conditions for organizations and programs that are at the cooperation or coordination stage (and have an interest in or previous experience working together) to form an interorganizational network.

Table 12.1 Why Do CBOs Develop Interorganizational Networks?

Reason	Importance
Internal reasons	
To enhance services or expand portfolio	Organizations recognize that their clients have multiple needs, often for comprehensive services.
To move into other areas	Agencies sometimes expand their geographical focus to respond to the needs of clients in underserved related areas.
To share and acquire expertise	Organizations need expertise related to the development and management of particular kinds of programs or services or of ways to serve clients from particular communities.
To reduce or share costs	Working with others allows agencies to share staff and reduce unit costs.
To access other opportunities	Collaborations present agencies with new opportunities to access resources, partners, and funding.
To enhance program reputation	Being sought-after and a good partner increases the reputation of an organization and its ability to develop programs, influence policy, and raise funds to support its work.
Funder-related reasons	
To achieve scale	Collaborations allow funders to add organizational capacity to their enterprises and develop them at a scale that is large enough to be visible and have an impact on the community.
To cash in on affinities	Collaborations allow funders to build networks between organizations that they work with that have similar or complementary styles, missions, services, or clients.

To spread contracts and risk	Funding multiple organizations in a collaborative allows funders to experiment with different organizational approaches to service delivery and allows organizations to learn from each other, thus minimizing the risk of loss.
To disseminate services	Collaborations provide a structure and a pool of knowledge and expertise that enables the systematic development of additional services for clients of the various organizations.
To serve numerous constituencies	Collaborations allow funders to include and serve more constituencies, whether in several communities or in sub-segments of a given community.
To engage a variety of expertise	Collaborations allow funders to draw from a diverse pool of experts and support personnel.
Government-related reasons	
To spread contacts	Collaborations enable governments to apportion contracts among many constituencies without having to administer multiple contracts.
To diffuse risk	Collaborations enable governments to diffuse the risk of failure or noncompliance.
To build community infrastructure	Collaborations enable governments to develop organizational infrastructure across communities.

Government-related reasons

Similarly, there are government-driven external reasons for a collaborative to apply for funding from a government agency, or for a government agency to seek a collaborative to develop a particular program. In the latter case, governments like to spread their service contracts among many constituencies without having to administer multiple contracts, and by working with collaboratives governments diffuse the risk of failure or noncompliance with the conditions of the contract. Finally, governments may seek to fund community collaboratives in order to provide resources to many organizations and help build a broad community infrastructure.

What Are the Factors Associated with the Success of CBO Workforce Development Networks?

In spite of the many accomplishments and positive contributions to the development of communities, organizations, and individuals on the part of CBO networks organized around workforce development and related social service areas, our case studies suggest that there are also many challenges to their successful design, development, management, and maintenance. Studying these challenges can help us understand the factors related to the success of CBO networks.

CCRP proved to be a successful collaboration in that four of the original six groups agreed to set up an incorporated entity to manage the collaboration and develop programs. There were, however, two organizations that exited the collaboration: One left and the other was asked to leave. The NSP has accomplished many goals, but as a collaboration it has had serious difficulties at two of its three sites with respect to the management and development of the network. CET has also had mixed results as a collaboration and administered its programs as a stand-alone organization with very limited partnerships with other local CBOs.

CCRP did have some problems, but the collaboration seems to have worked well for the remaining four organizations. The relationship between the CDCs that belong to CCRP was described to me in some of the interviews as a good example of repeat contracting by organizations that have worked well together and have benefited from working with one another. The participating CDCs moved mostly from housing redevelopment and management into other social service functions and worked on collaborating with each other when they were expanding services and planning the development of new initiatives and programs.

Some of the reasons why CCRP worked as a collaboration are consistent with the factors listed in the literature on collaborations (Mattessich and Monsey 1992): a selection of organizations with a track record; a history of work in the community and some assets and capacity; an active and professionally led planning process with significant community involvement; and opportunities to engage in activities, to discuss common interests, and to build trust among the participating organizations.

However, other factors that contributed to CCRP's success are not mentioned in the literature. First, CCRP encouraged the organizations to build the collaboration and created opportunities for them to do so. The participating agencies had many opportunities to meet and interact with one another and to develop a planning process that recognized the particularities of each community and organization yet at the same time allowed each organization and community to benefit from the work of others. A second important factor that helped CCRP was the decision to selectively target both the types of services it would provide and the communities where it would provide them. Unlike NSP, which relied on building multiagency collaborations in each neighborhood, CCRP selected one lead agency in each neighborhood and sought to link agencies across neighborhoods and communities. This proved to be a good decision because agencies could focus on identifying the needs in each community and could work on developing their social service niche in concert with broader CCRP programs. They did not have to spend a significant amount of time negotiating "turf" issues within their neighborhoods, but instead could devote their energies to service provision and to program development and management.

In terms of targeted services, CCRP organizations worked together in the development of employment services (the organizations shared a curriculum, a case management system, and other components of the program) while at the same time retaining the freedom to design and experiment with their own job placement programs. This combination of guidance, centralization, and flexibility (or "flexible centralization") resulted in organizations deriving the best advantages from the collaboration while being able to retain relative autonomy to develop (and share) focused solutions to specific program and service challenges in their communities.

Another factor that contributed to the success of CCRP as a collaborative had to do with the fact that the initiative began with manageable, concrete, and visible projects that were able to show clear gains early on. This indicated to observers and participants that the initiative was a serious endeavor, allowed the participating organizations to actively build their relationships, and by producing some visible results it gave them an incentive to continue to work together. Last, and perhaps paradoxically, one of the factors that allowed CCRP to succeed was that it was able to manage the exit of two organizations from the original six that were members of the initiative. One of the lessons from CCRP is that when building organizational networks there needs to be a mechanism, with clear rules and procedures, that regulates entry into and exit out of the network, as well as a protocol that establishes clear decision-making procedures and rules of accountability. When trust does not exist or is not built, the relationship is likely to languish and break down. In some instances, collaborations do not work because there is a change of direction or leadership on the part of one of the partners. Sometimes these changes in focus can be anticipated, but at other times they are quite complex and idiosyncratic and must be managed by the remaining partners.

An additional point to discuss is the issue of homogeneity versus heterogeneity in CBO collaborations. CCRP seems to have been a grouping of relatively heterogeneous organizations, in terms of clients and services, that provided services to a variety of constituencies within their neighborhoods, whereas NSP was more of a heterogeneous grouping of many homogeneous organizations. In NSP many different organizational actors felt as though they were in competition with one another: they had different interests and resources, different views of the collaborative, different connections to various constituencies in their communities, different definitions of the problems they faced, and, in some instances, different understandings of the solutions to the main problems in their communities. In contrast, the organizations involved with CCRP embodied, to varying degrees, some of the conflicts within their communities but shared many views on the nature of the social problems in their communities, on program development, and on the potential of the collaborative for bringing resources to their organizations and communities. In their official NSP evaluation, Pitt, Brown, and Hirota (1999) discuss some of the main obstacles encountered by NSP and confirm many of our observations. They report that the obstacles involved 1) translating a shared vision into action, 2) involving neighborhood residents and negotiating neighborhood politics, 3) establishing collaborative governance and effective management, and 4) balancing institutional and collaborative interests.

Based on a review of the literature, interviews, and analysis of materials from case studies, we find that there are 13 key factors that seem to be consistently related to the success of interorganizational networks among CBOs engaged in workforce development and related initiatives, and that planners, program administrators, researchers, and others need to keep in mind when designing, developing, and managing these networks.[6] Some of these factors are related to the formation, development, and management of CBO networks; others are related to the sustainability, maintenance, and growth of these networks (Table 12.2).

1) The first factor is an explicit mechanism for the selection of participants and the development of concrete criteria that emphasize a track record and a history of programs and other work in the community. CCRP, for example, grew out of a selection of organizations with some assets and a demonstrated capacity to carry out new commitments and programs with other organizations.
2) The second element relates to the importance of developing mutual respect, understanding, and trust. Organizations in a network must have trust in the other organizations, their mission, their capacity to accomplish goals, and their leadership.
3) Third is an active and professionally led planning process with significant community involvement, which allows the collaboratives to be known in the community, to work together with the community, and to learn about the specific program and resource needs of local residents, businesses, and others.
4) Fourth, members must all have a stake in the process and outcome. Actors involved in the network must organize discussions that build a consensus around goals, programs, and practices, particularly among initial members of the network.
5) Successful networks create opportunities for the organizations involved in the collaborative to engage in concrete activities

with one another, to discuss common interests, to develop clear expectations, and to build trust. When agencies have open channels of communication and many opportunities to meet, interact, and engage in a planning process, they work better together. This also lets them recognize the particularities of each community and organization while allowing each to benefit from the work of others.

6) Another important factor in the development and maintenance of successful interorganizational networks is the engagement and involvement of the community. Identification and involvement of community stakeholders in the development and planning of network programs and activities allows the initiative to build a constituency, to develop support and legitimacy in the community, and to acquire valuable information and resources that can be instrumental in the assessment, management, and planning of social services.
7) The successful development of interorganizational networks depends on an ability to compromise: organizations must develop a system to achieve consensus and resolve disagreements on goals, programs, and procedures.
8) There must be clear organizational roles and policies. Each organization must have its particular, defined role, and the policies and procedures for participation in the network should be clearly established, agreed upon, and made explicit.
9) Open and frequent communication through established formal and informal communication links is essential to the flow of information that builds confidence and trust, and to the learning that should take place between organizations involved in a collaborative. Multiple channels of communications between residents, administrators, and the staff of the various organizations are critical to the successful development of interorganizational networks.
10) Member organizations must be clear and selective in targeting both the types of services that are going to be provided and the communities where they will be provided. Targeting of services (having a clear definition of the services that will be provided) and of the areas of service (also clearly defining who the clients are going to be) focuses the energies and interven-

tions of participating organizations and is vital to the success of collaborative efforts.

11) As exemplified by CCRP, the initiative should begin with concrete and visible projects that are able to show clear gains early on, reflecting the seriousness of the initiative and giving participating organizations an incentive to continue to work together to achieve positive results.
12) There must be a process to develop concrete, long-term goals and objectives for the network. The network can then periodically take stock of its activities and agree on whether to continue projects and programs based on organizational capacities, available resources, and community needs.
13) CCRP succeeded because it was able to manage the exit of two organizations from the original six that belonged to the collaborative. One of the lessons learned from CCRP is that there needs to be a mechanism in interorganizational networks that regulates entry into and (voluntary or involuntary) exit from the network, complete with clear decision-making procedures, rules of performance, and processes of accountability.

Qualifications and amendments to the literature

Our research suggests there are a number of factors mentioned in the literature that are relevant but not necessarily central to the success of CBO workforce development networks.[7] I will discuss these qualifications to the literature following the schema presented in Mattessich and Monsey (1992): factors related to the environment, to issues of membership, to process and structure, and to communications, purpose, and resources. Our analysis suggests that some of the factors they list are necessary but not sufficient, while others seem to have a different relationship to the success of networks depending on the context.

In terms of the *environment,* we found that all of the programs that we studied had a legitimate history of work in the community. They were also organizations that were perceived as leaders in their communities. These two factors, then, are necessary to the success of a network but not sufficient. In terms of a favorable social and political climate it is important to make distinctions between the operation of political forces at the community, metropolitan (city), state, and national levels. Thus, Meléndez and Harrison (1998) have shown that part of the CET

Table 12.2 Factors Related to the Development of Interorganizational Networks

Factor	Action directive	Source
Formation		
Selection of participants	Have concrete criteria for the selection of organizations that are going to be part of the network.	Suggested by case studies
Mutual respect, understanding, and trust	Organizations should know about, appreciate, and respect each other's missions, goals, procedures, and programs.	See Mattessich and Monsey (1992)
Planning process with some community involvement	Involve the community in the early stages of the planning; analyze community needs.	Suggested by case studies
Development		
Members share a stake in process and outcome	Build consensus among initial members of the network around goals, programs, and practices.	See Mattessich and Monsey (1992)
Concrete opportunities to build trust, develop common interests, and collaborate	Engage in program development and design at initial stage in order to establish a working relationship between organizations.	Suggested by case studies
Engagement and involvement of community in programs	Involve community stakeholders in the planning and development of network programs and activities.	Suggested by case studies
Ability to compromise	Organizations must develop a system to resolve disagreements on goals, programs, and procedures.	See Mattessich and Monsey (1992)

Management		
Clear organizational roles; clear policy guidelines for network	Each organization must have a particular role. The policies and procedures of the network should be established and made explicit.	See Mattessich and Monsey (1992)
Open and frequent communication in the network; established formal and informal communication links	Have multiple channels of communication between residents, administrators, and staff of the various organizations and between groups.	See Mattessich and Monsey (1992)
Targeting of services and areas of service	Provide clear definitions of the services to be provided, the populations to be served, and the criteria for participation.	Suggested by case studies
Visible early gains	Begin by developing manageable, concrete, and visible projects that will show clear gains early in the process and build support.	Suggested by case studies
Sustainability and Growth		
Concrete goals and objectives	Establish a process to develop concrete, long-term goals and objectives for the network, enabling periodic evaluation.	See Mattessich and Monsey (1992)
Exit rules and procedures	Establish procedures allowing for entry into and exit from the network.	Suggested by case studies

formula for success was based on building organic relationships with both employers and community. There are organizational barriers to network building and maintenance, but city policy also has an impact. For example, the New York City Department of Employment (DOE) implemented new screening and assessment mechanisms whereby contracts were divided between assessment and placement and the assessment functions were centralized among a few providers. These changes seem to have contributed to severing the networks between the Center for Employment and Training (CET) and other CBOs. The DOE's reason for establishing a centralized screening and referral system was based in part on the argument that "cozy" relations between programs led to "creaming" (or selecting the clients with more strengths and fewer needs) and, thus, to inflated program results. However, it could very well be that strong networks between organizations lead to more comprehensive interventions, better services, more effective case management, and better outcomes.[8] Separating the assessment from the training functions was a metropolitan level policy decision that had an impact on interorganizational networks and illustrates the role of city policies in the formation, management, and chance of success of interorganizational networks.

In the area of *membership,* the literature suggests that an appropriate cross section of members is important to the success of networks, but some of the networks we reviewed raise questions about the merits of heterogeneity of representation within organizations versus heterogeneity of representation in collaboratives. Our case studies suggest that organizations that share certain methods, characteristics, and approaches seem to make better partners and form stronger networks than organizations that are different. Also, the literature suggests that members perceiving where their self-interest lies is important to the success of networks; but self-interest is not sufficient, and too much emphasis on it, particularly during the middle stages of a network, can lead to difficulties in building trust and, potentially, to failure. Organizations have to bring more than self-interest to the table; they also have to bring resources to invest in the network.

In the area of *process and structure,* our case studies suggest that multiple layers of decision-making can create obstacles to the success of networks, and that when many structures exist, leadership, accountability, and responsibility can be diluted. In terms of flexibility, it helps for organizations to be open about different ways of organizing the collaborative, but there have to be some boundaries to the discussions, and there has to be a mechanism in place to settle differences of opinion. Each interorganizational network has to find a governance structure that is particularly suited to the kinds of organizations, services, and communities that are involved in the collaboration. Similarly, adaptability to changes in the environment is critical to the success of networks—but then, adaptability is part of the analytical definition of a successful network.[9]

In terms of *purpose,* most of the organizations in the collaboratives we reviewed shared a vision, but they did not always share methods, styles, emphases, or approaches to the articulation and implementation of their particular vision. It is important for a network to have a unique purpose, but this purpose has to be consistent and compatible with the goals and possibilities of the member organizations. If "uniqueness" involves the creation of parallel organizational or managerial structures there can be a perception of duplication among some of the organizations, which can create legitimacy problems for the network. Last, in terms of *resources,* the collaboratives we studied had significant resources and skilled conveners. All of the organizations we looked at had professional leadership and competent staff. These elements are necessary but not sufficient, however, for the success of CBO networks. Though adequate resources and a skilled convener are important, once they are present other factors become more salient with respect to the success of networks.

CONCLUSION AND SUGGESTIONS FOR FUTURE RESEARCH

This paper has examined networks among community-based organizations involved in workforce development programs and initiatives and has tried to answer two research questions: Why do CBOs enter into networks with one another? And, what are some of the main factors associated with successful networking between community-based organizations engaged in workforce development and related initiatives?

As organizations develop, they face two choices: to partner and collaborate with others or to try to expand and develop more internal, independent capacity. How are organizations making decisions about which strategy or course of action to follow in the current policy environment? For the organizations that try to develop linkages with others, what are some of the challenges involved in network formation in relation to the various actors in the workforce development system: employers and corporations; educational and training institutions (schools, community colleges, and universities); government agencies and officials; other organizations, agencies, and service providers in the nonprofit sector; other business groups; and foundations and other types of funders?

From a research perspective, we need better theory, hypotheses, data, and measures with respect to the factors that are mentioned in the literature and suggested by case studies as being related to the success of CBO networks (Mulroy and Shay 1998). Whether organizations are increasing internal capacity or partnering, we know very little about the main challenges faced by CBOs in the areas of program management, case management, documentation of their efforts, and program evaluation. Researchers involved in the evaluation of community-based workforce development programs need to better understand organizational-level processes and incorporate the role of organizational-level characteristics (such as organizational resources, structure, and practices) into the analysis of individual-level outcomes. One of the main reasons data on the individual characteristics of program participants are collected is to be able to know who is best suited to benefit and for whom the various programs will work best. Another is to be able to evaluate whether individuals are actually benefiting from various interventions and program investments (Mueller and Schwartz 1998). Similarly, at the organizational level there is a need to know more about the impact of various program characteristics on participant outcomes. Policymakers need information on ways they can make programs more efficient by stimulating research and providing the resources and expertise needed to support the most effective organizational-level practices. In spite of the many challenges to CBOs engaged in workforce development, the promise of networks seems to be that they allow organizations to acquire and share knowledge, experience, expertise, and valuable resources, and that they can help many CBOs bring these resources to their areas in the form of more efficient, stable, and responsive services and programs for their communities.

Notes

The author would like to thank the Community Development Research Center and the Ford Foundation for their support in the preparation of this manuscript. I appreciate the comments received from James DeFilippis, Ronald Ferguson, Edwin Meléndez, Maria Victoria Quiroz, and the late Ben Harrison. I am also grateful for assistance from Ana Calero, Johana Herrera, Katia Flores, Wendy Garcia, and Tracy Chimelis. All disclaimers apply.

1. See Connell et al. (1995); Ferguson and Dickens (1999); Fulbright-Anderson, Kubisch, and Connell (1998); Harrison and Weiss (1998a); and Pitt, Brown, and Hirota (1999).
2. I use the terms interorganizational network and collaboration interchangeably to mean a sustained effort between two established community-based programs to provide social services under a common organizational structure. Following the literature (Mattessich and Monsey 1992), I make a distinction between coordination (or an informal arrangement), cooperation (involving project specific planning, organizational interaction, and shared management), and collaboration (or an interorganizational network), which entails the development of a common vision, a clear organizational structure, comprehensive integrated planning, concrete dedicated linkage between groups, shared resources, and integrated management. In order to build, maintain, and sustain effective interorganizational networks with the various actors in their immediate environment, organizations must have some experience cooperating on and coordinating activities and programs with others.
3. A successful network is one where organizations acknowledge that they have benefited from working together and seek to continue to do so. My focus is on the functioning of the network itself and not directly on the outcomes of the individual participants in the programs run by the network, though they are clearly related.
4. The two main pieces of legislation were the Personal Responsibility and Work Opportunity Reconciliation Act (PRWORA), which changed the welfare system, and the Workforce Investment Act (WIA), which repealed the Job Training Partnership Act (JTPA) and introduced and defined the new workforce development system.
5. Mattessich and Monsey (1992, p. 41) reviewed 133 studies that seemed to have some relevance to CBO collaborations. Upon analysis they reduced the studies to 62, which they then further pared based on the following criteria: "Studies were dropped because they did not address the major research question adequately; the projects did not meet our definition of collaboration, they did not include empirical observations, or they did not address the topic of success" (p. 42). The process left them with 18 studies to include in an analysis of the factors leading to successful collaborations. For more on the literature on CBO networks built around social services, see Winer and Ray (1997).

6. Here I discuss factors related to the success of the network itself, which are not necessarily the same factors that are associated with the outcomes of individual participants in collaborative based employment training programs and initiatives.
7. The analysis of the material from our case studies raises issues and qualifications about 12 of the 19 factors related to successful collaborations that are listed in Mattessich and Monsey (1992).
8. The key question at this point for the DOE is whether it has in place a mechanism to analyze current assessment and placement policies and distinguish between the two hypotheses.
9. Also, empirically it seems to me that adaptability is potentially difficult to carry out and measure and that it is more a dependent than an independent variable. To measure the success of networks is in a large way to measure their adaptability to a changing environment.

References

Bonavoglia, Angela. 1999. *A Guide Toward Better Jobs and Stronger Ties: Launching Economic Development and Community Building Initiatives*. New York: New York Community Trust.

Connell, James P., Anne C. Kubisch, Lisbeth C. Schorr, and Carol H. Weiss, eds. 1995. *New Approaches to Evaluating Community Initiatives.* Vol. 1, *Concepts, Methods, and Contexts.* Washington, DC: Aspen Institute.

Ferguson, Ronald F., and William T. Dickens. 1999. *Urban Problems and Community Development.* A project of the National Community Development Policy Analysis Network. Washington, DC: Brookings Institution Press.

Friedlander, Daniel, David H. Greenberg, and Philip K. Robins. 1997. "Evaluating Government Training Programs for the Economically Disadvantaged." *Journal of Economic Literature* 35(4): 1809–1855.

Fulbright-Anderson, Karen, Anne C. Kubisch, and James P. Connell. 1998. *New Approaches to Evaluating Community Initiatives.* Vol. 2, *Theory, Measurement, and Analysis*. Washington, DC: Aspen Institute.

Galaskiewicz, Joseph. 1985. "Interorganizational Relations." *Annual Review of Sociology* 11(1985): 281–304.

Gueron, Judith M., Edward Pauly, and Cameran M. Lougy. 1991. *From Welfare to Work.* New York: Russell Sage Foundation.

Harrison, Bennett, and Marcus Weiss. 1998a. *Workforce Development Networks: Community-Based Organizations and Regional Alliances.* Thousand Oaks, CA: Sage Publications.

———, eds. 1998b. *Networking Across Boundaries.* Vol. 1, *Community-based Organizations as Workforce Development Hubs.* Boston: Economic Development Assistance Consortium.

———, eds. 1998c. *Networking Across Boundaries.* Vol. 2, *Peer-to-Peer Workforce Development Networks.* Boston: Economic Development Assistance Consortium.

———, eds. 1998d. *Networking Across Boundaries.* Vol. 3, *Regional Intermediaries Bridging Job Training with Business and Community Development.* Boston: Economic Development Assistance Consortium.

Keyes, Langley C., Alex Schwartz, Avis C. Vidal, and Rachel Bratt. 1996. "Networks and Nonprofits: Opportunities and Challenges in an Era of Federal Devolution." *Housing Policy Debate* 7(2): 201–230.

Manski, Charles F., and Irwin Garfinkel, eds. 1992. *Evaluating Welfare and Training Programs.* Cambridge, MA: Harvard University Press.

Mattessich, Paul W., and Barbara R. Monsey. 1992. *Collaboration: What Makes It Work.* St. Paul, MN: Amherst H. Wilder Foundation.

Meléndez, Edwin. 1990. "Towards a Good Job Strategy for Latino Workers." *Journal of Hispanic Policy* 4: 39–51.

———. 1996. *Working on Jobs: The Center for Employment and Training.* Boston: Mauricio Gaston Institute for Latino Community Development and Public Policy, University of Massachusetts Boston.

———. 1997. "The Potential Impact of Workforce Development Legislation on CBOs." *New England Journal of Public Policy* 13(1): 175–186.

Meléndez, Edwin, and Bennett Harrison. 1998. "Matching the Disadvantaged to Job Opportunities: Structural Explanations for the Past Successes of the Center for Employment Training." *Economic Development Quarterly* 12(1): 3–11.

Mueller, Elizabeth, and Alex Schwartz. 1998. "Leaving Poverty Through Work: A Review of Current Development Strategies." *Economic Development Quarterly* 12(2): 166–180.

Mulroy, Elizabeth A., and Sharon Shay. 1998. "Motivation and Reward in Nonprofit Interorganizational Collaboration in Low-Income Neighborhoods." *Administration in Social Work* 22(4): 1–17.

OMG Center for Collaborative Learning. 1994. *First Annual Assessment Report: The Comprehensive Community Revitalization Program, Covering Program Start-Up through First Year Operations, April 1, 1992–December 31, 1993.* Philadelphia: OMG Center for Collaborative Learning.

———. 1995. *Second Annual Assessment Report: The Comprehensive Community Revitalization Program in the South Bronx.* Philadelphia: OMG Center for Collaborative Learning.

Pitt, Jessica, Prudence Brown, and Janice Hirota. 1999. *Collaborative Approaches to Revitalizing Communities: A Review of the Neighborhood Strategies Project.* Chicago: Chapin Hall Center for Children, University of Chicago.

Podolny, Joel M., and Karen L. Page. 1998. "Network Forms of Organization." *Annual Review of Sociology* 24 (1998): 57–76.

Spilka, Gerri, and Tom Burns. 1998a. *Final Assessment Report: The Comprehensive Community Revitalization Program in the South Bronx.* Philadelphia: OMG Center for Collaborative Learning.

———. 1998b. *Summary of Final Assessment Report: The Comprehensive Community Revitalization Program in the South Bronx.* Philadelphia: OMG Center for Collaborative Learning.

Stone, Rebecca, ed. 1996. *Core Issues in Comprehensive Community-Building Initiatives.* Chicago: Chapin Hall Center for Children, University of Chicago.

Sviridoff, Mitchell, and William Ryan. 1996. *Investing in Community: Lessons and Implications of the Comprehensive Community Revitalization Program.* New York: Comprehensive Community Revitalization Program.

Winer, Michael, and Karen Ray. 1997. *Collaboration Handbook: Creating, Sustaining, and Enjoying the Journey.* St. Paul, MN: Amherst H. Wilder Foundation.

13
Corporate-Community Workforce Development Collaborations

Stacey A. Sutton
Rutgers University

The literature addressing strategies for connecting low-income, typically low-skilled job seekers to the labor market has grown substantially over the past decade and a half. Improved school systems, better school-to-career feeder programs, employment training programs, and vocational certification and credentialing are examples of supply-side workforce development strategies that seek, by investing in individuals, to increase their capacity to obtain gainful employment. This literature, which emphasizes improving human capital, is a direct response to the research undertaken in the late 1970s and early 1980s that focused on supply-side factors as explanations of income inequality (Becker 1975, 1985). More recent supply-side workforce development literature has addressed additional inhibitors of sustainable employment and advancement for many low-income entry-level workers: the unavailability of child care, problems of transportation and housing, and issues related to work ethic and attitude. A major criticism of supply-side literature, however, is that it is too narrowly focused on developing individual capacity. It predicates employment opportunities on the behavior of low-income people while neglecting a broad array of issues related to public policy, employer practices, and corporate culture, as well as the political, economic, and social context in which they are embedded. Moreover, the needs and expectations of employers are also under-attended. Economic restructuring, the vagaries of employer demand for workers, the proliferation of part-time and temporary workers coupled with the reduction of internal career ladders and living wage opportunities, and mutated forms of employment discrimination and exploitation—none of these are factored into supply-side discourse.

In order to begin to more effectively accomplish the formidable task of creating seamless workforce development systems, it is important to better understand what employers are looking for. The extent to which employers are willing to participate in forming partnerships with other workforce development stakeholders, specifically community-based organizations (CBOs), and the factors that lead employers to collaborate with CBOs are both under-explored. Examining employers' internal systems designed for supporting the acclimation, development, and advancement of nontraditional workers (workers on the periphery of the labor market) provides insight into the nature of corporate-community collaborations. Firms without the necessary support systems—those important for labor market attachment, retention and advancement of nontraditional workers—may rely on CBOs as natural partners for enhancing corporate capacity to successfully bring workers out of the periphery and into the workplace, and for helping workers advance in the work environment. Corporations and CBOs form tight collaborations in such instances. In contrast, firms with greater internal capabilities may have a looser relationship with CBOs, whereby CBOs merely serve as brokers for connecting firms to a new pool of labor. It is important to explore a range of corporate practices and policies that contribute to successful collaborations, as well as those factors that seem to inhibit their success.

The purpose of this paper is to delve more deeply into the structure of employer-based workforce development strategies. More specifically, it is to explore employer perspectives, needs, and expectations with respect to building and sustaining collaborations, particularly with CBOs. It also purposes to look at the usefulness of such collaborative relationships in creating opportunities for disadvantaged job seekers. Over time, collaborations, and the new institutional relationships between corporations and CBOs have the potential of becoming embedded within a broader web of social networks, norms, and policies, thereby creating a more seamless connection between nontraditional job seekers and employers. Until then, however, particular attention should be given to the structure of these nascent and often fragile relationships. This research focuses on the employer side of the collaboration with CBOs. I explore three things: 1) the level of corporate involvement with CBOs, which is referred to as external or corporate connectedness; 2) the level of internal corporate support for and integration of workforce development practices, which is the corporation's level of cohesiveness; and 3) the extent to which a combination of connectedness and cohesiveness produces different labor market outcomes.

Based on a small yet diverse sample of corporate cases, I found that firms with high levels of both connectedness and cohesiveness are more likely to provide good jobs—those providing living wages, benefits, and the potential for upward mobility. By way of contrast, firms with low to moderate levels of connectedness and cohesiveness are more likely to provide dead-end jobs—those with fairly low wages, low job security, and little mobility. Accordingly, this research fine-tunes Harrison and Weiss's (1998) thesis that argues for the importance of institutional networks for connecting nontraditional job seekers to the labor market and for optimizing their outcomes. Although optimal collaborations or networks—those that produce good jobs—have both high levels of connectedness and cohesiveness, if we look at workforce development collaborations from an employer perspective, external connectedness seems to matter less than internal cohesiveness in producing good jobs for disadvantaged job seekers.

Over the next few sections of the paper, I present a review of the literature on the role of employers in workforce development and their approaches to collaborations with CBOs. I seek to highlight the role of employers' programs in promoting the employment and advancement of low-skilled and entry-level workers. In the following section, I present examples of the different approaches deployed by firms that have led the way in workforce development. For the purpose of organizing the discussion, I have divided the corporate cases selected for the study into four categories. These categories are based on an assessment of the structure of the relationship between the corporation and its partnering CBOs as defined by the corporation's efforts to build capacity at the community level. The corporation may choose to integrate workforce development programs into its core operations (vertical integration), or instead it may promote a strategic alliance, or structure programs as joint ventures.

WORKFORCE DEVELOPMENT AND THE ROLE OF EMPLOYERS

Harrison, Weiss, and Gant (1995) make an important distinction between employment training and workforce development. They state that the intent of workforce development is much more comprehensive than merely training employees; it includes services such as collaborating with other organizations, recruiting job seekers, job matching, mentoring, addressing issues of retention, and following up. Later, Harrison and Weiss (1998) embark on an understudied aspect of the workforce development process. From the community-based organization's perspective they analyze the structure and utility of the relationships or networks that CBOs develop with employers. Additionally, they create conceptual models for better understanding the operations of these relationships and the benefits they produce. Because workforce development extends beyond employment training and job placement into areas of retention, supervisory training, and advancement, it has become increasingly important to integrate the supply side of labor market participation—training, education, and job search strategies—with the demand side, employer needs and expectations. Harrison and Weiss argue for the instrumentality of formal and informal inter-organizational networks for integrating the two sides of the labor market with existing workforce development practices.

Job seekers often utilize informal networks—family, friends, and neighbors—to gain valuable information about economic opportunities. Similarly, employers often rely on word of mouth referrals to gain access to pools of labor. However, the formal relationships being forged between CBOs and employers "hold out the promise of building relationships of trust and competence that can, over time, reduce the individual and social costs of job search" (Harrison and Weiss 1998, p.1). As community organizations attract employers by leveraging long-standing relationships to community members, employers capitalize on these preexisting relationships and provide job seekers with economic opportunities. These mutually beneficial relationships can potentially redistribute jobs, income, and experience in areas hit hard by economic restructuring and public disinvestment. Harrison and Weiss's work was groundbreaking within workforce development research. However, it became increasingly important to better understand the sustainability of

CBO and employer collaborations. In addition to examining workforce development networks from a CBO perspective, researchers have to further explore employer needs and expectations. Using interviews of employers engaged in what they classify as workforce development, this research begins to create a conceptual framework for understanding the under-explored dimension of workforce development collaborations from the employer perspective.

Policymakers and practitioners have also begun to talk about demand-side workforce development strategies. Demand-side strategies seek to address employers needs, wants and expectations, and to be sensitive to how employers hire and what stimulates employer interest in additional semiskilled applicants. Demand-side workforce development strategies attempt to adapt to fluctuations in labor demand and the ensuing income inequality. For example, the skills mismatch argument is essentially a demand-side explanation for labor market inequality that explains the expanding employment gap between educated and less educated workers as a function of disparate technical skills and technological advancement. Moreover, demand-side workforce development attempts to engage in collaboration, recruitment, job matching, mentoring, and retention by paying particular attention to the all too familiar restructured economy. The new economy and changing labor market dynamics in the United States include a transition from a manufacturing economy to a service economy (Bluestone and Harrison 1982; Harrison 1994; Herzenberg, Alic, and Wial 1998), an increased utilization of domestic and international outsourcing, unprecedented pressure to be globally competitive, the spread of new technologies, the trend toward more casual employment relationships and the loss of job security (McCall 2001), and what Howell (1997) describes as an infectious acceptance of "low-road" strategies toward labor. All of these have contributed to the dismantling of career ladders, a growth in inequality, and a collapse in real earnings, particularly at the bottom of the skill distribution.

Yet another approach for connecting low-skilled job seekers to the labor market accentuates the institutional—especially the network—connections between supply and demand. Significant contributions to this body of work highlight sectoral initiatives as well as the role of networks (social networks between family and friends and institutional networks among workforce development intermediaries, CBOs, government agencies, and employers) in matching the disadvantaged to sustainable job opportunities (Harrison and Weiss, 1998; Meléndez and Harrison 1998; Falcón and Meléndez 1996; Granovetter 1973, 1974). It is now generally accepted, however, that many black and Latino job seekers pursuing entry-level jobs in the low-wage segment of the labor market are often impeded by a complex array of barriers such as inadequate technical preparation, untimely or inaccurate information about job opportunities, the physical and social distance between suburban employers and inner city laborers, and manifestations of institutionalized racism.

In addition to encountering labor market obstacles, racial and ethnic minorities pursuing entry-level jobs frequently have the misfortune of being connected to the wrong types of networks (Meléndez and Falcón 1999). In other words, the natural friendship and familial relationships, or strong ties, that most low-income people have tend to be with other low-income people. As a result, the necessary links to information regarding living-wage jobs do not exist for many low-skilled workers and job seekers. The rampant underemployment and unemployment that plagues many inner-city communities at levels that are usually at least twice that of other urban areas can be only partially attributed to inadequate market resources and to structural adjustments caused by plant closings, businesses relocating, and corporate downsizing (Lichter 1988). But beyond that, the absence of valuable marketplace connections developed through formal relationships, or institutional brokers, precludes inner city blacks and Latinos from finding gainful employment.

Workforce development practitioners, researchers, and policymakers alike are increasingly turning to sectoral strategies for linking job seekers to the mainstream economy. Sectoral strategies are considered promising because they target regional growth industries and occupations; therefore, workforce development becomes a customized product based on the needs of employers (Theodore and Carlson 1998; Parker and Rogers 1998). Once promising sectors are identified and targeted, workforce development organizations can efficiently enhance the human capital of job seekers by providing technical training based on employer requirements and specifications. Recent literature on sectoral strategies (Meléndez 1996; Meléndez and Harrison 1998; Parker and Rogers 1998) emphasizes the benefit of encouraging employer participation in the workforce development process from its inception. Ideally, employers should be regarded as active partners in a seamless process, as opposed being seen as the final destination in the workforce development delivery network. Firms such as United Parcel Service (UPS), Sprint, and Salomon Smith Barney work with community organizations that have the capacity to train potential employees in soft skills as well as in technical skills directly applicable to the jobs they will perform. In turn, these firms assist training organizations in designing and implementing customized curricula.

WORKFORCE DEVELOPMENT IN THE NEW ECONOMY

The effectiveness of all these workforce development approaches—those emphasizing human capital, those focusing on employer demand, and those stressing connections and networks—must be considered in the context of the economic restructuring of the 1990s and the sluggish recovery since 2000. While the new economy of the 1990s was robust and more than 12 million jobs were created (Giloth 1998), for all intents and purposes too few good jobs were accessible to members of low-income communities. The downward spiral in wages for low-skilled workers, which traditionally hits blacks and Latinos hardest, has led to an unprecedented rise in wage inequality (Blau and Kahn 1992; Mason 1995; McCall 2001; Rodgers 1997). There is also a heightened level of job insecurity caused by a complex array of factors: deunionization, corporate restructuring, downsizing, outsourcing, a dismantling of career ladders, and increased utilization of contingent labor. In all, many economists and policy analysts suggest that shifts from manufacturing to services, coupled with globalization (the rapid and accelerating worldwide movement of technology, goods, capital, people, and ideas), have had a disastrous effect on many of America's inner cities (Sugrue 1996). These low-road trends have been in existence long enough to make plain that the workers most vulnerable to changing employment practices are those on the periphery of the labor market: people without college education, the young, and nonwhites (Bernhardt and Bailey 1997).

A large and possibly growing incidence of short-term employment contracts, as opposed to career ladders and long-term investments in employees, characterizes the new economy. Other characteristics include the measurement of corporate health by a firm's ability to reduce costs through efficient uses of fixed costs; corporate restructuring and reengineering being used as synonyms for downsizing, layoffs, and lateral transfers; rapid technological change; deregulation; and freer global trade arrangements. Consistent with that is the widespread policy of outsourcing systems and departments while hiring contingent, part-time, and temporary workers to perform both highly skilled and menial jobs. Now more than ever, firms are becoming interested in developing innovative strategies for accessing new sources of labor. Since the tight labor market of the late 1990s, corporations have become more involved in external workforce development systems. Many firms realize the economic benefit of hiring employees after they have been screened, and to some extent trained, by external organizations. These benefits are proving to be incentives for firms to build relationships with CBOs and participate in the external workforce development process.

One can only speculate that the "lean and mean" firms of the nineties may have been preparing for tougher economic times. In doing so, they were perfecting what seemed to be a just-in-time human resource management system to fill positions at all levels of the firm. Many firms already have long-established relationships with universities, colleges, and private sector headhunters, and these labor market suppliers usually provide training in the technology, operations systems, and business practices necessary to fill managerial positions at many of the largest employers. One could easily draw parallels between these relationships and the networks that firms are currently creating with CBOs for filling entry-level positions.

Flexible and nimble firms drive the engine of America's economic system. Accordingly, it is rational for employers to work with labor force suppliers to obtain trained staff as needed instead of investing internally in the recruitment, training, and development of job candidates, especially for jobs that traditionally have high rates of turnover. CBOs and community colleges, for their part, have cultivated the niche of identifying "employable" pools of entry-level labor and are making capital investments in technology and operations management systems in order to provide more effective training. They are also designing customized curricula based on employer specifications.

It is evident from the above discussion that the context for the implementation of employer-based workforce development programs depends on the approaches deployed by both the employers and their community partners, and on broader economic trends not easily influenced by any one organization. In the next section of the paper, I explain the method used to assess the structure of the relationships and other factors affecting the implementation of employer and communities partnerships.

METHODS

I conducted interviews with human resource directors and staff, corporate foundation officers, and corporate community relations managers at eight large firms (those with more than 500 employees) from industries as diverse as financial services, package distribution, aircraft manufacturing, and life sciences. There were three primary criteria for inclusion: first, firms must have ongoing relationships with CBOs. These could be either tacit or explicit commitments to a CBO or a community. An agreement to hire graduates from training programs, or some other arrangement whereby the firm contracts with the CBO to provide products or services, would qualify. Second, employers must intend to create sustainable jobs (as opposed to seasonal or other temporary work) specifically geared toward low-income men and women from the inner city. And third, employers must be cognizant of the many issues associated with hiring nontraditional employees. The employers interviewed recognized the need to provide support for newly hired entry-level employees. However, this did not necessarily mean that they designed or implemented new policies and procedures; rather, they acknowledged the need to make a concerted effort to help acclimate new hires in ways that might be different from existing protocol.

Identifying firms that met these three criteria was not difficult. I selected eight cases that are representative of a much larger group of corporations actively engaged in developing and sustaining workforce development programs. This new corporate-community activism is related in part to the effects of the Personal Responsibility and Work Opportunity Reconciliation Act (PRWORA) of 1996, which redesigned the welfare system, shifting it from an income maintenance system to a work-based system.[1] As human resource managers grappled with the question of corporate participation in welfare reform, they often asked questions about the "appropriate" role of firms in workforce development and Welfare-to-Work.

FACTORS THAT DETERMINE CORPORATE INVOLVEMENT IN WORKFORCE DEVELOPMENT COLLABORATIONS

So far as profit driven corporations are concerned, their most obvious role in workforce development is, clearly, to provide employment opportunities for qualified job seekers. It is important to differentiate, however, between the formal workforce development practices most large firms are involved in through their internal labor market and the various external arrangements firms enter into with other workforce development stakeholders such as CBOs and state agencies, which is really the focus of this paper. Within a firm's internal labor market (Doeringer and Piore 1971; Osterman 1994), there is a clear incentive to engage in workforce development so as to improve human capital and, subsequently, increase productivity as well as competitive positioning. If our understanding of work is restricted to paid activities performed within a large firm, and we accept Harrison, Weiss, and Gant's (1995) definition of workforce development, which encompasses more than employee training by including the process of inter-organizational collaboration, recruiting job seekers, job matching, mentoring, and addressing issues of retention and follow-up, then it is easy to understand how workforce development becomes a reiterative process during the life of most workers. Moreover, internal human resource management has become so indispensable to corporate management that departments have emerged to train and retrain employees as they move horizontally and vertically. The cultivation and acculturation of employees is typically an internal function, although more and more employers are outsourcing the responsibility for human resource development to specialists, including independent private sector training firms and community colleges. This is especially true with respect to technical and managerial functions.

Another common strategy used to attract talent is to offer an efficiency wage, paying somewhat above what a given employee might be worth in order to quickly obtain employees who have acquired industry-specific knowledge and skills. For low-wage, entry-level positions, however, on-the-job training remains the standard. We are unlikely to hear about employers offering significant training to their low-wage, entry-level workers unless the labor market is so tight that even entry-level workers have leverage. Generally, employers anticipate that such an investment would be a sunk cost, owing to the expected high levels of turnover of these positions.

In contrast, the external workforce development networks in which firms participate emphasize the human capital development of a pool of potential entry-level applicants, rather than the training and maturation of specific employees. It is through such external systems that employers work with various labor suppliers, such as CBOs, governments, and educational institutions, to build human capacity and expand the pool of skilled job seekers. In both internal and external workforce development, corporations frequently employ human resource managers, or "buffers," whose responsibility it is to recruit and train new hires and acculturate them to the corporation. The level at which individual buffers are interested in, and receive internal support for, using unconventional practices to connect entry-level workers to a firm often dictates the scope of the partnership between CBOs and that firm. Moreover, the degree to which other firms in a given industry are involved in corporate-community partnerships sways an ambivalent firm's inclination to try these nontraditional arrangements. Consequently, the tight labor market of the 1990s also forced firms to be increasingly innovative and more liberal about implementing strategies to attract workers.

For many low-wage positions, points of entry into firms have expanded with changing corporate structures and changing organization of work (Cappelli et al. 1997). But as firms have become physically and socially disconnected from urban neighborhoods and inner city dwellers, they lose their ability to effectively marry employees to jobs and determine who will be productive workers. Research has shown that many potential applicants for low-skill, entry-level jobs, especially blacks and Latinos from the inner city, are intimidated by traditional cold calling on employers and filling out applications, on account of their fear of labor market discrimination and rejection (Newman 1996). Therefore, informal hiring networks based on word-of-mouth referrals among the friends and family of employees often benefit firms and represent more comfortable options for such applicants. As we previously observed, however, these informal networks among low-income workers do not regularly produce living wage opportunities. The networks proving to be most lucrative for firms and disadvantaged job seekers alike come from a combination of formal and informal relationships, which describes the role of many CBOs. Community-based organizations serve as the employment broker, as they both cultivate corporations as contacts and prepare job seekers for opportunities.

The role of community-based job developers has expanded as state employment systems have been revamped because of their inability to effectively match job seekers and employers. By utilizing community institutions, firms can choose among a pool of applicants that have been previously screened for all the basic indicators of poor employment performance, thereby increasing the probability of a good fit.

For example, Salomon Smith Barney has a partnership with Wildcat Service Corporation, a CBO that specializes in workforce development. Job seekers who have successfully completed Wildcat's fairly rigorous 16-week internal training program may be placed in a four-month internship at Salomon Smith Barney. During this four-month period job seekers remain Wildcat trainees, and Salomon pays Wildcat for the temporary help. Job seekers use the internship to get acclimated to the corporate culture, and Salomon uses the internship process as a strategy for trying out potential employees before making a commitment to them by offering full-time, permanent positions. (Recently, a similar process has been widely used by private temporary agencies to place highly skilled candidates in private sector positions.) The human resource manager at Salomon Smith Barney was comfortable using this recruiting technique as a nontraditional way to fill even entry-level administrative positions. The firm judged the idea to be an economically sound business decision and a socially responsible business practice.

To facilitate discussion of the cases examined in the study, I have categorized corporate involvement in workforce development systems depending on the nature of the external relationships cultivated with the CBOs and on the level of internal engagement in the process. I have grouped the cases into the following four categories:

1) Capacity building. Capacity-building strategies aim at improving the capacity of the community-based program participants.

2) Vertical integration. Corporations following this approach internalize most workforce development functions, from recruit ment to retention, and often do not create extensive partnerships with CBOs.
3) Strategic alliances. The most common way firms work with CBOs is through different types of strategic alliances in which participating institutions have common or mutually beneficial goals. Firms following this strategy bolster the organizations' ability to effectively manage networks, share information, and operate at scale.
4) Joint ventures. Although joint ventures are a form of strategic alliance, they represent the most cohesive possible partnership between firms and CBOs, whereby both parties have a vested interest in the success of the relationship.

Capacity Building

Both Johnson and Johnson and International Business Machines (IBM) used capacity building strategies to structure their participation in workforce development. Capacity building strategies do not bolster the firms' corporate workforce; instead, they enhance the capabilities of the CBOs by improving the capacity of the community-based program participants. This strategy indirectly increases the pool of qualified job applicants by improving the quality of supply-side strategies. Firms using it exhibit a fairly low level of internal cohesiveness toward workforce development. Capacity building strategies do not require employees to support corporate-CBO networks because firms are not recruiting new staff through this workforce development strategy. Rather, firms use it to develop or finance external human capital development programs such as summer internships for youth, school-to-work programs, technology-based in-kind donations, and technical assistance.

Johnson and Johnson is one of the largest manufacturers of health care products and pharmaceuticals in the country; it has its corporate headquarters in New Brunswick, New Jersey. Johnson and Johnson organized the Bridge to Employment program to provide opportunities for young people to receive the training and education necessary to pursue careers in health-related fields. The program is designed to help high schools and community colleges develop appropriate curricula by implementing work-based learning through internships, field trips, mentoring, and job shadowing programs. Johnson and Johnson offered grants of up to $90,000 over three years to groups selected to participate in the Bridge to Employment program. It uses the program as a corporate community relations strategy, which serves the dual purpose of facilitating collaborations with community organizations in disadvantaged neighborhoods and of improving the pool of local labor. The majority of the organizations receiving funds through the program develop stimulating health care–related curricula, pay stipends to interns, and cover operating expenses.

Within each site community collaborations are unique, although each usually includes high schools, local chambers of commerce, CBOs, community colleges, community foundations, and private sector employers. One primary or host organization (Johnson and Johnson requires that it be in proximity to a Johnson and Johnson office or operating company) is assigned to serve as the intermediary between Johnson and Johnson and the community. The collaborative structure is conducive to the multidimensional goals of the program. The goals include 1) building long-term partnerships among businesses, educators, community groups, and parents to develop effective education programs; 2) preparing young people who have dropped out of school, or are at risk of doing so, for the challenges involved in obtaining a job in the health care industry and for fulfilling the requirements necessary to succeed; 3) recognizing and advancing community efforts in locations that have a record of success in helping at-risk youth locate and sustain jobs; and 4) reinforcing parental involvement as an important link between young people and their schools.

"[Providing] internal employment opportunities is not the intention of the program," says Michael Bzdak, director of Bridge to Employment. "It is really designed to support young people in their pursuit of secondary education in health-related fields. If young people who have participated in the program come to us seeking employment after they have completed some secondary education, great. The program is part of corporate philanthropy, not human resources." Thus, for Johnson and Johnson, Bridge to Employment is a long-term workforce development strategy designed to ensure a pool of skilled labor for the future.

The IBM Corporation also used a capacity-building approach to establish partnerships with CBOs. IBM is one of the largest manufacturers of technology systems in the world; its corporate headquarters are in Armonk, New York. In response to the urban unrest and race riots that occurred in cities across the United States during the mid to late 1960s, largely due to inadequate economic opportunity, disenfranchisement, and embedded racial inequality, the IBM Corporation initiated a program to develop and support partnerships with community-based job training providers by donating equipment, supplies, technical services, and training. Since the initial partnership with the Urban League of Los Angeles was established, IBM has expanded its support to include more than 170 nonprofit job training centers throughout the nation and has invested over $26 million in technology and support. These centers have helped prepare more than 67,000 disadvantaged individuals for successful participation in the labor market. In 1996, IBM shifted its philanthropic strategy and created the IBM Workforce Development Technology grant program. This three-year demonstration program builds on IBM's long-standing commitment to and expertise in developing and supporting technology solutions for job training and adult education.

The IBM Workforce Development Technology grant program invested over $2 million in 10 nationwide projects, including CBOs, public-private partnerships, and schools, with the intent of building the projects' technological capacity and thereby increasing the scope, quality, and efficiency of their workforce development programming. The projects were located in more than 20 cities nationwide and collectively served about 6,000 people. The main goal of the program was to build organizational capacity in employment training by allowing organizations to use cutting-edge technology (such as distance learning, video conferencing, networking software, and Internet access) supplied and supported by IBM. In the process, inter-organizational collaborations were created, access to training was extended to disadvantaged people, and innovative curricula were developed and shared among organizations. Additionally, systems have been created to track programmatic outcomes and employment placements. Although job placement was not a primary goal for most of the organizations participating, they placed approximately 1,300 people in jobs paying between $6 and $13 per hour. Jobs included computer repair technicians, security guards, medical assistants, bookkeepers, customer service representatives, and environmental technicians.

All of IBM's programs connected people to job opportunities using technology. Doris Gonzales-Light, the IBM program manager, believes that the Workforce Development Technology grant program has been very successful in terms of helping nonprofit organizations enhance their internal capacity to implement employment training programs, track outcomes, and leverage resources to generate additional support. When asked how IBM will participate in workforce development in the future, Gonzales-Light responded that it would use another approach but continue its support. For example, IBM made a grant to the Welfare to Work Partnership in Washington, D.C., to help that organization upgrade its Web site and redesign its database. The Partnership database is intended to link job and training opportunities across regions and states; individuals can access the database to locate job openings, skill requirements, and facilities providing training.

In making its resources available to the Welfare to Work Partnership, IBM has moved away from building organizational capacity at the community level, which directly affects individual-level employment outcomes, toward institutional capacity building, in which individual outcomes are more nebulous. If we visualize the levels of capacity building using concentric circles, individual capacity is the micro-level at the center; organizational capacity is the meso-level; and institutional capacity, as with the Partnership, would be the macro-level, or the outer circle.

Vertical Integration

In contrast to the prior cases, Cessna Aircraft Company has a high level of internal cohesion and few external connections. The company's approach to workforce development can be understood as vertically integrated because it has internalized most workforce development functions, from recruitment to retention, as opposed to creating extensive partnerships with CBOs. Vertically integrating external workforce development is a strategy used by firms to reduce interdependencies with significant members of the environment, namely CBOs.

Cessna, a 9,400-person firm based in Wichita, Kansas, started an internal program called the 21st Street Project, a comprehensive job training program that targets welfare recipients as well as other community residents in need of work. As an aircraft manufacturer, Cessna requires a constant pool of trained or semiskilled laborers to fill entry-level positions, primarily in sheet metal work and administrative services or clerical positions. But rather than relying on capricious labor pool suppliers, who may or may not have access to timely information regarding job openings and may or may not have the capacity to train job seekers according to demand requirements, Cessna has integrated the process internally. (The recruiting and training of potential employees for sheet metal and administrative positions through the 21st Street Project, however, is distinct from the human resource management systems used for other technical and managerial positions in the firm.) Cessna attracts participants to the three-month-long pre-training program by posting announcements in public spaces believed to be accessible to and utilized by potential job seekers, such as on community bulletin boards, in local newspapers, and by distributing them directly to consumers at supermarkets. Cessna also received a pool of job candidates from the Kansas Department of Social Services, which referred welfare recipients ready to transfer to work.

Job candidates must take part in the 21st Street Project's pre-training program, designed to foster both basic academic skills and work ethic and soft skills, before they are allowed to apply for permanent Cessna positions in sheet metal or clerical. During the pre-training period Cessna has no formal commitment to participants, so participants are allowed to continue to receive public assistance. At the conclusion of the pre-training program, successful participants interview for sheet metal or clerical positions. Job seekers asked to participate in one of the 21st Street Project's training programs are considered full-time employees of Cessna. Trainees receive above-minimum wages, health benefits, and vacation time. Approximately 70 percent of trainees successfully complete the training, which includes a series of verbal and written exams, work-based evaluations, and regular progress reports.

Since the inception of the 21st Street Project in 1995, Cessna has expanded the program to address some of the common problems affecting many low-wage workers. Company executives found that the three most common factors impeding successful completion of training were inaccessible or unaffordable child care, the absence of reliable transportation to work, and abusive home environments. In response to an overwhelming need, Cessna expanded its training campus in November 1997 to include child care facilities and residential housing for trainees and for entry-level and lower-wage employees who have difficulty getting to and from work or are in need of more appropriate living conditions.

Although high costs are associated with developing and maintaining vertically integrated systems because of the additional staffing and overhead associated with the recruiting, training, and hiring process, there are clear economic benefits as well. By vertically integrating labor supply with demand, Cessna eliminates intermediaries and gains first-hand knowledge of potential employees. In a tight labor market, where employee turnover is costly, Cessna is able to make informed assessments about trainees' abilities to be productive and to acclimate to the corporate culture. Although CBOs engaged in workforce development strive to match employers' wants with job seekers' needs, the fit is not always ideal at either end. Vertical integration gives firms more control over their labor force by centralizing authority and decision making. At the same time, it also potentially minimizes opportunities for job seekers that may be excluded from the firm's hiring process, because there are no alternative points of entry.

Strategic Alliances

The most common way firms work with CBOs is through different types of strategic alliances in which participating institutions have common or mutually beneficial goals. Essentially, alliances bolster businesses' and CBOs' ability to effectively manage networks, share information, and operate at scale (Gouillart and Kelly 1995; Fombrun 1992). Since the term "strategic alliance" is quite broad, this section distinguishes among various types based on the degree to which corporate headquarters' commitment to the external workforce development process has permeated the firm, spreading into areas where it was not originally intended to apply. However, the strength of the alliance does not directly correlate with the number of people hired into entry-level positions. Strength is more often indicated by the flexibility of the corporate culture to engage in nontraditional relationships. Higher levels of corporate support for workforce development programs can be cultivated by charismatic human resource directors, or corporate buffers, who want to implement innovative strategies for attracting workers. Corporate cultures amenable to change often have established avenues to support new ideas.

The workforce development practices at United Parcel Service, United Airlines, Sprint, and Monsanto exemplify three variations of strategic alliances: highly decentralized (UPS), moderately decentralized (United), and centralized alliances (Sprint and Monsanto). In decentralized workforce development alliances, firms exhibit a commitment to integrating external partnerships throughout their regional offices as part of their corporate human resource practices, reflecting a resourceful approach to expanding the pool of labor. Firms engaged in a highly decentralized alliance customize external relationships to meet the specific needs of regional establishments; hence the environment and parameters of each relationship may be different. Regional offices partner with local CBOs to design and implement workforce development programs based on local or branch office employment needs.

UPS, a leader in package distribution and the third largest employer in the United States, has highly decentralized alliances with its CBO partners. The company has a long history of corporate citizenship and of hiring from within the communities it serves; its regional offices make a point of building partnerships with CBOs, churches, state and local government agencies, and schools. These formal and informal relationships with external organizations fulfill a dual need for UPS. They help the firm's local human resource departments develop qualified pools of applicants for positions at UPS, and they also help UPS achieve part of its corporate mission—specifically, to be a well-regarded employer that is mindful of the well-being of its community. UPS regards community involvement as essential to the fulfillment of its mission, says Kerry Benedetto, corporate community relations manager.

As a decentralized organization, UPS has given its regional offices the autonomy to design workforce development strategies based on local needs and resources. UPS personnel are able to develop decentralized workforce development programs because branch offices receive support from corporate headquarters. Indeed, regional offices have the autonomy to individually interpret the organizational philosophy and establish appropriate partnerships and programs that meet the common goal of workforce development. The UPS organizational philosophy and operational structure functions to help the firm do good while doing well. A description of the extent of United Parcel's participation in workforce development and community networks is beyond the scope of this chapter; instead, we take note of a few of the company's unique network relationships.

Although most UPS employees receive a starting wage of $11 an hour plus benefits, three-quarters of the workforce is employed part-time because of peaks and troughs in the company's delivery cycle. In an effort to provide full-time employment to more of its workers, in 1995 the Chicago branch office began an "Employee Sharing Program." In this program, a consortium of companies creates full-time hours for employees by combining compatible part-time jobs and creating a system of cross-referrals among employers. The employees gain greater work experience and earn additional income, and "the combination of jobs can be more interesting (or less boring), increasing their overall quality of life," says Benedetto. Employee sharing helps mitigate employers' fear of training entry-level workers only to have them leave for alternative economic opportunities. Moreover, the improved quality of life that employees experience has helped to increase retention rates.

The Employee Sharing Program has proven to be a mutually beneficial program. It satisfies UPS's need for employees who will work unconventional shifts, such as from 4 a.m. to 8 a.m., and at the same time it meets the needs of those participating employers, such as noncompetitive firms at a local airport or small businesses, that often cannot provide full-time work. Participating employers receive employees based on a referral from UPS, which includes a background check, drug testing, and training, along with a benefits package that often surpasses what these firms, particularly the small businesses, can offer part-time employees.

In addition to running the Employee Sharing Program, which is an internally operated, decentralized initiative, UPS offices partner with established and respected local CBOs, such as the Urban League, as well as with smaller organizations. UPS offices have long-standing partnerships with CBOs, and the company believes these partnerships are successful on account of the shared goals of providing economic opportunities, sustainable employment, and social welfare. Benedetto suggests that UPS is interested in building partnerships with CBOs that are forward-thinking and can provide employment training based on the needs and specifications of UPS. For example, UPS engages in workforce development partnerships with CBOs willing to provide off-peak training, such as the aforementioned early-morning shift of four to eight. CBOs also must be willing to provide both soft skills, such as punctuality, attention to detail, and physical fitness, and the hard skills, or technical skills, necessary to be a successful UPS employee, such as safe driving habits and technological acumen.

The difference between highly and moderately decentralized alliances lies in the level of corporate involvement and the degree of authority relinquished to regional offices to create and participate in external partnerships or commitments. In a highly decentralized alliance, external workforce development relationships may look different in each locale, but moderately decentralized alliances maintain a more uniform approach to regional workforce development.

United Airlines, based in Chicago, employs over 94,000 people, 37 percent of whom hold clerical and managerial positions, 29 percent of whom are mechanics, 24 percent flight attendants, and 10 percent pilots. United is the largest employee-owned company in the United States. In 1994, when Gerald Greenwald became chairman and CEO, he facilitated the company's transition to employee ownership. Greenwald saw United's long-term success and leadership in the airline industry as being dependent on creating a corporate vision that was shared by workers, management, unions, and shareholders. Early on, Greenwald made a corporate commitment to President Clinton that United would take a lead role in creating replicable strategies for corporate participation in the Welfare-to-Work program. United's core participation has evolved into a decentralized, regional office–based program whereby local, community-based partnerships are formed to fill entry-level reservations positions throughout the firm.

Although United serves approximately 100 domestic and nearly 40 international airports, its external workforce development partnerships operate primarily in 11 regional offices, with concentrated efforts in six: Chicago, Miami, New York, Denver, Los Angeles, and San Francisco. In each, United has created relationships with CBOs and government agencies, which perform the employment training and referral services in the workforce development network. According to Scott Gilday, director of people services for the airline, "United relies on external organizations to train job seekers in the soft skills, such as attitude, job performance standards, work ethic, and communication . . . United provides all new hires with the necessary technical skills in a six- to seven-week internal program."

Given the high costs associated with training new employees, United forms long-term relationships with CBOs such as the Urban League to increase the probability of a good fit. CBO partnerships are judged based on referrals' staying power, or the CBO's ability to refer job seekers who will remain on the job. Over 35 percent of unsolicited new hires leave United within a year, but referrals from CBOs and government agencies tend to produce a much greater success rate.

Eileen Sweeny, manager of civic affairs at United, offers an explanation for the company's seemingly high overall attrition rate and the significantly lower attrition rate for former welfare recipients. She notes that as part of the employee stock ownership program, in which over 55 percent of corporate personnel participate, wage concessions were made over a five-year period; as a result, newly hired employees, from front-line workers to pilots, received reduced benefits and salary. "An average hourly wage for newly hired front-line workers is $7.67," she says. "However, these newly hired workers may work beside coworkers, doing similar jobs, who earn $16 per hour because they were hired prior to the employee stock ownership program, enacted in 1994. This is bound to have a discouraging effect and create turnover." On the other hand, former welfare recipients are more inclined to stay with the company, she observes, because they have fewer leverageable skills owing to a lack of experience. They may also feel a sense of loyalty to the firm for giving them a chance.

The Welfare-to-Work program is a significant addition to the human resource practices of United Airlines. The airline expected to hire 2,000 people off of the welfare rolls by the year 2000. It has created new positions—so-called field employment staff—to execute and manage the program and to serve as links between the firm and CBOs. United views this human resource investment as an economically rational and efficient expense because the company is now able to reduce the high costs associated with turnover.

While United has made a considerable contribution to the Welfare-to-Work program, the overwhelming majority of its placements fill entry-level reservations positions, which typically have the highest rates of turnover in the industry. Even taking into account Sweeny's explanation, United's 35 percent attrition rate per year is curious. It leads one to question how much of the turnover can be attributed to the individuals involved and how much to the organization. Its efforts at cultivating a more dependent pool of labor, which leads to reduced turnover, does not suggest that the organization is inclined to address the underlying causes of job dissatisfaction.

The third and final form of strategic alliance, centralized alliances, reflects workforce development relationships designed and implemented centrally, within corporate headquarters as opposed to at regional offices. There seem to be two types of centralized alliances. Some, of which we give an example below, are not very different from decentralized alliances, except that they are designed to fill in-house job openings and provide limited employment opportunities. Others, as in the second example below, have firms that outsource more and more of their entry-level operations. Such firms are inclined to create centralized alliances characterized by a narrow span of control over workforce development and incorporating a limited interpretation of workforce development partnerships. Levels of cohesiveness and connectedness vary based on corporate culture and philosophy.

Sprint, whose headquarters is located in Kansas City, is a leader in the global telecommunications industry: a provider of local, long-distance, and wireless services and an innovator in the nationwide fiber optic network. By partnering with local CBOs, Sprint built a new call center in Kansas City's inner city to process long distance calls throughout the county. The facility is called the 18th and Vine Call Center or, informally, "The Jazz Rock" (reflecting the historic jazz district that flourished at 18th and Vine). The Kansas City Area Development Council, whose mission it is to bring jobs and businesses into Kansas City, encouraged Sprint to create jobs in the inner city by opening its call center there as opposed to in the suburbs, where Sprint already operates four centers. In addition to the Area Development Council, Sprint worked with the Black Economic Union to rebuild the site to house the call center, and with the Kansas City Urban League and the Full Employment Council to fill 60 new call center jobs. The demand for jobs in the area far outnumbered the supply: a job fair, held at the local community college, yielded more than 700 applicants for the 60 available slots.

Securing one of the available positions thus became a very competitive process. The Full Employment Council and the Urban League provided prescreening of job applicants (based on diction, telephone etiquette, work history, drug testing, and motor and cognitive skills) along with placement services and job training; applicants that passed the first round of screening participated in a training course administered by Sprint and Metropolitan Community College. Because call center employment is growing in the Kansas City area, Sprint helped design a six-week course to provide job seekers with the technical and soft skills necessary to obtain call center jobs with any of the city's major employers, including American Airlines, AT&T, and Sprint itself. The firm also made a significant investment in the training program by deploying staff to train community college trainers and by helping the college purchase equipment and technology to be used for training. Sprint expected its return on investment to be a pool of qualified job applicants, thereby lowering costs associated with turnover.

Another example of a centralized strategic alliance comes from Monsanto, located in St. Louis. Monsanto is a life sciences company that employs approximately 20,000 people; the business focuses on biotechnology in the areas of agriculture, food, and health. During the early 1990s Monsanto downsized and subsequently divested, or outsourced, most entry-level positions, including mailroom and printing, janitorial services, food services, laboratory glassware care, and some manufacturing, to independent firms that have become the firm's suppliers. Monsanto participates in workforce development by referring entry-level job seekers to its regional suppliers, such as Marriott and Pitney Bowes.

Deborah Patterson, a human resource director at Monsanto, says that the firm's current workforce development structure is best suited to Monsanto's needs. "Working with extraneous CBOs would require a lot of unnecessary paperwork," she says. "Moreover, most of the positions that Monsanto has to offer require at least an associate degree for entry-level technician jobs. Job seekers that have been successful with suppliers also have access to Monsanto's internal job postings, which is a way for applicants to join the Monsanto team after receiving the appropriate training." Monsanto's workforce development practices exemplify low internal cohesiveness and low external connectedness.

Joint Ventures

Although joint ventures are a form of strategic alliance, they represent the most cohesive possible partnership between firms and CBOs, whereby both parties have a vested interest in the success of the relationship. Joint ventures are often formed to reduce unpredictability in the environment. Within such arrangements, firms begin to depend on their CBO partners to supply pools of qualified and motivated job applicants, while CBOs rely on firms for support in designing curricula, offering real work experience, and hiring graduates from training programs.

Salomon Smith Barney (SSB), a leader in global financial services with corporate headquarters in New York City, has made a strong commitment to partnering with CBOs in order to expand its pool of qualified job applicants for entry-level jobs throughout the firm. Since mid-1995, SSB has partnered with Wildcat Service Corporation to provide Welfare-to-Work opportunities for single mothers receiving public assistance. The goal of Wildcat's Private Industry Partnership (PIP) project is to create a replicable, cost-effective way to significantly increase employment in growth-oriented industries and long-term job retention among public assistance recipients. The structure of the program allows individuals on public assistance to move through the three-step process of training at Wildcat, gaining on-the-job experience through an internship at SSB, and obtaining a living-wage career opportunity with SSB.

Wildcat provides vocational education and basic skills training through a 16-week program that focuses on life skills, basic education, computer skills, work ethic, and a general acclimation to the corporate culture. Timeliness and dressing appropriately for work are strictly enforced during training in order to foster favorable work habits among a population of people that have been out of the formal workforce for some time. In collaboration with SSB's human resource staff, Wildcat provides training in intermediate and advanced software applications that are compatible with SSB's systems.

At the conclusion of the training program at the Wildcat site, trainees have the opportunity to interview for a full-time paid work assignment (internship) at SSB. These internships last for an additional 16 weeks, during which time the trainee remains a participant in the Wildcat program. Thus, SSB pays Wildcat $8 an hour per intern, as opposed to the $20 an hour SSB would normally pay a temporary agency. This significant savings in labor costs was one of the main economic incentives for SSB's choosing to enter into a joint venture with Wildcat. During interns' tenure at SSB they develop new skills that are useful at SSB and transferable to other work settings. They also attend workshops at SSB targeted at helping them make the transition to a corporate environment, and covering topics such as conflict resolution and presentation skills. The workshops are open to all entry-level administrative and support staff at SSB; they are particularly illuminating, however, for the Wildcat interns.

During the course of the 16-week internship, interns undergo a written evaluation by their SSB manager. At the end of the internship, a hiring decision is made based on individual performance as well as the needs of the firm. Interns have attained permanent placements at SSB in departments such as research, legal, information systems, accounts payable, marketing, operations, public relations, and treasury. In 1998, salaries generally ranged from $22,000 to $28,000; also included is a comprehensive benefits package featuring stock options, tuition reimbursement, and access to backup child care.

Barbara Silvan, human resource director at SSB, and the program's champion, believes the program is so successful because "the managers at SSB really love Wildcats [the interns]. Where else can you try out employees for four months before you hire them? The Wildcats are highly motivated and well trained, they really want to work, and they've exceeded expectations. This was not initially designed to be a jobs program but rather an inexpensive way to fill numerous job openings. I could not have planned this better. The retention rate among the Wildcats is about 94 percent."

Both Silvan and Jeff Jablow, senior vice president at Wildcat, observe that one of the keys to the program's success is that it is a partnership between the corporation and the CBO. There is regular communication and continual follow-up, and since both parties want the partnership to be a success they actively engage in troubleshooting whenever a problem arises. Additionally, thc first 16-wcck training program remains flexible and adaptable to SSB's needs. Trainees, interns, and newly hired employees know they always have someone at Wildcat whom they can communicate with about problems or issues as they occur. The relationship does not end once a trainee is placed;

rather, a new type of relationship begins. And as a professional CBO, Wildcat conducts its business in such a way as to help its partner meet its corporate objectives.

What seems particularly interesting about joint venturing is the difficulty in encouraging firms to engage in external workforce development at this level despite the program's success in sustaining durable labor market connections. The SSB example suggests that success is contingent on the intellectual, emotional, and financial investment of participating institutions, sometimes spearheaded by charismatic leaders at corporations or CBOs. The leadership at SSB and Wildcat developed a professional relationship that fostered trust and understanding about the parameters and expectations of the partnership. What was particularly important for this relationship was the authority of SSB's human resource director (the buffer) to implement nontraditional and somewhat controversial connecting strategies that, nevertheless, quickly gained support at all levels of the firm.

MEASURES OF CORPORATE INVOLVEMENT

The eight case studies suggest that tighter (more connected) relationships between firms and CBOs lead to the creation of jobs in the short term and of career opportunities in the long term. Loose relationships, in contrast, simply build capacity in the short term and have the potential for job creation in the long term. Firms collaborate with CBOs to varying degrees; some firms create first-source hiring arrangements with CBOs, while others have informal agreements and merely pass along information about job openings. Collaborations tend to be structured in accordance with the overall corporate vision, or corporate culture, which becomes evident through its human resource practices. Corporate workforce development operations run the gamut, as we have seen, from centralized to decentralized initiatives, or from workforce development practices initiated and implemented through corporate headquarters to those initiated and implemented through regional offices.

Time and time again, firms express concern and uncertainty about collaborating with CBOs above and beyond traditional job placement relationships, and many firms exhibit reluctance to embark on a joint venture strategy, despite its significant returns. The tight labor market of a few years ago helped make unconventional working relationships more acceptable. Now we can expect that more and more firms will be pushed into alternative workforce development relationships as a result of their past success and the recognition of the importance of investing in relationships that attract and develop pools of entry-level workers. While employers are looking toward underutilized sources for pools of domestic labor, CBOs are becoming increasingly knowledgeable about designing training programs and brokering business relationships, with the goal of altering negative perceptions about nonprofit organizations and their constituents.

An important question remains. Now that the market has softened, will firms revert to their old ways of doing business, or have CBOs created relationships that are sustainable? It appears that some firms only tapped into the resources of CBOs during severe labor droughts but have since reverted to a range of more familiar practices for attracting entry-level job seekers. However, a cadre of savvy, forward-thinking CBOs engaged in workforce development did not relent when the labor market softened. Rather, these workforce developers focused on building sustainable relationships with a range of firms. They offered services that extended beyond increasing job placements to skill development and retention. The restructured economy and the proliferation of jobs in the service sector has created an even greater, albeit unfortunate, demand for low-wage, entry-level positions. As firms have become accustomed to outsourcing nonessential functions, reputable CBOs have emerged as the likely candidates to continue brokering entry-level positions, alleviating firms from being inundated with job applicants they do not want, and do not have the capacity, to process.

Although we do not know exactly what determines the structure of corporate-CBO relationships, we can see patterns in the types of jobs created. Using a conceptual framework to analyze corporate involvement in workforce development may be helpful. The level of cohesiveness represents the firm's commitment—reflected in its internalization of workforce development strategies (see Figure 13.1). Highly cohesive firms, such as Cessna, Salomon Smith Barney, UPS, and United Airlines, changed their organizational structure or protocol to adapt to new workforce development strategies. These firms utilized different external workforce development techniques, but each altered their old structure to incorporate new ways of attracting labor. United Airlines created new staff positions

Figure 13.1 Corporate Connectedness and Cohesiveness in Workforce Development

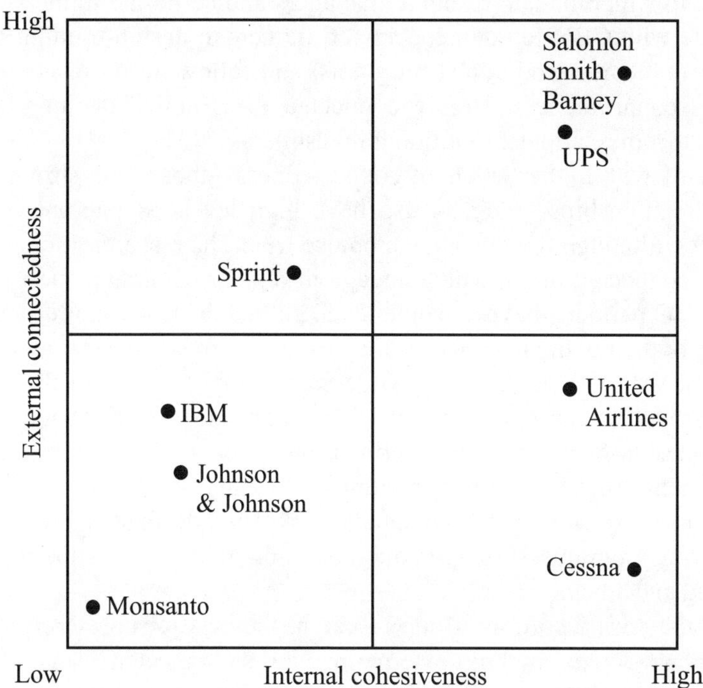

SOURCE: Author's calculations

to manage the influx, whereas Cessna made financial investments in infrastructure and personnel. The commitment within each highly cohesive firm was such that it altered "business as usual" at numerous levels within the corporation, not just in human resources or in the departments where new hires were working. This degree of commitment cannot easily be expressed in dollar terms because it encapsulates intangible aspects of the corporate culture. But we can, however, assert that firms engage in cohesive practices because they perceive them as a rational strategy for attracting employees given the constraints peculiar to those firms. Rarely do firms establish cohesive relationships based on purely altruistic intentions. Cohesiveness and altruism are not synonymous.

In contrast, the level of connectedness defines the strength of the relationship between firms and CBOs, specifically with respect to corporate involvement in external workforce development processes. The degree to which human resource managers and corporate trainers collaborate with CBO job developers and trainers to design training curricula, implement and adjust programs, and follow up on placements defines connectedness. Highly connected firms anticipate long-term benefits from relationship-building investments.

Firms with higher levels of connectedness—those with strong external relationships—tend to also have high levels of internal cohesiveness, although the reverse is not also true. The research found that highly connected firms, which engage in regular communication with their CBO partners, have, at some level, altered the tasks and responsibilities of their many human resource managers. And firms that actively network with CBOs tend to provide career opportunities in the long term as well as job opportunities in the short term. Highly connected and cohesive firms are more inclined, on account of their significant investment, to offer career opportunities to entry-level job seekers so as to ensure retention and job satisfaction. They do this by providing mentoring programs, skill upgrading, ongoing training, and supervisory training and advancement.

In the end, according to the research, the best jobs are created in firms characterized by both external networks (connectedness) and internal support (cohesiveness) with respect to utilizing the nontraditional pools of labor made up of former welfare recipients. So it is not just networks that matter in creating good jobs. Firms also have to be ready to embrace change.

Note

1. As of 1999 there was a list of over 7,000 employers formally participating in Welfare-to-Work through the Welfare to Work Partnership in Washington, D.C. The Partnership is a national effort on the part of the American business community to help move those on public assistance into private sector jobs. The mission of the Partnership is 1) to encourage firms to hire and retain former welfare recipients without displacing existing workers, and 2) to provide participating companies with the information, technical assistance, and support needed to create and manage successful programs. At the time this research commenced, the

Welfare to Work Partnership was in its infancy, with few corporate participants. All the firms included in this paper participate in the Partnership, although at different levels of engagement.

References

Becker, Gary. 1975. *Human Capital: A Theoretical and Empirical Analysis, with Special Reference to Education.* New York: National Bureau of Economic Research.

———. 1985. "Human Capital, Effort, and the Sexual Division of Labor." *Journal of Labor Economics*, 3(1): S33–S58.

Bernhardt, Annette, and Thomas Bailey. 1997. "Improving Worker Welfare in the Age of Flexibility." *Challenge* 41(5): 16–44.

Blau, Francine D., and Lawrence M. Kahn. 1992. "Race and Gender Pay Differentials." NBER Working Paper 4120. Cambridge, MA: National Bureau of Economic Research.

Bluestone, Barry, and Bennett Harrison. 1982. *The Deindustrialization of America: Plant Closings, Community Abandonment, and the Dismantling of Basic Industry.* New York: Basic Books.

Cappelli, Peter, Laurie Bassi, Harry Katz, David Knoke, Paul Osterman, and Michael Useem. 1997. *Change at Work: How American Industry and Workers are Coping with Corporate Restructuring and What Workers Must Do to Take Charge of Their Own Careers.* New York: Oxford University Press.

Doeringer, Peter, and Michael Piore. 1971. *Internal Labor Markets and Manpower Analysis.* Lexington, MA: D.C. Heath and Company.

Falcón, Luis, and Edwin Meléndez. 1996. *Social Network–Found Jobs and Other Labor Market Outcomes of Latinos, Blacks and Whites.* Boston: Mauricio Gaston Institute for Latino Community Development and Public Policy, University of Massachusetts Boston.

Fombrun, Charles. 1992. *Turning Points: Creating Strategic Change in Corporations.* New York: McGraw-Hill.

Giloth, Robert. 1998. "Jobs and Economic Development." In *Jobs and Economic Development: Strategies and Practice,* Robert Giloth, ed. Thousand Oaks, CA: Sage Publications, pp. 1–16.

Gouillart, Francis, and James Kelly. 1995. *Transforming the Organization: Reframing Corporate Direction, Restructuring the Company, Revitalizing the Enterprise and Renewing People.* New York: McGraw-Hill.

Granovetter, Mark. 1973. "The Strength of Weak Ties." *American Journal of Sociology* 78(6): 1360–1380.

———. 1974. *Getting a Job: A Study of Contacts and Careers.* Cambridge,

MA: Harvard University Press.

Harrison, Bennett. 1994. *Lean and Mean: The Changing Landscape of Corporate Power in the Age of Flexibility.* New York: Basic Books.

Harrison, Bennett, and Marcus Weiss. 1998. *Workforce Development Networks: Community Based Organizations and Regional Alliances.* Thousand Oaks, CA: Sage Publications.

Harrison, Bennett, Marcus Weiss, and Jon Gant. 1995. *Building Bridges: Community Development Corporations and the World of Employment Training.* New York: Ford Foundation.

Herzenberg, Stephen A., John A. Alic, and Howard Wial. 1998. *New Rules for a New Economy: Employment and Opportunity in Postindustrial America.* Ithaca, NY: Cornell University Press, ILR Press.

Howell, David. 1997. "The Collapse of Low-Skill Wages: Technological Shift or Institutional Failure?" Discussion Paper, Jerome Levy Economics Institute, Bard College.

Lichter, Daniel T. 1988. "Racial Differences in Underemployment in American Cities." *American Journal of Sociology* 93(4): 771–792.

Mason, Patrick L. 1995. "Race, Competition and Differential Wages." *Cambridge Journal of Economics* 19(4): 545–568.

McCall, Leslie. 2001. *Complex Inequality: Gender, Class and Race in the New Economy.* New York: Routledge.

Meléndez, Edwin. 1996. *Working on Jobs: The Center for Employment Training.* Boston: Mauricio Gaston Institute for Latino Community Development and Public Policy, University of Massachusetts Boston.

Meléndez, Edwin, and Luis M. Falcón. 1999. "Closing the Social Mismatch: Lessons from the Latino Experience." In *Moving Up the Economic Ladder: Latino Workers and the Nation's Future Prosperity,* Sonia Pérez, ed. Washington, DC: National Council of La Raza, pp. 186–209.

Meléndez, Edwin, and Bennett Harrison. 1998. "Matching the Disadvantaged to Job Opportunities: Structural Explanations for the Past Successes of the Center for Employment Training." *Economic Development Quarterly* 12(1): 3–11.

Newman, Katherine S. 1996. *Why Work: The Meaning of Labor and Sources of Dignity in Minority Adolescent Lives.* New York: Ford Foundation.

Osterman, Paul. 1994. "Internal Labor Markets: Theory and Change." In *Labor Economics and Industrial Relations,* Clark Kerr and Paul D. Staudohar, eds. Cambridge, MA: Harvard University Press, pp. 303–340.

Parker, Eric, and Joel Rogers. 1999. "Sectoral Training Initiatives in the US: Building Blocks of a New Workforce Preparation System?" In *The German System of Skill Provision in Comparative Perspective,* Pepper D. Culpepper and David Finegold, eds. New York: Berghahn Books, pp. 326–362.

Rodgers, William M. III. 1997. "Measuring Wage Discrimination During Periods of Growing Overall Wage Inequality." In *Race, Markets, and Social Outcomes,* Patrick Mason and Rhonda M. Williams, eds. Boston: Kluwer Academic Publishers, pp. 67–92.

Sugrue, Thomas J. 1996. *The Origins of the Urban Crisis: Race and Inequality in Postwar Detroit.* Princeton, NJ: Princeton University Press.

Theodore, Nikolas, and Virginia Carlson. 1998. "Targeting Job Opportunities: Developing Measures of Local Employment." *Economic Development Quarterly* 12(2): 137–149.

The Authors

Ramón Borges-Méndez is assistant professor of public policy at the University of Massachusetts Boston. In the past he has taught at Johns Hopkins University's School of Advanced International Studies, American University, and the University of Chile.

Héctor Cordero-Guzmán is an associate professor and the chair of Black and Hispanic Studies at Baruch College of the City University of New York. He is also a faculty member in the PhD programs in sociology and urban education at the CUNY Graduate Center.

Luis M. Falcón is vice provost for graduate education at Northeastern University. He is a professor and former chair of the sociology department there.

Joan Fitzgerald is an associate professor at Northeastern University and director of the Law, Policy, and Society Program, an interdisciplinary graduate program.

Sarah Gallagher is a senior program associate with Palladia Inc.

Lynn McCormick is an assistant professor in the Department of Urban Affairs and Planning at Hunter College of the City University of New York.

Edwin Meléndez is former director of the Community Development Research Center and a professor at the Robert J. Milano Graduate School of Management and Urban Policy at New School University.

Alexandra de Montrichard is an independent research consultant and project manager for several institutions. She formerly worked as a research associate for the Community Development Research Center at the Robert J. Milano Graduate School of Management and Urban Policy, New School University.

M. Bryna Sanger is a professor and former dean of the Robert J. Milano Graduate School of Management and Urban Policy at New School University. She has been a senior fellow at the Brookings Institution.

Alex Schwartz is an associate professor and chair of the Department of Urban Policy Analysis and Management at the Robert J. Milano Graduate School of Management and Urban Policy at New School University.

Lisa J. Servon is associate director of the Community Development Research Center and an associate professor at the Robert J. Milano Graduate School of Management and Urban Policy at New School University.

Michael A. Stoll is an associate professor of public policy and associate director of the Center for the Study of Urban Poverty at the University of California, Los Angeles.

Carlos Suárez-Boulangger is a counselor at the Nativity School in Boston. He is a researcher on educational programs for underserved populations who has worked as program evaluator for the Hyde Square Task Force in Boston and is completing a master's in counseling psychology at Boston College.

Stacey A. Sutton is a visiting fellow and lecturer at the Robert F. Wagner Graduate School of Public Service at New York University. She is also a doctoral candidate at the Edward J. Bloustein School of Planning and Public Policy and the Department of Sociology, Rutgers University.

Beverly Takahashi is a postdoctoral fellow at Wayne State University. She formerly taught at DePauw University. She has a doctorate in political science from the New School for Social Research.

Laura Wolf-Powers is an assistant professor of city planning in the Graduate Center for Planning and the Environment at Pratt Institute.

Index

The italic letters *f, n,* and *t* following a page number indicate that the subject information of the heading is within a figure, note, or table, respectively, on that page.

About the Institute

The W.E. Upjohn Institute for Employment Research is a nonprofit research organization devoted to finding and promoting solutions to employment-related problems at the national, state, and local levels. It is an activity of the W.E. Upjohn Unemployment Trustee Corporation, which was established in 1932 to administer a fund set aside by the late Dr. W.E. Upjohn, founder of The Upjohn Company, to seek ways to counteract the loss of employment income during economic downturns.

The Institute is funded largely by income from the W.E. Upjohn Unemployment Trust, supplemented by outside grants, contracts, and sales of publications. Activities of the Institute comprise the following elements: 1) a research program conducted by a resident staff of professional social scientists; 2) a competitive grant program, which expands and complements the internal research program by providing financial support to researchers outside the Institute; 3) a publications program, which provides the major vehicle for disseminating the research of staff and grantees, as well as other selected works in the field; and 4) an Employment Management Services division, which manages most of the publicly funded employment and training programs in the local area.

The broad objectives of the Institute's research, grant, and publication programs are to 1) promote scholarship and experimentation on issues of public and private employment and unemployment policy, and 2) make knowledge and scholarship relevant and useful to policymakers in their pursuit of solutions to employment and unemployment problems.

Current areas of concentration for these programs include causes, consequences, and measures to alleviate unemployment; social insurance and income maintenance programs; compensation; workforce quality; work arrangements; family labor issues; labor-management relations; and regional economic development and local labor markets.